The Social Organization of Hohokam Irrigation in the Middle Gila River Valley, Arizona

Artist's reconstruction of Hohokam workers cleaning out an irrigation canal near Snaketown Village, circa A.D. 1000, by Robert Ciaccio.

Gila River Indian Community
Anthropological Research Papers
Number 7

The Social Organization of Hohokam Irrigation in the Middle Gila River Valley, Arizona

by
M. Kyle Woodson

Gila River Indian Community
Cultural Resource Management Program
Sacaton, Arizona

About the Author

M. KYLE WOODSON, Ph.D., is the Director of the Gila River Indian Community's Cultural Resource Management Program, located in Sacaton, Arizona, USA. Dr. Woodson has studied the archaeology and history of southern Arizona for over 20 years with experience in tribal, academic, and for-profit cultural resource management (CRM) archaeology. He received B.A. and M.A. degrees in Anthropology in 1992 and 1995, respectively, from the University of Texas at Austin. He received his Ph.D. in Anthropology at Arizona State University in 2010, with a dissertation on the social organization of Hohokam irrigation organization in the middle Gila River Valley. His work focuses on southern Arizona, and his research interests include Hohokam canal irrigation agriculture, community organization, and ceramic production and technology, as well as Ancestral Puebloan migrations.

Cover: The front cover photo: Pima Men building a dam to turn water into an irrigation canal in Gila Crossing District, ca. 1900 (Image No. CHS-3609). (Courtesy of University of Southern California, on behalf of the USC Libraries.)
The back cover photo: Photo of Pima man maintaining canal ca. 1914 (courtesy the U.S. Bureau of Reclamation, Walter J. Lubken Collection). Top background, map drawn by Kino of southern and central Arizona (1701–1702). Bottom background, watercolor painting of an Akimel O'odham village by Seth Eastman.

Produced and Printed in the United States of America, by Statistical Research, Inc.

ISBN 978-0-9723347-6-1

Contents

List of Figures

List of Tables

List of Acronyms and Abbreviations

ASM	Arizona State Museum
ASU	Arizona State University
BOR	U.S. Department of the Interior Bureau of Reclamation
the Buttes	North and South Buttes
CAGR	compound annual growth rate
cfs	cubic foot/feet per second
CRMP	Cultural Resource Management Program
EMF	East Maricopa Floodway
GRIC	Gila River Indian Community
NRCS	Natural Resources Conservation Service
P-MIP	Pima-Maricopa Irrigation Project
SHESC	School of Human Evolution and Social Change
SWCA	SWCA Environmental Consultants, Inc.

Foreword

William E. Doolittle

In his best-selling book *Cadillac Desert*, Marc Reisner brought to public attention an old saying often heard in the American West: "Water flows uphill towards money." Although the ancient Hohokam did not have currency as we think of it today, wealth in the middle Gila River Valley 600–1,600 years ago was clearly centered at sites on Pleistocene terraces overlooking the river, in places that otherwise were high and dry.

Residents constructed more than a dozen elaborate canal systems around those sites. Main canals that carried water from the then-permanently flowing Gila River were large, up to 30 km in length and 4 m^2 in cross-sectional area. They transferred water to hundreds of smaller distribution canals that, in turn, carried water to thousands of smaller lateral canals that emptied into fields. At its zenith, upwards of 18,000 ha of desert were converted to an oasis of fertile farmland that fed more than 30,000 people.

But here is where the proverbial plot thickens. Focusing on four canal systems along the northern side of the river in the Gila River Indian Community (GRIC), M. Kyle Woodson contributes to at least two distinct lines of scholarship, each with several dimensions: irrigation studies and Hohokam archaeology.

According to Robert Hunt, there are perhaps 1,000,000 irrigation systems functioning around the world today. I have walked along the banks of many canals with Bob and have no reason to question his assertion. There were probably not as many canals functioning contemporaneously in centuries past as there are today, but there were a lot. Hundreds of them have been the focus of archaeological investigation in the Middle East, in northern and eastern Africa, around the Mediterranean, in South and Southeast Asia, in China, in the Andes, along the Pacific Coast of South America, in Mesoamerica, and even in Greenland. In almost every case, I dare say, canal studies include an assessment of adjacent settlements. Humans, after all, build canals, most often to irrigate crops they eat. And because their survival depends on the monitoring of fields, people have always resided near canals.

Living along canals—at their junctions with the river, at distal ends, and at points in between—has a host of implications, including demographics and social organization. Though not explanatory, small systems tend to involve small, scattered, loosely organized populations, whereas large systems tend to involve greater numbers of well-organized people living in nucleated settlements.

It is partly because of differences in size and partly because of data limitations that canal and settlement studies have been largely comparative in nature. Until now, there existed almost no data—archaeological, documentary, or ethnographic—that actually revealed how canal systems and their correlate settlements and organization evolved. The best we have been able to do is to examine small systems in one locale and infer the development of larger systems elsewhere. Rare are studies that actually investigate the evolution of individual canal systems over time, including settlements and social organization. And when such studies have been conducted, they have tended to treat growth as relatively simple and straightforward. The same holds true for the manner in which decline has been handled.

Woodson reveals something different in this book. Working in an area that has been little disturbed by twentieth- and twenty-first-century development, he was able to conduct detailed archaeological investigations using the latest analytical tools. His efforts have resulted in new and innovative insights into the expansion and consolidation of canal systems; the growth and decline of settlements, in terms of size and number; and the evolution of management and organizational systems. He demonstrates convincingly that canals were not simply extended but underwent constant re-engineering. Settlements changed in complex ways not previously recognized. Finally, and of the utmost importance in regard to anthropological theory, he is able to distinguish between single- and multiple-village irrigation management and elucidate how the latter developed out of the former and then persisted in a time of decline. Personally, I have long held a certain skepticism of interpretations of social organization based solely on archaeological data. Not in this case! Woodson has produced a benchmark volume, in no small way because of his thorough understanding and use of nuanced concepts such as intensification, least-cost principle, and labor requirements, to name just a few. Many scholars think they understand these issues, but few actually do. Woodson is one of the few, and he has now set a new and higher standard by which future irrigation studies will be measured.

In addition to contributing greatly to the literature on canal irrigation, this book is an important contribution to Hohokam archaeology. During the past 40 years, there has been a virtual explosion of archaeological projects focused on ancient irrigation in the American Southwest. Precipitated by urban sprawl and associated highway construction, much of that research has occurred in the greater Phoenix metropolitan area. The findings of those individual projects were major contributions in their own rights, but because of contractual restrictions, the studies tended to focus on specific locales through which canals passed. Information from those studies was synthesized masterfully by Jerry Howard into a valley-wide picture of ancient irrigation in the Salt River Valley. Still lacking, however, and indeed impossible to undertake, given urbanization, is a complete study of one or more canal systems in the area. That was not the case farther south, in the Gila Valley.

Prior to the 1970s, the most detailed studies of the Hohokam and their irrigation systems were undertaken at the site of Snaketown. Emil W. Haury began his investigations there in the 1930s and continued working through the 1960s. His work was excellent, with later research building on earlier findings. His methods and techniques changed over time, especially as new technologies became available. Then it came to an end . . . until the GRIC resumed archaeological research in the 1990s, thereby setting the stage for Woodson to begin his studies of ancient canals at the turn of the millennium.

Building on Haury's studies and those undertaken in the Salt River Valley and employing the latest methods and techniques, Woodson spent 12 years (and still counting) investigating not only Snaketown but the neighboring Granite Knob, Santan, and Gila Butte canal systems and settlements. This book is the culmination of his work to date, adopting innovative ways of establishing, for various time periods, the spatial extent of the habitation areas of sites, the irrigated hectarage, population sizes and rates of change, maintenance burdens, and administrative densities. In the process of doing so, factors such as crop calendars, variations in stream flow, periodic water scarcity, periods of channel downcutting and widening, and soil formation were included. It is all packaged with a marvelous array of maps that, by themselves, tell a fascinating story of the Hohokam.

I know not if Doc Haury ever owned a Cadillac, but he did work in the desert, and he knew a great deal about both irrigation and the Hohokam. He would be more than pleased with this book, with the work that went into it, and with M. Kyle Woodson.

PREFACE

The Huhugam prehistoric farmers of the Sonoran Desert of south-central Arizona constructed and maintained extensive irrigation-canal systems within the Gila and Salt River Valleys for over a thousand years. In accordance with the O'odham story of creation, the origin of the O'odham *Himdag* (Way of Life) began with the existence of human life in south-central Arizona. A central aspect of *Himdag* is a coexistence with the natural world that emphasizes survival and prosperity through cooperation. The Huhugam have a shared common agricultural interest in order to survive in the harsh environment, and this research provides practical insight into and considerations of the complexities in the social organization of canal-system management. Archaeologists use the term "Hohokam" to refer to these ancestors of the O'odham, but as employed, the two words have different meanings. "Huhugam" specifically refers to deceased members of the O'odham community, whereas "Hohokam" is used to designate the material cultural remains of the prehistoric inhabitants of southern Arizona. Because this study is focused on material cultural remains, the term "Hohokam" is employed throughout the manuscript.

This volume examines the social organization of Hohokam irrigation management through an analysis of canal systems and settlements in the middle Gila River Valley of Arizona during the Pioneer to Classic periods (A.D. 450–1450). This is the seventh publication in the Gila River Indian Community (GRIC) Anthropological Research Papers series. Extensive studies from archaeological investigations within the boundaries of the GRIC since 1993 provided the basis of the research in this volume. Most of those investigations were undertaken in conjunction with the Pima-Maricopa Irrigation Project, with funding from the U.S. Department of the Interior Bureau of Reclamation, under the Tribal Self-Governance Act of 1994 (Public Law 103-413), for the design and development of a water-delivery system utilizing Central Arizona Project water on the GRIC. This volume was originally published in 2010 as M. Kyle Woodson's Ph.D. dissertation, completed at the School of Human Evolution and Social Change at Arizona State University, in Tempe (Woodson 2010a).

Two research questions guide this study: (1) How was irrigation management organized in the middle Gila Valley? and (2) Given the significant changes during the Sedentary to Classic period transition, did the organization of irrigation management change in the Classic period? The investigation focuses on four canal systems (Granite Knob, Santan, Gila Butte, and Snaketown) and their associated settlements. Three aspects of the irrigation organizations are examined: internal structures, external relationships with the local political systems, and interrelationships among irrigation organizations. To achieve this, the study has three goals: (1) to describe and analyze canal systems and measure irrigation management complexity; (2) to describe and analyze settlements and evaluate settlement organization, and (3) to examine settlement organization and canal systems together, in terms of their implications for the organization of irrigation management.

This research concludes that single-village systems generally were managed as municipalities in which the authorities for the political institutions and irrigation organizations were the same. All four systems began in this form. Multivillage systems were managed by irrigation communities in which the authorities for the irrigation organizations and political institutions were separate. In the Sedentary period, three, and possibly all, of the systems were managed by irrigation communities. The settlement pattern changed dramatically in the Classic period, becoming dispersed and including a greater number of small habitations. Problems with water scarcity forced adaptive responses, including a decrease in canal capacities, the halt of new canal construction, demographic decline and the movement of people away from downstream systems, and the consolidation of canals to increase water supply in downstream canals, which would have required increased interaction among irrigation organizations in adjacent canal systems. Despite those changes, settlements remained organized in segmented communities along the branch canals (or main-canal reaches)—levels found to be important organizational units. The systems continued to be managed by irrigation communities, suggesting that no major internal changes occurred in irrigation management.

This report's conclusions suggest that locally managed irrigation systems have a long history in North America, extending back at least 1,500 years in the middle Gila River Valley of Arizona. This speaks to the persistence and adaptability of local, community-based irrigation organizations that have flourished around the world. Even today, it is estimated that the majority of the world's irrigated cropland still relies on hand-built, gravity-flow canal systems managed by local groups of farmers (Mabry 1996). These types of irrigation organizations that manage canal systems are embedded within traditional societies that often have long histories and deep ties to their lands. For this and other reasons, Woodson argues that the Akimel O'odham who farmed the middle Gila River Valley through historical-period times provide an appropriate ethnographic analog for the interpretation of prehistoric Hohokam canal-irrigation technology and irrigation social organization. An understanding of O'odham traditional practices and perspectives enhances the interpretation of Hohokam irrigation organization. This conclusion echoes those of ethnologists and other researchers who have highlighted the need for "bottom-up" or grass-roots institutions for successful and sustainable irrigation management (e.g., Hunt et al. 2005; Hunt and Hunt 1976; Mabry 1996; Tang 1992; Uphoff 1986). That applies as much to the modern industrialized world as it does to prehistoric or nonindustrial times.

-Barnaby V. Lewis, Tribal Historic Preservation Officer, Gila River Indian Community
- M. Kyle Woodson, Director, Cultural Resource Management Program, Gila River Indian Community

Acknowledgments

This study was made possible by the contributions and assistance of many people and institutions. The volume was originally published in 2010 as my Ph.D. dissertation, completed at the School of Human Evolution and Social Change (SHESC) at Arizona State University (ASU), in Tempe. I would first like to thank the Gila River Indian Community Cultural Resource Management Program (GRIC-CRMP), my employer for the past 19 years. The generous educational benefits offered by the GRIC allowed me to embark on my pursuit of a doctoral degree at ASU. In addition, the archaeological information generated by the GRIC-CRMP since its inception in 1993 formed the basis of the data utilized in this research, and I am grateful for the opportunity to integrate the information into this study. Most of the research at the GRIC-CRMP was undertaken in conjunction with the Pima-Maricopa Irrigation Project (P-MIP), with funding from the U.S. Department of the Interior Bureau of Reclamation (BOR), under the Tribal Self-Governance Act of 1994 (Public Law 103-413), for the design and development of a water-delivery system utilizing Central Arizona Project water. These studies have included extensive archaeological surveys and excavations and a series of thematic research documents written by GRIC-CRMP staff, as well as a long-term study of irrigation on the middle Gila River that I have directed for the last 17 years. I extend my thanks to Jon Czaplicki, retired archaeologist at the BOR, and Dr. David H. DeJong, project manager for the P-MIP, for their support.

My colleagues at the GRIC-CRMP made significant contributions to my doctoral studies and the ideas in this volume. John Ravesloot, former GRIC-CRMP coordinator, first supported my educational endeavor and continued to do so during and after his tenure at the GRIC-CRMP. He also served as a member of my Ph.D. committee. Andrew Darling, former GRIC-CRMP director (after John Ravesloot), continued to support my studies and helped me to see them to completion. I recognize these people and my fellow GRIC-CRMP supervisors, including current Project Managers Chris Loendorf and Teresa Rodrigues as well as past Project Directors Michael Foster, Robert Neily, David Jacobs, and David Wright. Scholarly discussion and interaction with them has helped me to better understand Hohokam prehistory over the years.

I offer my thanks to the GRIC-CRMP field staff for their efforts since 1993, which have led to the creation of one of the most extensive databases on Hohokam archaeology in Arizona. There are too many individuals to name here, but their work has contributed to advancing our understanding of Hohokam settlement and subsistence along the middle Gila River and made it possible to complete this study. I would like to give special thanks to Wesley Miles, GRIC-CRMP field supervisor, for his expertise and assistance in documenting canals on the GRIC and for being a sounding board for intellectual ideas and discussion. The GRIC-CRMP laboratory staff deserves much credit, as well, for their tireless work on artifact processing, analysis, data entry, and management of the artifact and photograph collections and computer databases.

Special thanks also are due to Lynn Simon, GRIC-CRMP cartography manager, who provided his expertise and time in producing the maps as well as some of the information in this volume. I am very grateful for his no-nonsense approach to work and his excellent cartographic skills. The cartographic efforts of Russ Talas and the late Brian Lewis also contributed to the maps.

I also thank GRIC Tribal Historic Preservation Officer Barnaby V. Lewis for being both a colleague and a friend for many years. Barnaby is a living example of a GRIC tribal member with a thorough knowledge and deep appreciation of the heritage and traditions of the GRIC. I have learned much from him over the years, and he has given me a much better perspective and appreciation of the Huhugam and Akimel O'odham oral traditions. This research has benefited from his influence.

I thank my Ph.D. committee for their guidance and support during my doctoral work. From the SHESC at ASU, I appreciate the contributions of Keith Kintigh (chair), Kate Spielmann, and David Abbott. Committee members from outside ASU were Robert Hunt, professor emeritus at Brandeis University, and John Ravesloot. All of my committee helped to shape my ideas during my doctoral work, and I sincerely appreciate their help and encouragement. Professor Hunt provided special guidance on concepts of canal irrigation and the social organization of irrigation, and he prodded me to think critically about my arguments. I am grateful for his tutelage.

I acknowledge the many scholars of Hohokam archaeology whose research and ideas have contributed to my understanding of the Hohokam and southern Arizona prehistory. Some of these archaeologists have passed on, and I was not able to meet them, such as Emil Haury, Harold Gladwin, Frank Midvale, and Richard Woodbury. It has been my privilege to know and learn from many other Hohokam scholars during my career, such as David Wilcox, the late David Gregory, David Doyel, David Abbott, Glen Rice, Jerry Howard, Patty Crown, Paul Fish, Suzanne Fish, Doug Craig, Kathy Henderson, Henry Wallace, Jonathon Mabry, William Doelle, Jeffrey Dean, Stephanie Whittlesey, Richard Ciolek-Torello, Bruce Masse, Jim Bayman, Charles Redman, Arelyn Simon, Owen Lindauer, Todd Bostwick, and Doug Mitchell. I also note the studies of Michael Waters, Gary Huckleberry, Fred Nials, and Donald Graybill, who advanced the understanding of geoarchaeology in the Hohokam region. There are still other Hohokam researchers I have not come to know, and I thank all of those researchers, because many of their ideas formed the basis of the concepts examined in this volume.

Finally, I am grateful for my wife, Stephani Etheridge Woodson, and my daughters, Adele, Maeve, and Esmée. Completing my Ph.D. was a long-time undertaking, and I would not have been able to complete the project without their love and support.

Chapter 1

Introduction

Anthropologists long have recognized that there is a unique relationship between canal irrigation agriculture and social organization. A key to this relationship is how a society is organized to handle the basic set of tasks that are necessary for successful irrigation management. That is, the users of a canal irrigation system have to coordinate and cooperate with each other in the construction, maintenance, and operation of the canal system; the allocation of water; and the resolution of conflicts that arise (Hunt 1988a; Kelly 1983; Mabry 1996). An irrigation organization is a social institution that manages and assigns the roles to accomplish these tasks. These institutions are focused on managing the commonly held resources—water, storage and delivery systems, and labor—that are critical to the success of indigenous societies that rely on irrigated agricultural production (Mabry 1996:22). As used in this study, "a *canal irrigation system* [or simply "canal system"] is composed of (1) a facility (gate and offtake) that takes water from a natural channel and moves it away from its natural downhill course and (2) the subsequent control works (canals, gates, and fields) that guide the water flowing on the surface to the agricultural plants, until that water either soaks into the earth or flows on the surface out of the control works" (Hunt 1988a:339–340, emphasis in original). When a canal system includes multiple main canals with proximate headgates, along with their subsequent works, it is identified as a "canal-system complex."

A persistent issue in social science studies of irrigation has been the structure of authority in the administration of canal irrigation systems (i.e., the irrigation organizations), especially how that authority is linked with the political system (see Hunt 1988a; Hunt and Hunt 1976; Kelly 1983). The topic garnered intense attention in the 1950s, beginning with Wittfogel's (1957) hydraulic hypothesis, which argued that irrigation was a prime mover in the origin of states. Specifically, he posited that the centralized coordination and direction of labor required by large-scale irrigation led to greater political integration and, ultimately, the formation of a state (see Mitchell 1973). Many researchers, though, brought evidence to refute the causal relationship between irrigation and the emergence of centralized political authority and early states (e.g., Adams 1966; Fernea 1970; Hunt 1988a; Mitchell 1973).

These debates led to more-nuanced examinations of the relationship between the authority structure in irrigation systems and political systems (e.g., papers in Downing and Gibson 1974). For example, an important point raised by some of these studies was that an irrigation organization has a management structure that is not necessarily the same as the authority for the political system (Hunt 1988a; Hunt and Hunt 1976; Hunt et al. 2005; Kelly 1983). In other words, the authority for managing an irrigation organization may be either embedded within the political structure or independent of it (autonomous). Other approaches have considered how irrigation agriculture can be used by elites in establishing and institutionalizing political power (e.g., Earle 1987, 1997; see Hunt and Hunt 1976). Elite control of the economy is identified as the primary basis of political power (Earle 1987:294, 1997:7, 12–13; Yoffee 1993:70). A key economic power strategy is staple finance, which is based on the ability of elites to mobilize and use food surpluses to finance themselves and their institutional activities (D'Altroy and Earle 1985; Earle 1987, 1997; Stein 1994). Staple finance requires control over productive land and the ability to mobilize large agricultural labor forces. Irrigated agricultural land represents the kind of concentrated, highly productive land that is ideal for elites seeking to control economic sources of power (see Earle et al. forthcoming).

These and other similar studies have indicated that the social organization of irrigation management cannot be fully understood without examining the link between irrigation organizations and political institutions. The nature of that link has implications for the potential level of control that political leaders have over the means of production. In addition, anthropological studies have identified two other key aspects of irrigation organizations: their internal structures and the interrelationships among different irrigation organizations. The internal structure of an irrigation organization revolves around several elements, such as the hierarchy of roles and the correlation of those roles to tasks at various operational levels of the canal system. The authority structure is a critical internal element—that is, whether or not an irrigation organization has a unified (or centralized) administrative structure (Hunt 1988a; Kelly 1983). Also important is examination of how labor is organized within an irrigation system. This issue has been addressed through the definition of task groups, which are linked to specific physical elements of an irrigation system (i.e., main, branch, distribution, and lateral canals) (see Howard 2006; Uphoff 1986). The labor requirements for managing a canal system (e.g., building and maintaining the canals) constitute another internal element that can inform on the size of the work force. Lastly, the analytical view can be widened to examine the interrelationships among irrigation organizations along separate canal systems sharing the same water source (Howard 1990, 1993, 2006; Hunt et al. 2005): is cooperation necessary between such institutions, and if so, what is the basis for cooperation?

Ethnographic and historical research has provided the basis of much of what we know about the social organization of irrigation management. On the one hand, ethnographic studies generally have dealt with the social, political, and economic aspects of irrigation organization. Often missing from such research are details on the physical elements and structure of a canal system (with notable exceptions in Downing [1974] and Lees [1973]). Moreover, with only a few exceptions (e.g., Downing 1974; Uphoff 1986), there is a lack of models of how these physical elements might relate to the social organization of irrigation (Howard 2006:6). Archaeology, on the other hand, can provide much information on the physical elements of a canal system, as well as on the settlements associated with the system. Few archaeological studies have explicitly examined the links between the physical structure of a canal system and the social organization of irrigation management. However, one region in which these links have begun to be addressed is the prehistoric Hohokam culture area in Arizona (see Howard 2006; Hunt et al. 2005).

The Hohokam were a group of farmers and artisans that flourished in the Sonoran Desert of south-central Arizona for a millennium, between roughly A.D. 450 and 1450 (Figure 1.1) (Bayman 2001; Crown and Judge 1991; S. Fish and P. Fish 2007; Gumerman 1991; Haury 1976). The geographic core of the Hohokam cultural tradition was the Phoenix Basin, which includes portions of two perennial rivers, the lower Salt and middle Gila Rivers. Hohokam culture history is divided generally into four time periods, which are subdivided into phases (Table 1.1) (see Dean 1991; Henderson 2001; Wallace et al. 1995). The Pioneer, Colonial, and Sedentary periods often are referred to collectively as the pre-Classic period. The Hohokam are known for their earthen public monuments (ballcourts and platform mounds) and distinctive craft items, such as red-on-buff pottery and marine-shell jewelry. They are noted especially for their construction of hundreds of kilometers of canals within numerous canal systems that irrigated thousands of hectares of land in the Phoenix Basin. Most of the Hohokam irrigation works in the lower Salt Valley, including Canal Systems 1 and 2 and the Scottsdale canal system, represent canal-system complexes. In contrast, most of the systems in the middle Gila Valley include only one main canal and headgate each and thus are best described as canal systems. The importance of irrigation agriculture to the Hohokam has drawn the attention of archaeologists and anthropologists interested in aspects of indigenous agricultural technology and the social organization of irrigation management.

Hohokam archaeologists have a long history of discourse on the social organization of irrigation management. The impetus for much of that research was Wittfogel's hydraulic hypothesis, because the Hohokam were cited as an example of a hydraulic society that would have required a central managerial authority. Like evidence from other areas of the world, the Hohokam evidence does not support the hydraulic hypothesis. Beyond agreement on that, there are divergent views on whether irrigation management was organized on a local, small scale or a centralized, larger scale. Also, there is a strong tendency in Hohokam irrigation studies to conflate the social organization of irrigation with political organization, which has led to an untested assumption that they are the same. A primary example is the use of "irrigation community" to refer to a political community that is coterminous with the set of sites along a canal system (Doyel 1980, 1981; Gregory 1991; Gregory and Nials 1985; Schroeder 1966). Such statements are based on an undemonstrated assumption that common use of the system created a basis for political integration. The concept has been applied commonly, if somewhat uncritically, to canal systems and associated settlements in the Hohokam region. Yet as noted above, the authority for an irrigation organization and the authority for its associated political institution may be different.

Two recent studies explicitly examined the organization of Hohokam irrigation along the canal-system complexes in the lower Salt River Valley (Howard 2006; Hunt et al. 2005). These studies made strides toward understanding irrigation organization, including its internal management structure and how that structure was connected to other institutions. In examining Canal System 2, Hunt et al. (2005) concluded that it had a unified (centralized) authority structure and probably had a communal form of irrigation organization. They could not determine whether the irrigation organization was coterminous with the political institution, and they found no ethnographic basis for positing the existence of a valley-wide management system. Howard (2006) examined Canal Systems 1 and 2 and elaborated the internal structures of the social groups that composed the irrigation organizations. He found that the task group consisting of the farmers who operated fields along a common distribution canal was an important organizational unit. Howard also found that villages were higher-level administrative nodes for irrigation management, whereas branch and main canals did not appear to play as vital a role. He concluded that rising water scarcity in the Classic period led to a need for cooperation between adjacent canal systems

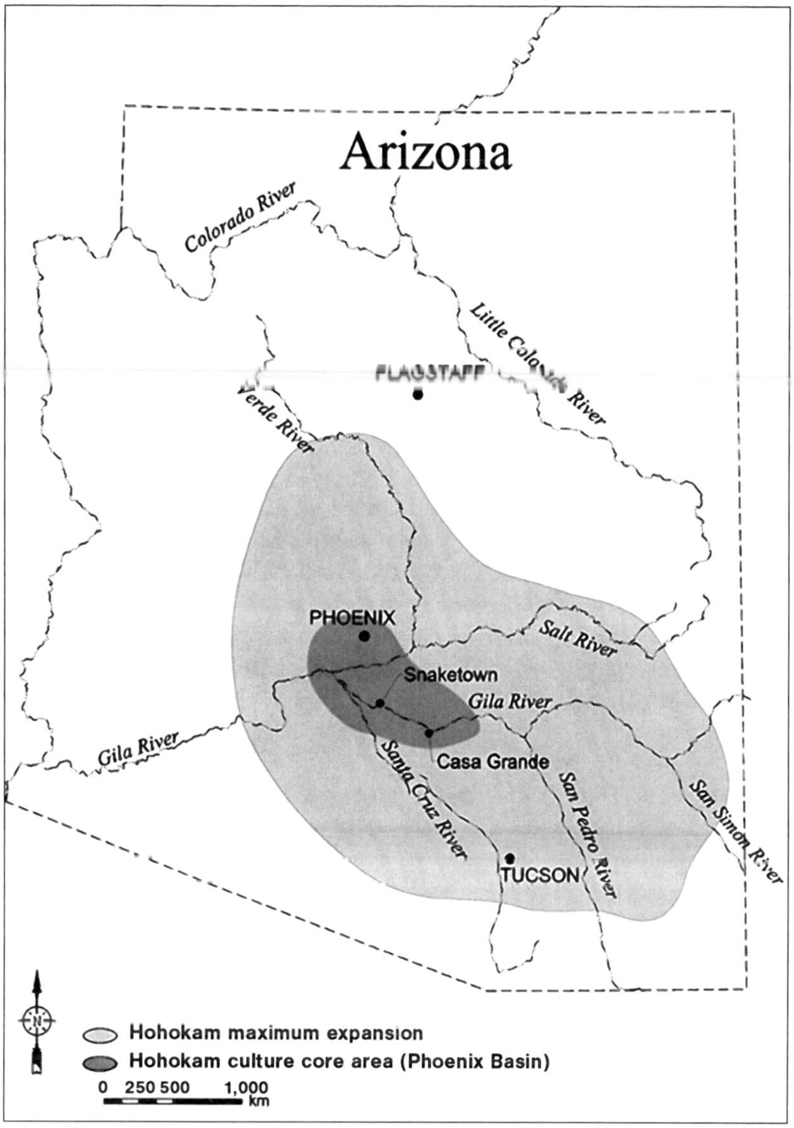

Figure 1.1. Map of the Hohokam culture area.

Table 1.1. Chronology of Hohokam Culture History

Period	Phase	Date Range (A.D.)
Pioneer	Red Mountain	100–450
	Vahki	450–650
	Estrella/Sweetwater	650–700
	Snaketown	700–750
Colonial	Gila Butte	750–850
	Santa Cruz	850–950
Sedentary	Sacaton	950–1150
Classic	Soho	1150–1300
	Civano	1300–1450

and among all systems in the valley. Interaction between systems was accomplished through negotiations among a hierarchy of corporate leadership roles, based at platform mounds. The social organization of Hohokam irrigation, then, is unresolved, and it deserves further attention.

Although many studies of Hohokam irrigation management have focused on Canal System 2 and the other canal-system complexes in the lower Salt Valley, the region presents obstacles to extending the inquiry into the social organization of Hohokam irrigation. The lower Salt Valley canal systems are large and complex, which makes it difficult to fully document and understand them and their associated settlements, both in synchronic and diachronic terms. Also, extensive historical-period agricultural development and modern urbanization have covered and obscured so much of the valley that gathering new data is laborious and limited in extent. In contrast, much of the middle Gila Valley landscape remains undisturbed by modern development; large block areas have been subjected to intensive archaeological surveys (Ravesloot and Waters 2004), and detailed studies have been made of the prehistoric canal systems (Woodson 2003, 2004, 2007, 2009, 2010a, forthcoming). We now have a comprehensive picture of the Hohokam canal systems and settlements along the middle Gila River (Figure 1.2). The strengths in the data are the number of and the precision and detail in the maps of the canals and settlements, the good documentation of the canals and settlements, and the relatively simple layout of the canal systems (especially when compared to the lower Salt Valley canal-system complexes). This data set allows for the description and analysis of geographically distinct Hohokam canal systems and settlements for which we have new and, in many ways, better data than we have for the lower Salt Valley. The archaeological resources of the middle Gila Valley thus present an opportunity to better address questions about the social organization of Hohokam irrigation management.

A general assessment of the middle Gila River data suggests that there were contrasts between canal systems, in terms of size and layout and in terms of the numbers, types, and sizes of settlements and the public architecture along the canal systems. These differences were partly related to the distribution of irrigable lands along the river, the locations of the canals along the river (in terms of upstream and downstream), the availability of reliable headgate locations, and other environmental conditions. The layout of some of the canal systems and the numbers and types of settlements along them changed from the Sedentary period to the Classic period. Those changes can be seen in the consolidation of some canal systems and settlement complexes along the middle Gila River. A settlement complex "consists of a central site with public architecture . . . surrounded by satellite settlements lacking such facilities" (Rice 2000:143). During the Sedentary period, there were 30 ballcourts at 21 settlement complexes along 8 canal systems, whereas during the Classic period, there were 12 platform mounds at 11 settlement complexes along 5 canal systems (Ravesloot, Rice, and Woodson 2005).

These changes occurred during the transition between the Sedentary and Classic periods, a time of sociopolitical transformation across the Hohokam region marked by "events and processes . . . [that] resulted in fundamental changes in Hohokam society" (Doyel 2000:222). During that interval, between around A.D. 1075 and 1200 (which Doyel [2000] referred to as the Santan phase), the Hohokam regional system appears to have weakened, as ballcourts and many sites in areas outside the Phoenix Basin were abandoned, and Hohokam populations settled primarily along major drainages (Crown 1991; Doyel 1991a; Wilcox and Sternberg 1983). The production of red-on-buff pottery decreased, while red-ware-pottery production increased, and an emphasis was placed on urn cremation burial (Abbott 2009; Doyel 1991:253). Some ancestral villages were depopulated, and the populations shifted and reorganized in nearby locations (Craig, ed. 2001; Crown 1991; Doyel 1980, 2000; Wilcox et al. 1981). A major landscape change, the downcutting and widening of the Gila River, also took place during that transition, between A.D. 1020 and 1160 (Waters and Ravesloot 2000, 2001; also Huckleberry 1993, 1995). Hence, the social organization of Hohokam irrigation management along the middle Gila River can be evaluated in the context of those important social, political, and environmental changes. That transition may represent a hinge point in both the internal structures and the external relationships of Hohokam irrigation organizations (see Abbott 2003; Howard 1990, 1993, 2006).

Goals of the Study

The central research question of this study is "How was irrigation management organized by the Hohokam in the middle Gila River Valley?" The question is examined through an analysis of canal systems and settlements during the Pioneer to Classic periods (ca. A.D. 450–1450). Given the significant changes in Hohokam society during the Sedentary to Classic period transition, an important secondary question is "Did the organization of irrigation management change in the Classic period?" The study focuses on the Santan–Gila Butte–Snaketown area of the valley, which included four canal systems (Granite Knob, Santan, Gila Butte, and Snaketown) and their associated settlements (see Figure 1.2 for canal-system locations). This area is situated on the north (or right) bank of the Gila River, between the Santan Mountains on the east and the area due north of Pima Butte on the west. The study area was chosen because it has been subjected to extensive survey and excavation, and much of the landscape is undisturbed (especially in the area around the ruin of Snaketown village). The sites contain archaeological evidence between irrigation organization and the political system. Was the authority of the organization that was responsible for irrigation management different from the authority of the political institution, or were they the same? If they were the same, for instance, a village administration (e.g., a council) for the primary village along a canal system would have supervised political matters as well as irrigation-management issues. This is a difficult issue to address, given current understandings of Hohokam political organization and because links may not be discernable in the archaeological record. The approach here is therefore simplified, extending from the analysis of settlement organization: when multiple focal villages occurred along a canal system, then the political system would have been segmented and not congruent with the entire canal system. By extension, the irrigation organization for the canal system must have been distinct from the political structure of each village. At that point in the analysis, the study also asks, "What was the most plausible type of irrigation organization for each canal system?"

Lastly, the third aspect of Research Goal 3 (interrelationships among irrigation organizations) is examined, by considering the circumstances of cooperation between farmers along neighboring canal systems. The decision to cooperate on a level external to the irrigation organization is directly related to the benefit of engaging in such a relationship (Howard 2006:218–219). The members of adjacent irrigation organizations could accrue benefits through cooperating in such tasks as construction or maintenance of infrastructure, conflict management, and the management of communally used or shared resources (see Howard 2006:219). In this study, I examine trends in subsistence and settlement as well as environmental data, to assess whether they reveal conditions that would have fostered cooperation between irrigation organizations.

Significance of Research

This study provides key insights into the social organization of Hohokam irrigation management in the middle Gila River Valley. The analysis examines four aspects of the internal structures of irrigation organizations. First, the four study area canal systems probably had unified (centralized) administrative structures from the earliest stages, or certainly by the early Colonial period. Second, the estimated population sizes along the canal systems were adequate to meet the minimum labor requirements for maintenance, as represented by the cleaning of the main canals. Third, a significant pattern in task-group organization is found at the branch-canal and main-canal levels of the canal systems. Fourth, along the multi-village canal systems, there was no obvious preeminent settlement along the Santan canal system that could have heavily influenced or dictated irrigation-management issues. Along the Snaketown canal system, though, Snaketown village appears to have been the preeminent pre-Classic period settlement and likely had a significant influence on matters of irrigation management. Maricopa Mound was preeminent in the Classic period and also could have been influential, but its unusual position at the tail end of the system would have limited its involvement in irrigation management.

Regarding external relationships between the irrigation organizations and political structures, the study suggests that the authorities for the organizations responsible for managing the canal systems were not always the same as the authorities for the political institutions governing people living along the systems. During the Pioneer period, the authorities for the irrigation organizations probably were the same as the authorities for the political institutions (i.e., the organization is characterized as a municipality). That continued to be the case for the Gila Butte system in the Colonial to Sedentary periods and for the Granite Knob system in the Colonial period. However, the patterns for the Snaketown and Santan systems in the Colonial to Sedentary periods (and probably for the Granite Knob system in the Sedentary period) suggest that the organization responsible for managing the systems was distinct from the political institutions governing people living along the systems (i.e., the organization is characterized as an irrigation community). By the Classic period, the consolidation of the canal systems was accompanied by the consolidation of the political communities. Although some changes in community organization were apparent, both consolidated canal systems probably continued to be managed by irrigation organizations that were independent from the political institutions.

A significant implication of the canal systems' being managed by irrigation communities is that the political leaders did not necessarily have direct control over the means of agricultural production at the level of the canal system. On the other hand, when a system was managed as a municipality, political leaders might have been able to exert a level of control over surpluses, by virtue of their likely involvement in co-managing both political and irrigation matters. The municipalities probably were short-lived, though, and because they occurred during the early stages of the systems, there likely was a lower potential for generating surpluses.

A major finding of this study is that problems arising from water scarcity in the Late Sedentary and Early Classic periods forced a response by Hohokam populations. Responses were reflected in the settlement pattern and the canal systems, including a decrease in main-canal capacities and the lack of new canal-system construction in the Classic period. Another key response was the movement of people away from downstream systems, as indicated by steep population declines. Segments of these downstream populations apparently moved to better-watered locales either farther upstream along the Gila River or along the lower Salt River. An important adaptation to scarcity was to increase the water supply in downstream canals through the consolidation of canals, which, I argue, led to the need for external interactions between the irrigation organizations in adjacent canal systems. These interrelationships may have been manifested in agreements or alliances for cooperation in water allocation, and possibly, there was cause for labor exchange in critical times. In all, these responses to conditions of water scarcity might have been key factors in the sociopolitical changes at this time. This study does not provide sufficient information to fully address the question of whether an arrangement or a larger type of management institution was created at a valley-wide level, integrating all 13 middle Gila Valley canal systems, during these periods.

The results of this study have significant implications for Hohokam archaeology. First, this research has considerably increased our understanding of the four study area canal systems, including their layout, size (command area), capacity, and sequence of development; the timing of their consolidation; the labor requirements for cleaning the main canals; and their levels of irrigation-management complexity. Second, a dramatic change in settlement pattern and demography between the Sedentary and Classic periods is clearly documented. Third, the study traces settlement-pattern trends that were important factors in the organization of agricultural labor and in the development of the political organization in the study area. Fourth, the study traces the formation and development of focal-village communities during the pre-Classic period. Fifth, a change in settlement organization between the Sedentary and Classic periods is clearly documented. Fifth, the research suggests that irrigators were experiencing problems with water scarcity by the Classic period. Sixth, the population movements documented within and outside the study area indicate that mobility was an adaptive strategy exercised by the Hohokam in the face of poor ecological conditions.

Some aspects of this research have broader relevance to both Hohokam archaeology and archaeological studies in the Southwest. The primary contribution is the explication of settlement organization through the use of a detailed, systematic site-function model (Wells et al. 2003, 2004). The site-function approach helps to avoid some of the problems with using spatial data alone in settlement-pattern analysis and provides a more-robust picture of the prehistoric landscape. A second contribution is the technique used for estimating population size. Estimating Hohokam population size has proven to be a difficult endeavor (Dean et al. 1994:70–71; Fish and Fish 1991). The level of detail of the current data allows a more-rigorous approach to population, which has revealed important trends in population growth and decline. A third contribution is the method developed for specifically defining the command area of the canal systems. Fourth, the study provides a solid approach to estimating labor requirements for canal maintenance.

Another aspect of the study relevant to southwestern studies is the examination of Hohokam adaptation to the streamflow and landscape changes that affected much of southern Arizona during the Sedentary to Classic period transition (see Graybill et al. 2006; Huckleberry 1993, 1995; Nials et al. 1989; Waters and Ravesloot 2000, 2001). These deteriorating conditions, in tandem with population growth, resulted in rising water scarcity, which presented a challenge for irrigators to maintain a reliable water supply in the canal systems, especially the downstream systems. They responded by consolidating canals while moving away from downstream canal systems. Lastly, the study contributes a perspective on the sociopolitical complexity of prehistoric southwestern societies as it pertains to the identity and role of Hohokam leaders at ballcourt and platform-mound villages (see Abbott 2000, 2003; Doyel 2007; Earle et al. forthcoming; Elson 1998; Redman 1991; Wilcox 1991). I conclude that the leaders probably were involved in matters of irrigation management at the levels of the focal-village communities (i.e., branch canals/main-canal reaches). Therefore, they probably had means of control over agricultural production and surpluses at those levels of the system, but they did not necessarily have the ability to exert control over the entire canal system.

The results of this study also speak to questions that are important to comparative irrigation studies. The Hohokam, with their large irrigation systems, were included in some of the debates in the anthropological community regarding Wittfogel's (1955, 1957) hydraulic hypothesis. Some scholars cited the Hohokam as an example of a hydraulic society that would have required a central managerial authority (e.g., Steward 1955:71–72). A number of cross-cultural irrigation studies have demonstrated that large-scale canal systems do not necessarily require centralized control by a state or central government (e.g., Hunt 1988a; Leach 1961; Millon 1962; Mitchell 1973). However, this study takes the perspective that the internal structure of an irrigation organization must be distinguished from the external articulation of irrigation roles to the political system, to clarify the meaning of "centralization" in both social spheres (Kelly 1983; see Hunt 1988a). I conclude that the management of each middle Gila Valley canal system required a centralized authority from the beginning, in the form of an irrigation organization. Although the authorities for these organizations may have been the same as the authorities for the political organizations in the early phases of irrigation, the two management spheres seem to have diverged as population size and sociopolitical complexity increased in the Colonial and Sedentary periods. It is feasible, then, that the "synergistic action of irrigation and its centralized coordination" resulted in greater political integration for the Hohokam (Mitchell 1973:533; also see Lees 1973). Hence, the cases studied here could be cited as support for a "modified" hydraulic hypothesis.

In addition, the analytical framework of the study successfully applies the ethnographic concept that the internal authority structure of an irrigation organization must be examined separately from its external relationship to the political system (Kelly 1983; also Hunt 1988a). This strategy promotes a more-nuanced understanding of the various levels of social organization. Another contribution of the current study is the level of detail presented for the physical structure and the sequence of development of indigenous prehistoric canal systems and their associated settlements. Few systems reported by ethnographers or archaeologists have been documented in such detail (although see Howard 1990, 1993, 2006), and this provides a basis for evaluation of some elements of irrigation organization. Lastly, the results of the study suggest that locally managed irrigation systems have a long history in North America, extending back at least 1,500 years in the middle Gila Valley. This study speaks to the persistence and adaptability of local, community-based irrigation organizations that have flourished around the world (see Mabry 1996; Tang 1992; Uphoff 1986).

Volume Organization

The results of the research are presented in eight chapters, including this introductory chapter. In Chapter 2, I outline the research background and framework for the study. Chapter 3 describes the study area. Chapter 4 describes the canal systems and addresses Research Goal 1. Chapters 5 and 6 address Research Goal 2 by describing the organization of settlements in Study Area 1 and Study Area 2, respectively. Chapter 7 addresses Research Goal 3 by examining settlement and population trends and the signatures of the social organization of irrigation. The conclusions of the study are presented in Chapter 8. The appendixes provide the background and additional descriptive data on the canal systems (Appendix A) and settlements (Appendixes B and C), including documentation methods.

Chapter 2

Research Background and Framework for Study

The research describes the Granite Knob, Santan, Gila Butte, and Snaketown canal systems and their associated settlements in the middle Gila Valley, in an effort to examine the social organization of Hohokam irrigation management. This chapter outlines the background concepts regarding the social organization of irrigation, reviews previous research on the organization of Hohokam irrigation, and presents the research goals and methods of the study.

The Social Organization of Irrigation

Anthropologists long have recognized that there is a unique relationship between irrigation and social organization (Downing 1974; Glick 1970; Fernea 1970; Hunt 1988a, 1988b; Hunt and Hunt 1976; Kelly 1983; Lansing 1991; Leach 1961; Lees 1973; Mabry 1996; Millon 1962; Mitchell 1973, 1976; Netting 1993; Scarborough 2003; Steward 1949, 1955; Uphoff 1986; Wittfogel 1955, 1957; see also papers in Coward, ed. [1979] and Downing and Gibson [1974]). The key aspect of that relationship concerns how a society was organized to handle the basic set of tasks necessary for successful local irrigation management. Social scientists recognize between 5 and 12 tasks (Hunt and Hunt 1976; Kelly 1983:882; Mabry 1996:14, citing Coward 1979; Uphoff 1986), and 4 of those can be considered the most fundamental tasks: "(1) the construction of irrigation facilities, (2) their maintenance and operation, (3) the allocation of water, and (4) the resolution of conflicts that arise" (Kelly 1983:882). The institution formed to manage and assign roles to accomplish these tasks represents the organizational unit of interest.

The hydraulic hypothesis of Wittfogel (1955, 1957) and Steward (1949, 1955) is one of the most influential models of the link between irrigation and social organization. The hypothesis posits that "large-scale irrigation requires centralized coordination and direction of effort, which, in turn, leads to greater political integration" (Mitchell 1973:532). By extension, irrigation is seen as a prime mover in the rise of states in arid or semiarid environments. Several studies (e.g., Adams 1966; Fernea 1970; Hunt 1988a; Mitchell 1973) have refuted the first aspect of the hypothesis, showing that large-scale irrigation does not always require centralized coordination of effort (i.e., control by a central government or state). Indeed, "it is mistaken to view irrigation by itself as the independent variable" (Mitchell 1973:533). Hunt (1988b:200) stressed that "*size alone* does not determine the charter of authority for a canal irrigation system (within the range of 700–458,000 ha). Any analyst who would infer political organization from only the size of an irrigation system is hereby cautioned" (emphasis in original). The second aspect of the hypothesis has been resoundingly rejected by many anthropologists and archaeologists. Global examples have been cited of the rise of states with no apparent use of canal irrigation (e.g., the Maya) and the rise of states before the use of large-scale irrigation (e.g., the Ur III Dynasty in Mesopotamia). These and other cases demonstrate that there is no a priori requirement that large-scale irrigation be present prior to the development of complex, hierarchical sociopolitical organizations.

Despite these critiques, the core concepts of the hydraulic hypothesis still can be usefully employed in analyzing the link between irrigation and social organization. Mitchell (1973:533; see also Lees 1973) argued that critiques of the hydraulic hypothesis "can be obviated by reformulating it: it is not irrigation itself, but the centralized coordination of irrigation activities that has important social consequences. It is the synergistic action of irrigation and its centralized coordination that results in greater political integration." The concept of "centralization" as used by Wittfogel and Steward has to do with the total society; that is, the meaning "concerns the kind of linkage between the authority roles of an irrigation system and external entities, usually the state" (Hunt 1988a:341; see also Hunt and Hunt 1976:392; Kelly 1983). However, Kelly (1983:883; see also Hunt 1988a:340–341; Scarborough 2003:27) advised that the concept of centralized authority needs to be broken down into two components: "the *internal* configuration of authority among roles performing irrigation tasks and the *external* relationship or connection of these irrigation roles to those in other social systems, most notably the general political system (the state)" (emphasis in original). Elucidating the internal coherence of authority and the structure of water-management roles indicates "the degree to which irrigation roles are hierarchically configured and authority in irrigation-task performance is concentrated [or centralized]" (Kelly 1983:883). The external linkage has to do with "whether authority over the decisions and activities within the irrigation system is located within the irrigation system or external to it" (Hunt 1988a:341). Thus an irrigation social organization may be autonomous or heteronomous, in terms of the locus of authority (Bolin 1993). In sum, the internal structure of an irrigation organization must be distinguished from the external articulation of irrigation roles to the political system, to clarify the meaning of "centralization" in both social spheres.

Many studies (e.g., Downing 1974; Hunt 1988a; Tang 1992; Uphoff 1986) have sought to identify the correlates that determine the internal management structure of local irrigation organizations within the canal systems themselves. What has been found is that there was no simple or direct correlation, as suggested by Hunt's (1988a, 1988b) conclusion that the charter of authority for an irrigation organization cannot be inferred from only the size of an irrigation system. Some general cross-cultural patterns, however, appear to be valid. For example, "if a canal system is composed of two or more villages, then a different (and probably special-purpose) organization has to exist" above the village level, to manage the system (Hunt 1988a:347). Another important pattern is that any canal system larger than 100 ha in size has a very high probability of having had a unified or concentrated administrative authority structure (Hunt 1988a:347; see also Tang 1992; Uphoff 1986). Such a structure implies a hierarchical configuration of irrigation roles managed by central officials, but not necessarily in a coerced or "despotic" order (sensu Wittfogel 1957).

Mabry (1996:10) suggested that "it is the *number of irrigators*, rather than the total number of people supported or the scale of the total command area, that creates 'scalar stress' in irrigation management" (emphasis in original). The concept of scalar stress (Johnson 1982) has been applied widely in studies of social organization in the Southwest (e.g., Cordell et al. 1994; Craig 1995; Johnson 1989; Kintigh 1994) and is amenable to analyzing irrigation social organization. The theory posits that a consensual decision-making organization tends to have a limit of about 6 participants (although there may be as many as 15), above which the organization experiences stress and tends to either fission into smaller units or develop into a hierarchical decision-making structure. Thus, whereas a small irrigation system (i.e., less than 100 ha) with a few irrigators can be managed without a centralized authority, "many irrigators sharing common sources to irrigate larger areas must develop hierarchical decision-making institutions to manage more complex, integrated systems" (Mabry 1996:11).

A focus on how labor is organized within an irrigation system has led to the identification of a link between the physical structure of a canal system and social organization. Uphoff (1986:59–60) described how the physical elements of an irrigation system (i.e., main, branch, distribution, and lateral canals and water-control features) constitute levels of system control or levels of operation (Figure 2.1); the "'levels' within an irrigation system are socio-technical in that they can be defined by both physical structure and social organization. There are levels of operation that are established by physical points of water control—such as a gate or diversion structure—between the water source and the fields" (Uphoff 1986:59). These levels of operation correspond to certain task groups that must cooperate in operating that segment of the system. Thus, the physical structure of a canal system reflects the social organization of the groups living along it (or vice versa). The premise is that the labor requirements for canal irrigation and the ways in which that labor becomes organized structures social relationships into sets of spatial blocs with their own unique sets of concerns.

Following this model, Howard (2006) focused on defining task groups along two Hohokam canal systems in the lower Salt River Valley. Task groups were formed at different scales of canal-system operation and interaction, to meet the operational requirements and labor needs of the irrigation system. He based his approach on ethnographic case studies of irrigation communities that closely resemble Hohokam canal systems. Howard (2006:104–107) identified the command area, consisting of a set of fields receiving water from a common distribution canal and the cooperating farmers operating it, as a major level in the internal organization of an irrigation community. This should not be confused with the more general usage of "command area" as the total area of fields irrigated by a canal system. He argued that the command area represents the most basic organizational unit, which frequently has a legal charter, and is responsible for the organization of labor for operation and maintenance activities along the distribution canal. Howard (2006:107) also found organizational units at the level of the main canal and branch canal, but he suggested that these "may not be a strong organizational node as seen in the case studies." At a higher organizational level, Howard (2006:287) contended that "villages, particularly those within the residential zones and containing public architecture, are interpreted as administrative nodes focused on water scheduling, water allocation and local conflict resolution."

Uphoff (1986:59–60; see Howard 2006:9–10, 18–24; Hunt et al. 2005:442–449) suggested that measures of organizational differentiation should be used in examining the complexity of irrigation management. In contrast to measures of system scale (i.e., command area), Uphoff (1986:60) suggested that the number of organizational

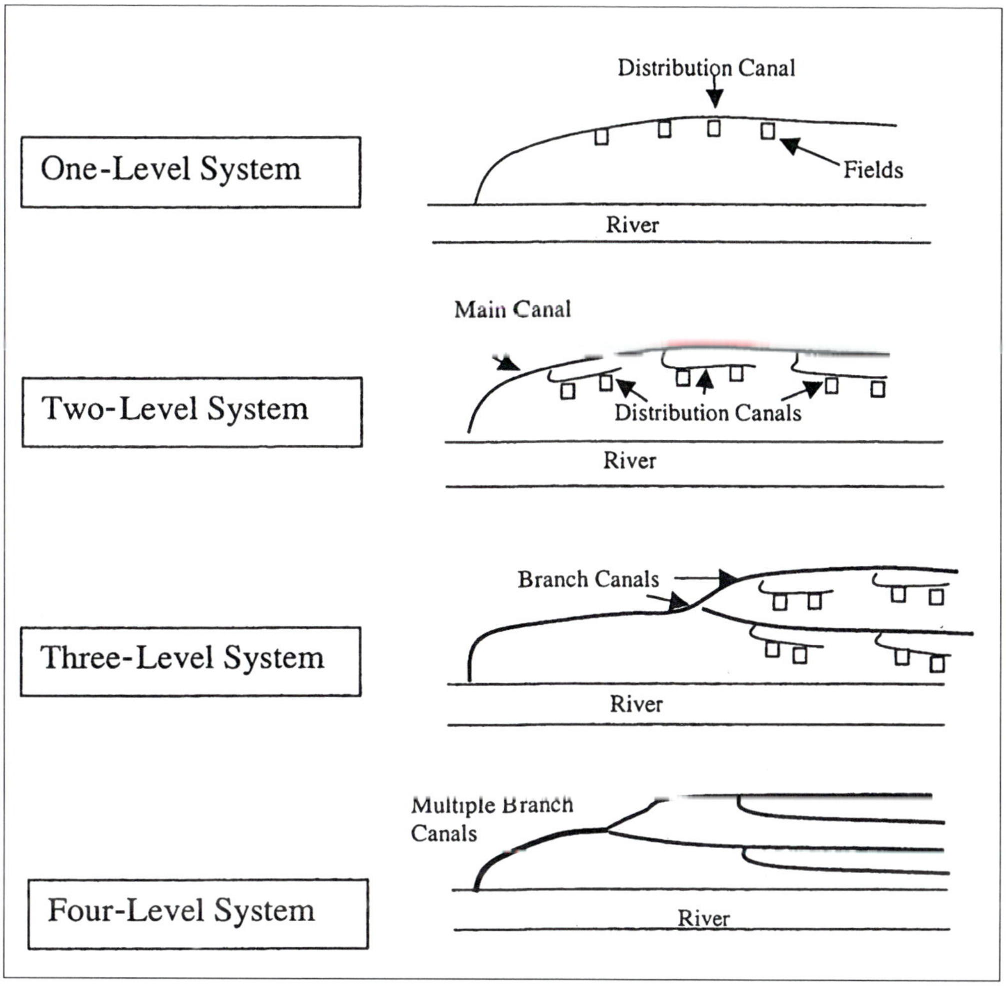

Figure 2.1. Schematic diagram of the number of organizational levels of canal irrigation systems (from Howard 2006:22, after Uphoff 1986:59–66).

levels is less ambiguous and more efficient in addressing the issues of communication and conflict management internal to a canal system. As diagrammed in Figure 2.1, canal systems generally range between one level (simple system) and four levels (often at a state-level system). Uphoff argued that the greater the number of physical levels in a canal system, the greater the complexity of irrigation management. That is, with an increase of each organizational level comes an increase in the hydrologic complexity and the needs for greater communication and interaction among the users and managers of the system.

Another aspect of a canal system that can disclose elements of an irrigation organization is the labor requirement for maintaining the main canal, which is one of the principal tasks for an irrigation organization. Whereas the construction of a new canal typically takes 1 or 2 years, canal maintenance is a persistent concern for irrigators (Woodson forthcoming). Maintenance of the main canal involves cutting off water flow, draining the canal, repairing/rebuilding the diversion dam, removing vegetation and debris, repairing breaks in the embankments and other areas, and cleaning out silt/sediments that have accumulated in the canal since the last cleaning. The most important maintenance event in many irrigation-using societies is preparing the main canal for the next agricultural cycle (see Castetter and Bell 1942:160; Unknown 1974:9–10). Ethnographic accounts of irrigation have indicated that, unlike the construction of new canals and irrigation works, the maintenance of existing main-canal facilities tends to be conducted at regular intervals (annually or biannually), is organized at a local level, and can be highly formalized or ritualized (Castetter and Bell 1942:160; Crawford 1988; Fernea 1970:129–130; Glick 1970:48–51; Lees 1973:29; Lewis 1991; Mitchell 1976:36; Sheridan 1996:41; Unknown 1974:9–10). Work on at least the major canals is communally organized and usually requires a large number of people. The annual "general cleaning" event common to many communities that rely on canal irrigation systems lasts 1–8 days and, in many cases, has been reported to take between 4 and 7 days.

The two particular aspects of main-canal maintenance that can be addressed are the labor requirements for cleaning and the distance between the heading and the nearest habitations. If assumptions are made regarding the amount of soil a worker can move in a day and the duration of the cleaning event, an estimate can be made of the sizes of the work crews that would be needed for the project. These measures provide insight into the number of members in the irrigation organization and the size of the population using the canal system. The diversion structures at the canal heading are ephemeral, and a sudden increase in the water-flow rate (e.g., a flood) can wash them away and cut off water flowing into the canal. This can be detrimental if the water is needed at the time it happens. The heading must be repaired, but how do the irrigators know about the problem, and how do they mobilize to fix it? If they live near the heading, it may not be a problem, but if they live far away, then it potentially is an issue. The distance from the habitations to the heading can indicate how well situated and well prepared the irrigators are to deal with problems with the heading. An effective solution where the main settlements are located far from the heading would be for irrigators to have a station near the heading, to monitor its condition.

These patterns in the internal management structure of irrigation organizations represent important concepts that can be applied to the archaeological analysis of canal systems. Measurement of certain variables, such as system size and canal length, can facilitate an evaluation of the "complexity" of canal-system management, and the physical components of a canal system have been shown to correlate to the social organization of the groups living along it (Howard 2006; Uphoff 1986). Main-canal volume can be used to estimate labor requirements for cleaning, and distance can be measured between the heading and the closest habitations. Archaeological data also can be employed to examine two other aspects of irrigation organizations: their external relationships with the local political systems and the interrelationships among irrigation organizations. Although archaeological evidence alone is not sufficient to reveal the details of an irrigation organization, such data can be utilized to define the general parameters of the agricultural and social landscape that structure the organization of irrigation management. The approach taken in this study is to examine three aspects of the social organization of Hohokam irrigation management through an analysis of canal systems and settlement systems. The framework for this approach is described below.

Previous Research on the Social Organization of Hohokam Irrigation

Hohokam archaeology has a long history of discourse on the social organization of irrigation, especially as it relates to sociopolitical organization. Table 2.1 provides a summary of the major previous models. The impetus for much of this research was Wittfogel's (1955, 1957; see also Steward 1955) hydraulic hypothesis, which proposes that large-scale irrigation in arid regions requires mass labor efforts that must be directed by a centralized authority, which, in turn, leads to greater political integration (Mitchell 1973:532). The Hohokam, with their large irrigation systems, were cited as an example of a hydraulic society that would have required a central managerial authority (e.g., Steward 1955:71–72). However, several prominent researchers (e.g., Haury 1976; Woodbury 1961:556) have contended that clear archaeological evidence of a central managerial authority for the Hohokam is lacking. Although some (e.g., Gregory and Nials 1985) have argued that large Classic period platform-mound sites represent evidence of a managerial elite, the construction of large-scale canal systems was accomplished long before the appearance of such mounds. Both perspectives contradict the hydraulic hypothesis. This apparent contradiction is supported by cross-cultural irrigation studies demonstrating that large-scale canal systems do not necessarily require centralized control by a state or central government (e.g., Hunt 1988a; Leach 1961; Millon 1962; Mitchell 1973).

Most of the models in Table 2.1 emphasize the relationship between labor inputs for canal construction and maintenance and the need for centralized management. Basically, centralized management is assumed to have been necessary where labor requirements are seen to have been high, and vice versa. Hohokam irrigation is variously concluded to have had an egalitarian organization with no central authority (Haury 1976; Woodbury 1961; Woodbury and Ressler 1962) or a complex organization with a central managerial authority (Gregory and Nials 1985; Howard 1993; Nicholas 1981; Nicholas and Neitzel 1984). That is, irrigation management was organized either on a local, small scale or on a centralized, larger scale. Some researchers have surmised that irrigation could have been organized at an inter-system or valley-wide level in the Classic period (Howard 1993, 2006; Masse 1981; Nicholas and Neitzel 1984). Howard (1993:317–318) even suggested that irrigation communities in the Salt and Gila Valleys may have become politically integrated in the Classic period. Other approaches have been offered by Doyel (1981), Ackerly (1982), Crown (1987), Rice (1998), Abbott (2000, 2003), and Hunt et al. (2005). It is notable that nearly all the models in Table 2.1 were based on particular cases, such as Canal System 1 or 2 in the Salt Valley or the Snaketown and Casa Grande canal systems in the Gila Valley. Therefore, the claims may not be applicable to all Hohokam canal systems.

An important concept that emerged from these studies is the "irrigation community," which has been used as a model for characterizing the social organization of prehistoric Hohokam populations along canal systems in modern-day Arizona. Hohokam scholars generally have assumed that "where multiple villages depended upon

Table 2.1. Previous Models of Hohokam Irrigation Organization

Researcher(s)	Basic Description of Model
Woodbury (1961), Woodbury and Ressler (1962), Haury (1976)	Small-scale, egalitarian social systems, accretionary model of canal system growth = labor requirements not very high. Simple traditional agreements would be sufficient for cooperation in irrigation management.
Doyel (1981)	An "irrigation community" is a fundamental unit of Hohokam sociopolitical organization comprising the set of interrelated sites sharing a common, integrated canal system.
Masse (1981)	Centralized control and coordination needed for Canal System 2; valley-wide management organization was needed for water scheduling and allocation.
Ackerly (1982)	No support for "regulated competition" model of water allocation or intersystem management institution; some support for "unregulated" model, but decision making offices (if they existed) at the canal-system level weren't concerned with allocation.
Nicholas and Neitzel (1984)	Major building episodes required over short periods; Canal System 1 doubled in size in the Sedentary period; a complex, centralized sociopolitical organization (that also managed irrigation) developed by the early Sedentary period; intersystem or river-wide management organization was needed in the Classic period.
Gregory and Nials (1985)	Managerial requirements of irrigation were major factors in the development of social organization. Regular spacing of Classic period platform-mound sites along canals implies that farmers practiced water regulation. The need to cooperate and coordinate efforts in system operation was a force for integration into the larger sociopolitical unit (i.e., irrigation organization).
Crown (1987)	Spacing of platform-mound sites in the Casa Grande canal system suggests that they represent significant water-management units in the irrigation community; intervillage water management must have existed; no evidence of intersystem or river-wide management authority.
Nicholas and Feinman (1989)	Based on aerial-photograph analysis, they concluded that there was no basin-level management system in the Salt River basin.
Howard (1990, 1993)	Canal System 2 required a complex, centralized administration by the Colonial period; changes in the Classic period may reflect development of sociopolitical integration at an inter-irrigation-community level in the Salt Valley, and possibly integration between irrigation communities in the Salt and Gila Valleys.
Rice (1998)	Segmentary opposition model, whereby settlements on long canal systems could relate to each other on the basis of force and cooperation. Segments would oppose each other at one level but cooperate in opposition to other segments at a different level.
Abbott (2000, 2003)	A communally organized decision-making body managed Canal System 2 until the early Classic period. Political elites may have taken control of hydraulic works during the Late Classic period, when environmental and social conditions were on the decline.
Hunt et al. (2005)	Canal System 2 managed by communal irrigation organization (irrigation community, municipality, or district), but it is unclear whether the organization was coterminous with the political institution. There probably was no institution for intersystem canal management or for managing all the systems in lower Salt Valley. However, it is plausible that a consortium of communal irrigation organizations in contiguous canal systems cooperated with each other in certain tasks.
Howard (2006)	The physical structure of the canal system is connected with the social organization of groups along it. The "command area" and villages were important organizational units internal to the irrigation community. Rising water scarcity in the Sedentary period led to a need for external relationships between communities, and at valley-wide level, in the Classic period.

a single canal, some form of inter-village management, including agreements on water allocation, had to be in effect" (Haury 1976:149). The concept of the irrigation community was proposed by Schroeder (1966) and has been examined by others (e.g., Doyel 1980, 1981:59–60; Gregory 1991; Gregory and Nials 1985; Howard 1987, 2006). Doyel (1981:59–60) was one of the first to postulate that Hohokam social organization in the Sacaton phase was based on irrigation; specifically, a "local irrigation community" was formed as a result of local villages' relating to each other in terms of a larger irrigation system. He visualized an irrigation community as consisting of at least one large population center with ceremonial architecture (i.e., ballcourts and/or platform mounds)—which could be construed as the ranked village—that served as a focus of integration for surrounding, smaller settlements. Thus, the community should reflect a hierarchy of site types that included the larger ceremonial center (i.e., primary village) and the smaller, agriculture-oriented sites (Howard 1987:212). The irrigation community would have been isomorphic with the larger canal-system entity only when the system included one primary village and its associated populations (Gregory and Nials 1985:384). However, an irrigation community also can refer to a canal system with multiple primary villages. Later studies specifically have identified the irrigation community as a social *and* political unit—above the level of individual settlements—that was concerned with the organization of irrigation tasks, regardless of the number of platform-mound settlements along the canal system (Crown 1987; Gregory 1991; Howard 1987, 2006). The irrigation-community concept has promoted a better understanding of the organization of Hohokam society in recognizing that people and settlements along a canal system clearly were dependent on each other for coordination in certain tasks, such as canal cleaning and maintenance and water allocation. It has forced archaeologists to examine the links among people and settlements along a canal system and to focus on the organizing principles of the community itself.

Many of the models listed in Table 2.1 conflate irrigation social organization with the overall political organization, with the exception of those from Crown (1987), Abbott (2000, 2003), Hunt et al. (2005), and Howard (2006). Yet there is no unambiguous correlation between these two organizational realms, and they may be mutually exclusive (Kelly 1983; Hunt 1988a). This problem is apparent in the usage of "irrigation community," as noted above. In ethnographic accounts, irrigation communities are types of irrigation organizations that represent "institutions for managing commonly held resources—water, storage and delivery systems, and labor—for irrigated agricultural production" (Mabry 1996:22–23). Irrigation communities are alliances of water users that are "autonomous, self-contained organizations . . . supported by consensual, mutually beneficial institutional arrangements" (Mabry 1996:9, citing Hunt 1989). They are, by definition, not controlled by an external authority structure, although they may be articulated with outside institutions (Hunt 1988a:342–343).

A detailed examination of Hohokam irrigation organization was offered by Hunt et al. (2005), who reconsidered the social organization of Hohokam irrigation by evaluating Canal System 2 in the lower Salt Valley in light of the known ethnographic forms of irrigation social organization: acephalous, politically centralized (state or province of a state), private, and communal. These organizational forms can be summarized as follows:

- Acephalous: The canal system has no recognized authority figure to supervise irrigation management. A canal system larger than 100 ha has a very high probability of having a unified or concentrated administrative authority structure (Hunt 1988a:347; see also Tang 1992; Uphoff 1986). Also, it is implausible that a system 1,000 ha or greater in size is acephalous (Hunt et al. 2005:449).

- Politically centralized: "This form of organization is dependent upon the existence of a state, and a fairly strong state at that. As there is no evidence that the Hohokam had a state (Crown 1991; Fish and Fish 2000[b]), this form of irrigation social organization would seem to be implausible" (Hunt et al. 2005:450).

- Private: The "few cases of private charter occur in monetized economies where it is easy to convert assets into money, move the money to other places, and convert that money back into labor and materials. They also involve substantial economic stratification. As neither a money economy nor substantial stratification seem to [have been] characteristic of Hohokam social organization, it follows that . . . a private charter for irrigation seems implausible" (Hunt et al. 2005:450).

- Communal: Having eliminated the previous three forms, Hunt et al. (2005:450) considered the plausibility of the various communal forms of irrigation social organization. In a communal (or community-based) irrigation organization, the charter of authority for the chief administrative officer lay with the members of the group (Hunt 1988a; Hunt et al. 2005:441). The three kinds of communal charter of authority include the "*Irrigation Community*, a corporate group of all and only the users; *Municipality*, the local territorial unit; and *District*, a territorial unit larger than a village created by a state, which is granted management authority over the irrigation facilities" (Hunt et al. 2005:441, my emphasis). An irrigation community includes only farmers as members and is a separate organization from the political administration. A municipality is a situation in which a political-administration system that includes a settlement or set of settlements along a canal system also unifies them for the purposes of irrigation tasks. Hunt et al. (2005:450) noted that a single "village" complex can manage a 1,000-ha system, but a command area in the 1,800-ha range must cover several villages. A district is essentially a modern mode of organization within states (Robert Hunt, personal communication 2009). The example given by Hunt et al. (2005) was Bali, where priests in a system of water temples managed a complex set of irrigation systems through ritual practices (see Lansing 1991).

Hunt et al. (2005) concluded that the various communal forms of irrigation organizations are the most plausible for the Hohokam farmers of Canal System 2 in the lower Salt Valley: "Ethnographically each seems viable. The major question is whether that organization is single purpose (irrigation alone, as in the irrigation communities) or multiple purpose" (Hunt et al. 2005:452). The municipality is isomorphic with the political organization and hence is a multiple-purpose institution; this contrasts with the irrigation community, which is a single-purpose institution. Hunt et al. (2005) were not able to determine whether the irrigation organization of Canal System 2 was coterminous with the political institution(s). More recently, though, Hunt (personal communication 2009) expressed that the district concept is not well developed, in terms of its definition and its applicability to the Hohokam. All the known examples exist within the context of a state, and that may be reason enough to downplay the plausibility of their existence for the Hohokam.

Hunt et al. (2005) also considered whether the Hohokam in the lower Salt Valley had institutions for managing irrigation across canal systems (i.e., inter-system management), or even for managing all the canal systems in the valley. They found no ethnographic basis for positing an institution of either kind, because such institutions have rarely occurred, even in the context of state societies (Hunt et al. 2005:451). However, they suggested that communal irrigation organizations that managed contiguous canal systems may have cooperated with each other in certain tasks, such as water allocation. This is analogous to a consortium of communal systems. As examples, Hunt et al. (2005:441, 451) cited two cases of irrigation-community consortia documented in medieval Valencia in Spain and the Kings River Water Association in Fresno, California. Such a consortium also is seen as a plausible form of organization for large canal-system complexes like Canal System 2 (Hunt et al. 2005:451).

The assessment of irrigation social organization for Canal System 2 presented by Hunt et al. (2005) is not to be construed as meaning that the same kind of irrigation organization has been, or should be, found in canal systems throughout the Hohokam region. The region exhibits considerable spatial variation in geography, subsistence technology, demography, and political economy, and it cannot be assumed that either irrigation or irrigation social organization is homogeneous. Likewise, the ethnographic literature has demonstrated that different kinds of irrigation and irrigation organizations can occur in different settings within the same political territory. Thus, irrigation and irrigation social organization should be approached as an empirical problem for each Hohokam subregion, and this study endeavors to do so.

Most recently, Howard (2006:285) has elucidated a model of the Hohokam irrigation community that contends that the "sociopolitical organization of the irrigation community operates on two distinct levels concurrently, those internal to the irrigation community (the community level) and [those] external to the community (regional and state levels of interaction). It is suggested that in most cases control is vested in both levels, with communities typically executing the majority of the regulatory functions and the daily operation of the irrigation system." As described in the first section of this chapter, Howard (2006) elucidated the internal structure of the irrigation organization by identifying task groups formed at different scales of canal-system operation and interaction to meet the operational requirements of the irrigation system. In regard to external relationships, Howard (2006:281) suggested that "the context of external relationships is one of water-shortages." He (2006:289) argued that pre-Classic period irrigation communities mostly operated independently, without any significant external interactions. But an increase in water shortages during the Sedentary period "created a need for communal resource management that initiated a trajectory of social and political change . . . . The need to retain water rights established new relationships between irrigation communities based on negotiation."

Two other prominent issues have been examined in previous studies of the social organization of Hohokam irrigation and also will be addressed in this volume. First, the Classic period is identified as an important hinge point in the social organization of irrigation. Howard (1993:315) suggested that a complex, centralized administration may have been in place by the Colonial period in Canal System 2. The expansion of irrigation and population in the remainder of the lower Salt Valley reached a peak and possibly a critical threshold at the end of the Sedentary period. Thereafter, the many changes in the Classic period might be primarily reflections of sociopolitical integration on an inter-irrigation-community level (Howard 2006:247–251). Abbott (2003) suggested that a communally organized decision-making body managed Canal System 2 up until the Early Classic period. During the Late Classic period, however, elites may have taken control of the hydraulic works. Gregory (1994) observed that platform mounds were absent from several canal systems along the middle Gila River in the Classic period. In contrast to other models that have argued that platform mounds were related to the organization and administration of labor associated with canal irrigation (e.g., Crown 1987), Gregory (1994:188–189) suggested that "their absence suggests that such organizational functions were not needed, were carried out without the degree of centralized control inferred from the presence of platform mounds, or were directed from elsewhere." He (1994:189) further posited that the mounds "were not simply expressions of a more complex organization required by the presence of multiple settlements along a canal. Rather, they appear to represent the identity and relative autonomy of individual settlements." Elson (1998; also Elson and Abbott 2000) espoused a similar view of platform mounds. Although these changes in irrigation management are not well defined, it is clear that major sociopolitical changes occurred between the pre-Classic and Classic periods, and these provide a backdrop against which to evaluate possible alterations in irrigation social organization.

Second, the regular spacing between ballcourt and platform-mound settlements along canal systems is thought to have been partly related to the administrative requirements of irrigation (e.g., Crown 1987; Fish and Fish 1991; Gregory 1991; Gregory and Nials 1985; Masse 1991). That is, the spacing was related to the length of canal that could be successfully maintained by a single settlement (Crown 1987:154). This inference is based on the Chisholm (1979) proximity-access principle, which posits that settlement location was prescribed by the need to minimize nonagricultural use of irrigable land while minimizing distance to intensively used farmlands (see Crown 1987). In this model, land use in agrarian societies develops with respect to optimal distances of agricultural travel. Chisholm (1979:127) argued that a distance of more than 3–4 km between a settlement and associated fields necessitates an adjustment in settlement. The fact that these major settlements include public architectural features, which are seen as loci of ceremonial and political authority, leads to the implication that irrigation social organization may be tied to other management (e.g., ceremonial or political) institutions.

Recent scholarship (e.g., Elson 1998; Elson and Abbott 2000) has supported the notion of multiple management functions for platform mounds, including ceremony and possibly irrigation. Hunt et al. (2005:450) also supported this notion for ballcourts and platform mounds, observing that this pattern of spatial organization was widespread in the Hohokam region, "including areas like the Tucson [B]asin that are not suitable for large-scale irrigation. . . . Furthermore, hierarchy and power relationships associated with centralized ritual at community centers do not appear to [have been] uniquely tied to irrigation." These arguments are better grounded than arguments based simply on the settlement-spacing data. In fact, Chisholm (1979:61) emphasized that the limiting distance beyond which agriculturalists are unwilling to travel on a daily or semi-daily basis is on the order of 6–11 km where pressure on resources is severe and/or farming is more intensive. Historical-period Pima farmers sometimes would travel from their residences to cultivate fields in other irrigation districts, and even across the river (see Castetter and Bell 1942:126). These distances are far greater than the 3–4 km normally cited by Hohokam researchers.

On the Use of Historical-Period Pima Ethnographies

The above researchers of Hohokam irrigation technology and irrigation organization have not been unanimous on the applicability of ethnographies on historical-period Akimel O'odham (Pima) irrigation. Only a few (e.g., Haury 1976; Howard 1993; Woodbury 1961) have made direct and explicit use of Pima ethnography. Others have not referred to it at all, whereas a few have dismissed using it, entirely. Hunt et al. (2005:435) observed that "the Pima ethnography is nearly silent on crucial questions of irrigation." Moreover, in reference to a statement by Doyel (1991b:226), Hunt et al. (2005:435) concluded that "there seems to be no reason to use the Pima ethnography as a guide for interpreting the vastly larger systems the Hohokam built and operated on the Salt River."

While recognizing that the Hohokam may have surpassed the Pima in the scale of population, public works, and regional economy (cf. Doyel 1991b:226; Hunt et al. 2005:435), I suggest that the Gila River Pima provide an appropriate analog for the specific arena of Hohokam canal irrigation and irrigation organization in the middle Gila Valley. First, many similarities may be drawn between the Hohokam and Pima, including the landscape and environment that had to be managed, canal-irrigation technology, water source, canal-system size (command area) and layout, and ranchería-settlement pattern. Many of the individual Pima canal systems are quite comparable to the Hohokam systems in their layout and size. Indeed, many of the Pima main canals closely followed the alignments of the Hohokam main canals. Yet the total irrigated land that was cultivated by the Pimas only reached a maximum of about 6,000 ha in the mid- to late 1800s (DeJong 2009; Olberg 1919:58–60, 69; Wilson 1999). That is considerably less than the 12,000–19,000 ha estimated to have been irrigated by the Hohokam (Woodson 2010b) (this estimate is discussed in Chapter 3).

Second, Pima ethnographies and other historical documentation have actually provided much information on irrigation, such as canal lengths and discharge, command areas, crop productivity, and land tenure (e.g., Castetter and Bell 1942; Hill 1936; Meskimons 1955; Russell 1975; Southworth 1914–1915, 1919; Wilson 1999). These sources include specific observations about how the Pimas built and maintained the canals, how they organized the labor to do the work, how ownership of irrigated land was assigned and inherited, and how they allocated irrigation water. Although these sources were based on observations made after the onset of Euroamerican influences on Pima irrigation (see Hunt et al. 2005:434–435), I suggest that ignoring the Pima ethnographic record inhibits a more-robust explication of Hohokam irrigation and irrigation organization.

Research Questions and Goals

The central research question guiding this study is "How was irrigation management organized by the Hohokam in the middle Gila River Valley?" An important secondary question is "Did the organization of irrigation management change in the Classic period?" Three aspects of Hohokam irrigation organizations are examined in this study: their internal structures, their external relationships with the local political systems, and the interrelationships among irrigation organizations. In order to address these elements, the study has three research goals: (1) to describe and analyze canal systems and measure their irrigation-management complexity, (2) to describe and analyze settlements and evaluate settlement organization, and (3) to examine settlement organization and canal systems, together, in terms of their implications for the social organization of Hohokam irrigation management. This section outlines the theoretical basis for each of these goals and the framework for the study, including methods.

Research Goal 1: To Describe and Analyze Canal Systems and Irrigation-Management Complexity

An important part of defining the parameters that would have structured the organization of irrigation management is a detailed understanding of the canal system. This includes canal-system layout, the number and types of canals in the system, the location of irrigated fields, the command area (size), and the sequence of development. These would have represented key elements of the built landscape for Hohokam residents living along the middle Gila River. As presented in Appendix A, we now have a detailed understanding of these aspects of the canal systems in the study area.

In addition, it is posited that the irrigation-management complexity of a canal system may have been a significant factor in the organization of irrigation management and, potentially, of settlements. That is, some canal systems may have required more labor, as well as interaction and cooperation, than other systems, to maintain effective irrigation management. The political systems associated with such canal systems may have become more integrated than those associated with less-complex canal systems did. In some ways, this concept is an extension of the hydraulic hypothesis, as argued by Mitchell (1973:533), who emphasized the "synergistic action of irrigation and its centralized coordination that results in greater political integration." Gregory and Nials (1985:384) also recognized that there probably was variability in the irrigation-management complexity of canal systems.

Irrigation-management complexity is characterized by four measures of a canal system: the number of organizational levels, the maintenance burden, the administrative density, and the labor requirements for cleaning the main canals. These measures provide a way of "ranking" the canal systems in terms of their complexity in irrigation management, both within a single system and between multiple systems. It should be instructive to examine variation in the measures, both within and between canal systems. The measures also are helpful in evaluating the links between the irrigation organization and the political organization (as discussed below, in the Research Goal 3 section). As described above, Uphoff (1986:59–60) argued that the number of organizational levels in a canal system is a useful measurement when inquiries are made into the issues of communication and conflict management internal to a canal system. In his model, the greater the number of physical levels in a canal system, the greater the complexity of irrigation management.

Two other measures that can inform on irrigation-management complexity are the maintenance burden and the administrative density of a canal system (Hunt 1988a). Hunt (1988a:344) stated that the ratio of system size (i.e., command area) to the total length of canals in the system would serve as a proxy for maintenance burden. Essentially, this is a measure of the amount of land irrigated per kilometer of canal. He also suggested that this ratio might correlate to variation in administrative structure for a canal-irrigation system, but he was not certain whether it does. Hunt (1988a:344) also discussed an index of administrative density, expressed as a ratio of the number of canal gates to the size of the whole system. He said that this would be a useful measurement of system size, "for it would identify the number of decision points in the system (each gate must be operated; and the more gate operations, the more decisions taken)." Density is posited to increase as a function of the increase in the number of decision-making points. In an archaeological context, it is not possible to confidently identify all canal gates in a system. In lieu of that, administrative density could be expressed as the ratio of the main canal plus the number of distributary canals (1 + n) to the system size (i.e., command area). That would be congruent with the number of gates, because, I assume, the main canal and each distributary canal would have been supplied through a gate. A greater number of gates would have existed, since the laterals also would have had gates, but the number of main and distribution canals will serve as a rough proxy of the total number of gates. Also, the consolidation of two canal systems (i.e., joining them together into one system) most likely would have been accompanied by an increase in maintenance burden (i.e., more canal to maintain) and administrative density (i.e., another decision point).

Lastly, canal-maintenance labor estimates provide a more concrete measure of a major part of the maintenance burden. As noted earlier in this chapter, the best way to measure that is to focus on the annual main-canal cleaning event. If the volume of the canal sediment is known, and assumptions are made regarding the amount of soil a worker can move in a day and the duration of the cleaning event, then an estimate can be made of the sizes of the work crews that would have been needed for the project. These measures provide insight into the number of members in the irrigation organization and the size of the population using the canal system. Also, distance can be measured between the headings and the closest habitations, to evaluate how well situated irrigators were to deal with managing and repairing the heading.

Table 2.2. Canal-System Variables

Variable	Definition/Basis for Measurement	Measurement Value(s)
Composition	number, lengths, and types of canals in the system	main, distribution, lateral (number and length)
Time period	period(s) during which the canals were used	Colonial, Sedentary, and Classic periods
Layout	layout of the whole system: a long, thin, "linear" one with few branchings and few levels (of distributary canals), and a dendritic one, with many branchings and levels	linear, dendritic, combination
Organizational levels	the physical elements of an irrigation system (i.e., main, branch, distribution, and lateral canals and water-control features) constituted levels of system control or levels of operation (Uphoff 1986:59–60; see Howard 2006:22)	1 (simple system) and 2–4 (complex system)
Organizational units	territorial units within a system that represent social organizational units in ethnographically documented irrigation societies (Hunt et al. 2005:442–449)	field, field cluster; lateral, distributary, and main canals
Irrigable area	the amount of land that *potentially* could be irrigated under a canal system	hectares
Size (command area)	size, or extent, is equivalent to command area (or irrigated lands), which is the land under the system irrigated regularly, or at least once	hectares
Maintenance burden	the ratio of system size to the length of canals in the system serves as a proxy for maintenance burden (Hunt 1988a:344); here, though, I use a ratio of length to size, so that higher values equate with a higher burden	kilometers/hectares
Administrative density	the ratio of the number of canal gates to system size (Hunt 1988a:344); alternatively, the ratio of the main canal plus the number of distributary canals to system size	number of main and distributary canals/ hectares
Main-canal cleaning—labor	if the volume of the canal sediment is known and assumptions are made for the amount of soil a worker can move in a day and the duration of the cleaning event, then an estimate can be made of person-days of labor and work-crew size	person-days of labor; work-crew size
Distance to heading	the distance between the heading and the nearest habitation site	kilometers
Consolidation	the connection of two or more separate canal systems into a single system; potentially, this included the merging of the two irrigation social organizations	present/absent
River position	the location of the headgate in regard to upstream vs. downstream	rank (1, 2, ...n) from upstream
Heading reliability	reliability of the water supply at the intake/heading location, based on geology (i.e., bedrock reefs) and historically observed patterns	good, fair, poor (rank = 1, 2, 3)

Methods for Canal-System Analysis

Chapter 1 includes the definitions for basic concepts about canal systems used herein, such as "canal system" and "irrigation organization." Other definitions are given in Table 2.2, which lists the variables that were measured for the canal systems. The methods used in documenting the canal systems are described in Appendix A, including mapping the canal systems, determining the ages of canals, estimating canal-system size (command area), and defining irrigated field areas. Some of these are new methods or refinements of old methods that were developed by the author. The basic documentation of the canal systems represents the culmination of many years of field study and analysis (e.g., Woodson 2002, 2003, 2004, 2007, 2009, 2010b). Irrigation-management complexity was examined by assessing the number of organizational levels, the maintenance burden, and the administrative density in the canal systems (as described above). One difference here is that the maintenance burden was calculated as the ratio of the total length of canals in the system (km) to the system size (multiplied by 1,000), so that higher values equated to a higher burden. These variables were considered internally for each system, as well as being compared between the canal systems. The number of levels was measured on a rank scale that correlated to a hypothetical level of complexity in irrigation management (Uphoff 1986). The other two variables were measured on a ratio scale.

Determining the labor requirements and work-crew sizes for cleaning a main canal involve the following steps: (1) calculate the volume of dirt excavated for canal cleaning, (2) convert those volumes to estimates of person-days required for cleaning the canal (labor requirement), and (3) convert the estimates of person-days of labor to work-crew sizes (see Woodson forthcoming). To calculate volume for canal cleaning, I followed the method outlined by Howard (1990, 1993:283–291), who used the following formula:

$$\text{Volume} = [(A_1 + A_2)/2] * x$$

where A_1 = the cross-sectional area of Point 1, A_2 = the cross-sectional area of Point 2, and x = the linear distance between Points 1 and 2.

The regression formula for reduction in canal cross-sectional area was used to estimate cross-sectional area at given intervals:

$$\hat{y} = z(\log(x+1)) + (\text{y intercept})$$

where $\hat{y}$ = the data point with the known cross-sectional area, x = the distance from the canal head, z = the multiplicative constant (slope), and y intercept = the cross-sectional area at the canal heading (Howard 1990, 1993). The estimation of cross-sectional area for each point was adjusted for the amount inferred to have been cleaned, assuming sediment accumulated from one-quarter to three-quarters of the postulated water-level depth.[1] To convert canal volume into an estimate of the labor requirements for cleaning, I assumed that a person could loosen, contain, and move 3 m^3 of dirt in a person-day of effort (based on studies by Erasmus [1965] and Mabry et al. [2008]). To estimate the sizes of work crews, the person-days of labor were divided by the duration of the cleaning event (I assumed that 1 week and, at most, 2 weeks were reasonable estimates for this; see Woodson [forthcoming]).

Research Goal 2: To Describe and Analyze Settlements and Evaluate Settlement Organization

The organization of the settlements in the study area was evaluated in terms of community organization, through an analysis of spatial, temporal, and functional data on sites and canals. As discussed by Fish and Fish (1991), Hohokam social organization usually is viewed from a political perspective. In their analysis, they distinguished between social-organizational levels that should be interpreted on a kinship basis and those that should be interpreted on a political basis. Fish and Fish (1991:162) argued that intrasite social organization should be viewed primarily on the basis of kinship principles or social structures, whereas multisite organizations are better viewed on a political basis. Kinship-based organizations are evident at the levels of the household, courtyard group, and village segment. *Communities* are political-based organizations that are conceptualized as "supravillage interactive organizations that satisfied requirements for mating, risk management, labor procurement, craft production, and so forth. . . . [They] embody institutions that integrate various settlements into bounded territorial units centered on pivotal sites" (Fish and Fish 1991:162). A community is a kind of civic-territorial organization that consists of "a set of interrelated sites within a bounded community territory . . . [that] contains a center with public architecture" (Fish and Fish 2000a:378). The integrative foundation of these communities primarily was based on ideology rather than kinship, and the "architectural symbols of integration would be comprehensible within an ideology of community identity and territorial affiliation" (Fish and Fish 2000b:164). Fish and Fish (2000a:378–379) observed that southwestern communities are defined by (1) boundaries that are indicated by settlement falloff and (2) an array of community configurations "that may be recognized through a replication of pattern elements at intervals." This model of Hohokam community organization has become known as the focal-village model. The concept is analogous to the settlement complex, which "consists of a central site with public architecture . . . surrounded by satellite settlements lacking such facilities" (Rice 2000:143).

In the Hohokam region, the focal villages included ballcourts and platform mounds and would have served as integrative nodes and administration centers for that community. The political authority for the community was located in the focal village. An assumption of the focal-village model is that each community maintained its own network of social, economic, and political ties (see Abbott et al. 2006:298). Where more than one focal-village community was located along a canal system, for instance, then they could be seen as competing centers pursuing their own interests. Such communities would clearly have needed to interact in certain matters, such as hydraulic management. Also, each one could have been aligned with communities in other canal systems. Along multi-village canal systems, one focal village sometimes appears to have been the preeminent settlement, based on its large size or the number and prominence of its public monuments (see Howard 1987, 2006; Wilcox 1991). Sociopolitical power may have accrued to such preeminent sites on the basis of their being founding villages or being situated closest to either the canal heading or the largest expanse of agricultural land, or some combination of all of these.

The convergence of average distances between pre-Classic period ballcourts (5.5 km) and Classic period platform mounds (5 km) "is highly suggestive of continuity in a basic integrative unit size between the Sedentary and Classic periods" (Fish and Fish 1991:163). Fish and Fish (1991:166) noted that this pattern appears to describe Hohokam settlement in irrigated and unirrigated areas, implying that this is "an abstract structural model for multisite integration, symbolized in public architecture, [that] was held by groups in both core and noncore subareas." That is, this "template" for sociopolitical organization is not necessarily coupled with irrigation systems. There is a consensus among many Hohokam scholars that supports this model of a supravillage, civic-territorial entity (e.g., Crown 1987; Fish and Fish 1991, 2000a, 2000b; Gregory 1991; Wilcox and Sternberg 1983).

Some researchers have surmised that there was a political-organizational unit above the level of focal-village communities that integrated all persons along a canal system (e.g., Abbott et al. 2006; Doyel 1980, 1981; Gregory and Nials 1985). An early version of this model was proposed by Doyel (1980, 1981:59–60, after Schroeder 1966) and "involved a hierarchy of settlement types in which sites along each canal network represented an *irrigation community*. Common use of the system created a basis for sociopolitical integration embodied at larger administrative sites or centers" (Fish and Fish 1991:163, my emphasis). Gregory and Nials (1985; see Crown 1987) later observed that large sites were spaced at regular intervals along canal systems, which, they argued, implies that the farmers practiced water regulation in the system. In this model, "the managerial requirements of the hydraulic works were a major factor in the development of Hohokam social organization in the major river valleys, making political communities coterminous with entire canal systems" (Abbott et al. 2006:290; see Gregory 1991; Gregory and Nials 1985). As described previously, managerial requirements would have included construction, operation, and maintenance of canals and water allocation.

The irrigation-community concept is commensurate with the linear-community model, which "envisions an elongated [political-community] arrangement integrating populations distributed along the routes of irrigation canals" (Abbott et al. 2006:285). The model "questions the existence of a single blueprint for sociopolitical organization implied by the focal village model" (Abbott et al. 2006:291). Abbott et al. (2006:290) also noted that large canal-system complexes (like Canal Systems 1 and 2 in the lower Salt Valley) could have been subdivided into multiple linear communities based along each main canal (see Hunt et al. 2005).

Abbott et al. (2006:290–291) acknowledged that the linear-community and focal-village models are not mutually exclusive concepts. The essence of the difference is the pattern of interaction, and distinguishing the difference is not possible with settlement-pattern data alone. In concept, when a canal system had only one primary village with public architecture, the settlement pattern would have been non-segmented, and the political community essentially would have been isomorphic with the canal system under both community models (see Abbott et al. 2006:290; Gregory and Nials 1985:384). However, where more than one focal-village community occurred along a canal system, the linear community network can only be revealed through patterns of interaction. Analyses of ceramic exchange during the Classic period in Canal Systems 2 (Abbott 2000) and 7 (Abbott et al. 2006) in the lower Salt Valley suggested that social interactions regularly occurred along an entire canal system, rather than strictly around focal-village communities. If these patterns truly represent the network of a political community, then an interesting implication is "What role did the central sites play in irrigation management in a non-segmented community?" For instance, Abbott et al. (2006:300; see Elson 1998; Elson and Abbott 2000) suggested that during the Classic period, the platform mounds were directly linked to ancestor veneration and represented a symbolic legitimization of claims to hereditary territory, including irrigation facilities and cultivated fields. On a functional level, then, the mounds would have served primarily as ceremonial centers for people in surrounding settlements, but perhaps they did not play such a pivotal role in irrigation management for an entire canal system (see also Gregory 1994:188–189).

This research proceeds from the assumption that no Hohokam model has clearly defined a multi-village political structure at the level of a canal system that existed irrespective of the need to cooperate in order to meet the managerial requirements of the canal system. Despite that issue, it is recognized that a canal-wide political institution might have existed along multi-village canal systems. The detection of interaction patterns is outside the scope of this study; so, it is not possible to effectively test the linear-community model in these cases. One alternative line of evidence that is considered here consists of signatures of inter-village dynamics along canal systems, as reflected in the settlement pattern. For instance, some have assumed that the largest village along a canal system was the preeminent settlement and could have used its higher social status and influence to exert a measure of control over other settlements (e.g., Crown 1987; Howard 2006; Rice 1998). Also, the founding village may have taken precedence over subsidiary, or "daughter," villages in certain areas, such as ceremonial matters, as noted in historical accounts among the Tohono O'odham (Underhill 1939; see P. Fish and S. Fish 2007). Certainly the dynamics of cooperation and competition among villages would have affected aspects of irrigation management, such as water allocation (see Hunt and Hunt 1976; Mabry 1996). Although these preeminent villages probably were influential in many situations, their assumed superiority does not necessarily indicate the existence of a multi-village polity. Where notable, some speculation is offered regarding the plausibility of a canal-wide political institution in these cases, but the settlement-pattern data can only be used as circumstantial evidence to support that concept.

For the purposes of the research herein, the primary information required about settlement organization concerns the functional differentiation and spatial arrangements of sites, the distribution of habitation sites and population along the canal systems, the nature of the settlement pattern (e.g., segmented or non-segmented, dispersed or nucleated), the location of focal villages (villages with public architecture), and the interpretation of the focal-village-community territories. The largest civic-territorial unit that is confidently defined here is the focal-village community. The approach assumes that the focal-village communities represent important political-organization units, in accordance with the concepts described above. The inability to confidently assess the existence of a canal-wide polity (e.g., using the methods outlined by the linear-community model) does not present major issues to the analyses, although some uncertainty is introduced into the examination of the external relationship between the irrigation organization and the political structure (discussed below, in the Research Goal 3 section).

Settlement Patterns and Labor Organization

In examining a settlement pattern, one must keep in mind its implications, not only for community organization, but also for labor organization. The two organizational forms are interrelated and can influence each other. There are two separate aspects of labor to consider, because they have been organized differently in the majority of known ethnographic cases: (1) canal labor and (2) field labor. Canal labor mostly falls under the purview of the irrigation organization. Howard (2006, following Uphoff 1986) argued that the physical structure of a canal system is connected with the social organization of the groups living along it. Different types of task groups are associated with the various physical levels of the irrigation system. The distribution of settlements and population in relation to distributary canals (i.e., distribution and main-branch canals) is of particular relevance here. Howard (2006:104–107) identified the "command area," consisting of a set of fields receiving water from a common distribution canal and the cooperating farmers operating it, as a major level in the internal organization of an irrigation community. This notion of "command area" should not be confused with its usage in reference to the land under a canal system that is irrigated regularly. The command area is shown to represent the most basic organizational unit, which frequently had a legal charter and was responsible for the organization of labor for operation and maintenance activities along the distribution canal. At a higher organizational level, Howard (2006:287) interpreted villages, especially those with public architecture, as important administrative nodes that are "focused on water scheduling, water allocation and local conflict resolution." However, he found that main and branch canals do not appear to have operated as strong organizational nodes (Howard 2006:110).

The second case is field labor, which was not managed by the irrigation organization. A pivotal question is "Did irrigation agriculture affect settlement decisions and the settlement pattern?" Pertinent to this issue is a theory of agrarian settlement by Glen Stone (1996:56) that described the phenomena that "produce constraints and tendencies for subsistence and peasant farmers cross-culturally." Stone's case study of Kofyar dryland farming in the Nigerian savannah is not directly analogous to the intensive irrigation agriculture of the Hohokam, but the analytical concepts he employed are useful to the current study. Specifically, they are useful to the analysis of the settlement pattern/settlement organization in relation to agriculture and field-labor organization. Both the Kofyar and the Hohokam were intensive agriculturalists. I suggest that the settlement trends that Stone identified as responses to the needs for field-labor organization operated for the Hohokam, too. Although those trends operated parallel to the settlement trends that occurred in response to the needs for canal labor, I argue in the following chapters that the aspects of labor organization for canals and fields would have mutually reinforced each other.

Stone (1996:28) started "with what we know of food production systems and then link[ed] these agricultural considerations with settlement decisions." He showed "how it is specifically interaction in agricultural production that affects site spacing, and how the relationship can be understood only by first understanding the social organization of agriculture" (Stone 1996:22). Stone analyzed the relationships between agricultural production and settlement pattern, to isolate the factors that drive agrarian settlements. His model focuses on the agricultural changes that occur with population pressure, which have profound effects on settlement. Stone's theory is grounded in the Von Thunen and Chisholm land-use model and the proximity-access principle: "the greater one's need to access any landscape feature, the greater the premium on residing near that feature" (Stone 1996:14). The Chisholm (1979) land-use model posits that land use in agrarian societies will develop with respect to optimal distances for agricultural travel. When distances extend beyond a 3–4-km zone from existing settlements, the tendency is for new settlements to be established in the farmed areas outside that zone.

Stone (1996) focused on changes in agrarian settlement in relation to agricultural intensification, which is the process of increasing production concentration (i.e., output per unit of land). For Boserup (1965), intensification refers to "changes in fallow from long-fallow to short-fallow to annual cropping to multiple cropping" (Hunt 2000:261). Turner and Doolittle (1978) later pointed out that intensification must be defined as increasing agricultural output per unit of land *and* per unit of time (Hunt 2000:261; Stone 1996:29). In most usage by archaeologists, "intensification" is defined as an increase in one or more *inputs* into a plot land, such as labor, technology, or fallow time (e.g., Adler 1996:343; Redman 1999:160, 166). However, an increase in inputs does not always lead to intensification (Hunt 2000:261). Hunt (2000:272) suggested that changes in technology are at the core of the intensification process, and he proposed the term "agricultural development," defined as "changes in technology that increase the output per unit of land and time." For the purposes of the current study, the types of intensification that are plausible are irrigation (which is certain) and double cropping (which is almost certain, according to Hunt and Ingram [2007]). Other inputs are possible, such as changes in fallow time or addition of fertilizers, but our ability to decipher these for the Hohokam is limited, and that deciphering would not be feasible (see Howard 1993:305).

For Boserup (1965), the driving force for increased production concentration is population pressure, or "a rising ratio of food demand to the quantity and quality of productive land" (Stone 1996:30). However, factors other than population pressure (e.g., market demand, risk aversion, or social production—which are not necessarily relevant to subsistence agriculture) can induce intensification, and also, actions other than intensification (e.g., migration, conflict, or trade) can occur in response to population pressure (Netting 1993; Stone 1996:28–40). Moreover, local ecological conditions can significantly affect agricultural potential and output efficiency, and these conditions figure prominently in farmers' decisions to intensify (Stone 1996:34–40). The Boserupian model is general and thus requires assumptions. Nevertheless, the Boserupian model of agricultural change—emphasizing rising population density as the primary variable influencing cultivators toward agricultural intensification—generally has proven to be a good predictor of intensification for situations in which production concentration can be raised, but at the expense of lowered efficiency (Adler 1996:343; Netting 1993; Stone 1996:31). Stone (1996) took into account the challenges to the model and thus extended the concept of population pressure by elucidating how *land pressure*, the ratio of population to productive land, leads to either intensification or abandonment/migration. This concept was found to be useful in the current analysis.

By proceeding from these basal theories, Stone (1996:43) argued that residences are "pulled" toward plots by intensification, a process he called "settlement dispersal," which "is a measure of how close the population lives to the fields it cultivates" (see Chisholm 1979:113). Another element that contributed to a dispersed settlement pattern was land tenure, since residing near intensively cultivated plots allows for individuals to better assert control over the land (Stone 1996:43; see also Netting 1993; Smith 1972:415). Thus,

> [in] other words, increasing *population density* should lead to each farmer's operating on less land and investing more labor, usually requiring more trips to the plot or plots. Increasing population in villages leads to expansion of the cultivation radius at the same time that it demands intensification. Farmers must spend more time on plots that tend to be farther away. This should encourage social units of production to be pulled away from the village, placing a premium on *settlement dispersion*" [Stone 1996:43–44, my emphasis].

Stone (1996:48–49) pointed out that even where population density, agricultural intensity, and land tenure are highly correlated, such as in highland New Guinea (Brown and Podolefsky 1976), these cases exhibit more settlement dispersion than is often recognized by anthropologists.

At the same time, Stone (1996:44–50) observed that there are several factors that pull settlements together (i.e., agglomeration, or "settlement gravity") and can lead to aggregation, which operates against the tendency toward settlement dispersal. These factors dilute the pull of the proximity-access principle to any plot (Stone 1996:49). Such pulls toward aggregation have included military threat/protection, attraction to central places, and reliance on fields in multiple locales (field fragmentation); labor organization/mobilization is easier in aggregated settlements (see Stone 1996:48–50; see also Cordell and Plog 1979). Stone (1996:51) argued that "whatever the factors favoring agglomeration of intensive farmers (see Glassow 1977), the result is a spatial contradiction—a pull toward the farm for agroecological reasons and toward the nucleated settlement for social, economic, military, or other reasons (Bunge 1962; Richards [1978])." Where the pull toward dispersal is matched or overridden by a pull toward a nucleated settlement, "we should expect the development of *satellite settlements*" (Stone 1996:48, emphasis added). These satellites vary in the intensity of their occupation, but they may move along a spectrum and evolve into homes (Stone 1996:51). Such a change "may result from the variables of distance to plot and agricultural intensity as described above: as more labor is invested in the satellite farm, there is increasing utility in the workers' spending more time close to the plot" (Stone 1996:51).

A second, related question to consider is "Does the organization of field labor influence settlement and the distribution of population?" Stone (1996:53–56; see also Stone et al. 1990) demonstrated how the organization of labor and labor scheduling have been most instrumental in the shaping of Kofyar settlement patterns. The proximity-access principle applies to accessing neighbors' plots as well as one's own: workers collaborate more willingly if they live closer (Stone 1996:55; see Erasmus 1956:446). This is a major influence on settlement where cooperative labor, or labor pooling, is important for field work. This tendency of regularly working others' fields means that residences are pulled not only to their own plots (settlement dispersal) but also to other residences (settlement gravity).

It is unclear whether cooperative labor for field work is an important element in settlement decisions for irrigation agriculturalists (including the Hohokam), as it was in the Kofyar case. For intensive agriculture, such as irrigation agriculture, the general position is that irrigated farms are worked by the landowners and their families (e.g., Hunt et al. 2005:443; Netting 1993). Occasionally, there are reports of cooperative labor, such as transplanting in wet rice systems in southeast Asia. Castetter and Bell (1942:126) stated that among the Pima, "there were no community fields, but families worked reciprocally." In another Pima account, Hill (1936:587) observed that

> [t]he responsibility for the development of the assigned plot was purely individual, *though communal labor was often involved in clearing and harvesting*. The family, occasionally with the help of neighbors, cleared the land, fenced it when necessary, and built and maintained the lateral or feeder ditches. *Any outside assistance was always paid for in kind or in produce* [my emphasis].

Table 2.3. Site Variables Measured in the Settlement-System Analysis

Variable	Definition/Basis for Measurement	Measurement Value(s)
Site type	site type as defined by archaeological survey, based on observations of surface remains, features, and artifacts	village, habitation, artifact scatter, canal, etc.
Time period	period(s) during which the settlement was occupied, based on surface-artifact collections	Colonial, Sedentary, and Classic periods
Site area	spatial area of a site within the defined boundary	square meters/hectares
Public architecture	the type, number, and size of public architecture (ballcourts or platform mounds) present at a settlement	ballcourt, platform mound
Site function	function as determined by the Wells et al. (2003, 2004) model using density and diversity measures of surface artifacts	village, habitation, camp, canal, multiple-activity area, limited-activity area
Settlement/habitation type	settlements that are typed as habitations are further classified as one of four types in the settlement hierarchy, based on definitions in Gregory (1991)	village, hamlet, camp (farmstead or field house)
Settlement-hierarchy levels	scholars (e.g., Doyel 1980; Gregory 1991; Wilcox 1991) have argued that Classic period settlements were organized into a hierarchy of four to five levels, with the uppermost/most-complex political tier composed of sites with platform mounds, Casa Grande tower, ball-court, and numerous compounds	village with public architecture, village without public architec ture, hamlet, farmstead, field house
Distance between settlements	linear distances/spacing between settlements (habitations)	kilometers
Settlement distribution	general distribution of habitation sites within the zone of occupation along a given canal system	nucleated, dispersed
Distance to canals	linear distances between permanently occupied habitation sites (villages and hamlets) and the nearest canal	meters
Distance to fields	linear distances between the center of each permanently occupied habitation site (villages and hamlets) and the closest field (minimum) and farthest field (maximum); maximum distances do not overlap with those measured from other, closest habitations; averages of minimum and maximum distances per period, respectively, are used in analysis	meters
Population size (based on irrigated land)	size (ha) of irrigated lands can be used to estimate the amount of food that could be grown and, further, to generate a rough estimate of the number of people that could be supported annually on those crops	size (ha) of irrigated lands
Population size (based on residential-site area)	population size is estimated through a proxy measure of residential-site area (in ha) and inferred density (10 persons/ha and 20 persons/ha), as per Kowalewski et al. (forthcoming)	size of residential area (ha) in settlements

Thus, cooperative labor on irrigated fields has been documented, including for the Pima, but that does not appear to have been the norm. There was, of course, cooperative labor on the irrigation system, but that is always seen as distinct from work on the farmlands. They are, in effect, almost always two different work environments (and property environments, as well; see Netting 1993). The irrigation organization is responsible for managing and organizing labor for the irrigation system (especially the larger, more labor-intensive tasks). However, the settlement trajectories that emerge as a result of the interaction between settlements and fields have an indirect effect on irrigation organization. An element of how this might occur can be seen in Uphoff's (1986; see also Howard 2006) model, which asserts that the physical structure of a canal system is connected with the social organization of the groups living along it (which also may constitute the task groups responsible for managing a particular segment of the system).

Methods of Settlement-System Analysis

The variables that were measured in the settlement-system analysis are described in Table 2.3. The methods used in documenting the settlements are provided in Appendix B, including the definitions of site functions and habitation sites, as well as time-period designations. Briefly, a site is a bounded area that includes at least 30 surface artifacts or one feature and is separated from other sites by at least 100 m. A locus is similar, except it is separated from other loci by less than 100 m and is contained within a site boundary. Habitation sites are where people resided either year-round or on a seasonal basis, as distinguished by residential features such as trash mounds, architecture or structural mounds, public architecture (ballcourts and platform mounds), and cemeteries. Settlement hierarchy provides a measurement of the political organization, and ballcourts and platform mounds represent "the architectural symbols of integration [that] would be comprehensible within an ideology of community identity and territorial affiliation" (Fish and Fish 2000b:164).

Site types were assigned during survey fieldwork. However, more-specific site-*function* designations were based on an approach developed by Wells, Rice, and Ravesloot (2003, 2004) that uses density and diversity measures of surface-artifact collections to evaluate the function of a given site or locus (see Appendix B for details). The method is quite useful in assessing sites typed as artifact scatters, because these constitute roughly 70 percent of recorded sites on the Gila River Indian Community (GRIC). The measures were compared against baseline measures for sites of known function, then each artifact scatter was assigned to one of the functional categories, based on the best fit. By coding sites based on a functional designation (e.g., village, activity area, or field house), I suggest, it is possible to achieve a more detailed picture of the structure of Hohokam communities along the Gila River.

The assessment of settlement organization is based on the concepts of the political-organization models described above. The primary focus in terms of organizational nodes is at the level of the village and focal-village community. A focal-village community is recognized as a set of interrelated sites within a bounded territory that has a center with public architecture (the focal village). The focal villages tend to be distributed at regular intervals, and the community boundaries may be indicated by settlement falloff. Settlement-pattern data can be used to identify such communities, as determined through an analysis of spatial, temporal, and functional data. The analysis focuses on the arrangement of various types of sites, defined on the basis of the site-function model, with a focus on habitation sites and their associated activity areas. This evaluation is operationalized by examining the spacing and distribution of settlements (according to site function) and population in relation to canals and fields along the canal system. The protocol for defining community-territory boundaries is described below.

Where multiple such communities exist along a canal system, the settlement pattern is described as segmented; where only one occurs, it is non-segmented. In essence, this is analogous to a nucleated or dispersed settlement pattern, respectively, as determined by the distribution of permanently occupied habitation sites. Where such communities are identified, they are examined to see if they contain similar proportions of site types. The objective is to ascertain if the site-type proportions in the communities are reasonably similar to each other (but not necessarily statistically significant).

In regard to assessing which settlements are associated with certain canal systems, an assumption is made regarding the proximity of the residences of irrigators to their fields and the canal system. I assume that the vast proportion of Hohokam farmers resided along the canal system in proximity to their fields. Both Howard (2006) and Clark (2004) found this to be generally true in their ethnographic case studies of irrigation societies. Membership in the irrigation social organization may be determined by co-residence, kinship, geographic proximity of irrigated properties, or some combination thereof (Clark 2004:165). Yet co-residence is not mandatory (Mabry 1996:13), and in some cases, farmers will travel great distances from their homes to their fields. Chisholm (1979) indicated that farmers might travel 6–11 km, whereas Castetter and Bell (1942:126) stated that the Pima would travel 6–8 miles [9.6–12.8 km] each day (however that was during the height of Apache raiding, when the Pima were living in nucleated settlements for protection). The validity of that assumption may be higher for the early periods of Hohokam irrigation but may diminish for later periods, when farmers' descendants moved away from the ancestral homes but retained land or water rights in the ancestral canal system.

Community-Territory Boundaries

In order to define a political community in archaeological terms, it is necessary to draw a boundary around the community territory. For a focal-village community, the general concept is that each community includes a set of interrelated settlements within a bounded territory that has a center with public architecture, and the focal villages are distributed at regular intervals. The proportions of site functional types encompassed by the territories should be similar to those in other communities for each time period. For linear communities, the territory is, by definition, commensurate to the extent of the canal system.

During the initial analyses for this research in Study Area 1, circles were used to define the focal-village-community territories (Figure 2.2a). When the interval distance between central sites was established for each period, the territory was identified by placing a circle on a map (centered on a central site) with a diameter equivalent to the interval. The community would consist of the settlements within the circle. However, this generic boundary was found to be unsatisfactory after the analysis had proceeded to advanced stages for Study Area 1. First, there was a lack of settlement falloff between the focal villages; that is, there was not a clear spatial separation of settlements among the inferred territories. Second, the settlement falloff to the north and south of the focal villages occurred too rapidly. Third, two community boundaries overlapped each other, so the sites in the overlap zone were not associated clearly with one or the other community (or both communities).

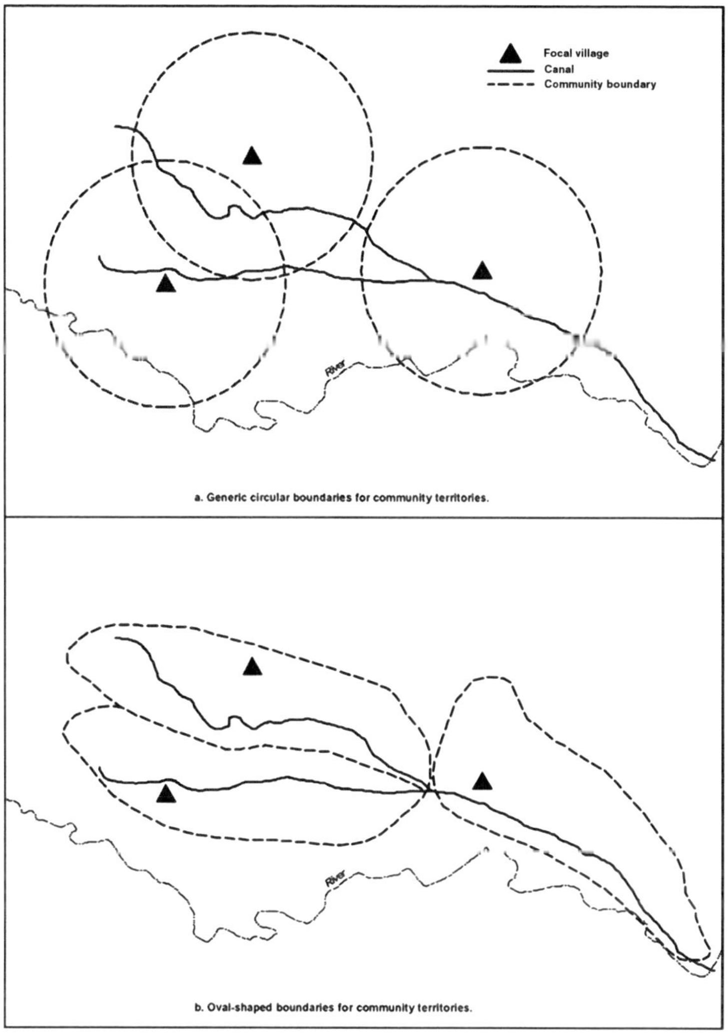

Figure 2.2. Diagram showing two ways of defining community-territory boundaries.

Lastly, there were some camps that did not fall within any of the community territories.

Further analysis indicated that the community territories could not be defined without reference to the physical layout of the canal system, the locations of settlements along the system, the inferred priorities of the Hohokam in deciding where to locate new settlements, and the natural geographic features that probably served as a kind of social boundary (albeit a permeable one). As described in Appendix B and Chapter 5, the focal villages in Study Area 1 were founded at or near the tail ends of the three principal main-canal segments, each concurrent with the building of each new segment. Instead of using a circle to model the community territories, it was found that the territories could be modeled better by oval-shaped boundaries that extended upstream from the focal villages, along the main-canal segments (see Figure 2.2b). The oval length was roughly equal to the spacing interval between one village and the next upstream village for a given time period. In this way, the focal villages were situated at or near the tail ends of the major main-canal segments, and the constituent settlements of each community extended upstream from the focal village, along the canal. Most of the caveats noted in the previous paragraph for the circular territory were resolved by this approach: (1) there was no longer a rapid settlement falloff to the north, south, and west of the communities, and so, the territories did not encompass too much "empty" space; (2) the two community boundaries no longer overlapped but, instead, were divided along a natural wash drainage that probably represented a natural boundary during prehistory; and (3) the camps that were not encompassed within any of the circular territories were more clearly associated with communities. One issue that was not completely resolved by this revised community-boundary method was the clear identification of boundaries between communities for which there was no settlement falloff or natural boundary. In those instances, other criteria were used to mark boundaries in the most appropriate locations, such as the oval territory length (based on village-spacing intervals) and territory boundaries established from the previous time period.

From an irrigation-management perspective, the oval-shaped community-territory configuration that extends upstream along the canal from the focal village also makes more sense than a circular one. For instance, by using the oval territory, the settlement near the head of the Study Area 1 canal system was linked with Snaketown village. This is important, because it is critical for farmers and residents along a canal system to have control of the headworks, to ensure a proper supply and regulation of water. Another argument in favor of the oval territory is that it encompasses the settlements distributed along the branch canals and their respective distribution canals, since these canals appear to have been an important basis for social organization (see Howard 2006; Hunt et al. 2005). These kinds of communities could be commensurate to what Howard (2006:26–29) described as "branch canal task groups," which are amalgamations of "command area task groups."

Settlement Distribution and Population Size

Population size and settlement distribution also were analyzed during the test of the community models. Attention was given to the distances between habitation sites, especially between villages with public architecture, and to the distances between settlements and fields. The general distribution of population along the canal system (e.g., nucleated/dispersed, linear, or clustered) also was considered. Another aspect that was examined was where new settlements were founded in relation to the canals and fields. These settlement decisions probably developed with respect to optimal distances for agricultural travel, as a result of least-cost-principle rules.

Considerations of population size were integrated into the analysis. Following Kowalewski et al. (forthcoming), two methods were used to estimate population. One estimate was based on the size (or command area, in hectares) of irrigated lands for each canal system, which could be used to generate a rough estimate of the number of people that could be supported annually on the crops. Castetter and Bell (1942:54–56) reported that a Pima (Akimel O'odham) family of five cultivated an average of 0.86–2.15 ha (2–5 acres) of irrigated land per year (or 0.17–0.43 ha per person, per year). Hunt and Ingram (2010) reported that Castetter and Bell stated in their field notes from Sacaton (ca. 1938–1939) that the average household could operate about 2 ha (5 acres). For a household of five people—which is based on Padre Kino and Manje's observations of early-historical-period Pima families in 1699 (Ezell 1961:16)—this equates to 0.4 ha per person. Likewise, Kowalewski et al. (forthcoming) assumed that roughly 0.4 ha of irrigated land was required per person to fulfill basic subsistence needs. Population size was calculated here at 0.4 ha per person, per year.[2]

The second population estimate was based on residential-site area at habitation sites. Generating population estimates from residential area is possible by using a multiplier for population density, but density in Hohokam settlements is still a debated issue. Kowalewski et al. (forthcoming) found that primary villages in the Hohokam region had low internal-population densities, in the general range of 5–20 persons per hectare. That assessment was based on a survey of Hohokam population studies. Referring to Craig's (2000) study of the Grewe site, they used a density of 10 persons per hectare for pre-Classic period villages in the middle Gila Valley. Kowalewski et al. (forthcoming) observed that Classic period villages with compound residential architecture exhibited similar density ranges, with the exception of some pueblo-style and *trincheras* sites. Yet they also noted that villages with 10 persons per hectare would have been an unusually dispersed pattern for a society with intensive agriculture requiring coordinated labor on canal systems (Robert Hunt, personal communication 2006; Kowalewski et al. forthcoming). My own analysis of the data from the 2.1-ha portion of the Grewe site investigated by Craig (2001a) indicated that the population density varied between 9.8 and 22.1 persons per hectare between the early Pioneer and Middle Sedentary periods, with an average of 20.4 persons per hectare over those periods (assuming that houses were replaced every 25 years). Whether that density can be extrapolated to the entire Grewe settlement is unclear, but it provided an empirically based calculation. In this study, I used a range of 10–20 persons per hectare for the population estimates.

Two last issues are relevant to the estimation of population size. First, many of the settlements were occupied for several centuries, and fields were farmed for equally long periods. It was therefore necessary to address potential problems in estimating population size. An effort was made to quantify the area of irrigated lands and residential-site area by time period, based on the methods outlined above. That provided a level of temporal resolution sufficient for both methods of population estimation in this study. Second, as will be made clear in subsequent chapters, the population estimates based on command area were all larger than the largest estimates based on residential-site area (at 20 persons per hectare), with the exception of the Santan canal system in the late Colonial and Sedentary periods. This could indicate that more than 0.4 ha per person was required for subsistence, that not all of the command area was farmed at any one time, or that population density was higher than 20 persons per hectare—or a combination of all three. Another factor that is relevant to the exception noted for the Santan system is that produce from non-irrigated fields may have provided additional subsistence for people. In general, then, the population estimate based on command area might have set a theoretical upper limit on the actual population size. The more important estimate for the purposes of the ultimate arguments in this study is the one based on residential-site area.

Research Goal 3: To Examine Settlement Organization and Canal Systems as They Pertain to the Social Organization of Irrigation Management

The primary thrust of the study is to examine the political organization of the settlements and the canal systems, together, in terms of their implications for the social organization of irrigation management. Three aspects of Hohokam irrigation organizations are examined: their internal structures, the external relationships with the local political systems, and the interrelationships among irrigation organizations. The framework for discussing these three elements was provided by the analysis results for the canal systems (Research Goal 1) and the settlement organization (Research Goal 2).

Internal Structure

Internal structure was explored by focusing on what the results of Research Goals 1 and 2 informed us in regard to the trends in canal-system layout and size, settlement organization and the distribution of settlements and population, canal-labor requirements, and labor organization. The four elements addressed and the methods for addressing them were the following:

1. Unified administrative authority. If the command area of a canal system is over 100 ha, then the irrigation organization probably had a unified (or centralized) authority structure.

2. Adequacy of the population to meet the labor requirements for canal maintenance. The minimum work force requirements were compared to the minimum population size as calculated by residential-site area.

3. Task-group organization. The distribution of habitation sites and population in relation to the primary elements of the canal system were examined as described earlier in this chapter (Howard 2006; Uphoff 1986).

4. Dynamics of inter-village relationships along multi-village canal systems and their effects on irrigation management. How irrigation management may have been influenced if a preeminent site was present along the canal was considered, especially if it had a position near the canal heading or expansive agricultural land.

External Relationship with the Local Political System

Examination of this aspect asks, "Were the organizations that were responsible for irrigation management different from the political institutions, or were they the same?" Another way to ask this is "Were irrigation tasks managed or controlled by authorities that administered other political tasks?" That is, "Were the middle Gila River irrigation social organizations multiple-purpose entities?" Unfortunately, this is a difficult issue to assess for the Hohokam, because the decision-making loci within these organizational units are not clearly reflected in the archaeological record. The approach taken in this study is therefore a simplified one and extends from the analysis of settlement organization as described in the Research Goal 2 section, above. The assessment is most focused on the organizational nodes represented by focal villages and focal-village communities. Where multiple focal-village communities existed along a canal system, the settlement pattern is described as segmented; where only one occurred, it is described as non-segmented.

Addressing this question of the link with the political system is directly relevant to evaluating the type of irrigation organization that managed the canal system. Based on the analytical guidelines by Hunt et al. (2005), which are summarized above, my initial assessment of the middle Gila Valley canal systems suggests that they were managed by one of the three communal forms of irrigation organization (irrigation community, municipality, and district). As in the lower Salt Valley, there is no apparent evidence to suggest that the Hohokam living along the middle Gila River had acephalous, private, or politically centralized (i.e., on the state level) irrigation organizations (see Hunt et al. 2005:449–450; see also Crown 1987:156). As was also noted above, Robert Hunt (personal communication 2009) now considers the district concept to be weak and probably irrelevant to Hohokam irrigation studies. I concur with that opinion, and this study therefore will not utilize the district concept. The other two communal forms are defined largely on the basis of their relationships with the local political systems. An irrigation community is a separate organization from the local political administration. In the case of a municipality, the irrigation organization would be articulated with the local political administration, including a situation in which it links several settlements along a canal system (see Hunt et al. 2005). By extension, the irrigation community is a single-purpose institution, whereas the municipality is a multiple-purpose one.

Based on these perspectives, it is posited that two basic situations should occur in the study area:

1. If there is only one village with public architecture along a canal system, then the settlement pattern would be non-segmented (and contiguous with the canal system). In this case, it is more plausible that the authority for the political institution also had authority over the decisions and activities within the irrigation organization (i.e., a municipality), because there is only one community/one political structure along the canal system. The territory of the political community is essentially the same as that covered by the irrigation organization, so the irrigation authority role could feasibly be embedded in the political leadership roles. Yet an irrigation community still cannot be ruled out as a possible form of the irrigation organization in this case.

2. On the other hand, if there are two or more villages with public architecture along a canal system, then each focal village and its associated community will have its own political institution/structure. The settlement pattern would be segmented, and the political structure, fragmented among the multiple communities. I argue that the authority for managing the irrigation organization along the canal system would have been independent of these political structures. In such a case, the evidence of irrigation organization would be analogous to that of an irrigation community. If the authority for the irrigation community was independent, it still could have been—and probably was—linked with the political institutions for each of the separate village communities.

The relevance of this distinction is the locus of authority for the irrigation organization. In a municipality, the authority for the irrigation organization probably was the same as the political authority. The significance is that the political leaders may have had more direct control over the means of agricultural production at the level of the canal system. Irrigated produce would have been ideal for Hohokam leaders or aggrandizers seeking to control economic sources of political power. In the case of an irrigation community for which the irrigation-authority position feasibly was independent of that of the political authority, there would have been less potential for political leaders to control the means of production at the canal-system level.

One caveat for the second scenario is that multiple focal-village communities along a canal system feasibly could have been integrated into a canal-wide polity. The irrigation organization might then have been analogous to a municipality. As noted previously, Hohokam researchers have not developed a consensus on how to recognize a multi-village polity, because there is not a clear archaeological signature for it (other than the sharing of a canal). The linear-community model examines interaction patterns as evidence of such an institution, but that approach has problems and is also beyond the scope of this study. Some attention is given to inter-village dynamics as evidenced in settlement pattern, such as the role of the "preeminent" settlement, but that approach also has limitations.

Interrelationships among Irrigation Organizations

Finally, other data are brought to bear in the examination of the interrelationships among separate irrigation organizations. These relationships might have involved formal negotiations or larger-scale alliances (Howard 2006:212). For example, Hunt et al. (2005:441) cited two ethnographic cases of irrigation-community consortia, which developed when a "number of contiguous irrigation systems organized as irrigation communities combine in a consortium to manage some of their affairs." The decision to cooperate on a level external to the irrigation organization is directly related to the benefit of engaging in such a relationship. These benefits fall into three general categories: construction of infrastructure, a higher level of conflict management, and communal resource management (Howard 2006:219). The last category is concerned with the management of communally used resources that are necessary for the survival of an economic system (Howard 2006:222). In the case of the Hohokam, the clearest example of such a shared resource would be water, but it also could be labor. I suggest that the first category should include both construction *and* maintenance of infrastructure. The cases in the study area were assessed in terms of the benefits and costs of cooperating with other irrigation organizations in these contexts. However, the exact character of those interrelationships cannot realistically be observed in the archaeological record, because even the ethnographically known cases of intersystem-management institutions are nearly invisible in material terms (see Hunt et al. 2005:451). The current study considers whether the ethnographic examples of such interrelationships could plausibly have occurred among the Hohokam canal systems in the study area.

---

[1] I determined this by actually "drawing" the canal cross section at the area indicated by the regression formula, then "drawing" the sediment-depth lines at the given depths, and then calculating those areas. First, the maximum water level in the canal was assumed to have been equivalent to the wetted part of the canal, or roughly two-thirds of the maximum canal depth (which allowed for a one-third freeboard). Second, areas were calculated for a range of possible sediment-accumulation depths, from one-quarter to three-quarters of the postulated water-level depth. I found that, on average, the cross-sectional areas of the various sediment depths were equivalent to a certain percentage of the overall cross-sectional area of the canal channel. Those averages were 56.9 percent (the area of the channel with a one-third freeboard), 37.8 percent (the area at three-quarters full), 21.7 percent (the area at half full), and 7.8 percent (the area at one-quarter full).

[2] The focus was on irrigated agricultural land, but the Hohokam clearly cultivated crops above the floodplain on the *bajadas* using non-irrigation agricultural features, such as rock-pile fields, terraces, and grid gardens in the middle Gila Valley (see Crown 1987; Masse 1991). The question is whether any food crops (especially maize, beans, and squash) were grown in quantities that would have composed significant proportions of the average person's diet. Evidence from studies of non-irrigated fields in southern Arizona (e.g., Marana, Florence, and Safford Valley) indicated that agave was the crop most likely grown on a large scale in these fields (see Crown 1987; Doolittle and Neely 2004; Fish et al. 1992). The agave plants would have been used in the production of edible mescal and other inedible byproducts. In addition to agave, corn and/or cotton pollen also has been recovered from rock-mulched features, including near Florence (Crown 1987:152), at Hayden (Purcell et al. 1997), and in the Santan Mountains (Cantley 1991; Swarthout and Blank-Roper 1984:185). However, the tendency of rock piles to act as pollen traps for both prehistoric and modern pollen from nearby locales led to ambiguity in interpreting these remains as clear evidence of corn and cotton cultivation (Cantley 1991; Purcell et al. 1997). It seems more likely that maize or cotton could only have been grown in rock-mulched features, in places where supplemental water could be diverted to water these relatively moisture-dependent crops (Doolittle and Neely 2004:183). Therefore, I argue that the non-irrigated agricultural fields in the study area did not contribute significant amounts of food to the Hohokam diet.

Chapter 3

Study Area

This chapter describes the study area, including the environmental setting and previous research on the canal systems and settlements. The study area is located on the GRIC, in the middle Gila River Valley, in south-central Arizona (Figure 3.1). It was divided into two parts: Study Area 1 encompasses the Snaketown canal system and its associated settlements, and Study Area 2 includes the Santan and Gila Butte canal systems and settlements. Appendix A presents additional data on the canal systems. Additional data on the settlements are given in Appendixes B (Study Area 1) and C (Study Area 2). The primary data sources for the study were derived from the research conducted by the GRIC Cultural Resource Management Program (CRMP). The research on the middle Gila Valley canal systems represents a multiyear investigation of prehistoric canal irrigation and provides an excellent database for addressing the research problem (e.g., Woodson 2003, 2004, 2009). Some of the principal contributions of this ongoing study are a greatly clarified map of the canal systems (Woodson 2009) (see Figure 1.2), a major increase in the number of excavated canal segments, and a new understanding of the layout, size, and capacity of the canal systems and their development through time. The settlement data were based on the large-scale surveys of the GRIC conducted by the GRIC-CRMP (see Ravesloot and Waters 2004), as well as previous research. Most of the surveys and the work on the canals were conducted in conjunction with the Pima-Maricopa Irrigation Project (P-MIP), which is a component of the Central Arizona Project and is funded by the U.S. Department of the Interior Bureau of Reclamation (BOR). The results of the surveys in the study area have been published in previous P-MIP survey reports (e.g., Neily et al. 1999, 2000; Wells and Greenspan 2002; see also Gregory and Douglas 1994). The exception was a survey of a large area surrounding the village of Snaketown bounded by Interstate 10, Maricopa Road, Riggs Road, and the Gila River floodplain (within Study Area 1). The cultural remains in that zone were recorded as site GR-1157; the unpublished survey data were used in this research (and are summarized in Appendix B).

Environmental Setting

Physiographically, the study area is situated in the southern portion of the Phoenix (Salt-Gila) Basin, which lies within the Sonoran Desert subprovince of the Basin and Range physiographic province. The middle Gila Valley is conventionally described as encompassing a 120-km (72-mile) segment of the Gila River that begins at the North and South Buttes (collectively known as "the Buttes"), approximately 26 km east of Florence, and continues downstream to the confluence of the Gila and Salt Rivers (Gregory and Huckleberry 1994, Waters and Ravesloot 2000) (see Figure 1.2). The middle Gila Valley is broad, ranging from 5 km (3.2 miles) to over 20 km (12.5 miles) in width, and has a low gradient, descending only 176 m (579 feet) from the Buttes to the Gila-Salt River confluence, an average of 1.4 m (4.6 feet) per kilometer.

The climate of the middle Gila Valley is hot and arid (Sellars and Hill 1974). The mean annual temperature is 20.6° C (69° F), with July maximum temperatures averaging 41° C (106° F) and January minimum temperatures averaging 1° C (33° F). There is a slight moisture gradient from west to east, and mean annual rainfall ranges from 19 cm (7.5 inches) at Maricopa to 21 cm (8.3 inches) at Sacaton to 24 cm (9.4 inches) at Florence. The wettest months are typically July and August, during which afternoon thunderstorms develop and produce heavy, but localized, rainfall. A second period of precipitation occurs in the winter, when large storm systems from the Pacific Ocean enter the region.

Topographically, the study area is situated mostly on the second (early to middle Holocene, or T-2) and third (Pleistocene, or T-3) terraces, and it is bordered on the south by the modern Gila River streambed (Waters 1996) (see Figure 3.1). The eastern portion of Study Area 2 is located partly on the alluvial fan and bedrock outcrops of the Santan Mountains. The Santan Mountains, Gila Butte, and Pima Butte are the most prominent geographic features in the vicinity. Elevations range from 335 m (1,100 feet) above mean sea level, at the Gila River near Pima Butte, to 457 m (1,500 feet), on the top of Gila Butte, to over 945 m (3,100 feet) in the Santan Mountains.

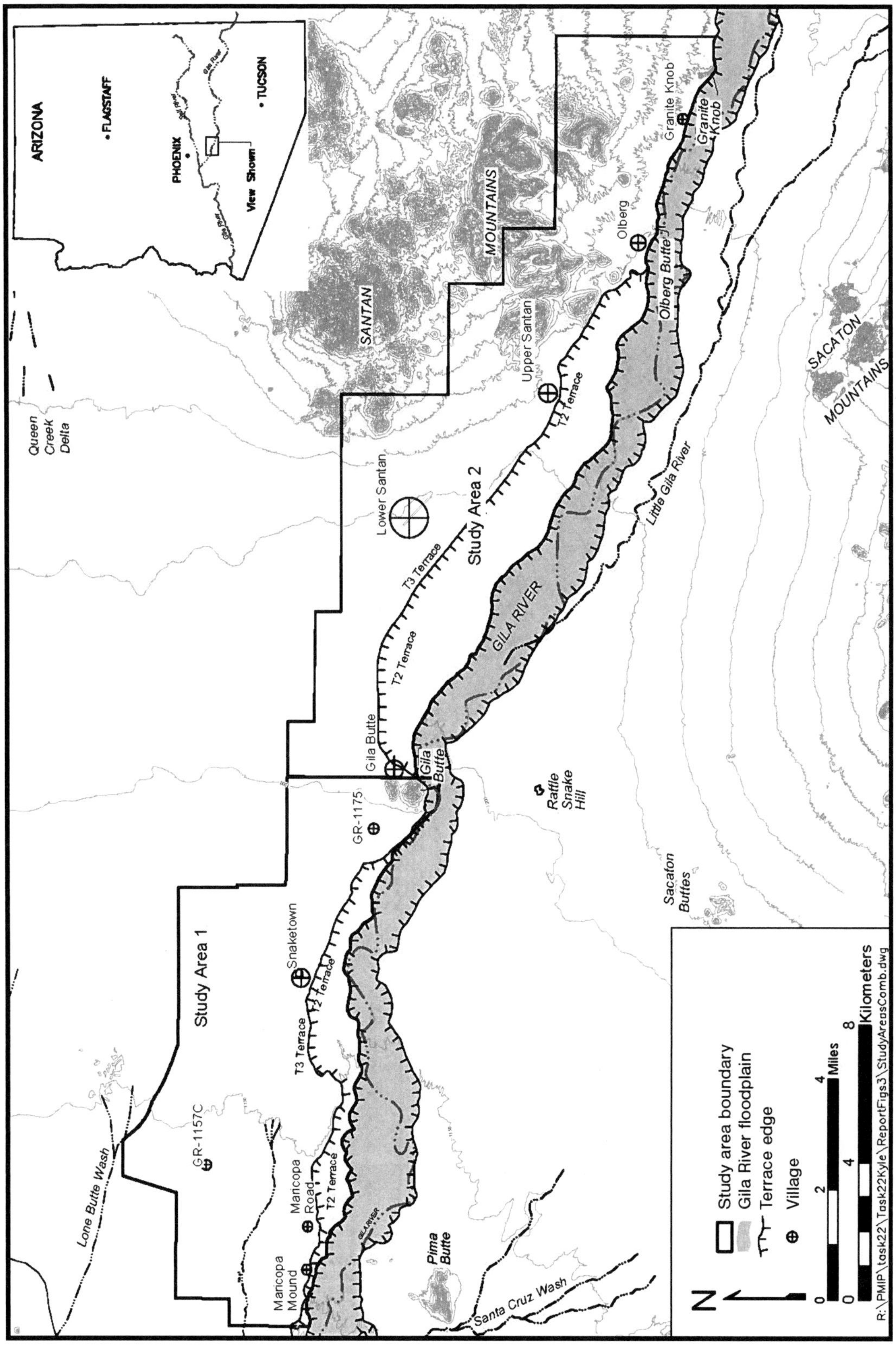

Figure 3.1. Map showing the location of the study area.

Vegetation in the study area is characteristic of both the Lower Colorado River Valley and Arizona Upland subdivisions of the Sonoran Desertscrub biotic community (Turner and Brown 1994). The Lower Colorado River Valley subdivision is predominantly characterized by the creosote bush–white bursage and saltbush series. This series also includes mesquite, palo verde, and ironwood trees and saguaro, barrel, and cholla cacti. At higher elevations along the *bajadas*, the paloverde–cacti–mixed scrub series appears in the transition to the Arizona Upland subdivision, which includes the creosote bush–crucifixion thorn series. A large portion of Study Area 2 has been altered as a result of previous and current agricultural development. Fallow or previously cultivated fields commonly contain grasses, forbs, and Russian thistle.

The main focus of the study is the Snaketown canal system and its environs (Study Area 1), because that area has the most detailed documentation of canals and settlements in the middle Gila Valley (see Figure 3.1). The most prominent settlement in Study Area 1, of course, is Snaketown village (Gladwin et al. 1937; Haury 1976; Wilcox et al. 1981). Study Area 1 measures roughly 79.63 km^2 (30.75 square miles) in area. Snaketown is located on the right bank of the Gila River and is situated on the edge of the upper (T-3) terrace, which is covered by an extensive Holocene aeolian sand sheet (Waters 1996). Facing south, toward the river, the site overlooks the lower (T-2) terrace and the modern Gila River streambed. The northern edge of Study Area 1 is bordered by an ephemeral drainage known as Lone Butte Wash, which represents part of the Queen Creek drainage, where it begins to rise to the surface after having submerged underground in a delta to the north of the Santan Mountains. Another minor wash extends through the west-central portion of the study area. Gila Butte is situated in the southeastern corner of Study Area 1.

The terrain in the Snaketown area is undeveloped and relatively undisturbed, having escaped the land subjugation of the twentieth-century agricultural-improvement programs. Although Akimel O'odham groups lived along the upper terrace in numerous small habitations until the 1940s, all historical-period agricultural activities occurred on the lower (T-2) terrace. These conditions present an ideal situation for the use of archaeological survey data to construct a detailed picture of the prehistoric landscape.

The settlements and canals along the Granite Knob, Santan, and Gila Butte canal systems (Study Area 2) are the secondary focus of this study (see Figure 3.1). Study Area 2 measures roughly 107.72 km^2 (41.59 square miles) in area and is situated directly upstream from Study Area 1. It is bounded roughly by the Gila River on the south, Granite Knob on the southeast, the Santan Mountains on the northeast, and Gila Butte on the west. The canal systems are located on the right bank of the river and are situated primarily on the T-2 terrace, with portions extending onto the T-3 terrace and the alluvial fan along the Santan Mountains and Gila Butte. The villages and primary settlements in Study Area 2 are located on the T-3 terrace and alluvial fans.

Study Area 2 has been more extensively developed and disturbed by historical-period and modern agricultural practices and habitation areas than the Snaketown area. The levels of archaeological preservation and of detail in the documentation of prehistoric settlements and canals are correspondingly lower than what is available for Study Area 1. In addition, historical-period flooding of the Gila River scoured away most of the T-2 terrace between Granite Knob and Olberg Butte and destroyed the canal system and portions of settlements in that zone. Despite those disturbances, archaeological documentation in the area is still very good, based on extensive survey coverage and numerous excavation results. Also, most of the villages are located on the T-3 terrace; so, they are better preserved than the sites on the T-2 terrace.

Gila River Channel and Streamflow Characteristics

Of particular interest to this study is the variation in channel morphology and streamflow of the Gila River, because these are the most significant environmental variables with which Hohokam irrigators would have had to contend, to operate their canals (see Graybill et al. 2006:69). The two primary sources of information on this are geological studies of the history of river environments and reconstructed annual streamflows based on tree-ring research. The geological studies have focused on the geomorphology and alluvial stratigraphy of the middle Gila River Valley (Huckleberry 1993, 1995; Waters and Ravesloot 2000, 2001) and have found that for much of the Hohokam occupational sequence, the Gila River was an aggrading regime with periodic overbank flooding that contributed to the build-up of the river terraces (Ravesloot et al. 2009; Waters and Ravesloot 2000, 2001). However, that was interrupted by one catastrophic period of downcutting and widening sometime between A.D. 1020 and 1160 (Waters and Ravesloot 2000, 2001). Following that episode of erosion, the Gila River returned to an aggrading regime for the remainder of the Hohokam period, and it was not until the late nineteenth century that the Gila and Salt Rivers underwent another regime shift, to a period of downcutting and erosion of river terraces. There is no geomorphic evidence that downcutting and channel widening contributed to the decline of the Hohokam tradition and their irrigation systems, at about A.D. 1400 or 1450.

Graybill et al. (2006) used dendrochronological analysis to reconstruct the annual streamflow in the Gila and Salt Rivers. It should be noted that these streamflow reconstructions do not account for additional input provided by the San Carlos or San Pedro Rivers (Graybill et al. 2006:80) or summer monsoon rainfall. These sources could have significantly increased the annual streamflow totals. In their analysis of the streamflow data, Graybill et al. (2006:85) focused on factors that likely influence channel morphology and change, including "mean flow; overall variability; the number, relative magnitude, and temporal spacing of high-magnitude annual discharges; and the number, severity, and duration of prolonged periods of low mean discharge characterized by low variability (droughts)." A "prolonged period of low flow" is defined as any period of 8 or more successive years during which the annual flow is consistently half a standard deviation beneath the average annual flow (Graybill et al. 2006:85). It is important to note here that periods of low flow do not necessarily result in water shortage (or scarcity)—a condition that must be defined as a function of supply in relation to demand (this is discussed further in Chapter 4).

Graybill et al. (2006:110) found that during most of the Pioneer period, from A.D. 450 to 700, the Gila River was characterized by "moderate to low variability and conditions that would have been generally favorable for irrigation agriculture." A marked increase in variability began in the Snaketown phase (A.D. 700–750), though, including several prolonged periods of low flow followed by extreme, high-magnitude annual flows. These less-than-desirable conditions continued through the next two intervals (A.D. 750–900 and 900–1150), which encompassed the Colonial and Sedentary periods (Graybill et al. 2006:112). The subsequent period, between A.D. 1150 and 1420, is described as generally favorable for irrigation agriculture (Graybill et al. 2006:115–116), until "the radical flows of the 1420s" (Graybill et al. 2006:119).

Ravesloot et al. (forthcoming) observed that Hohokam irrigators were adapted to floods and periods of low flow in the river that were high-frequency events (see also Ravesloot et al. 2009; Waters and Ravesloot 2003). Irrigators were capable of summoning the labor needed to rebuild their canal systems relatively quickly following floods, and their use of irrigation was not permanently disrupted by high-frequency floods. On the other hand, there are three factors that would have had a more critical effect on the adaptation of Hohokam populations to irrigation agriculture: (1) the occasional shift in "prolonged periods of low streamflow" from low-frequency events to high-frequency events, (2) shifts from century-long periods when the 50-year moving average was consistently above the mean flow (33 million acre-feet) to a prolonged period of below-average flow, and (3) the very rare occasions when the Gila River changed from an aggrading regime to a downcutting and widening regime (Ravesloot et al. forthcoming). The first two kinds of changes reduced the overall volume of water available for irrigation, and the third kind of change led to the erosion of some field areas and increased the difficulty of maintaining intake weirs at the headgates. The basis for this reasoning is Dean's (1988) concept of low- and high-frequency environmental change and adaptive responses. Humans are adapted to high-frequency processes that operate over short periodicities, whereas low-frequency processes may have more severe consequences. Human response to these changes varies depending on a number of factors; two of the most important are subsistence patterns and how close the population is to the carrying capacity of the land. If the populace is near capacity and using an intensive agricultural strategy, then landscape changes are critical to survival and require a rapid response to stave off disaster.

Considering the streamflow data presented by Graybill et al. (2006), Ravesloot et al. (forthcoming) observed that at five times during the Hohokam occupation of the Gila River, the "prolonged periods of low-flow" were low-frequency events: A.D. 615–696 (1 low flow), 814–881 (0 low flows), 927–1090 (2 low flows), 1258–1387 (1 low flow), and 1419–1500 (1 low flow). Thus, these times most likely were more favorable for agriculture, whereas the intervals immediately *following* these periods would represent shifts of low flows from low- to high-frequency events and may have been more detrimental in terms of agricultural adaptations. This suggests that, although Graybill et al. (2006) indicated less-favorable conditions between A.D. 700 and 1150, there were two intervals within that span when conditions probably were not so dire for irrigators. Also, the interval between A.D. 1090 and 1258 included significant prolonged periods of low flow as well as the downcutting and widening event, all of which would have been major factors to deal with during the Early Classic period. More-favorable conditions for agriculture persisted between A.D. 1258 and 1450 (essentially, the Late Classic period).

Ravesloot et al. (forthcoming) also computed 50-year moving averages of annual discharge reconstructed by Graybill et al. (2006) (Figure 3.2). Computing multiyear averages has the effect of damping out annual variability, to allow the recognition of longer-term trends in the data. The 50-year moving average focuses on low-frequency variability. Based on these averages, it becomes clear that the two centuries from A.D. 800 to 1000 were characterized by consistently above-average flow. The period between A.D. 1000 and 1160, which encompasses the time of the downcutting and widening event, was quite variable on the whole (as was also observed by Graybill et al. 2006). The following period from A.D. 1160 to 1280 (essentially equivalent to the Early Classic period) was characterized by consistently below-average flow (drought), which probably would have presented problems for irrigators. Thereafter, from A.D. 1280 to 1450 (essentially, the Late Classic period), streamflow returned to above-average flow, which would have improved the water-supply conditions for canal systems.

The downcutting and widening event between A.D. 1020 and 1160 occurred during the second half of the Sedentary period, which was a period of sociopolitical transformation across the Hohokam region (see Chapter 1). Similar stream-channel modifications and abrupt cultural changes occurred during this time across southern Arizona (Waters and Ravesloot 2001, 2003). The downcutting and widening events correlated to a wet climatic episode in Arizona that included a period of intense, high-magnitude flood activity in southern Arizona (Ely 1997; Waters and Ravesloot 2000:56, 2001:292). The Gila River event would have

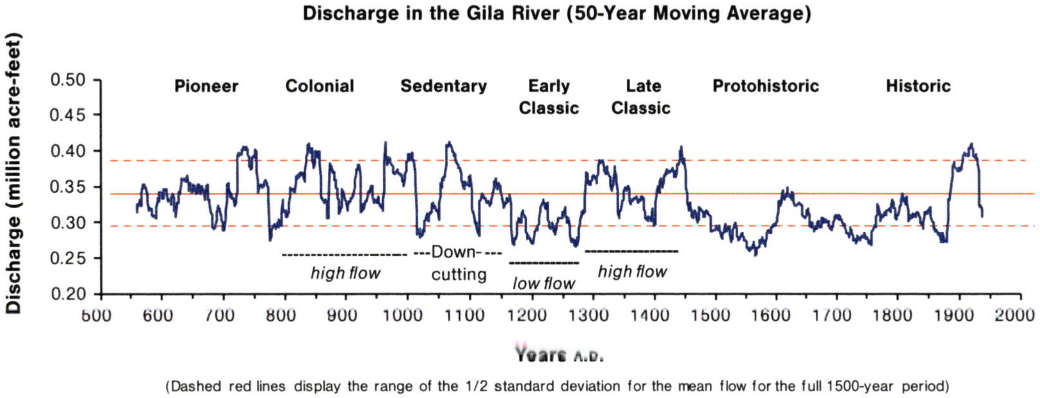

Figure 3.2. Graph of the 50-year moving averages of annual discharge for the Gila River (from Ravesloot et al. forthcoming, based on data from Graybill et al. 2006).

destroyed the riparian habitat along the river, disrupted nearly a millennium of floodplain stability, scoured or eroded fields along the former channel, and destroyed canal-system diversion structures and intakes (i.e., upper portions of the main canals) (Waters and Ravesloot 2000, 2001:292). The wider channel had a braided streambed that was more porous, and the main flow channel would have shifted over the streambed with each major flow. These changes would have affected marginal canal headings, resulting in irrigators' placing a premium on the most reliable headgate locations along the river (Ravesloot et al. forthcoming; Waters and Ravesloot 2000, 2001) (see below for a discussion of headings). Once the headings were re-established, irrigators would have had more difficulty diverting water into the canals in the shifting channel situation. Addressing that difficulty would have required additional labor and administrative oversight to maintain the diversion weirs or dams and intakes, in order to keep the canal systems in operation. These conditions would have lasted between 30 (Huckleberry 1995:177) and 100 (Ravesloot et al. forthcoming) years, as the channel progressively narrowed and aggraded until, once again, the river flowed through a single, relatively narrow channel.

In sum, the most critical period of river-channel and streamflow changes for Hohokam irrigators along the middle Gila River would have been during the Late Sedentary and Early Classic periods. The combination of the low-flow periods from A.D. 1160 to 1280 (Early Classic period) on the heels of the downcutting and widening event (between A.D. 1020 and 1160) would have presented a significant challenge for irrigators to maintain a reliable water supply in the canal systems. This issue is addressed further in the following chapters.

Previous Research on Canal Systems

The most recent map of the middle Gila Valley canal systems is provided in Figure 1.2 (Woodson 2009). However, this map was the culmination of a number of previous canal investigations in the study area (Woodson 2010b). Early researchers in the middle Gila Valley, like Bandelier (1892) and Fewkes (1913:113–115), noted their observations about canals but drew no maps. Charles Southworth mapped a few prehistoric canal segments during his Gila River survey in 1914–1915. The only segment mapped by Southworth that falls in the current study area, though, is next to Gila Butte, near the heading of the Snaketown canal. The first important map of middle Gila Valley canals was drawn by Larson (1926) and published by Cummings in 1926 (Figure 3.3). Larson's map focused on the Coolidge and Florence areas. The western edge of the map overlaps the current Study Area 2. It depicted a canal, which presumably represented Canal Santan, heading just upstream of Granite Knob and possibly terminating at Olberg Butte. The canal was shown as extending along the *north* side of Granite Knob, which clearly was an error, because that would have been difficult, if not impossible, using prehistoric technology.

Thereafter, Frank Midvale (1935, 1946, 1963, 1965, 1972) (whose last name was Mitalsky) made significant contributions to the mapping of canals and settlements along the middle Gila River during his survey efforts between 1918 and 1972. His 1963 map of the Casa Grande Ruins area is still used by many archaeologists today as a standard archaeological reference. Midvale's canal maps (1935, 1972) of areas downstream from Casa Grande were less detailed and have proven to be less accurate. Midvale's earliest sketch map (in 1935) depicted canals in the Santan, Gila Butte, and Snaketown areas and included both Study Areas 1 and 2 (Figure 3.4). It was actually the first published map of the Snaketown canal system. Midvale must have completed the map just after the Gila Pueblo excavations at Snaketown in 1934–1935 but before the publication of the excavation results (Gladwin et al. 1937). The map shows the heading of the Snaketown canal far upstream, at Olberg Butte, showing the Santan, Gila Butte, and Snaketown areas as all served by the same canal system. The map also showed a short canal on the lower terrace that headed at the foot of Gila Butte

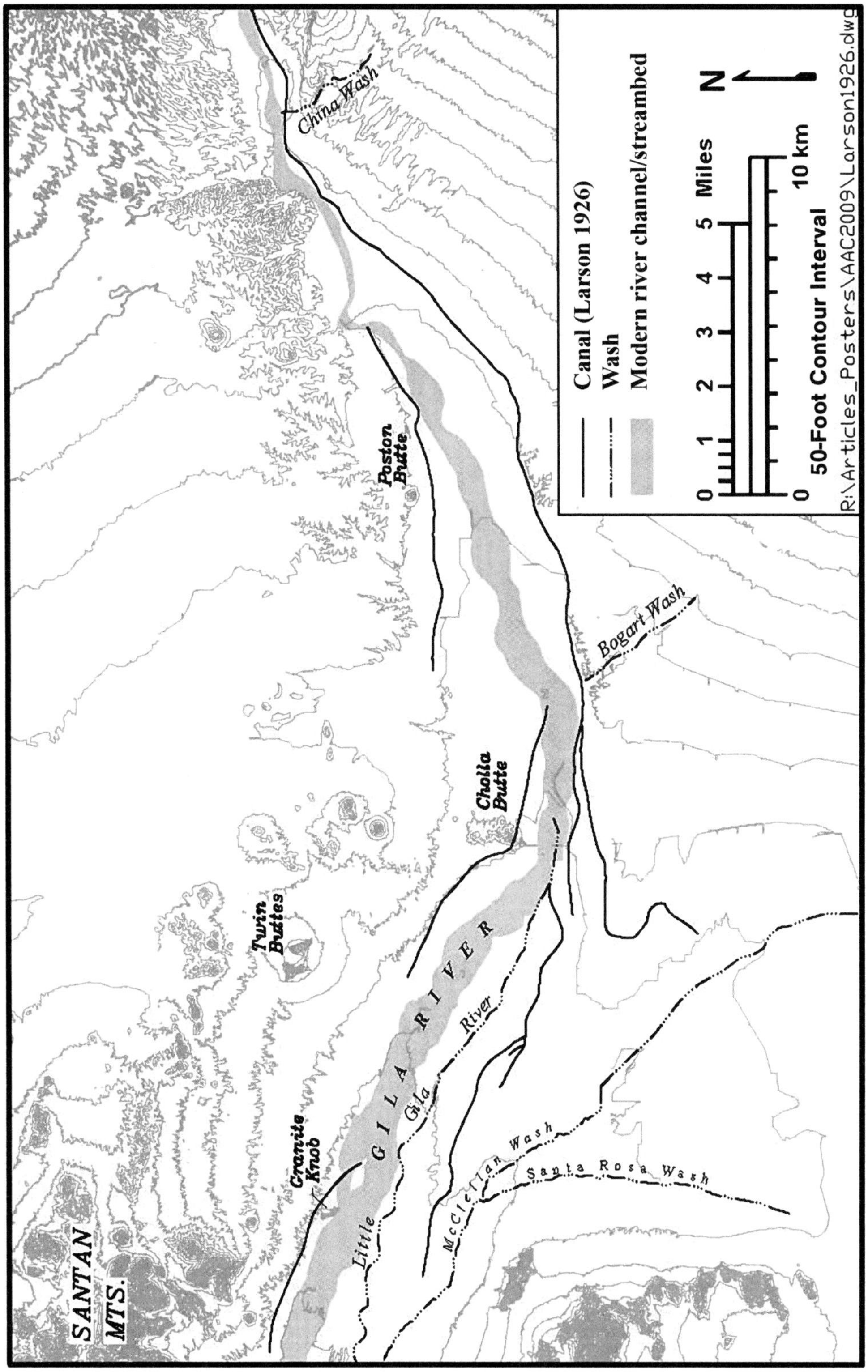

Figure 3.3. Prehistoric canals along the Gila River, mapped by Larson (1926).

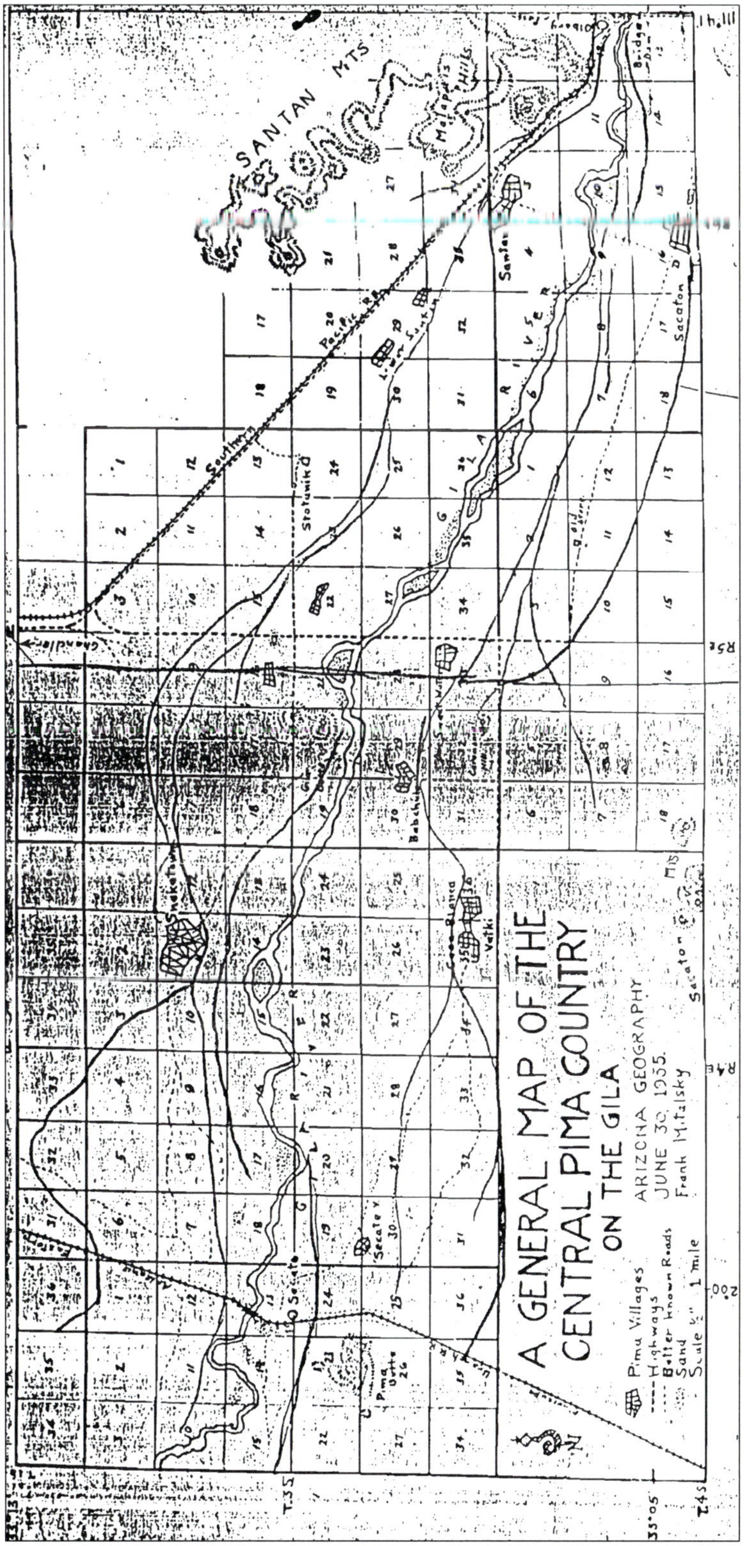

Figure 3.4. Map showing canals in the Snaketown, Gila Butte, and Santan areas, drawn by Frank Midvale in 1935 (from Mitalsky 1935).

(Haury's [1976] Diversion Point 1). In his later map of canals in the Casa Grande Ruins area, Midvale (1963) indicated that Canal Santan had its heading at Granite Knob. Midvale's last known map of the area (1972) depicted the Santan and Snaketown canal systems as separate, but it showed the Snaketown canal system as heading to the east of Gila Butte (Haury's [1976] Diversion Point 2). Midvale's 1972 map also showed two short canals on the lower terrace below Snaketown, with one canal heading at Diversion Point 1 and the other heading 5 miles farther downstream.

Emil Haury tested and extensively studied portions of the Snaketown canal system near Snaketown in 1934–1935 (Haury 1937), 1959 (Woodbury 1976 [West Fork excavation]), and 1964–1965 (Haury 1976:120–151). Figure 3.5 shows one of Haury's (1976:122) final maps of the canal system, along with other formerly used (historical-period) canals and currently used canals as of 1965. His efforts resulted in a more accurate map than Midvale's, identifying a 3.8-km segment of the main canal and a bifurcation point called the West Fork, where the canal divides into two branch canals. The map also identified the two points on the river that Haury (1976:123) suggested as possible headings: one at the foot of Gila Butte (Diversion Point 1) and one to the east of Gila Butte (Diversion Point 2). Haury (1976) also identified a segment of the earliest known canal along the middle Gila River, the Pioneer Canal, which was built in the Vahki phase of the early Pioneer period. Lastly, he also mapped a prehistoric canal segment at the end of the modern Santan Canal, just northeast of Gila Butte, that represents the tail end of what is now called the Gila Butte Canal.

Later excavations conducted near Gila Butte documented numerous canal segments that were part of the Gila Butte canal system and some that may have been linked with the Snaketown canal system (Howard and Rice 1982; Motsinger 1993; Rice et al. 1979; Swarthout and Blank-Roper 1984). Figure 3.6 is a map compiled by Motsinger (1993) showing the composite of canal features identified by these researchers in this area. Two of the studies (Motsinger 1993; Swarthout and Blank-Roper 1984), which are described in more detail below (see the Canal-System Heading section in Appendix A), suggested that one of the canals in their study area represented the "Snaketown canal" that headed at Diversion Point 2. The researchers came to different conclusions about when the Snaketown canal headed at that point: Swarthout and Blank-Roper (1984) contended that it was during the pre-Classic period, and Motsinger (1993) claimed that it was during the Classic period.

More recently, GRIC-CRMP researchers developed a version of the map of the Snaketown canal system and parts of the adjoining Santan and Gila Butte canal systems (Figure 3.7) (Ravesloot 2007; Ravesloot et al. forthcoming; Woodson and Ravesloot 2005). The canal alignments and site-type codes shown on this map were based on information from the large-scale surveys conducted by the GRIC-CRMP, in conjunction with the P-MIP, in the areas between the Santan Mountains on the east and Hidden Ruin on the west (Neily et al. 1999, 2000; Wells and Greenspan 2002). The map also included information from unpublished results of survey of the area surrounding the village of Snaketown bounded by Interstate 10, Maricopa Road, Riggs Road, and the Gila River floodplain (the cultural remains in this zone were recorded as numerous loci within GR-1157). Also, the map used data collected by the GRIC-CRMP as part of a survey of linear features (including canals, historical-period roads and ditches, and other feature types) between Gila Butte and Maricopa Road. The features near Gila Butte were reported by Neily et al. (2000), but the features in the Snaketown area have not been reported before now. The linear features initially were identified in aerial photographs and were given numeric designations, each beginning with "LB-" or "ST"—"LB-" for features in the Lone Butte management area, which includes the Snaketown area (the current Study Area 1), and "ST-" for features in the Santan–Gila Butte area (the current Study Area 2). Subsequently, most of the features were examined on the ground and mapped with a Global Positioning System unit by a CRMP survey crew. The crew recorded information on each linear-feature segment (segments were defined between the junctions/intersections of linear features). The information included a feature-type designation (prehistoric canal, historical-period road, historical-period ditch, or unknown), a physical description of the segment (concave or convex profile, vegetation alignment, ditch, etc.), a description of the junctions between linear features, and a description of the artifact assemblage along the segment. Although the GRIC-CRMP map in Figure 3.7 is more detailed than the Midvale and Haury maps, it lacks the details of the canal system that were determined during the current research of the study (as described in Chapter 4 and Appendix A).

The Granite Knob, Santan, and Gila Butte canal systems in Study Area 2 have been studied more intensively in recent years, including the studies cited in the previous paragraph. Survey and excavation around Gila Butte have examined the tail end of the Gila Butte canal system and the interface with the Snaketown canal system (see Figure 3.6). Surveys also have identified surface evidence of relict segments of the Granite Knob canal (Gregory and Douglas 1994), the Santan canal (Neily et al. 1999), and the Gila Butte canal (Neily et al. 2000). Over the last 10 years, the layouts of the Santan and Gila Butte canal systems have become much clearer, based on the findings of excavations conducted by the GRIC-CRMP as part of the P-MIP investigations (e.g., Loendorf et al. 2007; Miles 2009; Miles et al. 2008; Rodrigues et al. 2003; Waters and Ravesloot 2000; Woodson 2006) and tribal-housing and -infrastructure projects (e.g., Burt 2007; Fertelmes and Loendorf 2010; GRIC-CRMP Project 2006.36, Task 2, home-sites testing).

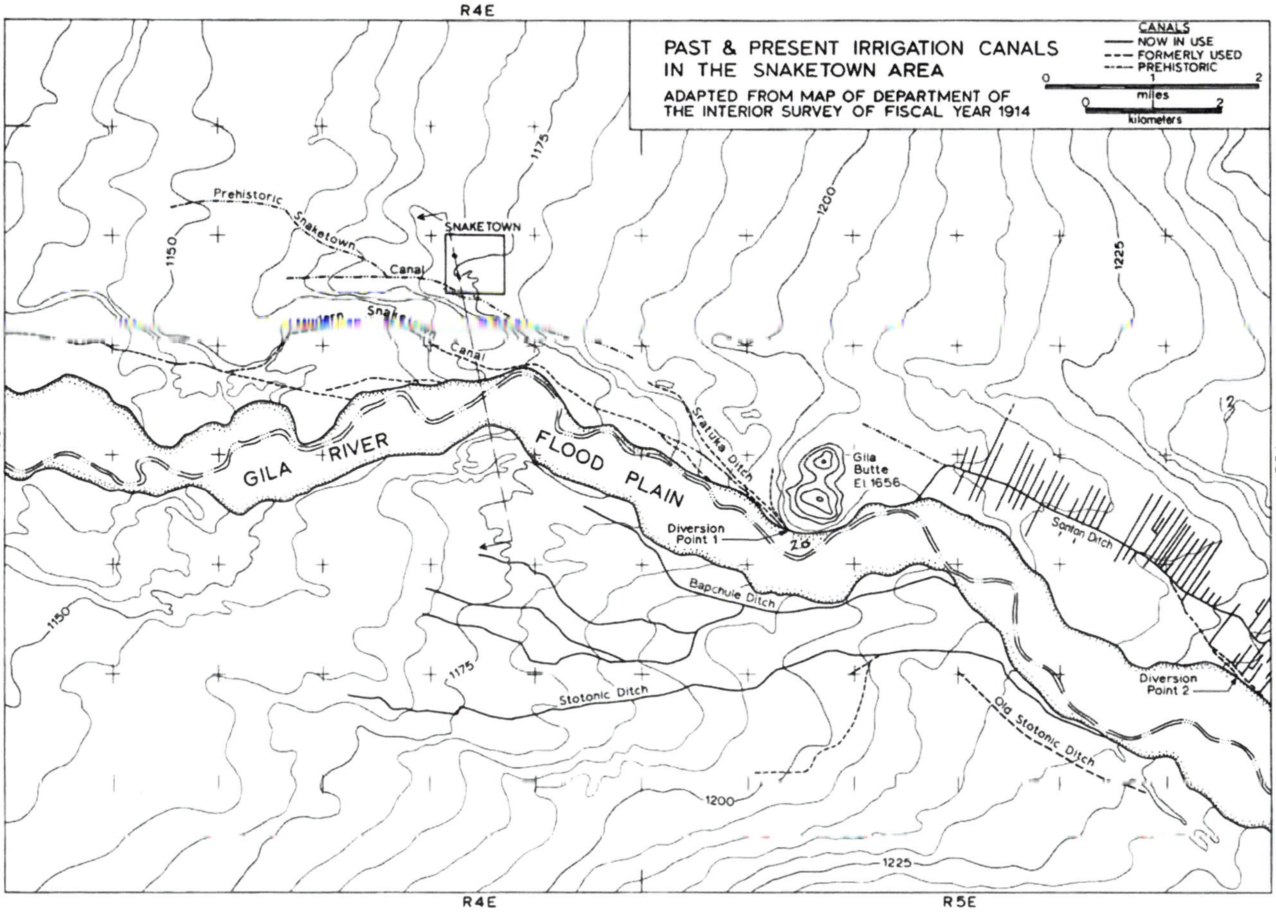

Figure 3.5. Map of the Snaketown canal system, other nearby canals, and diversion points, as shown by Haury (1976:122).

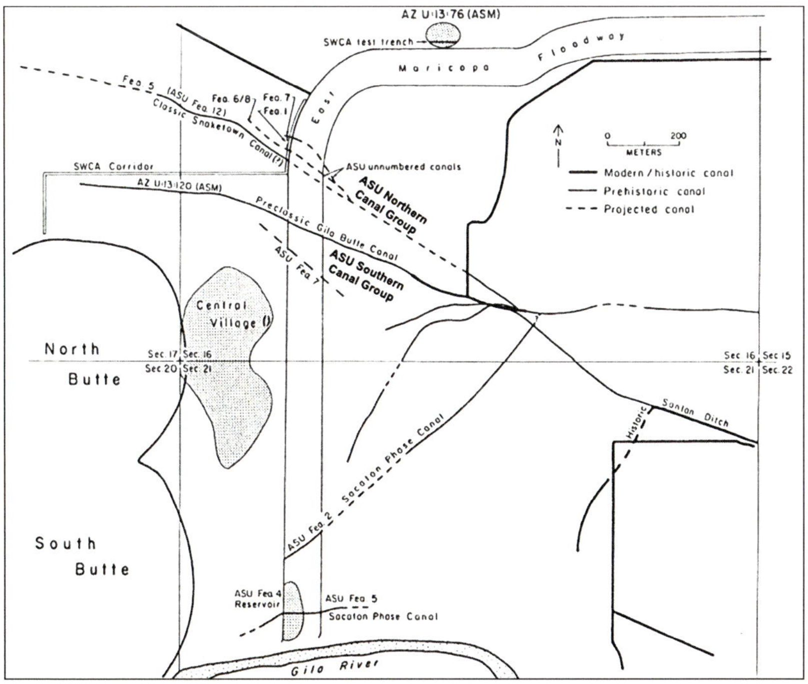

Figure 3.6. Map showing canal features identified in the Gila Butte area by researchers from Arizona State University and SWCA Environmental Consultants, Inc. (from Motsinger 1993:58, with added text).

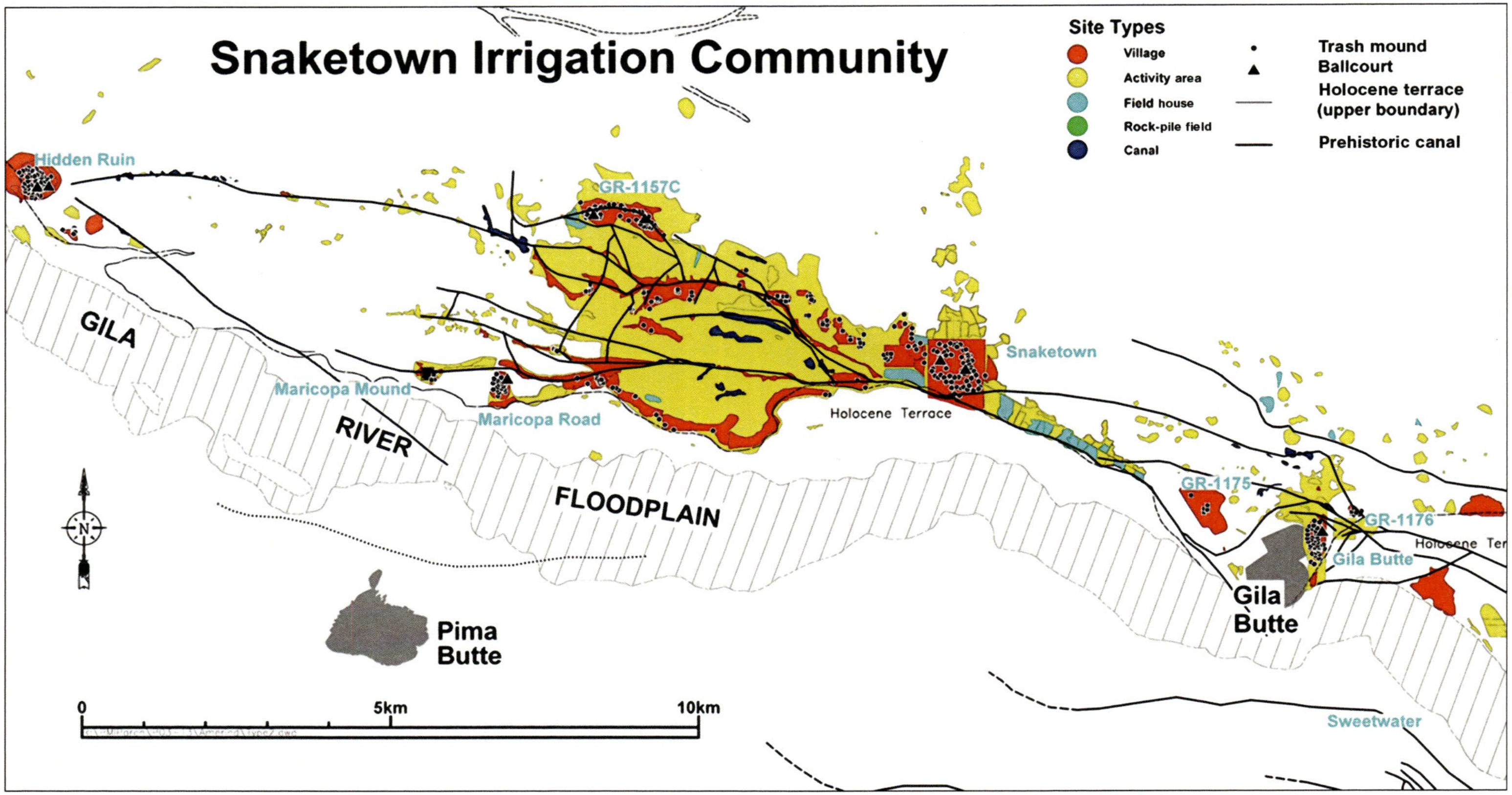

Figure 3.7. Initial map of site types and canals in the Snaketown "irrigation community" (from Woodson and Ravesloot 2005; see also Ravesloot 2007) prior to the current research.

Table 3.1. Hohokam Canal Systems along the Middle Gila River (Upstream to Downstream)

No.	Canal System	Main Canal Length (km)	Bedrock Reef at Head?	Command Area (ha)		Percentage of Total Irrigable Area along the Gila River
				Laterals = 500 m long	Laterals = 254 m long	
1	Grewe-Casa Grande	33.6	yes	3,607	2,374	18.6
2	Poston	12.0	no	544	297	2.3
3	Chee Nee	16.0	yes	839	458	3.6
4	Blackwater	14.4	yes	1,426	830	6.5
5	Sweetwater	10.3	no	830	457	3.6
6	Casa Blanca	24.2	no	3,389	2,342	18.3
7	Granite Knob	5.5	yes	186	133	1.0
8	Santan	26.6	yes	1,457	1,193	9.3
9	Sacaton	8.4	yes	808	469	3.7
10	Gila Butte	12.7	no	1,048	660	5.2
11	Snaketown	25.5	yes	2,660	1,492	11.7
	Pima Butte	*13.2*	*no*	-	-	-
12	Riverbend	23.6	yes	2,396	1,873	14.7
13	Gila Crossing	9.1	no	339	203	1.6
	Estrella	*7.7*	*no*	-	-	-
Total		242.7	8 = yes	19,531	12,781	100.0
Total length without possible canals:		221.8				

Note: Italics indicate possible canals.

Putting the Study Area Canal Systems in Perspective

The previous canal investigations in the study area were integral to the compilation of the most recent map of the middle Gila Valley canal systems shown in Figure 1.2 (Woodson 2009). Using the data from all areas of the middle Gila Valley, we can step back and examine the study area canal systems from a wider perspective (see Woodson 2010b). The Granite Knob, Santan, Gila Butte, and Snaketown canal systems are 4 of the 13 known canal systems along the middle Gila River. Table 3.1 lists these 13 canal systems in order of sequence upstream to downstream, the length of the main canal(s) in each system, whether the main canal headed on the river at a bedrock reef, and the estimated command area of each system (two values). There is inferential support for 2 other systems (Pima Butte and Estrella), shown in italics in Table 3.1. The main canals in the 13 well-documented systems have a total length of 221.8 km. The length increases to 242.7 km if the 2 possible systems are included. I estimate that the total command area of these 13 systems was between 12,781 and 19,531 ha (an explanation of the method of estimating command area is provided in Appendix A.) The command areas of the 4 study area canal systems totaled between 3,478 and 5,351 ha, accounting for 27.4 percent of the total irrigable area along the middle Gila River.

The first canals were built in the Vahki phase of the early Pioneer period (around A.D. 450–650) to serve the villages at Snaketown and Grewe. The Casa Blanca canal possibly was built at that time, based on a radiocarbon date from a possible subsurface canal found during a testing project (Waters and Ravesloot 2000:53). At least 1 canal system (Gila Butte) was built during the Snaketown phase of the late Pioneer period (A.D. 700–750) (Burt 2007; Swarthout and Blank-Roper 1984). Despite the lack of direct evidence of other Snaketown phase canals, data from sites along the canals support the contention that 6 other canals were built at that time: Casa Blanca (if it was not already built in the Vahki phase) as well as the Chee Nee, Santan, and Sweetwater canals and possibly the Granite Knob and Blackwater canals. Thus, by the late Pioneer period, 9 canal systems probably were in operation. Those early systems mostly were built out to their greatest extents in the Colonial period (A.D. 750–950). Two additional systems (Riverbend and Poston) were built in the early Colonial period, and the remaining 2 systems (Sacaton and Gila Crossing) may not have been built until the Sedentary period (A.D. 950–1150). All 13 systems were in operation during the Classic period (A.D. 1150–1450). Some systems were linked,

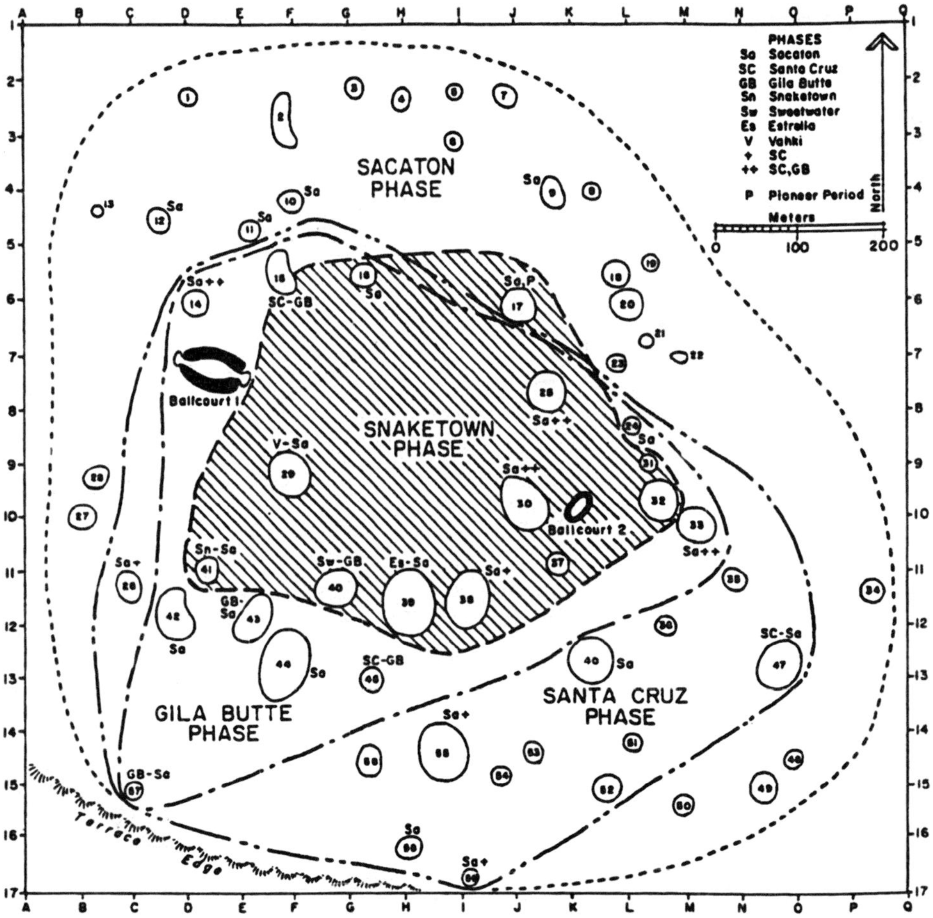

Figure 3.8. Map of Snaketown, showing village growth by phase (from Wilcox et al. 1981:18, based on Haury 1976:37, 81).

or consolidated, with other systems during their use-lives, evidently during the Sedentary and Classic periods.

The headings for the Granite Knob, Santan, Gila Butte, and Snaketown canal systems are numbered 7, 8, 10, and 11 in the sequence, respectively. These 4 systems thus were some of the last ones along the middle Gila River to receive water. Regarding the bedrock reefs, I am not aware of any published material that has clearly identified the locations of bedrock formations underneath the Gila River. Largely, archaeologists have assumed that if there is a bedrock mass (e.g., a butte or mountain) adjacent to the river, then there should be a "reef" that forces underflow to the surface (Gregory 1991:177; Gregory and Nials 1985; Haury 1976). These locations would be more reliable sources of surface water, particularly during low streamflow periods. Ravesloot et al. (forthcoming) posited that the heading for the Santan canal at Olberg was the best location, because there, the river passed between two mountain ranges, and the bedrock reef extends upstream for a distance of about 10 km, providing a long stretch in which the water could develop a strong surface flow. This reef area also would have benefited the Granite Knob and Sacaton canals. The only other canal that headed in an area between bedrock masses was the Grewe–Casa Grande canal. In sum, 8 of the 13 canal systems have bedrock masses adjacent to their headings. The other 5 main canals have no known bedrock outcrop (or an inferred underground reef) and thus are considered to be marginal headings. However, 2 of these canals (Poston and Gila Crossing) probably benefited from bends in the river or "underflow" below the surface.

Previous Research on Hohokam Settlements

This section briefly describes the previous research on the major settlements in the study area. The village of Snaketown, recorded as AZ U:13:1 (ASM) (also designated GR-898), is the most prominent settlement in Study Area 1, and it remains one of the most famous settlements in the Hohokam region (Figure 3.8; see Figure 3.1), largely because of the attention it has garnered since the major excavations conducted there by Gila Pueblo in 1933–1934 (Gladwin et al. 1937) and by Emil Haury, with the University of Arizona, in 1964–1965 (Haury 1976). Although Snaketown was known to be a preeminent Hohokam site prior to those studies, the large scope of those excavations provided a wealth of impressive results and data that fueled a whole generation of Hohokam research. Ideas and models of Hohokam prehistory formed on the basis of the Snaketown data were tested and debated in the following decades, including Hohokam chronology (e.g., Dean 1991; Gladwin 1948; Schiffer 1982), Hohokam origins (e.g., Wallace et al. 1995), site structure and organization (e.g., Wilcox et al. 1981; papers in Doyel [1987]), craft production and the Hohokam economy (e.g., McGuire and Howard 1987; Seymour and Schiffer 1987), irrigation agriculture and irrigation social organization (see Table 2.1), the connection between Mesoamerica and the Southwest (e.g., McGuire 1980; Nelson 1986; Wilcox 1986), and Hohokam ideology (e.g., Wilcox 1987, 1991; Wilcox and Sternberg 1983).

Surface features at Snaketown include at least 60 mounds, 2 ballcourts, and a central plaza (Haury 1976; Wilcox et al. 1981). Court 1, the large east–west-oriented court, was built in the Gila Butte phase, and Court 2, the smaller, north–south-oriented court, was built in the Sacaton phase. As defined by the maximum extents of mounds, Snaketown covers roughly 69 ha. Most of the mounds appear to have functioned as trash mounds, but 3 mounds (Mounds 16, 39, and 40) and possibly a fourth (Mound 38) were deliberately capped with caliche-rich layers and were used as platform mounds. Mound 40, built during the Snaketown phase, is the earliest known platform mound in the Hohokam region. A portion of the main irrigation canal traverses the southern edge of the site, at the interface of the upper and lower terraces. Below the surface, the excavations uncovered pit houses, pits, burials and cemeteries, caches, wells, canals, and the subsurface deposits (trash and/or culturally sterile materials) that formed the mounds. Snaketown was founded in the Vahki phase of the early Pioneer (or Early Formative) period. The most recent studies of Hohokam chronology have placed the Vahki phase between A.D. 450 and 650 (Henderson 2001; Wallace et al. 1995). By the Middle to Late Sedentary period (ca. A.D. 1050–1100), the village of Snaketown had been abandoned, and its inhabitants had moved elsewhere.

Of course, Snaketown did not exist in a vacuum. Other settlements in the vicinity were part of the social landscape and must be included in any consideration of community or irrigation social organization (Ravesloot 2007; Ravesloot et al. forthcoming). These other settlements are discussed in this study; some of them have been subjected to previous study and are mentioned here (see Figure 3.1). The Maricopa Road site, AZ T:16:13 (ASU) (also recorded as GR-1157, Locus V [GR-1157V]), is a Colonial to Sedentary period village located 6.4 km (4 miles) west of Snaketown and shared the same canal system (Ravesloot and Lascaux 1993) (see site maps in Appendix B). This village was considerably smaller than Snaketown, although it included a possible ballcourt. A mile (1.6 km) farther west from there lies the Maricopa Platform Mound site, AZ T:16:14 (ASU) (also recorded as GR-674A), the only Classic period platform mound located along the Snaketown canal system during the Classic period (Wells and Greenspan 2002) (see site maps in Appendix B). Four Classic period habitation sites are located just west of Snaketown: AZ U:13:21 (ASM), AZ U:13:22 (ASM), AZ U:13:23 (ASM), and AZ U:13:24 (ASM). These are among the sites posited to have been occupied by some residents who left Snaketown (Haury 1976:48–53). Haury (1976) tested these sites (all but AZ U:13:23 [ASM]).

A major survey was conducted by the GRIC-CRMP around Snaketown village, in the area bounded roughly by Interstate 10 on the east, the Gila River floodplain on the south, Maricopa Road on the west, and Riggs Road on the north (within Study Area 1). The cultural remains documented in this large area during that survey and my research included numerous main, distribution, and lateral canals and over 600 archaeological features, such as compounds and architectural mounds, trash mounds, ballcourts, and roasting pits (Neily et al. 2000; Ravesloot et al. forthcoming; Rice and Ravesloot 2002; Wells and Greenspan 2002). The extensive archaeological remains were recorded as numerous loci within GR-1157. Most of the canal alignments are visible in aerial photos and on the ground as vegetation lines or slightly raised earthen alignments, and the canals are littered with artifacts. The detailed documentation of this well-preserved area allows reconstructions of the canals, field areas, and settlements from the late Pioneer through Classic periods. These unpublished survey data are used in this research (see Appendix B for details).

Several other habitation sites lie to the east of Snaketown, around the flanks of Gila Butte. Pre-Classic period villages are present on the eastern side of the butte, at the Gila Butte site, AZ U:13:8 (ASM) (or GR-1167O) (Motsinger 1993; Neily et al. 2000; Rafferty 1982), and on the western side, at GR-1206 (Neily et al. 2000). A small, camp-size settlement dating to the pre-Classic period was documented at AZ U:13:9 (ASM), Area A (or GR-1184), on the southwestern edge of Gila Butte (Johnson 1964). These settlements were abandoned concurrently with the abandonment of Snaketown. A Classic period village is situated on the western side of the butte, at GR-1175 (AZ U:13:12/U:13:118 [ASM]), and a smaller Classic period settlement is located east of the butte, at GR-776D (AZ U:13:75 [ASM]) (Neily et al. 2000). Johnson (1964) documented two Early Classic period camps at AZ U:13:9 (ASM), Area B (at the southern end of GR-1205A), and at AZ U:13:11 (ASM) (adjacent to GR-1206A). Gila Butte was an important source of mica schist for temper in pottery manufacture (Rafferty 1982; Walsh-Anduze

1993). It also was situated at the primary heading of the Snaketown canal system and near the interface between the Gila Butte and Snaketown canal systems.

Study Area 2 encompasses the Granite Knob, Santan, and Gila Butte canal systems, which lie directly upstream from the Snaketown canal system. Extensive survey coverage is available for this area (e.g., Neily et al. 1999, 2000; Gregory and Douglas 1994; Gregory and Huckleberry 1994; Jacobs et al. 2010; Wood 1972), and numerous excavations have been conducted in certain portions (e.g., Burt 2007; GRIC-CRMP Project 2006.36, Task 2, home-sites testing; Loendorf et al. 2007; Motsinger 1993; Rodrigues et al. 2003; Swarthout and Blank-Roper 1984). There are several prominent prehistoric villages in Study Area 2, including Granite Knob, Olberg, Upper Santan, Lower Santan, and Gila Butte (see Figure 3.1). These villages are located on the right bank of the middle Gila River, on the edge of the upper (T-3) terrace or on the distal end of the alluvial fans emanating from the Santan Mountains.

Founded as a hamlet in the Estrella/Sweetwater phase of the late Pioneer period, Upper Santan village is the oldest prehistoric settlement in Study Area 2 (Figure 3.9). Facing south, toward the river, the site overlooks the lower (T-2) terrace, where an expanse of irrigated fields was situated between the two main-canal branches of the Santan canal system. Olberg village also was initiated as a hamlet, slightly later than Upper Santan, in the Sweetwater/Snaketown phase of the late Pioneer period. The Gila Butte site was founded as a hamlet by the Snaketown phase, and Granite Knob village may have been initiated as a camp at that time. By the early Colonial period, all four sites had probably developed into village-size settlements, and each had a ballcourt, except Olberg. A fifth ballcourt village was founded at Lower Santan in the early Colonial period (Figure 3.10). During the Classic period, platform mounds were constructed at Upper and Lower Santan. Upper Santan also included a possible second platform mound.

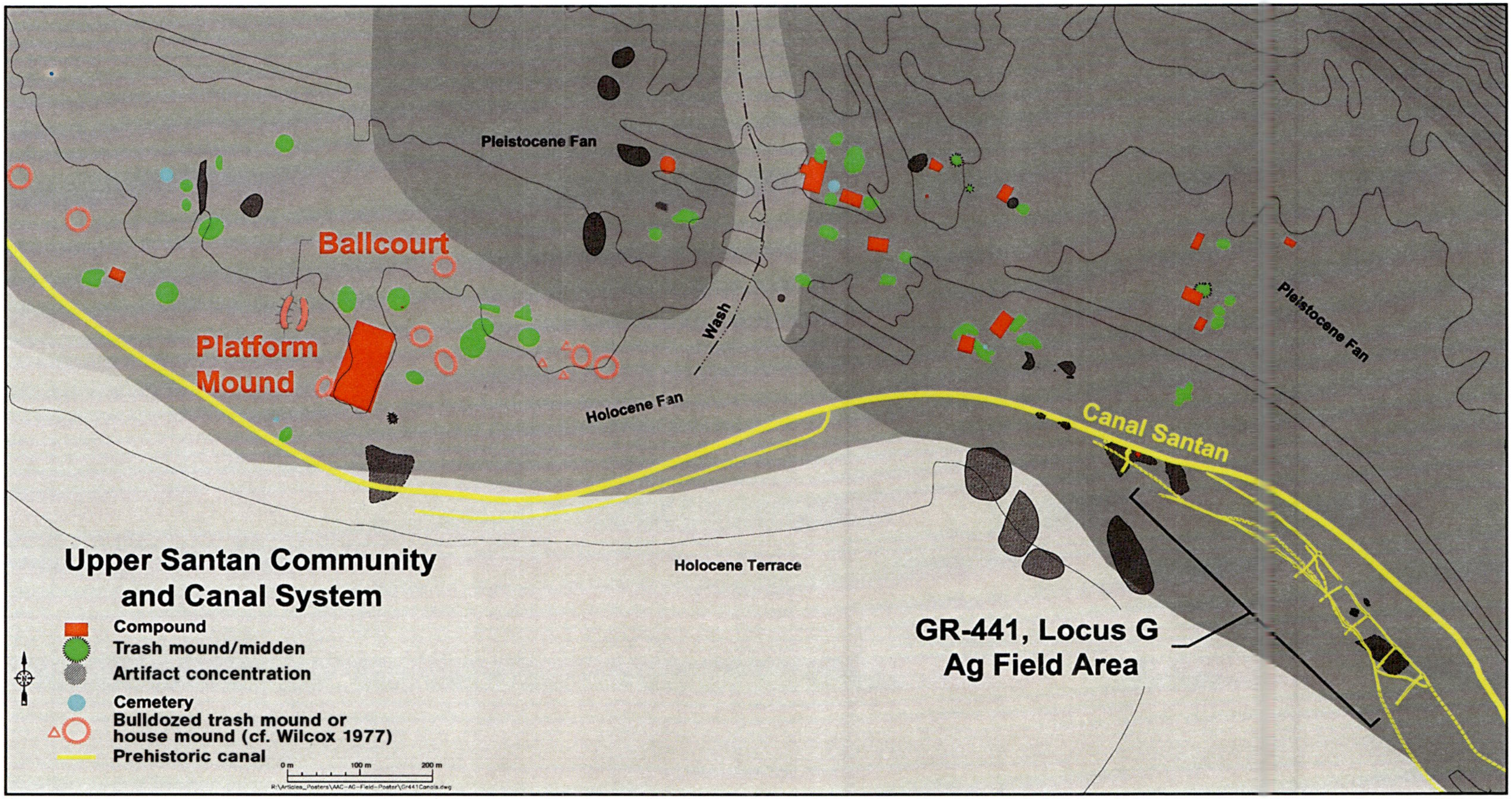

Figure 3.9. Schematic map of the Upper Santan village community and a portion of the Santan canal system (along the north branch of Canal Santan) (from Miles et al. 2008).

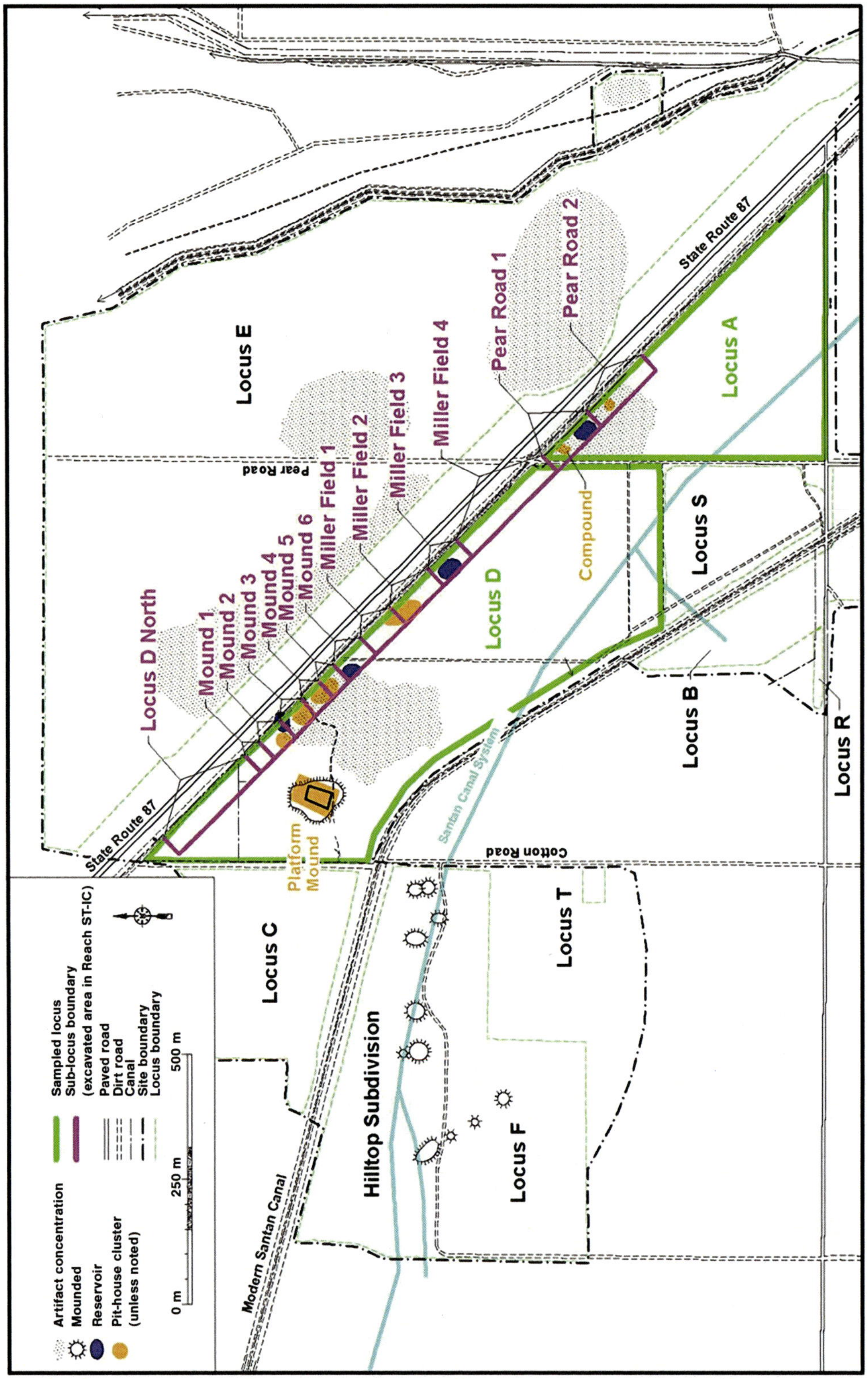

Figure 3.10. Map of Lower Santan village (in the northern half of GR-522), showing the distribution of known architectural units, trash mounds, reservoirs, and a portion of the Santan canal system (along the north branch of Canal Santan) (from Loendorf et al. 2009).

CHAPTER 4

Canal Systems

Four canal systems were located in the study area: the Snaketown canal system (in Study Area 1) and the Santan, Gila Butte, and Granite Knob canal systems (in Study Area 2). This chapter, which addresses Research Goal 1, examines these canal systems, describes their developmental sequence, evaluates their canal capacities and command areas, and evaluates their irrigation-management complexity. Appendix A provides a summary of the background and details of how reconstructions of the canal systems were created as part of this study, including the system layouts and irrigated field areas (command areas). Tables with canal lengths and sizes of individual field areas are given in Appendix A, as well. Through these efforts, this research has made several important contributions to our understanding of the middle Gila Valley canal systems, including a detailed map of the entire Snaketown canal system and the most detailed reconstructions to date of the Santan, Gila Butte, and Granite Knob canal systems.

Another significant contribution is the specific definition of the irrigated field areas in the Snaketown canal system. This is important because it allows an assessment of canal-system size, or command area, which is the portion of land under the system that was irrigated regularly (Hunt 1988a:344; Hunt et al. 2005:441). Understanding command area allows the estimation of agricultural productivity as well as population size. Using field evidence of lateral canals along the Snaketown system and a review of the average lengths of laterals in early-historical-period Akimel O'odham canal systems, I was able to determine the range and average length of the Snaketown laterals. It turned out that this correlated well to the lateral lengths inferred by Howard (2006:148) based on his study of field sizes in a portion of Canal System 1 along the lower Salt River. By applying what was learned in defining the Snaketown fields, it was possible to reconstruct field areas along the Santan, Gila Butte, and Granite Knob canal systems (where historical-period and modern land modifications have obscured surficial evidence of prehistoric fields).

Developmental Sequence of the Canal Systems

The first main canal in the Snaketown canal system was built during the Vahki phase of the early Pioneer (or Early Formative) period (Figure 4.1). As evidence of this, Haury (1976:135–136, 148) cited the recovery of Vahki Plain and Vahki Red sherds from the dipping pools in the floor of the Pioneer Canal (in the Pioneer Canal area).[1] This correlated well to the founding of the village of Snaketown in the Vahki phase and indicated that the residents began irrigating crops with canals concomitant with the settling of the area. The most recent studies of Hohokam chronology have placed the Vahki phase between A.D. 450 and 650 (Henderson 2001; Wallace et al. 1995). As argued by Woodson (2010b), canal irrigation probably was initiated during this phase in the Grewe–Casa Grande canal system (see Phillips and Craig 2001) and possibly the Casa Blanca canal system (see Waters and Ravesloot 2000; Woodson 2003). For comparison, canal irrigation had been established in the lower Salt Valley by the Red Mountain phase (A.D. 100–450) of the early Pioneer/Early Formative period in Canal System 1 (Ackerly and Henderson 1989) and Canal System 2 (Henderson and Nials 2004). The early Pioneer period canal in the Snaketown canal system headed on the Gila River at Diversion Point 1, located at the foot of Gila Butte (Haury 1976:150). The main canal measures roughly 7.5 km long from the diversion point to the western end of the Pioneer Canal area investigated by Haury (1976). Haury (1976:133) showed the canal as turning southwest at that point, but he did not clearly state whether the canal turned down onto the lower terrace or continued west along the upper terrace. Apparently this issue could not be resolved, because of the confusing array of overlapping channels from later time periods in this area, along with the erosion of the upper-terrace edge, both of which either destroyed or obscured the Pioneer Canal in this area (Haury 1976:132, 137).

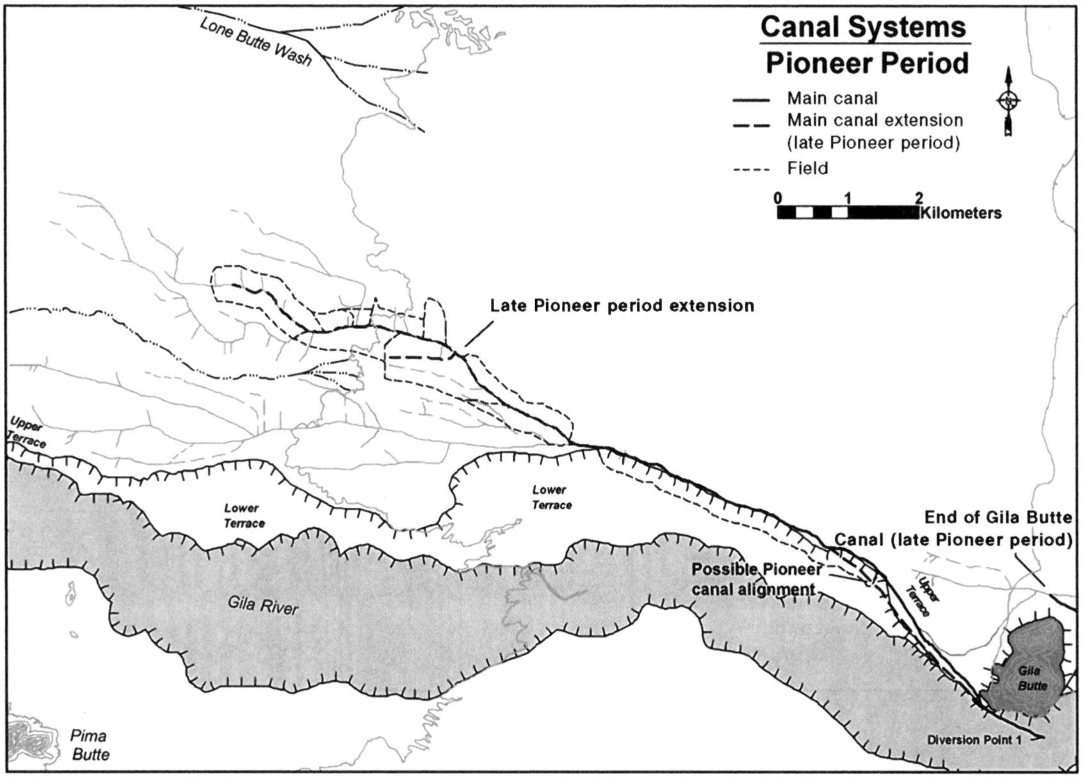

Figure 4.1. Map of the canal system and fields in Study Area 1 in the Pioneer period.

From an irrigation-technology point of view, it seems impractical that the irrigators would have turned the Pioneer Canal back down onto the lower terrace. Haury (1976:134–137) documented at least one turnout, and possibly several, along the Pioneer Canal that were the means by which water was diverted into lateral canals and thence onto fields on the lower terrace. There would have been no advantage to dropping the main canal back down onto the lower terrace and losing the command that had been established along the edge of the upper terrace. If the canal simply bent back to the west, it would have remained on the upper terrace. Assuming that was the case, the question then is "How much farther did the Pioneer Canal extend?" Haury (1976:147) noted some disturbances below the upper channels of the North Fork and South Fork canals (about 660 m downstream from the Pioneer Canal area) that "may represent traces of the Pioneer Canal, but tangible support for this idea was not forthcoming." Also, the GR-1157 survey to the west of Snaketown did not reveal any diagnostic ceramics earlier than Snaketown Red-on-buff. Based on the lack of early Pioneer period evidence to the west of the Pioneer Canal area, I argue that the Pioneer Canal terminated roughly near the West Fork. The main canal thus would measure 8.1 km long. All the fields irrigated during the Vahki phase were located on the lower terrace, and the estimated command area of the canal system at that time was 109 ha (see Appendix A).

The Pioneer Canal continued to be used into the late Pioneer period (Haury 1976:133–136) (see Figure 4.1). The late Pioneer period includes the Estrella/Sweetwater phase (A.D. 650–700) and the Snaketown phase (A.D. 700–750) (Henderson 2001; Wallace et al. 1995). Survey to the west of Snaketown along the north main-canal-branch alignment recovered Snaketown Red-on-buff sherds in sufficient quantities (i.e., more than incidental occurrences) to suggest that the main canal was extended another 6 km to the west in the late Pioneer period, which would bring the total main canal length to 14.1 km. This construction effort would have provided the opportunity to irrigate new field areas on the upper terrace that would have been free from the hazards of flooding that characterized the fields on the lower terrace. The estimated command area of the canal system at that time was 308 ha, assuming that the main canal was 14 km long. Of that amount, 109 ha were on the lower terrace, and the remaining 199 ha were located on the upper terrace (see Appendix A).

The Santan canal probably was built in the Estrella/Sweetwater phase of the late Pioneer period (Figure 4.2). This initial canal was about 9.3 km long, with an estimated command area of 421 ha (see Appendix A). All the irrigated fields were situated on the lower terrace. The layout of the Santan canal as shown in Figure 4.2 was inferred based mostly on survey evidence, since no excavations have documented a Pioneer period canal. The most intensively

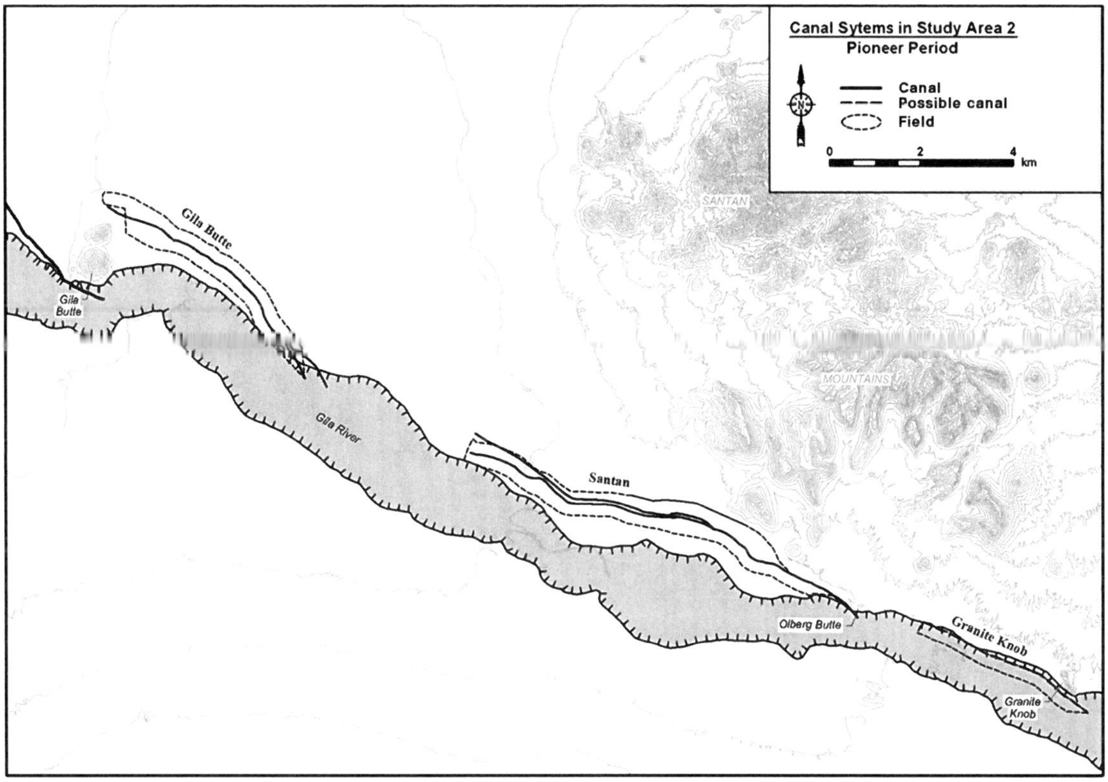

Figure 4.2. Map of the canal systems and fields in Study Area 2 in the Pioneer period.

used sites and loci, based on greater proportions of Snaketown Red-on-buff/-gray sherds, suggest that the initial main canal followed the trajectory shown on the map. The depicted canal followed the alignment of what later (after the expansion of the canal system) was designated the south branch of the Santan canal.

The Gila Butte canal was built by the Snaketown phase, as revealed by excavations (Burt 2007; Swarthout and Blank-Roper 1984). Based on the distribution of Snaketown Red-on-buff/-gray sherds, excavated canals, and linear features visible in aerial photos, it is posited that the Gila Butte canal headed about 5 km upstream of Gila Butte at that time (see Figure 4.2). This inferred heading is roughly 4 km downstream from Diversion Point 2, the more commonly cited heading for the Gila Butte canal. The initial canal was about 6.4 km long, and the command area is estimated at 300 ha (see Appendix A). The fields were on the lower terrace.

The lack of sites between Granite Knob and Olberg Butte with clear late Pioneer period components suggests that the Granite Knob canal had not been built yet. The dashed line in Figure 4.2 suggests a possible canal alignment, if it actually was in operation; if so, it was perhaps 4.2 km long, with an estimated command area of 100 ha (see Appendix A).

During the early Colonial period (Gila Butte phase, A.D. 750–850), the main Snaketown canal was re-engineered and rebuilt, and the system was constructed to its fullest extent (Figure 4.3). The new main canal was narrower and deeper than the Pioneer Canal, and it was shifted farther away (i.e., to the north) from the edge of the upper terrace (Haury 1976:138). The new canal continued to head on the river at Diversion Point 1 and extended 8.1 km to the West Fork, where it bifurcated into two branch canals. From there, the north main-canal branch extended 9.3 km and the south main-canal branch extended 8.1 km, for a total main-canal length of 25.5 km. In addition, at least 11 and possibly 13 distribution canals were built along the main canals (6 along Main Canal 1 and 7 along Main Canal 2). The 3 laterals documented along the Pioneer Canal (1-2–1-4) were abandoned, but at least 35 and possibly 42 new lateral canals were built in the early Colonial period. As noted above, it is almost certain that more lateral canals were used by that time, but their lack of visibility as surface archaeological features has prevented identification of all of them. A significant amount of new land on the upper terrace was brought under irrigation. The estimated command area of the canal system in the early Colonial period was 1,492 ha, of which 109 ha was on the lower terrace. This represents a nearly fivefold increase in command area from the late Pioneer period. On the upper terrace, 605 ha of fields were situated along the north main-canal branch, and 778 ha were located along the south main-canal branch (see Appendix A).

During the early Colonial period, the Santan and Gila Butte canal systems also were constructed to their fullest extents (Figure 4.4). The Santan canal still had its heading

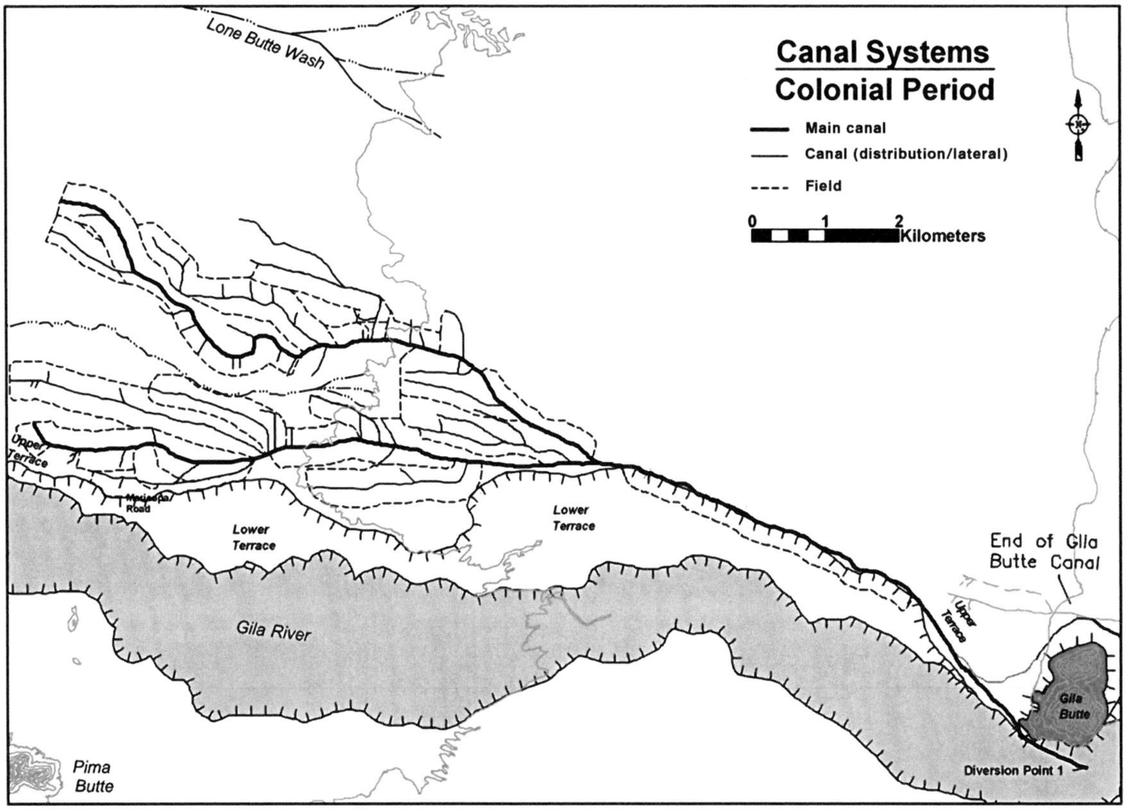

Figure 4.3. Map of the canal system and fields in Study Area 1 in the Colonial period.

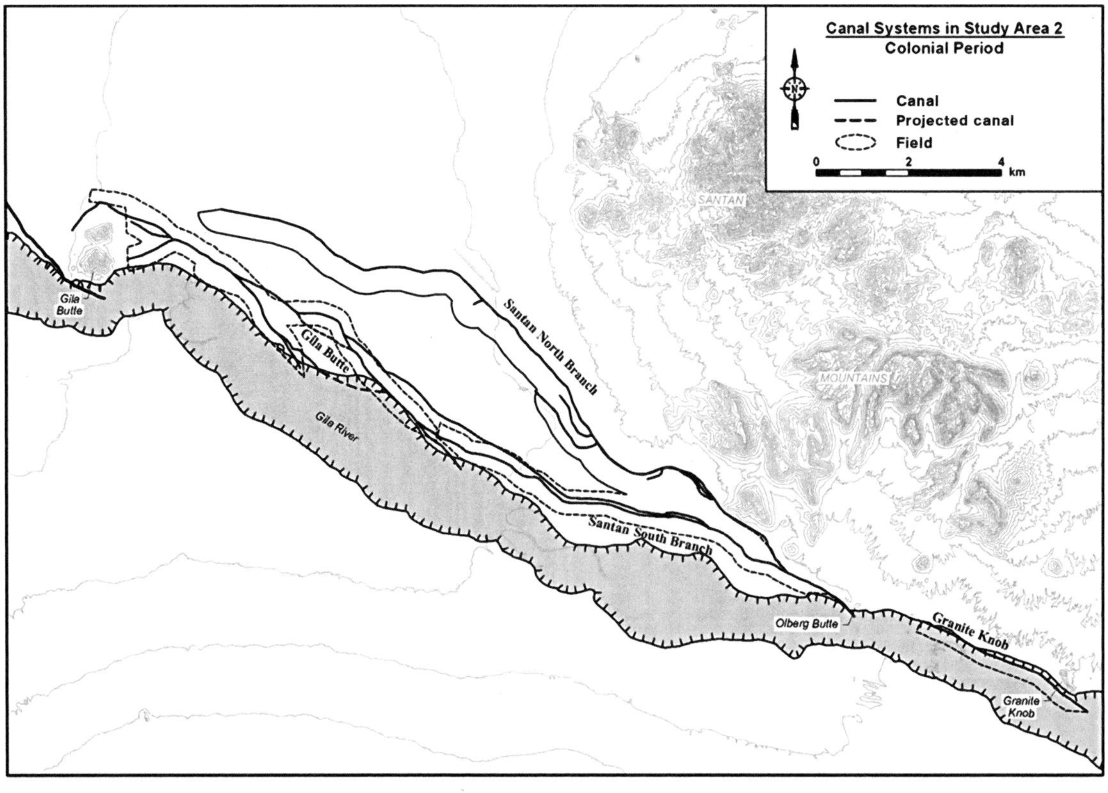

Figure 4.4. Map of the canal systems and fields in Study Area 2 in the Colonial period.

at Olberg Butte. A 15.3-km-long north main-canal branch was built out toward Lower Santan, and the south canal branch probably was extended by 2 km. The main canals measured 26.6 km in length, and the estimated command area was increased by 772 ha (along the north canal branch), to a total of 1,193 ha. Roughly 40 percent of these new field areas along the north-branch canal were situated on the upper terrace. Figure 4.4 (and the other figures for Study Area 2 in this chapter) actually depicts two parallel canals for the south-branch canal. The reason is that excavations have documented two parallel main-canal-size features in two separate locations along the south-branch alignment (GR-640, Features 6 and 9, and GR-1210, Features 2 and 3). Current data are insufficient to resolve whether or not the two main canals actually were contemporaneous and paralleled each other along the entire length of the south branch. Based on patterns observed in other middle Gila Valley canal systems, it seems more likely that the two canals were used in sequence, with one built to replace the other at some point in time. Further excavations in the area may help to resolve this issue or perhaps demonstrate that the inferred parallel alignments were configured differently from what is shown on the current map.

The Gila Butte canal heading appears to have been moved upstream to Diversion Point 2, implying that a new main canal was built at that time (see Figure 4.4). The Gila Butte canal extended to 10.4 km in length, and the command area was 600 ha. Historical-period scouring of the T-2 terrace by floods has obscured the southern part of the canal system; so, some of the distribution-canal alignments are unclear. As described in Appendix A, the main canal was extended around the northern side of Gila Butte to a hamlet at GR-1206. Survey, excavation, and aerial-photographic evidence suggest that the Santan and Gila Butte canals may have been connected by the early Colonial period, but each system still maintained its original heading. Some of the field areas at the end of the Gila Butte canal were on the upper terrace. The Granite Knob canal was definitely in use by that time, if it had not already been built in the late Pioneer period. The canal is estimated at 4.2 km long, with a command area of 100 ha. As noted above, our knowledge of this canal system is fragmentary, because a significant portion of the terrace between Granite Knob and Olberg Butte was scoured away by historical-period flooding, which destroyed nearly all of the canal system. However, all of the land irrigated by the Granite Knob canal would have been on the lower terrace.

The entire Snaketown canal system and field areas continued to be used in the late Colonial (Santa Cruz phase, A.D. 850–950) and Sedentary (Sacaton phase, A.D. 950–1150) periods, but no new main or distribution canals were built. However, a 1.2-km-long extension of the Gila Butte canal that connected with the Snaketown canal was built in the Sedentary period (Figure 4.5). The extension (designated ST-18) began at the terminus of the Gila Butte canal, within a village (GR-1206) on the western side of Gila Butte. This connecting canal probably functioned as a "waste ditch" to convey excess water from the Gila Butte canal to the Snaketown canal. The Gila Butte canal probably headed about 5 miles east of Gila Butte, at Diversion Point 2. It is estimated that the command area of the canal system remained at 1,492 ha, with 109 ha on the lower terrace.

The early Colonial period layouts of the Santan and Gila Butte canal systems mostly were unchanged in the late Colonial period, but a few changes occurred in the Sedentary period (Figure 4.6). The Granite Knob canal most likely was extended and connected with the Santan canal at that time. This assessment is based on the increased settlement and activity areas that "filled in" the zone between the former tail end of the Granite Knob canal and Olberg Butte. The canal measured 5.5 km long and had an estimated command area of 133 ha. The Santan canal definitely was connected to the downstream Gila Butte canal by the Sedentary period. The system command area remained at 1,193 ha. The Gila Butte canal system added a possible main-canal branch along the edge of the floodplain, based on the discovery of a main-canal-size feature during a monitoring project (Arizona State University [ASU] Feature 5) (Howard and Rice 1982) (see Appendix A). Also, the end of the Gila Butte canal was extended to connect with the Snaketown canal (as noted above). The Gila Butte canal then measured 11.6 km long and had a command area of 630 ha. Hence, the Granite Knob, Santan (south branch), Gila Butte, and Snaketown canals were joined by the Sedentary period, but each of the three original headings appears to have remained in operation (see Appendix A). The rationale for these consolidations is discussed below.

Survey data have suggested that nearly the entire Snaketown canal system was still being used during the Early Classic period (Soho phase, A.D. 1150–1300) (Figure 4.7). The extension of the Gila Butte canal (ST-18) continued in use. No new main canals were built, but another canal extension (designated ST-22) was built from the end of the Gila Butte canal, to connect with the Snaketown canal. Measuring 3.4 km long, this extension is commensurate with the previously mapped alignment of the "Classic period Snaketown canal." Survey data suggest that during the Late Classic period (Civano phase, A.D. 1300–1450), the Hohokam were still farming along nearly the entire system. The previously built extension (ST-18) may have been abandoned in the Late Classic period, but the ST-22 extension continued in use. Survey evidence also suggests that the heading at Diversion Point 1 *may* have fallen out of use in the Late Classic period. If that was the case, then the water in the Snaketown canal system was being supplied exclusively by the Gila Butte canal, which appears to have headed at Diversion Point 2. The estimated command area of the canal system throughout the Classic period was 1,492 ha, of which 109 ha were located on the lower terrace.

The three canal systems in Study Area 2 had been consolidated for a century by the Early Classic period, and the Gila Butte canal system had been linked with the downstream Snaketown canal system for a similar duration (Figure 4.8).

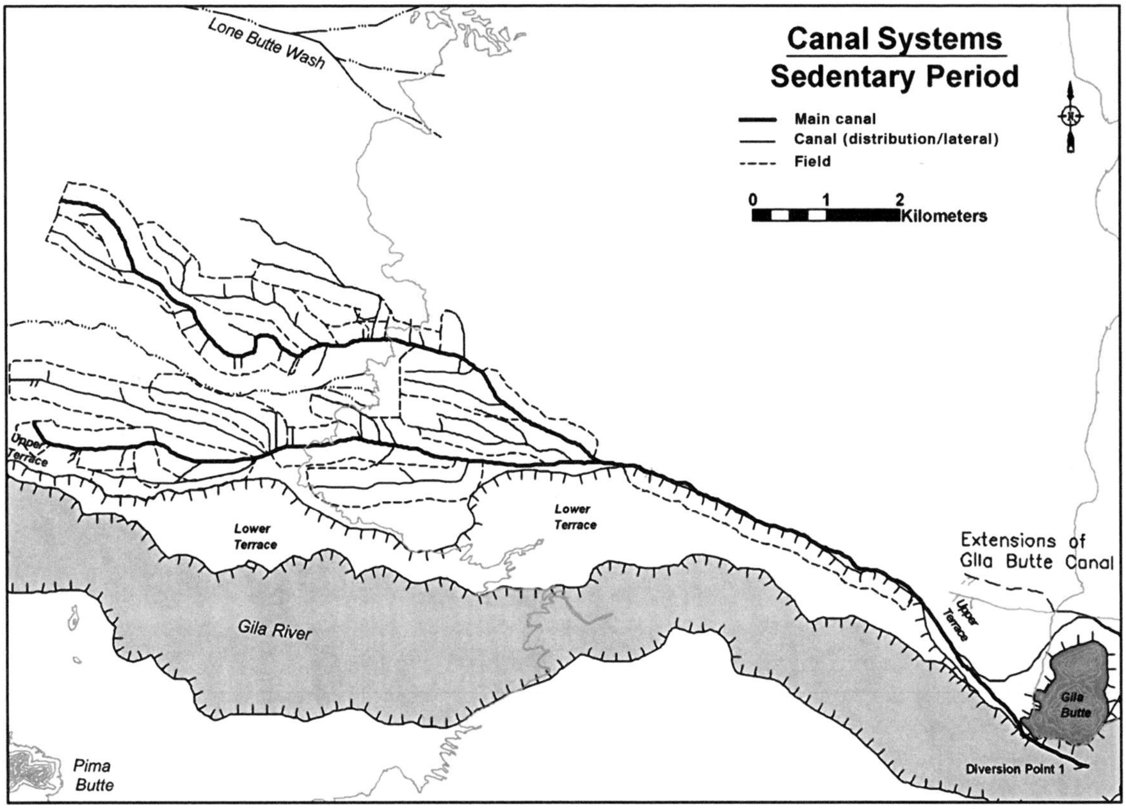

Figure 4.5. Map of the canal system and fields in Study Area 1 in the Sedentary period.

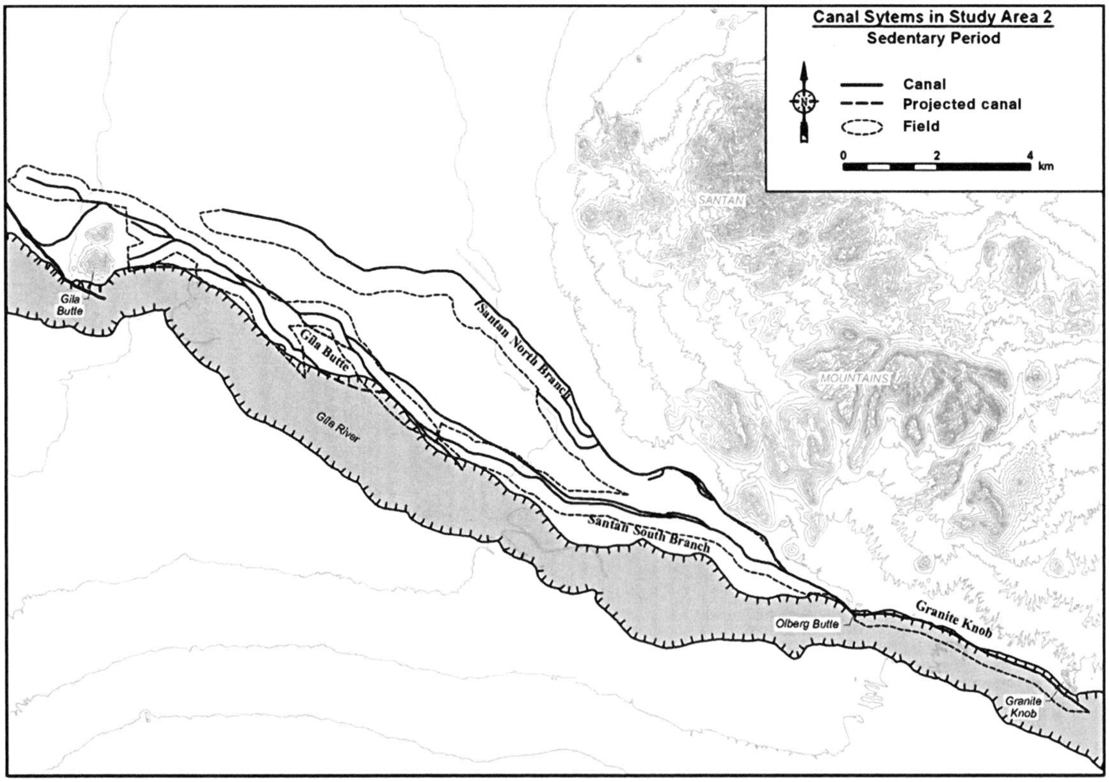

Figure 4.6. Map of the canal systems and fields in Study Area 2 in the Sedentary period.

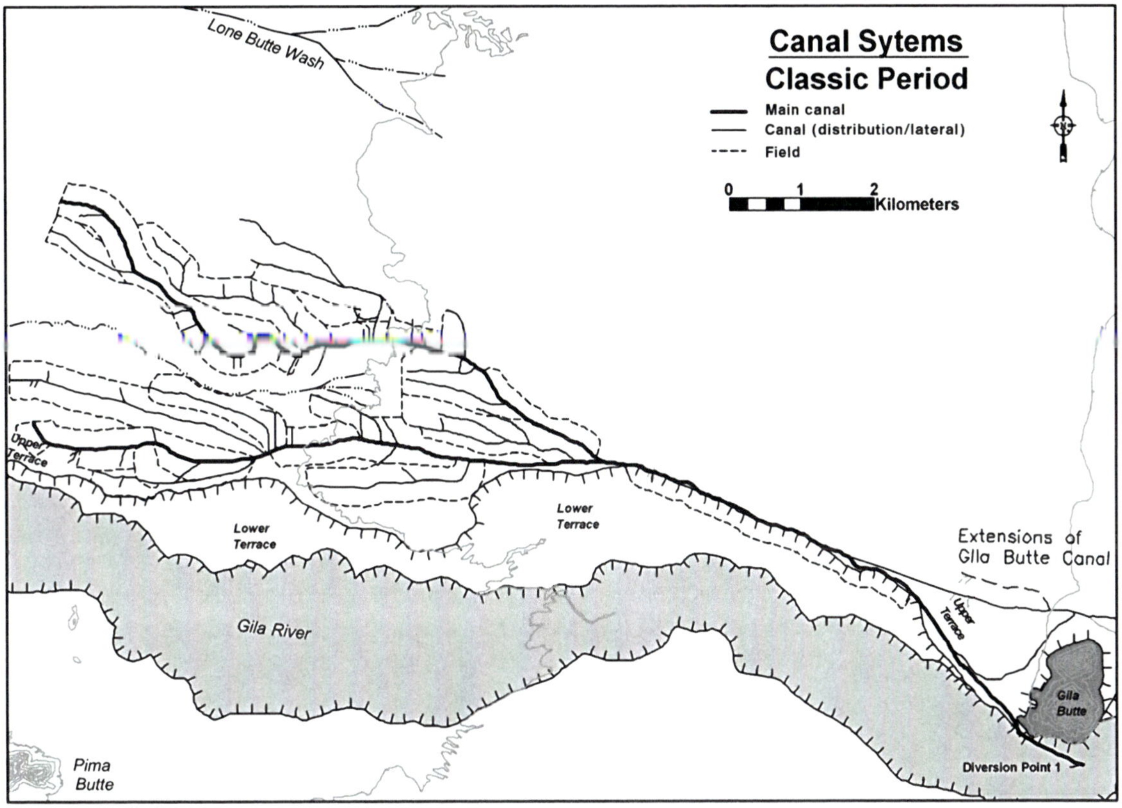

Figure 4.7. Map of the canal systems and fields in Study Area 1 in the Classic period.

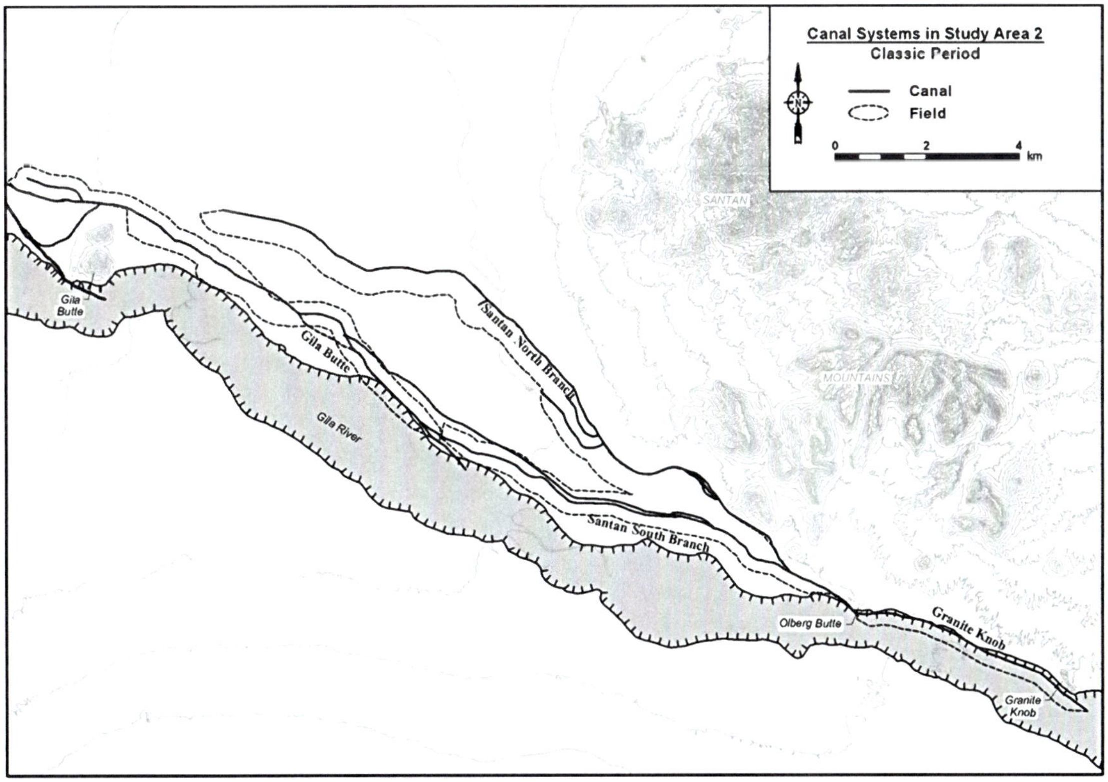

Figure 4.8. Map of the canal system and fields in Study Area 2 in the Classic period.

Their layout remained essentially the same as in the Sedentary period, except that another segment of the Gila Butte canal was extended to connect with the Snaketown canal. The command areas of the Granite Knob canal and the Santan and Gila Butte canal systems are 133 ha, 1,193 ha, and 660 ha, respectively.

A few changes to the canal systems in Study Area 2 occurred during the Late Classic period. It is possible that the Granite Knob canal was abandoned at that time, based on the lack of polychrome ceramics at GR-146, the only site with a preserved segment of the main canal, and the general decline in intensity of use and occupation along the canal. Also, the possible main-canal branch in the Gila Butte canal system, located along the edge of the floodplain, appears to have fallen into disuse, based on survey data, and therefore is not certain at this time.

Command Area and Canal Capacity

The maximum command areas for the study area canal systems were as follows: 133 ha for the Granite Knob canal system (Colonial to Classic periods), 1,193 ha for the Santan canal system (Colonial to Classic periods), 680 ha for the Gila Butte canal system (Classic period), and 1,492 ha for the Snaketown canal system (during the Colonial to Classic periods). Given these maxima, it is relevant to ask whether the main canals had sufficient capacity to irrigate these areas. Capacity, or discharge (Q), is the amount of water passing through a given canal-channel cross section in a given unit of time, measured in cubic meters per second (m^3/s). After discharge is calculated for an excavated canal segment, an estimation may be made of the amount of land that could have been irrigated by the canal. The estimates of irrigable area can then be compared to the estimates of command area.

Estimates of irrigable area are based on assumptions of the irrigation requirement for various crops, seepage and evaporation losses within the canal system, and efficiency of the water delivery to field areas (Woodson and Huckleberry 2002:136). Historical-period canal-irrigation analogs provide the basis for these estimations (Ackerly 1991). First, an assumption must be made about water duty for the canal. Haury (1976:144), apparently through reference to the BOR's (1951) *Irrigation Advisor's Guide*, assumed that 40–70 acres could be irrigated with each cubic foot per second (cfs) of discharge.[2] Second, the use of maximum discharge (as calculated from the maximum canal dimensions derived from excavated canal cross sections) results in dramatic overestimates of irrigable area (Ackerly 1991), primarily because of the uncertainty about the water levels in prehistoric canals (Howard 1990; Woodson 2007). Canals are not designed to carry water at bankful levels; rather, they incorporate a freeboard, to avoid bank erosion. Archaeologists thus commonly estimate the total number of irrigated acres by reducing the acreage derived from maximum discharge by 75 percent and then further reducing that result by 10 percent, to account for estimated water loss (hence, the final estimate is equivalent to 22.5 percent of the original maximum acreage calculation) (see Ackerly 1991; Howard 1990, 1993). The adjusted irrigable-acreage value is therefore equal to 22.5 percent of the value derived from maximum discharge at the heading. Even with these corrections, irrigable-area estimates should only be used as guidelines and not as absolute measures (Woodson and Huckleberry 2002).

Open-channel equations, as adapted from Chow (1959), were used to calculate cross-sectional area, hydraulic radius, velocity, and maximum discharge of the main canals in Study Areas 1 and 2 through time. The parameters were calculated based on excavated canal-segment dimensions considered to be the most representative of the main-canal size through time. In the cases considered here, these are the farthest-upstream excavated main-canal segments in the four canal systems. The estimated discharge at the canal heading was calculated based on the regression formula of cross-sectional-area reduction established by Howard (1990, 1993:287) (see Appendix A). The estimates of the maximum irrigable acreage were based on an assumed water duty of 70 acres per 1 cfs of discharge at the canal head. The estimated acreage was then adjusted by applying the 25 percent correction factor and a further 10 percent reduction for estimated water loss. Table 4.1 provides the relevant values for the main canals in each of the four canal systems.[3] The estimated command areas, as determined based on a reconstruction of irrigated field areas (see Appendix A), are given in the last column of the table for each main canal, by time period. By comparing the command-area estimates with irrigable-area estimates, an assessment could be made as to whether the main canals had sufficient capacity to irrigate the command areas.

The capacity of the Granite Knob canal far exceeded the estimated command area of 100 ha in the Colonial period and 133 ha in the Sedentary to Classic periods (Miles 2009). The possible exception was the Late Classic period, when the canal might have fallen into disuse (this is based on limited surface evidence and is a tentative conclusion). The excessive capacity of the Granite Knob canal may have been engineered to provide additional water to the adjacent downstream Santan canal, with which it was linked by the Sedentary period. However, the cross-sectional area and discharge of the excavated Granite Knob canal segment were smaller than those of the excavated segment of the Santan canal (see analysis in Appendix A). This suggests that the Granite Knob canal was not the sole source of water for the Santan canal. One reason for the discrepancy between the results of estimated discharge and cross-sectional area is that several assumptions have to be made in

Table 4.1. Estimated Discharge and Irrigable Areas for Main Canals, Based on Excavated Canal Segments

Canal-Segment Location	Time Period	A (m^2)	Q (m^3/s)	z Value	Distance from Heading (km)	Q at Head[a]	Change (%)	Maximum Irrigable Area at Canal Heading: @70 acres/cfs (Haury 1976)	25% of Previous Cell	Reduced by 10%	Converted to Hectares	Command Area (ha)
Granite Knob Canal												
GR-146 (Feature 1a)	Colonial	2.76	2.57	−1.65	3.00	4.86		12,013	3,003	2,70[illegible]	**1,094**	100
GR-146 (Feature 1b)	Colonial to Sedentary?	2.39	2.13	−1.65	3.00	4.41	−9	10,904	2,726	2,45[illegible]	**993**	133
GR-146 (Feature 1c)	Classic?	2.16	1.89	−1.45	3.00	3.90	−11.5	9,638	2,409	2,16[illegible]	**878**	133
Santan Canal												
GR-442 (Feature 25a)	Colonial to Sedentary?	4.30	4.21	−1.65	0.80	5.18		12,807	3,202	2,88[illegible]	**1,166**	1,193
GR-442 (Feature 25b)	Sedentary to Classic?	3.60	3.47	−1.25	0.80	4.21	−18.7	10,399	2,600	2,34[illegible]	**947**	1,193
Gila Butte Canal												
GR-1214 (Feature 2)	late Pioneer/early Colonial	1.53	1.07	−1.25	2.00	2.44		6,037	1,509	1,35[illegible]	**550**	300
GR-1220 (Feature 1a)	Colonial to Sedentary?	2.58	2.11	−1.75	2.90	4.49	92.0	11,106	2,776	2,49[illegible]	**1,011**	600-630
GR-1220 (Feature 1b)	Sedentary to Classic?	2.16	1.71	−1.25	2.90	3.41	−24	8,429	2,107	1,89[illegible]	**768**	680
Snaketown Canal												
Pioneer Canal Area/CT 6	Pioneer	1.76	1.25	−1.65	7.41	4.76		11,771	2,943	2,64[illegible]	**1,072**	109/308
CT 14	Colonial	3.40	3.36	−1.65	5.35	6.41	34.6	15,839	3,960	3,56[illegible]	**1,442**	1,492
CT 14	Sedentary	2.96	2.77	−1.65	5.35	5.82	−9	14,381	3,595	3,23[illegible]	**1,309**	1,492
CT 14	(Early?) Classic	1.44	0.99	−1.25	5.35	3.30	−43	8,156	2,039	1,83[illegible]	**743**	1,492?
CT 14	(Late?) Classic	1.09	0.72	−1.25	5.35	3.03	−8.1	7,489	1,872	1,68[illegible]	**682**	1,492?

[a] The regression formula of cross-sectional-area reduction established by Howard (1990, 1993:287) was used to retrodict discharge at the head of the canal: $\hat{y} = z(\log x+1)$ + (y intercept), where $\hat{y}$ = data point with known cross-sectional area (or discharge), z = multiplicative constant (slope), and x = distance from canal head. "z" values were determined for each main canal.

estimating discharge, causing potentially significant error ranges in the results. The Granite Knob canal traverses an area of the valley with large, incised wash channels; so, the canal may have been built larger than necessary for holding water in order to protect it from destructive flooding. Also, prehistoric canals probably were "overbuilt" in size, to facilitate periodic flooding in order to remove salts from fields and replenish fields with fresh deposits of silt (Woodson 2003). This assessment is based on observations of technologically similar historical-period Akimel O'odham canals (see Russell 1975:87; Southworth 1919:116). This means that the actual capacity of the canal may have been considerably lower than was calculated using maximum canal dimensions. In sum, we can surmise that the Santan canal probably maintained its own heading at Olberg Butte, and the end of the Granite Knob canal was joined to the Santan canal, to provide supplemental water.

For the Santan canal, no main-canal segments dating to the late Pioneer period have been excavated; so, it is not possible to assess whether the canal was sufficient to irrigate the estimated 421-ha command area. During the Colonial to Sedentary periods, the Santan canal appears to have had just enough capacity to irrigate its entire command area of 1,193 ha. By the Classic period, canal capacity was reduced by 18.7 percent, which may have resulted in problems with the canal system's ability to irrigate all its field areas. A mitigating factor against that was the supplemental water received from the Granite Knob canal, which probably made up for any shortfalls from the Santan canal heading.

The Gila Butte canal appears to have been sufficient to irrigate the 300–680 ha in its estimated command area until the Sedentary period. Like the Santan canal, the Gila Butte canal was reduced in capacity (29 percent) over the Sedentary to Classic periods. The Gila Butte canal was still large enough to irrigate its own fields in the Classic period. It also received supplemental water from the Santan canal, with which it had been linked in the Colonial period. However, the ability of the Gila Butte canal to provide additional water to the downstream Snaketown canal (with which it was linked in the Sedentary and Classic periods) may have been compromised in the Classic period.

The Snaketown canal had the highest capacity in the Colonial period, was lessened in the Sedentary period, and was significantly reduced (by 43 percent) during the Classic period. The figures suggest that the Snaketown canal had sufficient capacity to irrigate all command-area fields during the Pioneer (109–308 ha) through Colonial (1,492 ha) periods. In the Sedentary period, canal capacity had dropped since the Colonial period but probably was still adequate to irrigate all 1,492 ha with the supplemental water from the Gila Butte canal. By the Early Classic period, however, the capacity of the Snaketown canal probably was insufficient to irrigate the entire 1,492 ha, even with the additional water from the Gila Butte canal. We might surmise that the actual command area that could be irrigated was equivalent to the reduction in capacity of 43 percent, although this is unclear. Canal capacity decreased further by the Late Classic period. As noted above, the heading at Diversion Point 1 possibly was abandoned by the Late Classic period, which also would have contributed to the decreased water supply. This suggests that the Snaketown system irrigators were experiencing significant reductions in the water supply during the Classic period.

This analysis indicates that the capacity of the main canals in all four canal systems waned from the Colonial to Classic periods, with the largest declines over the Sedentary to Classic period transition. The Colonial period channels in these canals were deeper and had the greatest capacities, and the Classic period channels were shallower and had smaller capacities (which varied between 65 and 89 percent of the Sedentary period capacities). These reductions resulted from decreased water flow in the river in the Early Classic period, an increase in upstream canal-system diversions, a degradation in the efficiency of water diversion at the canal heading, or a combination of all three factors (see Chapter 3 for a discussion of river-channel and streamflow changes and the Gila River canal systems). The reductions also could have been related to less labor available to clean the canals, a topic that is discussed in the following sections. Despite these reductions, the three upstream main canals (in Study Area 2) appear to have been capable of irrigating their entire command areas throughout their use-lives. That does not necessarily mean that irrigators along these canals did not experience water scarcity, because the excavated canals, by themselves, did not provide information on water-supply levels. In contrast, the Snaketown canal probably could not irrigate its entire command area during the Classic period. Again, the series of assumptions that have to be made in the calculations of irrigable area might have produced enough error that these results could be called into question. However, the assumptions produced fairly conservative estimates; so, I would argue that they have utility in examining the issues of canal capacity and command area.

Irrigation-Management Complexity

This study posits that the irrigation-management complexity of a canal system may have been a significant factor in the organization of irrigation management and potentially in the organization of settlements. The canal systems with higher maintenance-burden and administrative-density values, as well as more organizational levels, could represent cases in which irrigation management was more complex. As such, management tasks may have required more interaction and cooperation among the members of the irrigation organization than in systems with fewer levels and decision points. The consolidation of two canal systems, for example, most likely would have been accompanied by an increase in maintenance burden and administrative density.

Table 4.2 provides the values for the canal-system variables measured for the Granite Knob, Santan, Gila Butte, and Snaketown canal systems (listed in order of the sequence of their headings along the river). The table includes the number of organizational levels, the maintenance burden, and the administrative density for each system, as well as whether the system was consolidated with another system. As described in Chapter 2, the number of levels was measured on a rank scale (from 1 to 4) that correlates to hypothetical levels of management complexity, with four levels being the most complex (Uphoff 1986). Maintenance burden is the ratio of the total length of canals in the system (km) to system size (ha), multiplied by 1,000. Higher values equate to a higher burden. Essentially, this is a measure of the length of canal (in meters) that must be maintained for each hectare. For comparison, the ratio of length of *main* canals (km) to size also is given. The maintenance-burden-ratio values differ when using either the entire system length or main-canal lengths, but the general trend by time period is similar. However, the values with main-canal lengths have a higher confidence level, because the main canals are documented better than the other types of canals (i.e., distribution or lateral) in the system. Administrative density is measured here as the ratio of the main canal plus the number of distributary canals (1 + n) to system size (in hectares), multiplied by 1,000 (see Hunt 1988a:344). When two canals are joined or consolidated, this is viewed as adding another canal or decision point to the system. Higher density values equate to a higher administrative requirement. Figures 4.9 and 4.10 graph maintenance-burden values (based on the ratio of main-canal length to system size) and administrative-density values, respectively.

All four canal systems were initiated in the simplest configuration, at one organizational level. The Snaketown system progressed to two levels in the late Pioneer period and then expanded to three levels by the early Colonial period. The Santan system also expanded to three organizational levels by the early Colonial period. These systems are quite similar to each other in layout (with a "fork" represented by two main-canal branches) and in total main-canal length (25.5 km in the Snaketown system and 26.6 km in the Santan system). The Gila Butte system expanded to two levels by the early Colonial period and possibly to three levels by the Sedentary period. The Granite Knob canal is listed as having only one organizational level, but it probably had at least one distribution canal, which would result in the canal system's being characterized as having two levels. It must be noted that the Granite Knob canal system is the least-well-documented system, for reasons cited above (see Table 4.2 footnote). The uncertainty about the layout and command area of the system is a caveat for the evaluation of the measures of irrigation-management complexity for it. In sum, the Snaketown and Santan canal systems had the most organizational levels, followed by the Gila Butte (although it may have had three levels) and Granite Knob systems.

The trends in maintenance burden are somewhat surprising in their similarities, except for the Snaketown canal system in the Pioneer period (see Figure 4.9). The high early Pioneer period value for the Snaketown system must be considered with care, because that incipient period is the least well known of the entire sequence. In the late Pioneer period, the Snaketown canal was extended, the system size nearly tripled, and an organizational level was added. The steep drop in the burden values suggests that the Snaketown irrigators reduced maintenance effort by modifying elements of the system. During the Colonial to Classic periods, the maintenance-burden values for the Snaketown, Santan, and Gila Butte systems were similar and all remained relatively flat. This suggests that they were similar in terms of their *relative* levels of effort required for maintenance, and it might indicate that they were operating at similar levels of efficiency. As will be seen below in the discussion of labor requirements for cleaning, though, there were clear differences among these systems in the work effort required for maintenance.

Some comment is needed for the Granite Knob canal system, which had a maintenance-burden level in the Colonial to Classic periods that was roughly twice as high as those of the other systems. That level may be misleading, because the command area irrigated by the canal possibly was larger than inferred here. If it was even 50 percent larger than estimated, the maintenance burden would be reduced to levels similar to those of the other canal systems. On the other hand, the Granite Knob canal traversed terrain along the distal end of an alluvial fan dissected by numerous washes, damage from which would have required additional maintenance effort.

Administrative density generally increased and was highest in the Classic period for the Snaketown, Santan, and Gila Butte systems (see Figure 4.10). Again, for the early Pioneer period Snaketown system, the higher density value may have been skewed because of the lack of information on this early stage. There was a notable rise in administrative density for these three systems between the late Pioneer and early Colonial periods, when the systems underwent their most dramatic expansions. The density was greatest for the Santan system from the Colonial to Classic periods. The increases in administrative density in the three systems during the Sedentary and Classic periods were due to the efforts involved in consolidating the canal systems, even though the command area remained essentially the same in each system. A notable observation is that the Santan canal system was linked to another system at both its head and tail ends, as was the Gila Butte canal system. As defined for the Granite Knob canal, administrative density actually decreased from the Colonial to Sedentary period and then remained the same in the Classic period. That runs counter to the pattern in the other systems, but again, the lack of clear definition for this canal system may have skewed this measure.

Table 4.2. Values of Measured Variables for the Canal Systems

Time Period	No. of Levels	Maintenance Burden						Administrative Density			Consolidated with Upstream Canal?
		Total System Length (km)	Size (ha)	Ratio Value (m/ha)	Main-Canal Length (km)	Size (ha)	Ratio Value (m/ha)	Main Canal and No. of Distribution Canals	Size (ha)	Ratio Value (m/ha)	
Granite Knob Canal											
Pioneer (?) to Colonial	*1*[a]	*4.2*	100	42.0	4.2	100	42.0	1	100	10.0	no
Sedentary to Classic	*1*[a]	*5.5*	133	41.4	5.5	133	41.4	*1*	133	7.5	no
Santan Canal System											
Pioneer	1	*11.0*	421	26.1	*9.3*	421	22.1	*1*	421	2.4	no
Colonial	3	30.0	1,193	25.1	26.6	1,193	22.3	12	1,193	10.1	no
Sedentary to Classic	3	30.0	1,193	25.1	26.6	1,193	22.3	13	1,193	10.9	yes[b]
Granite Knob–Santan Canal System (Consolidated)											
Sedentary to Classic	3	*35.5*	1,326	26.8	32.1	1,326	24.2	*14*	1,326	10.6	
Gila Butte Canal System											
Pioneer	1	*7.5*	300	25.0	6.4	300	21.3	1	300	3.3	no
Colonial	2	*13.0*	600	21.7	10.4	600	17.3	*4*	600	6.7	yes[c]
Sedentary	2/3[d]	*22.0*	630	34.9	11.6	630	18.4	*5*	630	7.9	yes[c]
Classic	2/3[d]	*25.9*	680	38.1	15.0	680	22.1	*6*	680	8.8	yes[c]
Snaketown Canal System											
Early Pioneer	1	8.1	109	74.3	8.1	109	74.3	1	109	9.2	no
Late Pioneer	2	15.1	308	49.0	14.1	308	45.8	2	308	6.5	no
Colonial	3	54.0	1,492	36.2	25.5	1,492	17.1	12	1,492	8.0	no
Sedentary	3	55.2	1,492	37.0	26.7	1,492	17.9	13	1,492	8.7	yes
Classic	3	58.6	1,492	39.3	30.1	1,492	20.2	14	1,492	9.4	yes
Gila Butte–Snaketown Canal System (Consolidated)											
Sedentary	3	*77.2*	2,142	36.0	38.3	2,142	17.9	*18*	2,142	8.4	
Classic	3	*84.5*	2,172	38.9	45.1	2,172	20.8	*20*	2,172	9.2	

Time Period	No. of Levels	Maintenance Burden						Administrative Density			Consolidated with Upstream Canal?
		Total System Length (km)	Size (ha)	Ratio Value (m/ha)	Main-Canal Length (km)	Size (ha)	Ratio Value (m/ha)	Main Canal and No. of Distribution Canals	Size (ha)	Ratio Value (m/ha)	
All Four Canal Systems (Consolidated)											
Sedentary	3?	112.7	3,468	32.5	70.4	3,468	20.3	32.0	3,468	9.2	
Classic	3?	120.0	3,498	34.3	77.2	3,498	22.1	34.0	3,498	9.7	

Note: Italicized numbers are estimates.

[a] Most of the Granite Knob canal and its field areas were scoured away by historical-period flooding of the Gila River, and it is unclear whether the main canal had any main-branch or distribution canals associated with it (therefore, the number of levels is listed as only 1).

[b] The Santan canal was consolidated with the Granite Knob canal on the upstream end in the Sedentary period but had been joined with the Gila Butte canal on the downstream end in the Colonial period.

[c] The Gila Butte canal was consolidated with the Santan canal on the upstream end in the Colonial period and was joined with the Snaketown canal in the Sedentary period on the downstream end.

[d] The Gila Butte canal may have had a main-canal branch, as suggested the documentation of canal Feature 5 near Gila Butte by Howard and Rice (1982) during monitoring, but that could have been a distribution canal; so, this is unclear.

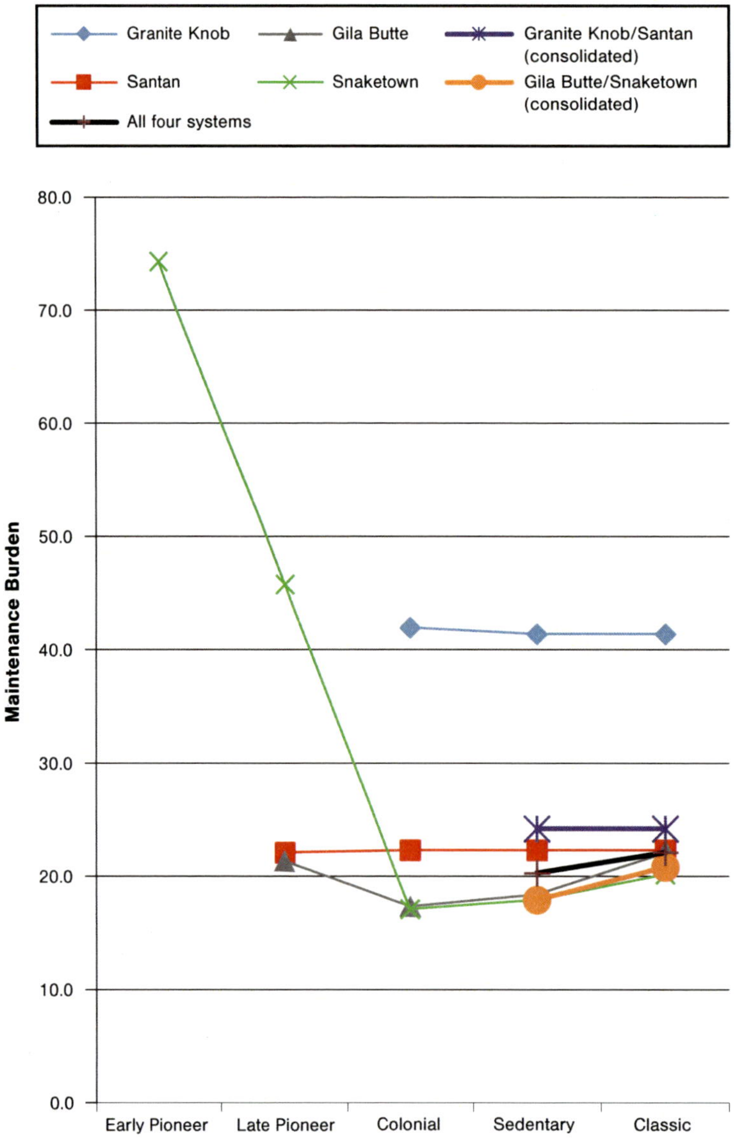

Figure 4.9. Graph of maintenance-burden values.

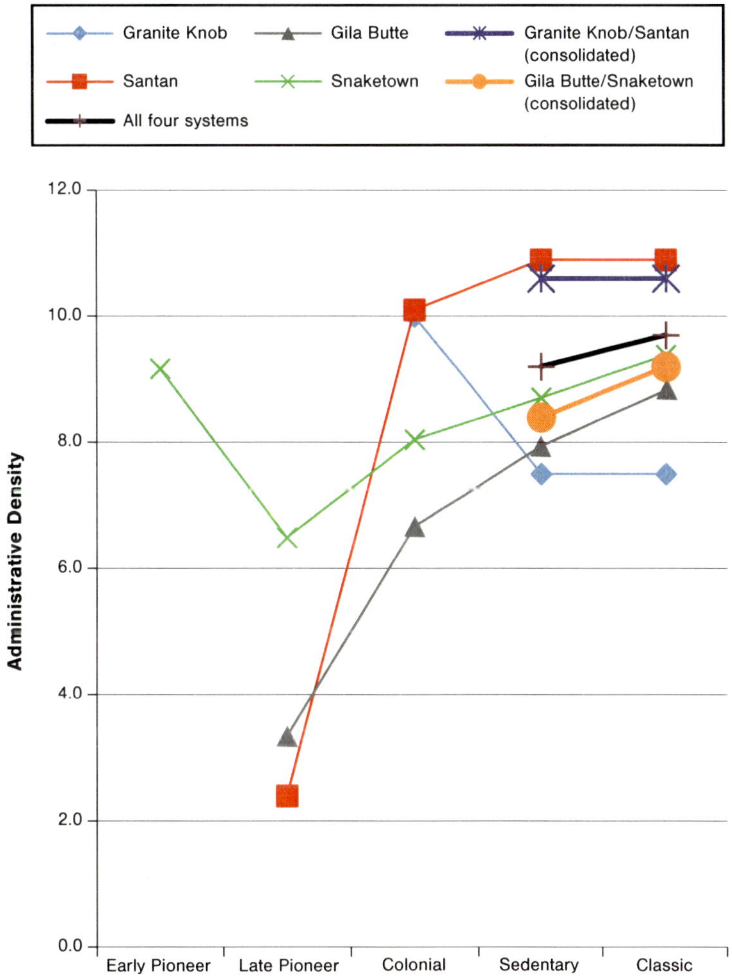

Figure 4.10. Graph of administrative-density values.

Interestingly, when the management-complexity values are calculated for the two inferred consolidated canal systems (Granite Knob/Santan and Gila Butte/Snaketown in the Sedentary and Classic periods), the maintenance-burden and administrative-density values are similar to those for the separate systems (see Table 4.2; Figures 4.9 and 4.10). Upon first consideration, one would assume that the values should increase, because the canal system becomes larger and more complex upon consolidation. The values do increase, but the values for the separate systems already had accounted for the linking points between the systems. Therefore, the management complexity of each of the two consolidated systems actually was similar to that of each of the separate systems (i.e., each consolidated-system value was essentially an average of its two component-system values). The two linked systems would still be considered to have three organizational levels. It should be noted that evidence indicated that the four main canals maintained their own separate headings through their use-lives, although the Gila Butte/Snaketown canals possibly were consolidated into one canal system with one heading (at Diversion Point 2) by the Late Classic period. The only case in which the consolidated-system values were appreciably different from those of its constituent two systems was for the Granite Knob/Santan canal system. There, the maintenance-burden value was considerably lower than that of the Granite Knob canal alone, whereas the administrative-density value was higher.

Lastly, values are given assuming that all four canal systems were consolidated into one large system that was managed as a unit. The likelihood that this was the case is quite low, as will become more clear in the settlement-pattern analysis. Still, it is somewhat surprising that the values were not much different from the values for the separate systems or for the two smaller, consolidated systems. Again, that is because of the same factors noted in the previous paragraph in regard to this scenario. It is not clear whether such a large system would still be considered to have three organizational levels.

Labor Requirements for Canal Maintenance

The maintenance-burden measure tells us the length of canal that must be maintained for each hectare of fields, but it does not indicate the level of effort involved in that maintenance. Here, I provide labor-requirement estimates for canal maintenance as a more concrete measure of the maintenance burden of each canal. The best way to measure this is to focus on the annual main-canal cleaning event (Woodson forthcoming). The calculation method is described in Chapter 2. Estimates are given for the sizes of the work crews that would have been needed for the yearly canal cleaning in Tables 4.3–4.6. The chart in Figure 4.11 depicts the work-crew sizes for cleaning each of the main canals in 1 week at one-quarter full, by time period. I assume that the cleaning was more likely to occur within 1 week, rather than 2 weeks, based on ethnographic accounts of this type of work. Sediment could have accumulated to a range of depths each year, but the one-quarter-full level is graphed as what is assumed to be more typical.

These measures indicate that there were *significant* differences among the four canal systems in the number of people required to clean each main canal. Generally, the size of the work crew co-varies with the length of the main canal; however, canal capacity (volume) is the other major factor. During the late Pioneer period, the Snaketown canal required the most people for the cleaning event, followed by the Gila Butte canal. No data are available for the Santan canal in the late Pioneer period; however, we may infer, based on its probable length of 9.3 km, that cleaning it required at least as many people as cleaning of the Snaketown canal. During the Colonial and Sedentary periods, the Santan canal required the most people for the cleaning event, followed by the Snaketown, Gila Butte, and Granite Knob canals. The Santan canal, by far, required the most people for cleaning in the Classic period, followed by the Snaketown, Gila Butte, and Granite Knob canals. The trend for the Classic period is notable for the steep decline in people needed to clean the Snaketown canal, which was a result of the dramatic falloff in canal capacity.

These measures provide insight into the number of members in the irrigation organization. The people involved in cleaning the canals probably were men (Burton and White 1984; Castetter and Bell 1942:160; Uphoff 1986:89), although cases in which women would help with such tasks are known (Castetter and Bell 1942:160–161). The men that cleaned the canals probably comprised the members of the water-user group. If that was the case for the Hohokam, then the size ranges of the irrigation organizations were equivalent to the work-crew-size ranges given in Tables 4.3–4.6.

By extension, workforce-size estimates have important implications for the size of the population living along a canal system (or, more specifically, the population using water for farms along a canal system). I assume that the average Hohokam household included five people, based on ethnographic accounts that reported that a Pima family or household included about five persons (e.g., Castetter and Bell 1942:54–56; Ezell 1961:16; see Craig 1995). If we assume that adult men were the only persons from each household to be involved with canal-maintenance tasks, then we can multiply the size of the workforce by five to estimate the size of the population living along the canal system. The population-size ranges for each period given in Table 4.7 were derived using the minimum and maximum numbers of people required for cleaning at either 1 or 2 weeks. These population estimates will be considered further in the following chapters.

Table 4.3. Labor Requirements for Cleaning the Granite Knob Canal

Duration of Cleaning Event	Volume of Dirt Cleaned (m^3)	Person-Days of Labor (@ 3 m^3/Person)	Work-Crew Size (Divided by the No. of Days)
<u>**Colonial Period (Canal Length = 4.2 km)**</u>			
Canal ¼ full of sediment			
1 week	1,076	359	51
2 weeks	1,076	359	26
Canal ¾ full of sediment			
1 week	5,316	1,772	253
2 weeks	5,316	1,772	127
<u>**Sedentary Period (Canal Length = 5.5 km)**</u>			
Canal ¼ full of sediment			
1 week	1,113	371	53
2 weeks	1,113	371	27
Canal ¾ full of sediment			
1 week	5,677	1,892	270
2 weeks	5,677	1,892	135
<u>**Classic Period (Canal Length = 5.5 km)**</u>			
Canal ¼ full of sediment			
1 week	988	329	47
2 weeks	988	329	24
Canal ¾ full of sediment			
1 week	5,391	1,797	257
2 weeks	5,391	1,797	128

Table 4.4. Labor Requirements for Cleaning the Santan Canal

Duration of Cleaning Event	Volume of Dirt Cleaned (m^3)	Person-Days of Labor (@ 3 m^3/Person)	Work-Crew Size (Divided by the No. of Days)
<u>**Colonial and Sedentary Periods (Canal Length = 26.6 km)**</u>			
Canal ¼ full of sediment			
1 week	4,283	1,428	204
2 weeks	4,283	1,428	102
Canal ¾ full of sediment			
1 week	20,757	6,919	988
2 weeks	20,757	6,919	494
<u>**Classic Period (Canal Length = 26.6 km)**</u>			
Canal ¼ full of sediment			
1 week	3,997	1,332	190
2 weeks	3,997	1,332	95
Canal ¾ full of sediment			
1 week	19,369	6,456	922
2 weeks	19,369	6,456	461

Table 4.5. Labor Requirements for Cleaning the Gila Butte Canal

Duration of Cleaning Event	Volume of Dirt Cleaned (m^3)	Person-Days of Labor (@ 3 m^3/Person)	Work-Crew Size (Divided by the No. of Days)
<u>Pioneer Period (Canal Length = 6.4 km)</u>			
Canal 1/4 full of sediment			
1 week	706	235	34
2 weeks	706	235	17
Canal 3/4 full of sediment			
1 week	3,323	1,108	158
2 weeks	3,323	1,108	79
<u>Colonial Period (Canal Length = 10.4 km)</u>			
Canal 1/4 full of sediment			
1 week	1,678	559	80
2 weeks	1,678	559	40
Canal 3/4 full of sediment			
1 week	8,204	2,735	391
2 weeks	8,204	2,735	195
<u>Sedentary Period (Canal Length = 11.6 km)</u>			
Canal 1/4 full of sediment			
1 week	1,748	583	83
2 weeks	1,748	583	42
Canal 3/4 full of sediment			
1 week	8,362	2,787	398
2 weeks	8,362	2,787	199
<u>Classic Period (Canal Length = 12.7 km)</u>[a]			
Canal 1/4 full of sediment			
1 week	1,775	592	85
2 weeks	1,775	592	42
Canal 3/4 full of sediment			
1 week	8,158	2,719	388
2 weeks	8,158	2,719	194

[a] Length would be 15.0 km if the ST-18 extension built in the Sedentary period continued to be used in the Classic period. If so, the volume would be 1,970 and 9,282 m^3 for 1/4 and 3/4 full, respectively.

Table 4.6. Labor Requirements for Cleaning the Snaketown Canal

Duration of Cleaning Event	Volume of Dirt Cleaned (m^3)	Person-Days of Labor (@ 3 m^3/Person)	Work-Crew Size (Divided by the No. of Days)
<u>Early Pioneer Period (Canal Length = 8.1 km)</u>			
Canal 1/4 full of sediment			
1 week	1,891	630	90
2 weeks	1,891	630	45
Canal 3/4 full of sediment			
1 week	8,910	2,970	424
2 weeks	8,910	2,970	212
<u>Late Pioneer Period (Canal Length = 14.1 km)</u>			
Canal 1/4 full of sediment			
1 week	2,439	813	116
2 weeks	2,439	813	58
Canal 3/4 full of sediment			

Duration of Cleaning Event	Volume of Dirt Cleaned (m^3)	Person-Days of Labor (@ 3 m^3/Person)	Work-Crew Size (Divided by the No. of Days)
1 week	11,654	3,885	555
2 weeks	11,564	3,855	275
Colonial Period (Canal Length = 25.5 km)			
Canal 1/4 full of sediment			
1 week	4,130	1,377	197
2 weeks	4,130	1,377	98
Canal 3/4 full of sediment			
1 week	19,769	6,590	941
2 weeks	19,769	6,590	471
Sedentary Period (Canal Length = 25.5 km)			
Canal 1/4 full of sediment			
1 week	3,540	1,180	169
2 weeks	3,540	1,180	84
Canal 3/4 full of sediment			
1 week	16,989	5,663	809
2 weeks	16,989	5,663	405
Classic Period (Canal Length = 25.5 km)			
Canal 1/4 full of sediment			
1 week	1,615	538	77
2 weeks	1,615	538	38
Canal 3/4 full of sediment			
1 week	7,556	2,519	360
2 weeks	7,556	2,519	180

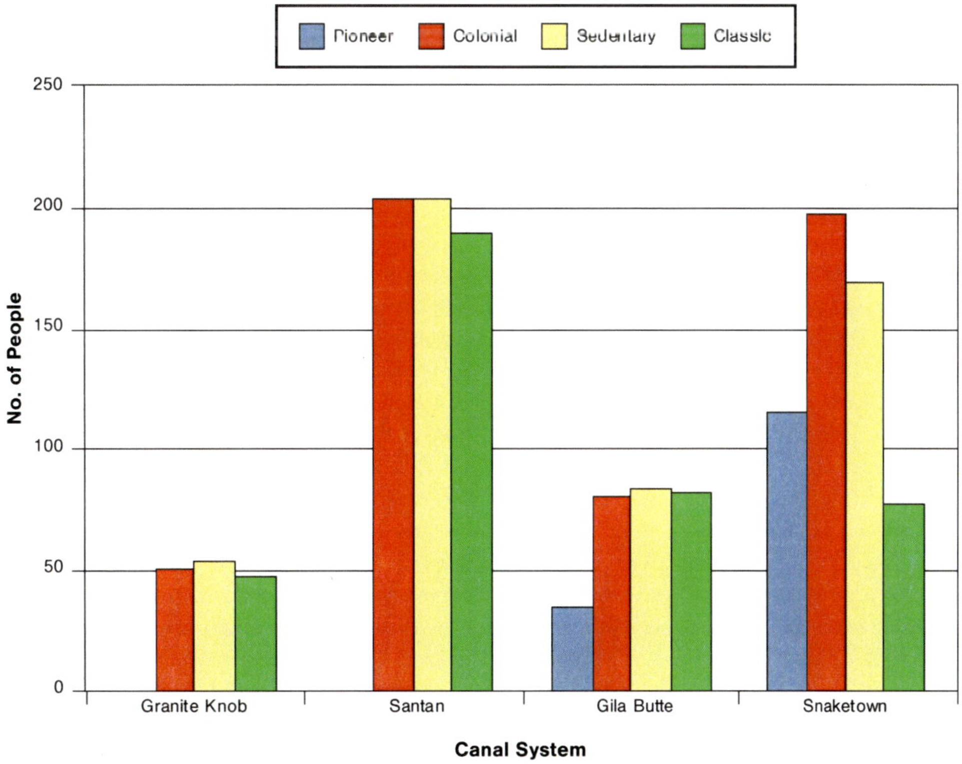

Figure 4.11. Graph showing work-crew sizes for cleaning the main canals in 1 week at one-quarter full.

Table 4.7. Population Estimates Derived from Work-Crew Sizes for Annual Canal Cleaning

Canal	Population, by Period				
	Early Pioneer	Late Pioneer	Colonial	Sedentary	Classic
Granite Knob			130–1,265	135–1,350	120–1,285
Santan		?	510–4,940	510–4,940	475–4,610
Gila Butte		85–790	200–1,955	210–1,990	210–1,940
Snaketown	225–2,120	290–2,775	490–4,705	420–4,045	190–1,800

Table 4.8. Distances (in Kilometers) between the Canal Headings and the Closest Habitation Sites, by Time Period

Canal System	Heading	Period						
		Early Pioneer	Late Pioneer	Early Colonial	Late Colonial	Sedentary	Early Classic	Late Classic
Snaketown	Diversion Point 1	6.8 [H]	*0.8 [C]*[a]	0.8 [C]	0.8 [C]	0.8 [C]	0.8 [C]	2.3 [V]
Gila Butte	Diversion Point 2		5.6 [H]	1.4 [C]	1.4 [C]	1.4 [C]	1.0 [C][b]	1.0 [C][b]
Santan	Olberg Butte	*6.0 [H]*[c]	1.1 [H]	1.1 [V]	1.1 [V]	0.7 [V]	0.7 [V]	0.7 [V]
Granite Knob	Granite Knob		*2.3 [C]*[d]	2.3 [V]	1.4 [V]	1.4 [V]	1.4 [H]	1.7 [H]

Note: The letter in brackets ([ ]) is the habitation type: V = village; H = hamlet; C = camp.

[a] This is the distance from the heading to GR-1184, which might have been established as a camp by this time (Johnson 1964). If it wasn't a camp until the early Colonial period, the distance would be 6.8 km to Snaketown.

[b] This is the distance from the heading to the nearest camp (GR-1208A), which was situated slightly upstream, along the south branch of the Santan canal. The nearest habitation (GR-775C) along the Gila Butte canal was 7.1 km downstream.

[c] This is the late Pioneer period distance from the heading to Upper Santan, which was founded slightly earlier than Olberg (which was considerably closer to the heading).

[d] The Granite Knob canal might have been built as early as the late Pioneer period, but this is unclear.

Another measure of maintenance is the distance between the canal heading and the closest habitation site, which is an indicator of how well situated irrigators were to deal with damage to the heading (i.e., how quickly they could identify a problem and mobilize to fix it). Table 4.8 provides these distances (representing a straight line between a heading and the center of the habitation site), by time period, for the four canal systems. The table also indicates the type of habitation from which the measurement was taken (the settlement analysis is discussed in Chapters 5 and 6). The longest distance between a heading and the nearest habitation was during the incipient phase of each canal system. Shortly after the initial phase of use, the residents along each system established a habitation site much closer to the heading. These new habitations were founded as camps, except in the Santan system, in which it may have been a hamlet. The habitations remained as camps in the Snaketown and Gila Butte systems, but they developed quickly into village-level settlements along the Santan and Granite Knob systems. Through the Sedentary period, each system maintained at least one habitation in close proximity to the heading. In that way, these settlements served as maintenance or "guard" stations that were well positioned to monitor and manage the canal headings. In the three downstream systems, these stations also were situated near the connection points with the next upstream systems, so they could also help manage these important links. The ramifications of these patterns for irrigation organization are discussed further in Chapter 7.

Some changes took place in the Classic period. By the Early Classic period, all four canal systems had become linked, yet I have argued that each of the four canal headings remained in use. Each heading probably would still have required a monitor, and that continued to be true for the Granite Knob, Santan, and Snaketown canals. Yet the camp near the Gila Butte canal heading (Diversion Point 2) was abandoned; so, the distance between the heading and the nearest habitation is somewhat unclear. Table 4.8 indicates that a camp was only 1 km away from the heading, but it was situated slightly upstream, along the tail end of the Santan canal. If that camp was related only to the Santan system, though, then the nearest habitation along the Gila Butte canal was 7.1 km away. That would be a significant change, and the distance would have prevented effective management of the canal heading and the link with the Santan canal. Therefore, it seems likely that the camp along the Santan canal probably assisted in managing the Diversion Point 2 heading (or that there was another habitation in the vicinity that is not currently identified). If so, it might be an indication of an effective cooperation that existed between irrigators along the Santan and Gila Butte canals. In the Late Classic period, some settlements were abandoned, and there was a slight increase in the distance between the headings of the Snaketown and

Granite Knob systems and the nearest habitations. Survey data for the Late Classic period, though, suggest that the headings for the Snaketown canal (at Diversion Point 1, by Gila Butte) and the Granite Knob canal (at Granite Knob) may have been abandoned. If these headings actually were abandoned, then the distances to the headings would not be applicable here.

Lastly, the management of the linking points between the main canals was important to the three downstream systems in the Classic period, because of increases in water scarcity (see the following section). Habitations were positioned directly adjacent to the links between the Granite Knob/Santan canals and Gila Butte/Snaketown canals, but the camp that was situated at the junction between the Santan and Gila Butte canals in the Sedentary period was abandoned in the Classic period. Although there were two camps located about 2 km away from the junction, these settlements were situated along the Santan canal system. Again, that situation may reflect a high degree of cooperation and interaction between irrigators along the Santan and Gila Butte canal systems.

Problems with Water Scarcity

Other factors that must be considered here in regard to their effects on irrigation and irrigation-management complexity are the streambed alterations and discharge changes that occurred along the Gila River (see Chapter 3). The most significant of these environmental events occurred during the Late Sedentary and Early Classic periods. As described below, the context in which those events occurred increased the probability that the canals in the study area experienced periods of water scarcity. Water scarcity is the product of a ratio of which the numerator is *demand* and the denominator is *supply* (Hunt and Hunt 1976:392). Estimating scarcity and excess in the water supply during prehistory is difficult, but multiple data sets now allow us to make inferences about supply and demand and whether certain canal systems were experiencing water scarcity.

Chapter 3 describes the variation in channel morphology and streamflow of the Gila River, the most significant environmental variables that affected Hohokam canal systems. The most important factors that potentially would have tipped the water-supply balance toward water scarcity were a catastrophic landscape-change event and the century-long period of low streamflow that followed. The downcutting and widening event occurred during the second half of the Sedentary period, between A.D. 1020 and 1160 (Huckleberry 1993, 1995; Waters and Ravesloot 2000, 2001). That event would have destroyed the riparian habitat and fields along the river, as well as the canal diversion structures and intakes. The resulting porous, braided streambed and shifting channel would have required additional labor and administrative oversight in order to maintain the diversion dams and canal intakes for 30–100 years. The subsequent shift to a period of low streamflow was highlighted by analysis of 50-year moving averages of the Graybill et al. (2006) streamflow data (see Figure 3.2). Ravesloot et al. (forthcoming) concluded that the period from A.D. 800 to 1000 was characterized by consistently above-average flow, and the period from A.D. 1160 to 1280 (essentially equivalent to the Early Classic period) was characterized by consistently below-average flow. The combination of this low-flow period on the heels of the downcutting and widening event (between A.D. 1020 and 1160) would have presented a significant challenge for period irrigators to maintain a reliable water supply in the canal systems. Thereafter, streamflow returned to above-average flow from A.D. 1280 to 1450 (essentially, the Late Classic period), which would have improved the water supply.

At the same time as these stream-channel and streamflow changes during the Late Sedentary and Early Classic periods, demand for irrigation water had reached its highest level. All 13 of the middle Gila River systems were in operation by the Sedentary period (A.D. 950–1150), bringing the total length of canals in use and the total command area to their highest levels (Woodson 2010b). The total command area of these 13 systems is estimated between 12,781 and 19,531 ha (see Chapter 3). All 13 systems remained in use during the Classic period. With demand at an all-time high and the onset of below-average-flow periods, the position of the canal heading on the river became very important to maintaining a sufficient water supply in the Classic period. For instance, the Diversion Point 1 heading for the Snaketown canal system is the third to last heading (number 11 of the 13 systems) as one travels from upstream to downstream along the middle Gila River. The headings for the Granite Knob, Santan, and Gila Butte systems are numbered 7, 8 and 10 in the sequence, respectively. Thus, these 4 systems were some of the last ones along the middle Gila River to receive water, making them "tail-ender" systems. These positions would have increased the chance of water scarcity, especially during low seasonal flows (see Hunt and Ingram 2007). The effects of the low-flow periods in the Early Classic period would have been multiplied in these tail-ender systems, with the probability of water scarcity becoming successively greater going downstream.

A recent study by Hunt and Ingram (2007, 2010) demonstrated how the position of the headgate on the river is of major importance. They used historical-period Gila River streamflow data (between 1912 and 1929, as measured at the Kelvin gage) to simulate Hohokam maize-production cycles along the middle Gila Valley canal systems. There are two maize cycles per solar year in the Phoenix Basin (Hunt and Ingram 2007, 2010; see also

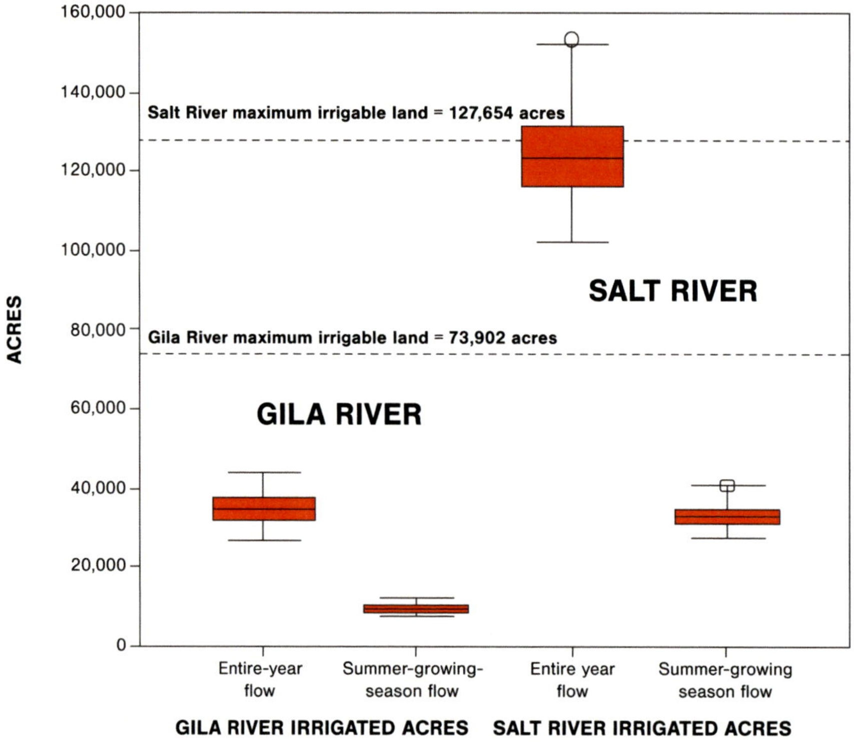

Figure 4.12. Box-and-whisker plots of the estimated ranges of irrigable acreage for the middle Gila and lower Salt Valleys, based on diversion of the entire year's flow and the summer-growing-season flow (from Woodson 2004).

Bohrer 1970). Hunt and Ingram demonstrated that, assuming all canal systems were operating simultaneously, there was a maize failure in 75 percent of the cycles for some of the downstream canal systems. A few of the upstream systems could have produced surpluses. However, there simply was not enough water to supply all the canal systems during some years. The potential problems of crop failure in the downstream systems led them to conclude that there should have been a steady pressure for irrigators to move upriver. Other plausible explanations include (1) the downstream systems were doing something besides growing corn and getting their corn from upstream systems (possibly through exchange), (2) the systems were not actually contemporaneous, and (3) the 1912–1929 sample of middle Gila River flow was substantially less than during the period when all the Hohokam systems were operating.

In a previous study, I examined the topographic and hydrological constraints on irrigable land along the middle Gila Valley canal systems in general (Woodson 2004). I found that despite large expanses of land, the amount of available water in the Gila River sets an upper limit on the amount of land that can be irrigated. The amount of *potentially* irrigable land is 29,000 ha (73,902 acres), which was calculated by measuring the area that could have been irrigated between the highest canal in a system and the river, on the basis of topography. I used the 50-year moving averages of the reconstructed annual discharges for the Gila River (see Chapter 3) as a basis for estimating maximum irrigable acreage. I projected potentially irrigable acreage using both the entire mean annual flow and the estimated split-summer flow (representing a 5-month irrigation season).[4] I made estimates based on diversion of the entire year's flow and the summer-growing-season flow and assumed a canal intake efficiency of 40 percent and an irrigation requirement of 3.75 acre-feet per acre, because it is probable that crops with "suboptimal" yields could be grown at that level (see Ackerly et al. 1987:12; Nials et al. 1989:70). If water was diverted the entire year, irrigators along the middle Gila River could have watered 10,900–17,800 ha (27,000–44,000 acres) of the available farmland (Figure 4.12). For diversion during the growing season only, irrigators could supply water to only a small fraction of the potentially irrigable land (2,914–4,735 ha, or 7,190–11,684 acres). As Hunt and Ingram (2010) observed, though, historical-period Pima ethnographies indicated that farmers diverted water between March and September (7 months). Therefore, the actual amount of farmland that the Hohokam could have irrigated probably was between the two ranges cited above. Also, the Woodson (2004) study was generalized, because it used means of the annual flows (and did not account for input from San Pedro River or monsoon rainfall). However, it showed that the amount of available water in the rivers (especially during the irrigation season) may have been considerably less than would have been required to irrigate all the potentially irrigable land. Competition for water would have been very high in such a situation, and the highest headgates on the river would have had the best water supplies. The scenario of low summer flows has been illustrated historically in observations that the Akimel O'odham utilized the entire flow of the Gila River during the summer months (Ezell 1961; Hackenberg 1974).

The problem of water scarcity was also noted by Graybill et al. (2006) in their analysis of the Gila River streamflow data. Graybill et al. (2006:108) observed that based on reconstructions of stream discharge between A.D. 1143 and 1426 and the estimated irrigable acreage under the first two systems on the middle Gila River (Casa Grande and Escalante/Poston), "about 15 percent of the time, these two canals would have had to capture between 50 percent and 100 percent of the total annual flow in order to irrigate the maximum acreage." Their assessment assumed that 6,247 ha were irrigated under these two canals, with an irrigation requirement of 5 acre-feet per acre. By my own estimations, the command area of these two systems was no larger than 4,151 ha (Woodson 2010b), and the irrigation requirement may have been as low as 2.5 acre-feet per acre (Woodson 2004; see Ackerly 1991). Therefore, the statement above might be an exaggeration of the actual prehistoric situation. Nevertheless, the "amount of available water was likely a limiting factor in Hohokam irrigation farming along the Gila River and . . . there were times when irrigation water may not have been available to downstream canal systems" (Graybill et al. 2006:108).

Other effects of the streambed and discharge changes were evident in the canals themselves (as described above). The capacity of the Snaketown canal was reduced during the Classic period, to the degree that it probably was insufficient to irrigate the inferred 1,492-ha command area. Thus, regardless of the stream-discharge pattern, it is clear that the Snaketown farmers were dealing with a reduction in the water supply. Also, the heading at Diversion Point 1 possibly was abandoned in the Late Classic period. If so, the failure of the heading may have been a result of the downcutting and widening. The capacity of the three main canals in Study Area 2 also diminished, but they probably were still adequate to irrigate their field areas. Still, the irrigators using these systems almost certainly were dealing with the same conditions of potential water scarcity as the Snaketown irrigators (but not necessarily to the same degree, because they had headings located higher up the river).

Because of the river-channel change and water-scarcity problems during the Late Sedentary to Early Classic periods, the maintenance-burden levels in the canal systems probably were more pronounced than indicated by the measures above. The stream-channel changes would have required a higher maintenance investment for the headings and intakes (upper segments of the main canals) for, perhaps, up to a century. The increase in difficulties in the process of water allocation would have led to stresses on the irrigators that were not reflected in the measures of irrigation-management complexity. Yet clearly, the problems would have required irrigation managers to increase their involvement and oversight, to ensure that allocation shares and rules were adhered to by the users (see Mabry 1996).

Several choices are available to irrigators in response to water scarcity (Hunt and Hunt 1976:392): increase the supply of water (i.e., expand supply with existing or new technology or locate a new source), place limits on demand (i.e., resist new uses), practice individual emigration, or shift allocation principles toward water monopolization. First, as evidenced by this chapter's analyses, the most significant response from irrigators in the study area was to *consolidate* each canal system with the next upstream system (see Ravesloot et al. forthcoming). The intent of the consolidations almost certainly was to increase reliability in the water supply for the downstream systems. The vulnerability of the downstream systems, in particular, would have exerted a steady pressure on irrigators to link with another canal system with a headgate higher up the river. As described in Chapter 3, the best headings were at Olberg Butte and Granite Knob. The Snaketown canal was joined with the Gila Butte canal by means of a built extension from the Gila Butte canal in the Sedentary period and another extension in the Early Classic period. The Gila Butte canal was consolidated with its upstream neighbor, the Santan canal, although that may have occurred during the Colonial period, which was before the downcutting and widening. The Santan canal was linked with the Granite Knob canal in the Sedentary period. These consolidations were accomplished because the effectiveness of the downstream canal-system headings had become degraded, the diversions by upstream canal systems were significantly reducing water levels in the river by that time, or the overall water supply in the river was reduced (or a combination of all three). Another contributing factor may have been the downcutting and widening of the Gila River between A.D. 1020 and 1160 (Waters and Ravesloot 2000, 2001), which could have affected marginal canal headings (this event is discussed further at the end of the this chapter).

Second, we can note that no new canal systems were built along the middle Gila River during the Classic period (Woodson 2010b). Nor do there appear to have been any new main canals built within any of the existing 13 canal systems in the Classic period. Exceptions to that might be the canal extension built from the Gila Butte canal to the Snaketown canal, the reconstruction of the Casa Grande canal in the Early Classic period, and its enlargement in the Late Classic period (Craig 2001b). Overall, though, the cessation of new canal construction could be seen as a choice made to place limits on demand.

In addition, the Hohokam in the study area may have chosen other responses to water scarcity during the Classic period that are not reflected in the canal systems. For instance, Hunt and Ingram (2007) suggested that Hohokam farmers along the downstream systems would have needed to obtain corn from upstream farmers on a regular basis. They may have relied on exchange relationships, such as in ceramics, to buffer the risk of crop shortfalls (see Graybill et al. 2006:113). Finally, the water-scarcity conditions would have "pushed" people to move to upstream locales (see Hunt and Ingram 2007). These may have been attractive choices to the study area populations, a topic that is discussed in subsequent chapters.

Summary

In conclusion, this analysis provides valuable insight into the irrigation-management complexity of the canal systems in the study area. First, with the exception of the Snaketown canal system in the Pioneer period, irrigation-management complexity generally increased over time for the Santan, Gila Butte, and Snaketown canal systems. These changes are not surprising, because environmental and social conditions and the canal systems themselves changed over time. The largest increases occurred in administrative density and organizational level during the Colonial period, when these systems were built out. The increases in management complexity in the Sedentary and Classic periods were mainly due to the efforts involved in consolidating the canal systems, even though the command areas remained the same. In the consolidation scenario, the users of the downstream system probably were responsible for cleaning (or helping to clean) the canal extensions/connections from the upstream system, and the additional decision-making points required further administrative attention. Management complexity in the Sedentary and Classic periods probably was even more pronounced than indicated by these measures, because irrigators were dealing with significant water-scarcity problems. This probably involved negotiation and cooperation (and perhaps conflict) with upstream irrigators, to try to secure an adequate water supply. The pattern for the Granite Knob canal is somewhat unclear, but it seems to have remained at about the same level through time.

Second, it is interesting to observe how little variability in irrigation-management-complexity values there was between systems through time. Again, the exception is the Snaketown canal system in the Pioneer period; also, the Granite Knob system remains uncertain. The canal systems followed similar developmental trajectories. The similar maintenance-burden levels indicated that they were operating at similar levels of efficiency. In each system, irrigators kept the distance between the heading and the nearest habitation site quite short, to facilitate quick repairs to the heading.

Third, although the internal measures of management complexity did not exhibit a high degree of variability between systems, it is clear that there were significant differences in labor requirements for maintenance, as indicated by the labor estimates for main-canal cleaning. Generally, the Santan canal required the most people for the cleaning event during the pre-Classic period, followed closely by the Snaketown canal. The labor needed for these two canals exceeded that for the Gila Butte and Granite Knob canals by factors of two and four, respectively. In the Classic period, the Santan canal still required the most people for cleaning, but the second-largest labor force was required for the Gila Butte canal, followed by the Snaketown and Granite Knob canals. The drop for the Snaketown canal was due to its decline in capacity.

Finally, it would appear that the Santan canal system was the most complex, in terms of overall irrigation-management requirements. It required more labor for cleaning and more interaction and cooperation than the other systems to maintain effective irrigation management. Closely following the Santan canal system, the Snaketown canal system was the next-most-complex system, and third was the Gila Butte canal system. The Granite Knob system was the least complex, but its pattern is somewhat uncertain, because of the reasons cited above. These issues will bear upon the discussion in the following chapters, in terms of how irrigation-management complexity relates to political organization of the settlements along the canal systems.

---

[1] In contrast to Haury's (1976) conclusion of a Vahki phase origin for the Pioneer Canal at Snaketown, Wilcox and Shenk (1977:180) cited three reasons they thought that the canal was not used until the Snaketown phase of the late Pioneer period (this view also seems to be supported by Howard [1993:294]): (1) the absence of evidence of erosion and rebuilding of the canal, indicating that it had a relatively short use-life; (2) the presence of Snaketown Red-on-buff sherds in the canal fill; and (3) a suggestion that canal irrigation may not have been necessary for the establishment of the village in the Vahki phase. Wilcox and Shenk (1977:182) further suggested that a late Pioneer period development for irrigation makes more sense, because it would have been correlated to a population increase at Snaketown and elsewhere in the Phoenix Basin. I do not think that these points are sufficient to undermine the argument that the Pioneer Canal was used initially in the Vahki phase and continued to be used through the Snaketown phase. It is true that the investigated segment of the canal was short, and its condition from erosion and overlapping canals left many details unclear (Haury 1976:133). Still, Haury (1976:135–136) found several contexts in which sherd collections from the canal fill included only Vahki Plain and Vahki Red sherds. Another important, but indirect, supporting reason is that Snaketown village was founded in the Vahki phase, and it is improbable that its residents would have located the settlement where it is unless a canal had been built concurrent with the village founding. Haury (1976:9) observed that the site location was chosen for its access to shallow groundwater through the digging of wells, its nearness to arable land on the lower terrace, and its position along the trajectory of canal that could be

diverted from the river several miles upstream. The residents were growing maize and possibly beans, squash, and cotton in the Vahki phase and probably harvesting two plantings a year (Bohrer 1970). These cultigens could be more reliably grown using canal irrigation. For the Pima, three to five irrigations generally were necessary to mature a crop (Castetter and Bell 1942:170). Craig (2001b:142, 144) reached a similar conclusion for the Grewe site, even though direct evidence was not found there for a Vahki phase canal. Although it is possible that floodwater farming first was used by the early Pioneer period farmers (see Cable and Doyel 1987; Wilcox and Shenk 1977:181), I would argue that one of the primary "pulls" for the people who moved into the middle Gila Valley and founded Snaketown and Grewe was the opportunity to build new canals and irrigated fields.

[2] Ackerly (1991:52) determined that early-historical-period, predam Euroamerican canals in Arizona and New Mexico irrigated approximately 86 ± 23.64 acres (62–110 acres) for each cubic foot per second of average canal discharge. That range, though based on empirical analysis, probably exceeds the average range of prehistoric canals, because the efficiency of historical-period Euroamerican canals is thought to be higher than that of prehistoric canals, and the water requirements of modern crop varieties commonly are thought to be greater than those of their prehistoric counterparts (Ackerly et al. 1987; Robert Hunt, personal communication 2010; Nials et al. 1989). I therefore assume that this water-duty estimate is higher than what would have been used by the prehistoric Hohokam and use Haury's (1976:144) estimate of 70 acres per cubic foot per second as a maximum value.

[3] The average dimensions of the Snaketown Pioneer Canal are difficult to ascertain, because the 75-m-long section of the canal investigated by Haury (1976:132–141) has variable dimensions, includes three possible lateral turnouts, and has been impacted by the construction of later, overlapping canals, as well as subsequent erosion. Along the upper 50 m of the canal segment (where it is not overlapped by later canals), the width varies between 2.85 and 5.20 m, and the depth is 0.66 m. I chose an average width of 4.0 m and a depth of 0.66 m as representative dimensions of the canal in this location, resulting in an inferred capacity of 4.76 m^3/s at the heading—*far* larger than was necessary to irrigate the command area inferred for the Pioneer period (see Table 4.1) and larger than needed to feed the inferred population. Although it is possible that the irrigators intended this, the large difference seems to be a discrepancy that could be due to one or more of the following: (1) the canal dimensions used were too large, (2) the heading was closer than Gila Butte, (3) the regression formula for retrodicting canal discharge at the heading is not appropriate for this situation, or (4) the command area actually was much larger than reconstructed here. I believe the dimensions used probably were too large, because the canal may have been purposely built wider in this location to manipulate water flow in order to facilitate diversion of water into lateral canals, allow use of the dipping pools, and enable the curve in the canal at the western end of the Pioneer Canal area. If the width is reduced to 3.0 m and the distance to the heading is reduced to 6 km, the capacity at the heading is 4.46 m^3/s, which is still much larger than necessary. Perhaps the regression formula is not well suited to this situation; the canal area may not have reduced longitudinally as expected in the formula. Even if that is the case, the capacity of the Pioneer Canal would be larger than required for the command area. As revealed in the next section, that overbuilding also would have led to considerably high labor requirements to clean the canal. These aspects may have been the impetus for re-engineering and rebuilding the main canal in the Colonial period.

[4] Nials et al. (1989:70–75) calculated the split-summer discharge (estimated flow for May and June of the current year and July–September of the preceding year) for their five Salt River streamflow periods. The average split-summer discharge ranged from 25.7 to 27.4 percent (the overall percentage was 26.6 percent) of the average annual discharge for the five streamflow periods. Summer discharges of the Gila River between 1920 and 1997 represented 29.7 percent of the annual flow, which was 1 percent higher than the 28.7 percent for flows of the Salt River between 1914 and 1997 (Graybill et al. 2006). For the purposes of estimating the summer Gila River flow, I assumed that the long-term average split-summer discharge was 27.6 percent of the average annual discharge (1 percent higher than the average 26.6 percent for the Salt River) in the reconstruction presented by Graybill et al. (2006).

CHAPTER 5

The Organization of Settlements along the Snaketown Canal System

This chapter examines the settlements along the Snaketown canal system (Study Area 1) and addresses Research Goal 2, to describe and analyze settlements and evaluate settlement organization. The settlement and population trends are described, and the settlement pattern is defined as either segmented or non-segmented for each period, through an analysis of spatial, temporal, and functional data. The analysis then evaluates the settlement pattern in terms of community organization and examines possible signatures of inter-village dynamics. Study Area 1 includes 295 archaeological sites and loci (within sites) situated along or near the Snaketown canal system. Appendix B provides the data for all sites and loci in the study area and includes a summary of the settlement-analysis results (including information on the site-type designations and all habitation sites) and a description of the settlement trends through time. The information in Appendix B and Chapter 4 (canal systems) forms the basis of the discussion in this chapter.

Settlement Trends in Study Area 1

This section provides a summary of the settlement and population trends through time in Study Area 1, in relation to the canals and fields. Appendix B provides a more detailed description of the settlement trends, with a focus on site function, accompanied by figures that display site function by time period in conjunction with the definition of habitation sites. This section draws from the appendix, focusing on the inferred community territories and habitation sites. The community-territory boundaries shown on the maps in this chapter are the same as those shown in Appendix B. The boundaries reflect the most practical configurations, based on application of the principles of the focal-community model and the boundary-definition criteria described in Chapter 2.

This section also discusses the trends in the distribution of settlements and population, utilizing the information given in the next three tables. Table 5.1 provides data on the number of focal villages, the average distances between adjacent focal villages and between all permanent habitations, and the general settlement distribution. The table also gives the average distances between the permanent habitations and the nearest canals and the average minimum and maximum distances to irrigated fields. Table 5.2 provides population estimates for each period, based on the total habitation-site area and total command area. Ranges of population sizes for the residential areas are given, based on the assumption that the population density was 10 or 20 persons per hectare. These population sizes were used to compute the compound annual growth rates (CAGRs) between periods (based on Hassan [1981:140]). Population sizes for the command areas are given assuming that 0.4 ha of irrigated land per person was needed for subsistence. Table 5.3 breaks down the population size by main-canal branch for each period, based on residential-site area for each branch. The data are given for the main-canal branches because they were found to represent a possibly important organizational level for the settlements in Study Area 1. The trends in population and annual growth rates are addressed at greater length in Chapter 7.

Pioneer Period

Snaketown was founded as a hamlet in the early Pioneer period and was situated near the end of a canal built at the same time (Figure 5.1). This site is the only known settlement in the study area at that time. Snaketown was situated roughly 400 m from the Pioneer Canal; however, with a walk-in well inside the village, the residents would have had a closer source of domestic water (Haury 1976). The settlement distribution was nucleated, because all of the population was living at Snaketown. The settlement pattern was non-segmented in structure. The minimum distance between Snaketown and the irrigated fields was 440 m, and the maximum distance was 3,400 m. The population of Snaketown is estimated to have been between 46 and 92 people, based on residential-site area. The canal system could have irrigated 109 ha, which, if fully farmed, could have supported 273 people.

Table 5.1. Variables Measured for Settlement Distribution in Study Area 1 (Hypothesis 3), by Time Period

Period	No. of Focal Villages	Average Distance between Villages (km)	Average Distance between all Permanent Habitations (km)	Settlement Distribution	Average Distance to Canals (m)[a]	Average Minimum Distance to Fields (m)[a]	Average Maximum Distance to Fields (m)[a]
Early Pioneer	—			nucleated	400[b]	440	3,400
Late Pioneer	1	6.5[c]	6.5[c]	nucleated	400[b]	440	5,800
Early Colonial	3	5.6	4.5	nucleated	100	370	2,680
Late Colonial	3	5.6	4.5	nucleated	100	370	2,680
Sedentary	3	5.6	4.5	nucleated	100	370	2,680
Early Classic	1	13.2[d]	3.0	dispersed	200	213	1,897
Late Classic	1	13.2[d]	2.8	dispersed	200	213	1,897

[a] As measured from the center of each permanently occupied habitation site (villages and hamlets, including "dispersed" ones) to the closest field (minimum) and the farthest field (maximum). Maximum distances don't overlap with those measured from other, closest habitations.

[b] Although this distance might seem high, Snaketown also had a walk-in well within the site.

[c] Although only one focal village was in Study Area 1, this spacing is based on the distance to the Gila Butte site and GR-1157C.

[d] This is the distance between the Maricopa Platform Mound and GR-1175, a village without public architecture.

Table 5.2. Population Estimates for Study Area 1, Based on Habitation-Site Area and Command Area, by Time Period

		Based on Habitation-Site Area				*Based on Command Area*	
Period	No. of Years	Total Habitation-Site Area (ha)	Population Size (@ 10 Persons/ha)	Population Size (@ 20 Persons/ha)	*Annual Growth Rate (%)*[a]	Total Command Area (ha)	Population Size (@ 1 Person/0.4 ha)
Early Pioneer	200	4.61	46	92		109	273
Early to late Pioneer					*1.78*		
Late Pioneer	100	26.91	269	538		308	770
Late Pioneer to early Colonial					*1.06*		
Early Colonial	100	77.00	770	1,540		1,492	3,730
Early to late Colonial					*0.28*		
Late Colonial	100	101.44	1,014	2,029		1,492	3,730
Late Colonial to Sedentary					*0.21*		
Sedentary	200	153.81	1,538	3,076		1,492	3,730
Sedentary to Early Classic					*−0.34*		
Early Classic	150	92.21	922	1,844		1,492	3,730
Early to Late Classic					*−0.12*		
Late Classic	150	76.72	767	1,534		1,492	3,730

[a] The compound annual growth rate (CAGR) = $(p2/p1)^{1/n} - 1$, where $p2$ and $p1$ are the numbers of people at the end and beginning of the phase, respectively, and n is the number of years in the phase (see Hassan 1981:140).

Table 5.3. Estimated Population Sizes along the Three Main-Canal Branches in Study Area 1, by Time Period

Period	Main Canal (Snaketown)			North Branch (GR-1157C)			South Branch (Maricopa Road Site)		
	Habitation-Site Area (ha)	Population Size (10 Persons/ha)	Population Size (20 Persons/ha)	Habitation-Site Area (ha)	Population Size (10 Persons/ha)	Population Size (20 Persons/ha)	Habitation-Site Area (ha)	Population Size (10 Persons/ha)	Population Size (20 Persons/ha)
Early Pioneer[a]	4.61	46	92						
Late Pioneer[a]	26.91	269	538						
Early Colonial	37.73	377	755	23.22	232	464	16.05	161	321
Late Colonial	51.89	519	1,038	33.50	335	670	16.05	161	321
Sedentary	86.25	863	1,725	51.51	515	1,030	16.05	161	321
Early Classic	31.90	319	638	40.45	405	809	19.90	199	398
Late Classic	22.08	221	442	34.74	347	695	19.90	199	398

[a] During the Pioneer period, only one main-canal "branch" was in use.

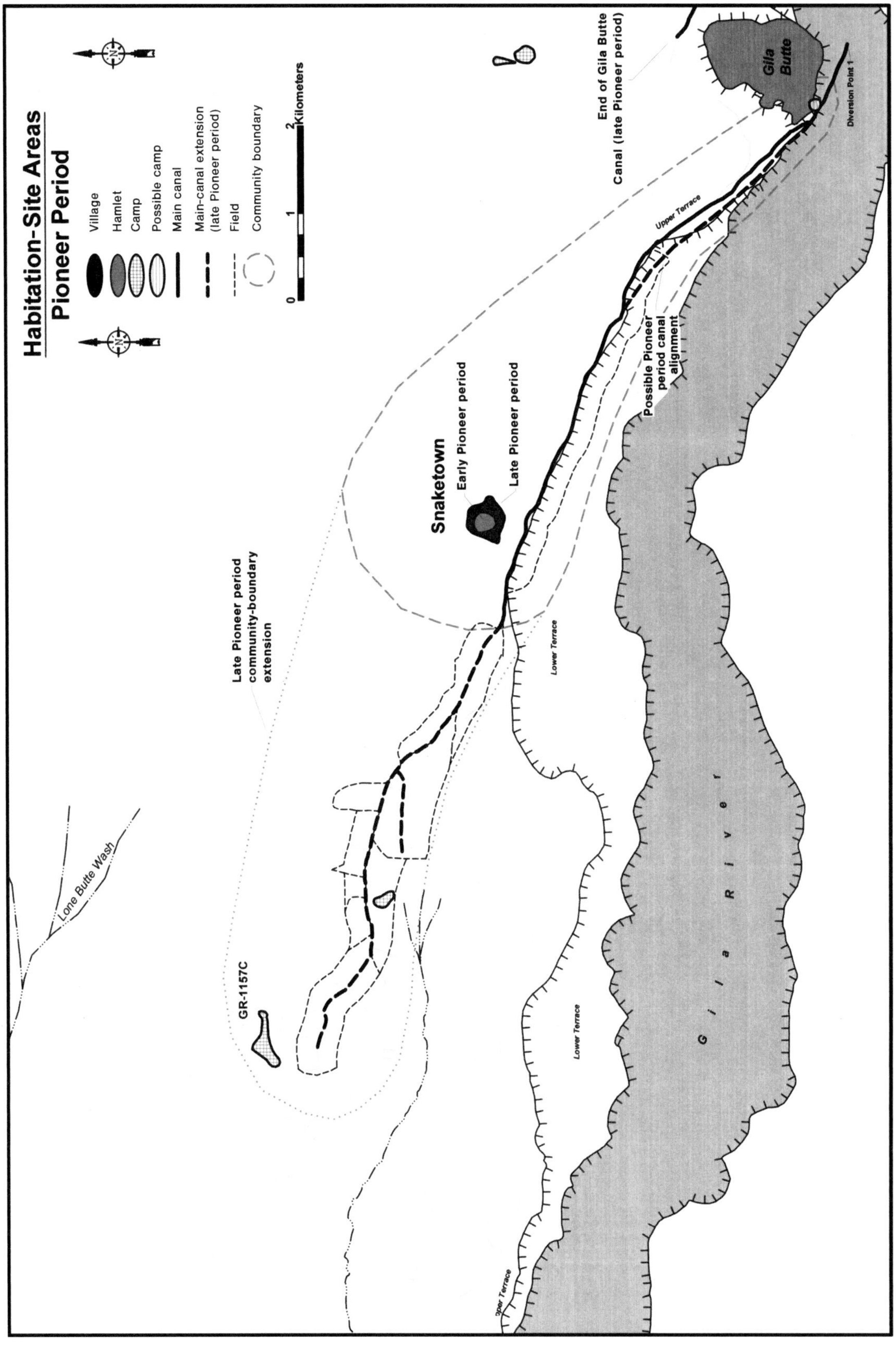

Figure 5.1. Map of the habitation sites, canals, and fields in the Snaketown canal system during the Pioneer period.

In the late Pioneer period, Snaketown more than tripled in area, growing to village size, and residents built a platform mound (Mound 40), making the site a "focal village" (see Figure 5.1). The Pioneer Canal was extended 6 km to the west, for a total main-canal length of 14.1 km. GR-1157C and GR-1157I East were founded as camps at 4.5 and 6.5 km to the west of Snaketown, respectively, along the inferred canal extension. A third possible camp was established at GR-1184, near the Diversion Point 1 heading. A hamlet known as the Gila Butte site was founded 6.5 km to the east, on the eastern side of Gila Butte, and two camps to the north of the butte were used. The settlements at GR-1157C and the Gila Butte site did not include public architecture at that time, but they both would become primary villages with ballcourts in the subsequent early Colonial period. Because both sites were located 6.5 km away from Snaketown, the provisional spacing between primary sites is 6.5 km. Also, the settlement distribution was nucleated, because most or all of the population was living at Snaketown. The settlement pattern remained non-segmented in structure.

The minimum distance between Snaketown and the late Pioneer period fields was 440 m, and the maximum distance was 5,800 m. The latter distance may be somewhat overestimated, because that is the distance from Snaketown to the tail end of the Pioneer Canal extension, near the camps at GR-1157C and GR-1157I. During the parts of the agricultural cycle that required high labor inputs, workers would have been living in these camps closer to the fields, in the lower part of the canal system. The population along the Snaketown canal system is estimated to have exploded fivefold to between 269 and 538 people, based on residential-site area. The canal system could have irrigated 308 ha—nearly triple the previous command area—which, if fully farmed, could have supported 770 people.

Early Colonial Period

During the early Colonial period, Snaketown grew further in size and added the large, east–west-oriented ballcourt (Ballcourt 1) (Figure 5.2). The camp at GR-1157C expanded to a village with two possible ballcourts (along the north branch of the Snaketown canal). The camp at GR-1157I expanded into a hamlet, and three additional hamlets were founded near it, making this "I Group" on par with a "dispersed village." Also, a new village with a probable ballcourt was founded at the Maricopa Road site, 7.3 km west of Snaketown (along the newly built south branch of the Snaketown canal), and a hamlet was established at GR-1206, near Gila Butte. The settlement distribution was nucleated, because most of the population was living at the three focal villages and the hamlets. The settlement pattern became segmented at that time. The average spacing between the primary villages was 5.6 km, and the spacing between habitations was 4.5 km. Two camps also were founded along each of the canal branches, and a camp had definitely been established at GR-1184 by this time.

The average distance between the villages and hamlets and the nearest canal reduced to 100 m in the early Colonial period. If the distances between the camps and the nearest canal also are included in those calculations, the average distance is approximately the same. The only camp that was not located within 400 m of a canal is GR-1157DD (roughly 700 m from a canal). This camp was situated at the southern perimeter of the canal system, overlooking the lower terrace, and includes two roasting pits. It may have been located near a canal on the lower terrace (none are currently known in the area) or near some other unknown resource area, such as a mesquite bosque. Likewise, the camp might be near a currently undefined canal along the south main-canal branch, on the upper terrace. No rock-pile fields are in the area.

The minimum distance between habitations and the early Colonial period fields was 370 m, and the maximum distance was 2,680 m (see Table 5.1). That was a substantial decrease from the late Pioneer period. The population of Snaketown and the other permanent habitations was estimated to have tripled in size to between 770 and 1,540 people, based on residential-site area. The canal system could have irrigated up to 1,492 ha—nearly five times the previous command area—which, if fully farmed, could have supported 3,730 people (see Table 5.2). The population was divided among the villages and other settlements along the three main-canal branches (see Table 5.3). The majority (377–755 people) were living along the main canal, compared to 232–464 people along the north-branch canal and 161–321 people along the south-branch canal.

Late Colonial and Sedentary Periods

The settlement pattern of the early Colonial period evidently continued into the late Colonial period (Figure 5.3) and the Sedentary period (Figure 5.4), but with further growth. Snaketown residents built two additional platform mounds (Mounds 16 and 39) and possibly a third (Mound 38), as well as a second, north–south-oriented ballcourt (Ballcourt 2). The settlement distribution was nucleated, because most of the population was living at the three focal villages and the hamlets. The settlement pattern remained segmented. The average spacing between the primary villages was 5.6 km, and the spacing between habitations was 4.5 km. The average distance between the villages and hamlets and the nearest canal remained at 100 m in the late Colonial and Sedentary periods (see Table 5.1). If the distances between the camps and the nearest canal also are included in these calculations, the average distance is approximately the same. As in the early Colonial period, the only camp that was not located within 400 m of a canal is GR-1157DD.

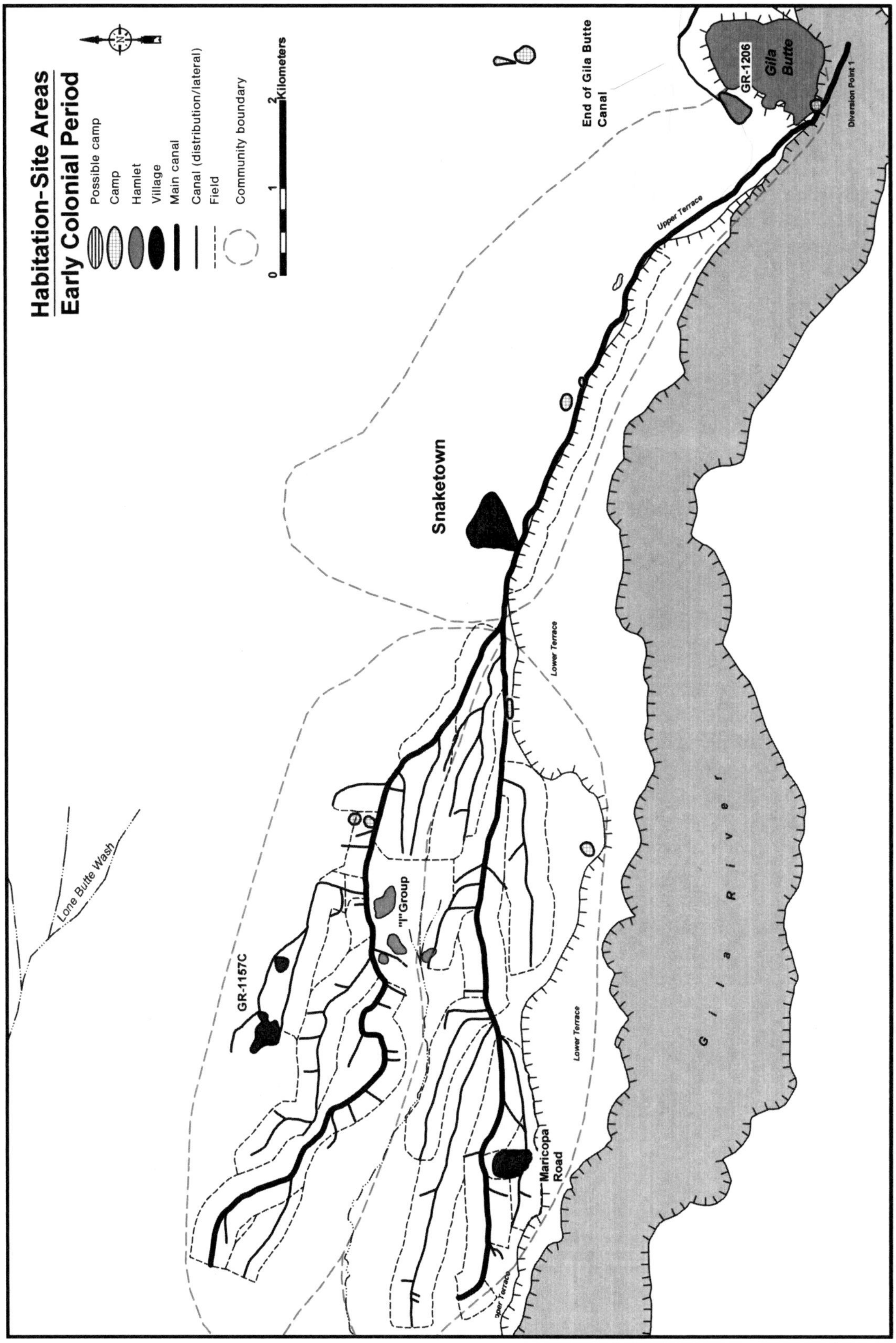

Figure 5.2. Map of the habitation sites, canals, and fields in the Snaketown canal system during the early Colonial period.

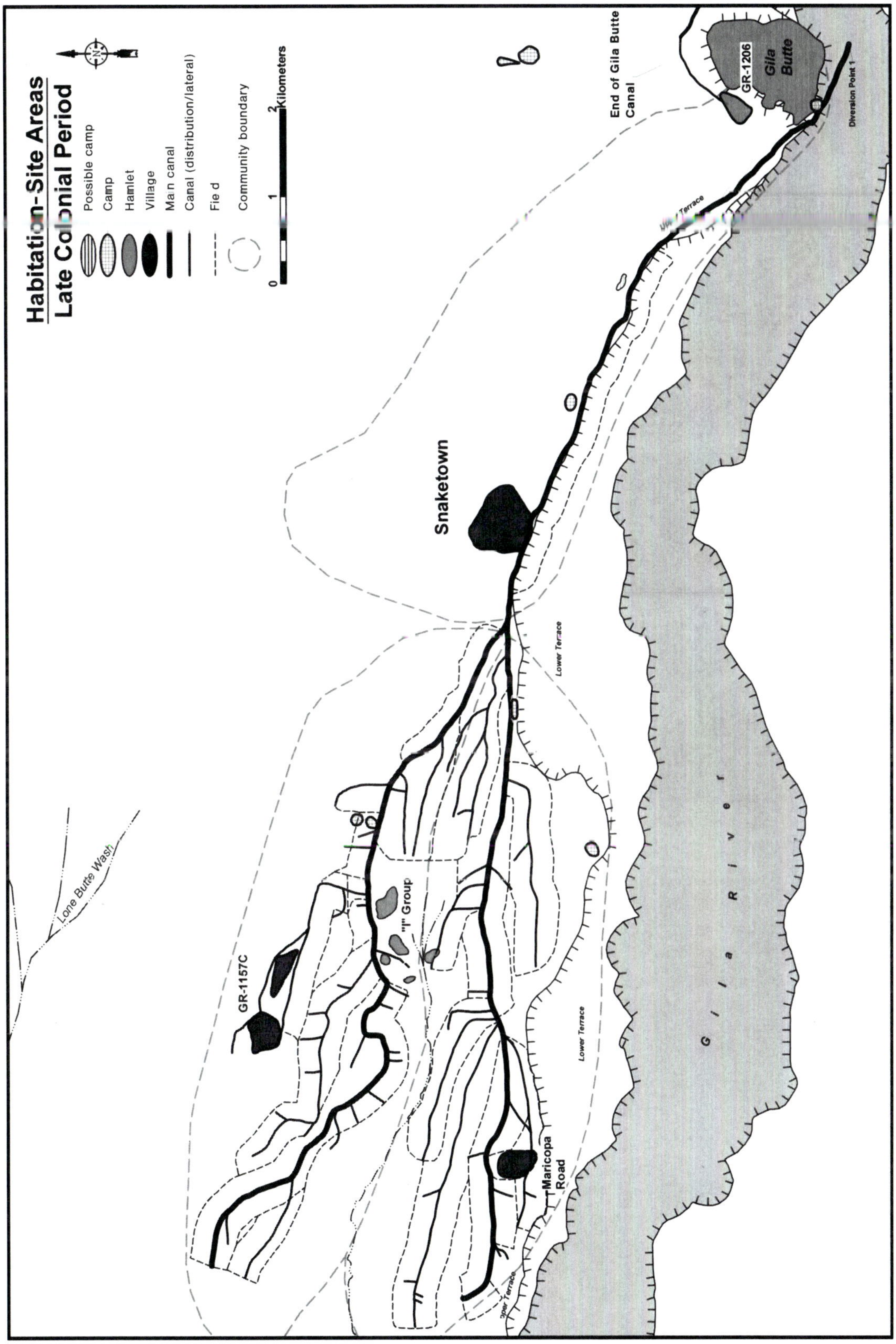

Figure 5.3. Map of the habitation sites, canals, and fields in the Snaketown canal system during the late Colonial period.

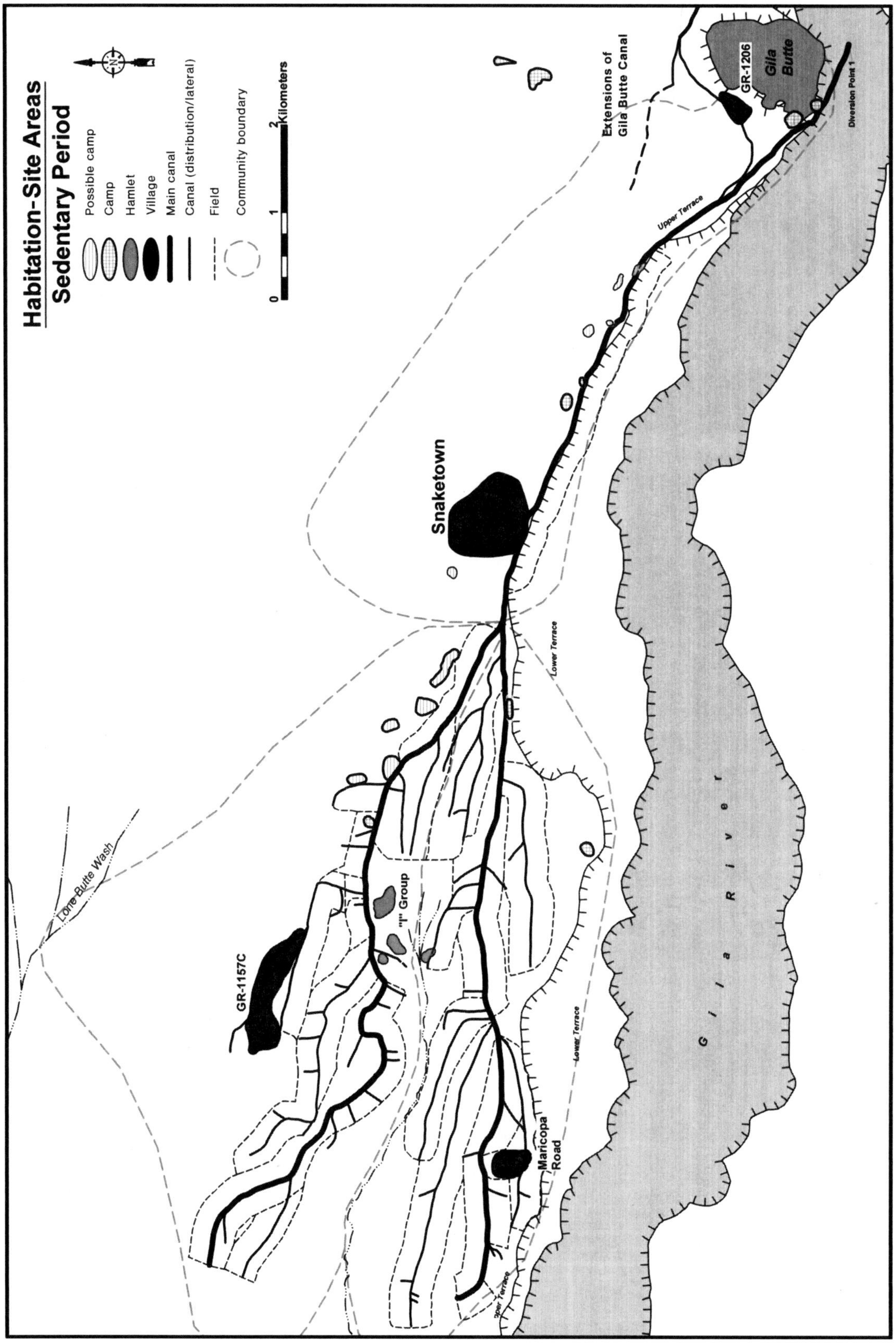

Figure 5.4. Map of the habitation sites, canals, and fields in the Snaketown canal system during the Sedentary period.

As addressed in Appendix B, the six possible camps shown in Figure 5.4 between Snaketown and the I Group (GR-1157, Loci Y, BB, TT, WW, XX, and LLL) probably were not initiated until after Snaketown had been abandoned, in the Middle Sedentary period. The minimum distance between habitations and fields remained constant at 370 m, and the maximum distance was 2,680 m for both the late Colonial and Sedentary periods. These distances are the same as those in the early Colonial period, suggesting an overall stability in the settlement pattern from A.D. 750 until at least 1050.

Further population growth occurred in both periods at Snaketown and GR-1157C, but at a much lower rate than before. The I Group expanded in the late Colonial period and then reduced back to its previous size in the Sedentary period. The hamlet at GR-1206 appears to have reached village size in the Sedentary period. The late Colonial period population of Snaketown and the other permanent habitations, based on residential-site area, is estimated to have been between 1,014 and 2,029 people, an increase of 32 percent (see Table 5.2). During the Sedentary period, the estimated total population size increased another 52 percent, to between 1,538 and 3,076 people, and that was the peak population size for the entire sequence of occupation. The canal system in both periods could have irrigated up to 1,492 ha, which, if fully farmed, could have supported 3,730 people.

The population still was divided among the villages and other settlements along the three main-canal branches (see Table 5.3). The population size increased along the main canal and the north branch. The majority were living along the main canal (Snaketown community), with 519–1,038 people in the late Colonial period and 863–1,725 people in the Sedentary period (based on residential-site area). Along the north-branch canal (GR-1157C community), the late Colonial period population is estimated to have been between 335 and 670 people, and the Sedentary period population is estimated to have been between 515 and 1,030 people. Along the south-branch canal (Maricopa Road community), the population size remained steady at 161–321 people during both periods. That level is the same as in the early Colonial period, indicating that the south-branch canal did not witness population growth during the Colonial or Sedentary period.

Classic Period

By the beginning of the Early Classic period, or more likely at the end of the Middle Sedentary period, the 3 ballcourt villages (Snaketown, the Maricopa Road site, and GR-1157C) had been abandoned, and a series of smaller settlements had been built in their place (Figure 5.5). The other nearest primary (ballcourt) villages to the east (Gila Butte site) and west (Hidden Ruin) of the study area also had been abandoned by this time. One new village with public architecture was built at the Maricopa Platform Mound site, at the far-western end of the canal system, on the south-branch canal. One other village was located 13.2 km upstream from the mound, at GR-1175, near Gila Butte. Between were five main foci of habitation, including four hamlet clusters (I, Y, U, and VV Groups), each of which represents a dispersed village. The Y and VV Groups feasibly could have been grouped together into one dispersed village. The fifth focus of habitation is a cluster of camps just west of GR-1175 (FFFF Group) that probably represents a dispersed hamlet. The residents had redistributed themselves into a greater number of small habitation sites that were more evenly dispersed and separated by shorter intervals than in the Sedentary period. Compared with the Sedentary period, the number of permanently occupied habitation units was dramatically higher in the Early Classic period—2 villages and 18 hamlets vs. 4 Sedentary period villages and 4 hamlets. In addition, 9–11 camps were used during this period. Although the settlement distribution was dispersed, the settlement pattern still could be characterized as segmented when examined in general across the entire canal system. That is, there are essentially three clusters of permanently occupied habitation sites that coincide with the three main-canal branches.

The spacing of primary settlements during the Classic period was difficult to assess, because only one "central site" was present during this time (Maricopa Mound). The closest platform-mound site (on the northern side of the Gila River) was at Lower Santan village, which was located roughly 22 km to the east, on another canal system. The closest "true" village without public architecture was 13.2 km upstream, at GR-1175, or possibly 8 km upstream, at the VV Group (if it represents a village). Any of these distances is far greater than the average spacing of focal villages in the pre-Classic period. The average spacing between permanently occupied habitations along the canal system was 2.8 km, a significant decrease from before.

It is probable that the former Gila Butte community became integrated into either the Snaketown or the Lower Santan community in the Early Classic period. This will be discussed further in Chapter 6, but the abandonment of the Gila Butte site left no villages along the Gila Butte canal. A second extension of the Gila Butte canal was built to connect with the Snaketown canal at that time. Also, the Gila Butte canal system was connected to the Santan canal system on the upstream end. However, the village at GR-1175 was technically situated at the tail end of the Gila Butte canal and also at the heading of the Snaketown canal. If the consolidated Gila Butte/Snaketown canal system is a better representation of the community-organization framework in Study Area 1, then the average settlement spacing was 2.9 km, the average distance to canals was 205 m, and the distance to fields was between 200 and 2,200 m.

Many fewer activity areas were evident between the habitations, suggesting that activities were more restricted to the habitation areas. The exception would be the canal areas, including the associated fields, which were still being used.

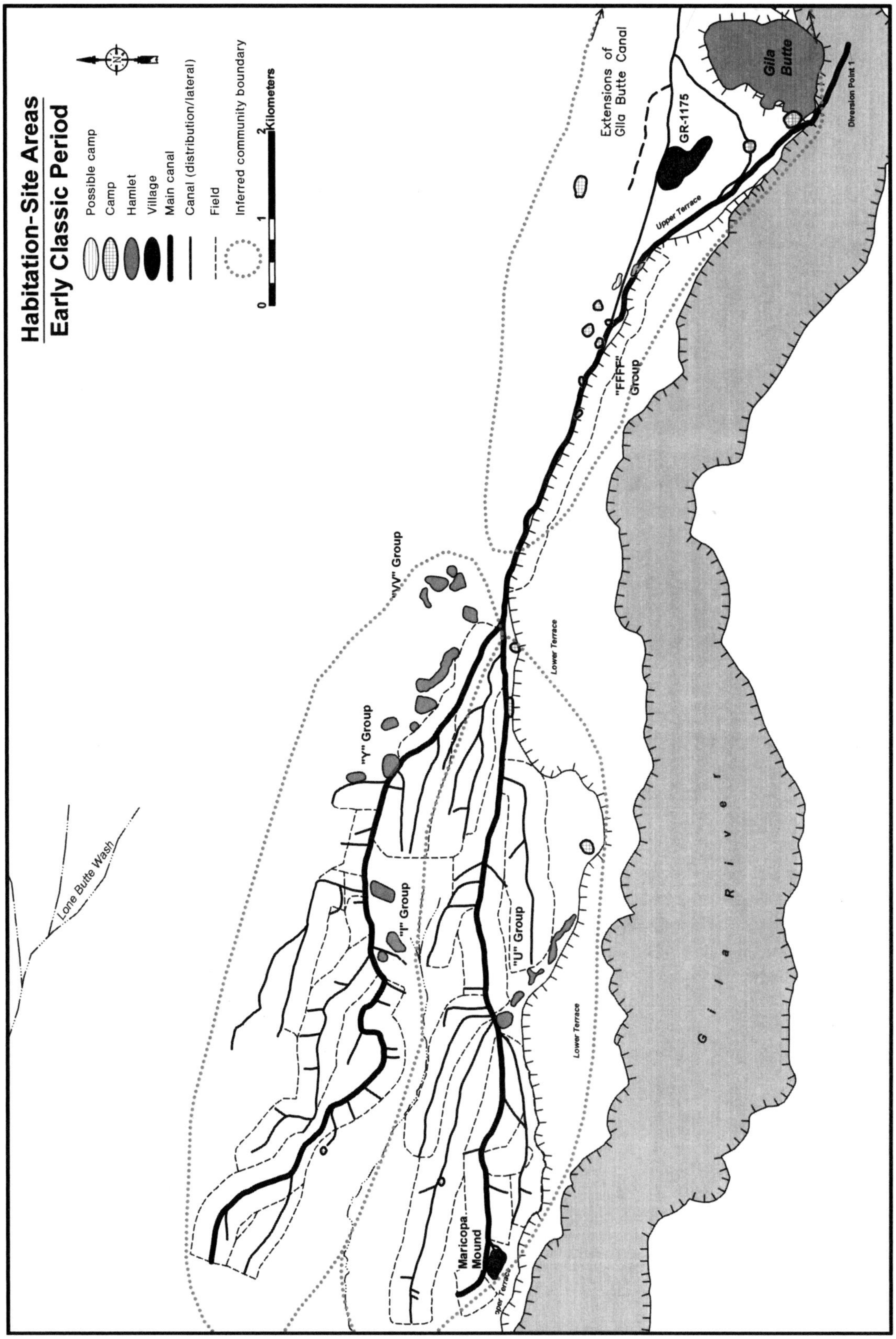

Figure 5.5. Map of the habitation sites, canals, and fields in the Snaketown canal system during the Early Classic period.

The analysis in Appendix B also suggests that the trail corridors extending north toward the lower Salt Valley either ceased to be used or declined significantly in use. That may have been related to the collapse of the trade networks associated with the distribution of red-on-buff pottery and the ballcourt system (see Abbott 2009; Abbott et al. 2007; Doyel 1991a, 2007). When considered along with the dramatic changes in Hohokam lifeways during the Sedentary to Classic period transition, the dispersed settlement pattern during the Classic period suggests that the settlement system along the Snaketown canal was characterized by a more insular socioeconomic interaction sphere. A similar pattern has been noted for the Hohokam living along Canal System 2 in the lower Salt Valley (see Abbott 2003). It would seem that the collapse of the Hohokam ballcourt system and the abandonment of the ballcourt villages in the study area were concomitant with a significant change in settlement organization.

The same settlement pattern characterized Study Area 1 in the Late Classic period, except that some of the previous settlements were abandoned at that time (Figure 5.6). It appears that three hamlets between Locus Y and the VV Group hamlets were abandoned, or the intensity of their occupations was dramatically reduced. Four of the camps and the two possible camps near Gila Butte and along the upper reach of the main canal were abandoned, too. This contributed to a slightly more-clustered appearance of the hamlet groups and the camp group. One new camp at GR-1157K was occupied. Thus, although the settlement distribution was dispersed, the settlement pattern remained segmented.

The average distance between the villages and hamlets and the nearest canal increased slightly, to 200 m, for the Early and Late Classic periods. The minimum distance between habitations and fields was 213 m, and the maximum distance was 1,897 m for the Classic period (see Table 5.1). Thus, although these habitations were situated farther away from the nearest canals than in the Sedentary period, they were considerably closer to the fields throughout the Classic period—the closest average distance for the entire occupational sequence.

The overall population size, based on residential-site area, dropped by 41 percent in the Early Classic period (n = 922–1,844) and by another 16 percent in the Late Classic period (n = 767–1,534) (see Table 5.2). The significant drop in the Early Classic period clearly indicates that a large segment of the Sedentary period population moved out of the study area (this issue is addressed further in Chapter 7). The same situation may have occurred in the Late Classic period, but the smaller proportion of the drop leaves this unclear. The proportion of the population as it was distributed along the three main-canal branches changed during these periods. The majority were living along the north-branch canal (the former GR-1157C community), with 405–809 people in the Early Classic period and 347–695 people in the Late Classic period (see Table 5.3). Along the main canal (the former Snaketown community), the Early Classic period population is estimated to have been between 319 and 638 people, and the Late Classic period population is estimated to have been between 221 and 442 people. Along the south-branch canal, the population size increased to between 199 and 398 people during both periods. Roughly the same number of people were living along the south-branch canal and the main canal by the Late Classic period.

The distribution of settlements along the canal system in both the Early and Late Classic periods suggests that farming might have occurred in the entire command area of 1,492 ha. Another canal in the Gila Butte canal system was extended to the Snaketown canal, probably to further augment the water supply. If all the fields were being farmed, the produce could have supported 3,730 people. However, that is considerably more than the population size of 1,534–1,844 people that was inferred based on residential area. Also, as noted in Chapter 4, the large reduction in main-canal capacity by the Early Classic period was such that it probably was insufficient to irrigate the entire 1,492 ha that was inferred for the command area. Canal capacity decreased further by the Late Classic period, and the heading at Diversion Point 1 possibly was abandoned. The canal-capacity reductions likely are an indication that the command area, and possibly the lengths of the canals in use, was reduced by the same (or nearly the same) percentage in the Classic period. If so, the number of people that could be supported by the farms would have been more in line with the inferred population size. These traits of the canal system, along with the significant population decrease, indicate that residents along the Snaketown canal system were experiencing significant water reductions during the Classic period.

Settlement Organization in Study Area 1

The objective of this chapter is to evaluate the settlement organization in Study Area 1. Through an analysis of spatial, temporal, and functional data, the settlement pattern is defined as either segmented or non-segmented for each period, and then it is evaluated in terms of community organization. The primary focus, in terms of organizational nodes, is at the level of the village and focal-village community. Where such communities are identified, they are examined to see whether they contained similar proportions of site types. Lastly, the possible signatures of intervillage dynamics, as reflected in the settlement pattern, are noted, especially where they are relevant for inferring the existence of a canal-wide political institution.

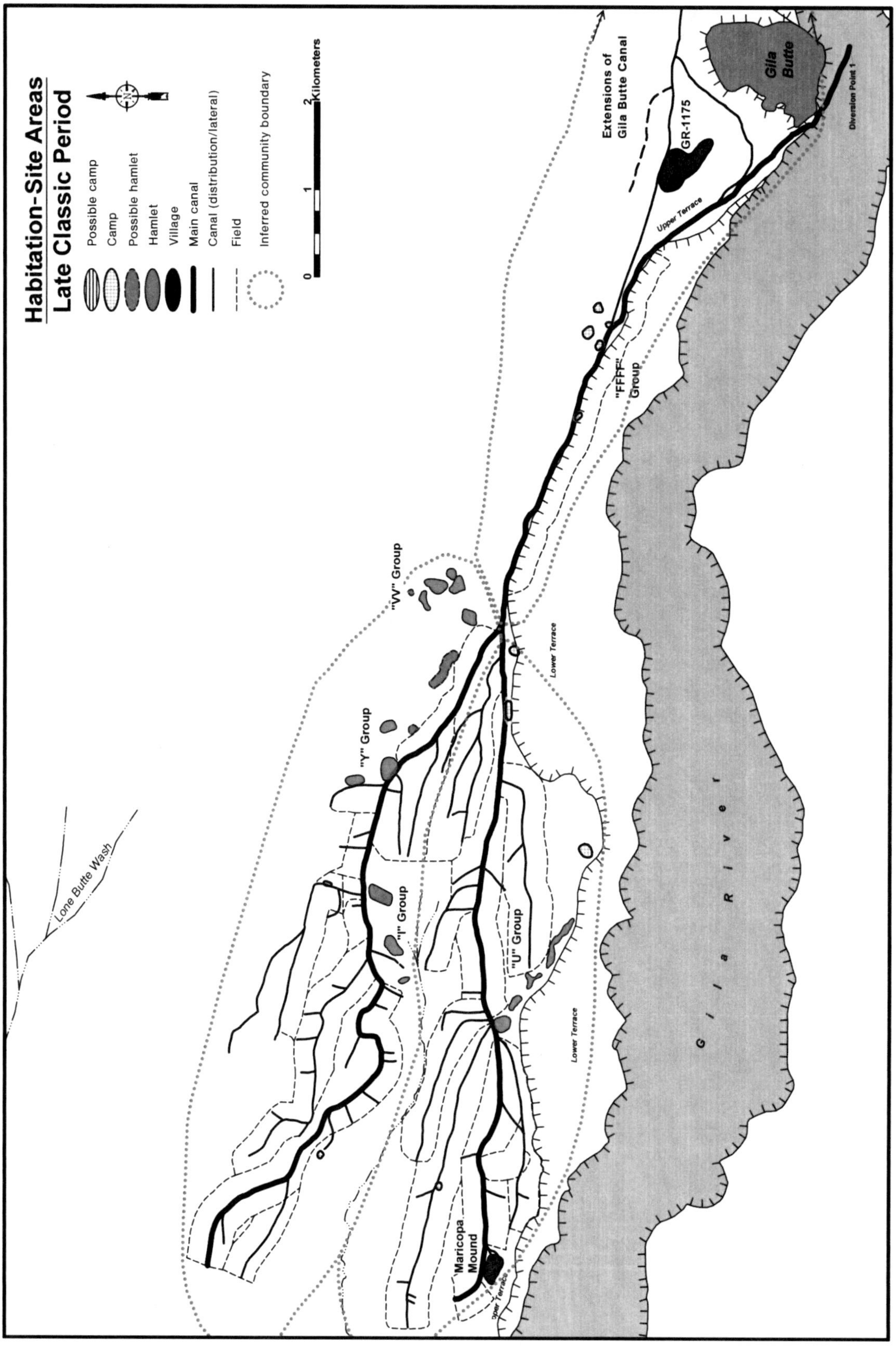

Figure 5.6. Map of the habitation sites, canals, and fields in the Snaketown canal system during the Late Classic period.

In general terms, the settlement pattern in Study Area 1 was non-segmented in the Pioneer period, but it became segmented in the Colonial to Sedentary periods, as the population became nucleated into three villages. The pattern remained segmented in the Classic period, even if one assumes that the Gila Butte and Snaketown canal systems had been consolidated, but the population was much more dispersed than before.

Pioneer Period

In the early Pioneer period, Snaketown was a hamlet situated near the end of the Pioneer Canal, and it is currently the only known settlement along the canal (see Figure 5.1). No public architecture had been constructed; so, Snaketown in this period does not fulfill the definition of a "central site" or meet the criteria for a focal village. Little other data are available for the canals or settlement system in this period. The settlement pattern was non-segmented; so, the inferred political community was coterminous with the canal system. In concept, without a focal village, it could not be classified as a focal-village community. Feasibly, the settlements could be considered to have been organized as a linear community, with the caveats noted for that concept in Chapter 2.

During the late Pioneer period, Snaketown developed into a focal village with public architecture (Mound 40, a platform mound), and two camps were founded along the newly extended main canal (see Figure 5.1). The new camps were founded along the canal extension in a position for Snaketown farmers to have satellites for farming activities in areas that were over 4 km away (see Chisholm 1979). In concept, when a canal system has only one primary village with public architecture, the settlement pattern would be non-segmented, and the political community essentially would be isomorphic with the canal system under the focal-village-community or linear-community model (see Abbott et al. 2006:290; Gregory and Nials 1985:384).

Colonial Period

In the early Colonial period, the distribution of settlements was segmented within three nucleated ballcourt villages and two hamlet areas (see Figure 5.2). The population was living primarily in the three villages. The Maricopa Road site (a village with a probable ballcourt) was founded 7.3 km west of Snaketown, and GR-1157C grew to village size and added two possible ballcourts. By factoring the distance intervals between Snaketown and these two primary villages, the average spacing was 6.7 km. If the distance from GR-1157C to Maricopa Road is factored in (3.4 km), the average spacing is 5.6 km. If the distance from Snaketown to the Gila Butte site (6.5 km) is considered in this equation (although it is on a separate canal system), then the average spacing is 5.8 km (which is nearly the same as 5.6 km). That interval remained constant through the late Colonial and Sedentary periods.

The inferred community organization was considerably different from that of the Pioneer period. Two focal villages, a group of hamlets, and several camps were founded along the north and south main-canal branches. The two new ballcourt villages were located at relatively similar distances from Snaketown, near the ends of their respective main-canal branches. The new villages were not as large or as impressive as Snaketown (e.g., the ballcourts and trash mounds were significantly smaller). Given the primacy of Snaketown as the founding and largest village, the two new villages probably were "daughter villages" composed of relatives and descendants of Snaketown residents and possibly newly arrived migrants.

As discussed in Chapter 2, early analysis efforts for this project revealed that the structure of the community territories could not be understood without reference to the physical layout of the canal system, the inferred priorities of the Hohokam in deciding where to locate new settlements, and natural geographic features that probably served as a kind of social boundary. It is argued that the community territories are best modeled by oval-shaped boundaries that extend up the main-canal segments from the focal villages. These new villages along the branch canals appear to represent the centers for distinct communities organized in a similar fashion to Snaketown and its associated settlements along the original main canal. In other words, the evidence suggests that the settlement organization was most consistent with the focal-village-community model.

To test this proposition, the site-type proportions in each focal-village community were compared to each other (Table 5.4). The counts in Table 5.4 were modified from those given in Appendix B, to address the caveats listed as footnotes in those tables, including the case in which more than one hamlet was found inside a locus (Locus I), the case in which a single village (Snaketown) was encompassed by more than one archaeological locus, and the case in which a camp was probably part of a village. In addition, the site types *activity area* and *canal area* are combined in Table 5.4. The rationale for that was that the sites/loci coded as *canal areas* represented arbitrary divisions of canal alignments, based on surface evidence observed during survey. It is therefore unclear whether they can be considered discrete activity areas along canals. The canal area also is a specialized type of activity area; so, the two site types are combined for the purposes of the subsequent analysis. The types *camp* and *possible camp* also are combined as one type (*camp*); the few cases classified as possible camps are assumed to have actually been camps.

Using the column percentages shown in Table 5.4, Figure 5.7 depicts the site-type proportions in each inferred focal-village community during the early Colonial period. This bar chart shows that the Snaketown and Maricopa Road communities had very similar site-type proportions. The GR-1157C community was similar to the other two communities, but it appears to have had a higher proportion

Table 5.4. Modified Site-Type Counts and Percentages for Three Focal-Village Communities in Study Area 1 in the Early Colonial Period

Site Type	Snaketown	%	GR-1157C	%	Maricopa Road	%
Village	1	*1.4*	1	*3.7*	1	*2.2*
Hamlet	1	*1.4*	3	*11.1*	1	*2.2*
Camp	4	*5.6*	2	*7.4*	2	*4.3*
Activity/canal area	64	*90.1*	20	*74.1*	41	*89.1*
Roasting area	1	*1.4*	1	*3.7*	1	*2.2*
Total	71	*100.0*	27	*100.0*	46	*100.0*

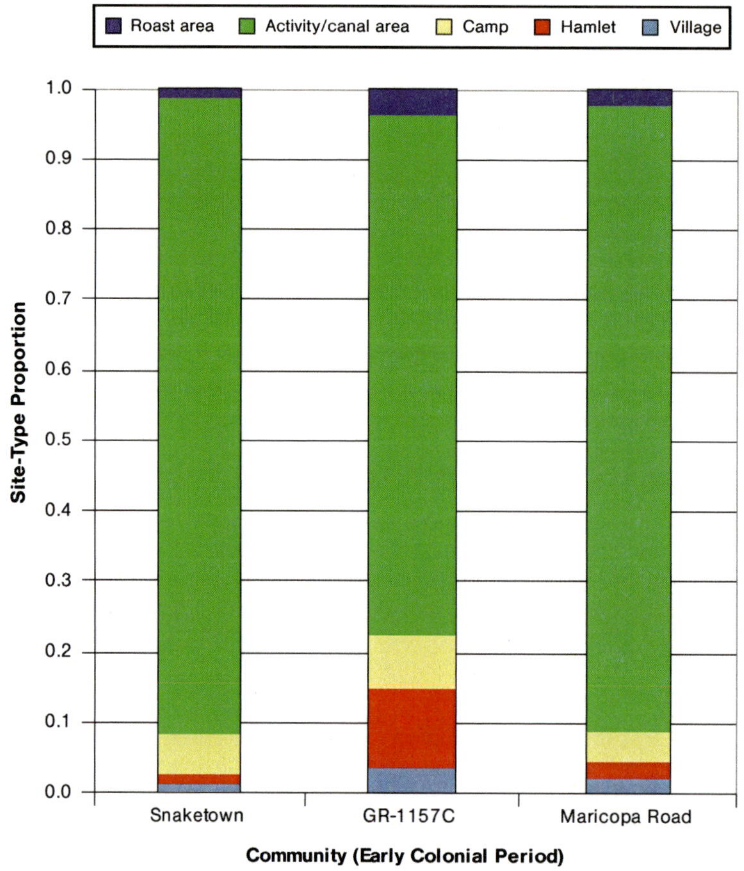

Figure 5.7. Bar chart of site-type proportions in the early Colonial period, by community.

of hamlets (the I Group) and camps. If the I Group is considered to represent one dispersed village, the GR-1157C proportions are closer to the other two. Otherwise, it can be seen that the site-type proportions in the inferred focal-village-community territories are quite similar to each other. The inferred communities included similar sets of site types (with similar ranges of functions). The early Colonial period communities along the Snaketown canal system thus are most consistent with the focal-village-community model.

The late Colonial period patterns were similar to those of the early Colonial period. The distribution of settlements was segmented within three nucleated ballcourt villages and two hamlet areas, and the average spacing between focal villages remained at 5.6 km (see Figure 5.3). The late Colonial period site-type distributions in the inferred communities were compared in the same manner as above. Table 5.5 provides the modified site-type counts and percentages, using the protocols described above. Using the column percentages given in the table, Figure 5.8 depicts the site-type proportions for each inferred community during the late Colonial period. Overall, the chart suggests that the site-type proportions in the inferred late Colonial period focal-village-community territories were very similar to each other. Like the early Colonial period graph, the slightly higher proportion of hamlets in the GR-1157C community shown in Figure 5.8 would be lessened if the I Group hamlets were considered to constitute a dispersed village.

Sedentary Period

The Sedentary period patterns were similar to those of the late Colonial period. The distribution of settlements was segmented within three nucleated ballcourt villages, one village without public architecture, and one hamlet area. The average spacing between focal villages remained at 5.6 km (see Figure 5.4). The same approach as above was applied to comparison of the site-type distributions in the inferred communities in Sedentary period. Table 5.6 provides the modified site-type counts and percentages, using the protocols described above. Using the column percentages shown in the table, Figure 5.9 displays the site-type proportions for each inferred community during the Sedentary period. This chart shows that the site-type proportions in the inferred Sedentary period focal-village-community territories were very similar.

In sum, the key to the territorial extent of the communities during the Colonial to Sedentary periods appears to have been the main-canal branches. The pre-Classic period focal-village communities had an elongated form that correlated to the branch canals. The diversity and proportions of site types within the inferred focal-village communities were very similar. As will be discussed further in Chapter 7, it is significant that the three community boundaries not only encompassed the branch-canal task groups and their constituent command areas but also included the three focal villages. Thus, the two most important organizational nodes, as defined by Howard (2006), were included in each community territory.

Classic Period

By the Early Classic period, the settlement pattern was dramatically different, with a much more dispersed character (see Figure 5.5). A series of new, smaller settlements were founded in the wake of the abandonment of the Sedentary period villages. This period witnessed the greatest number of individual habitation sites (n = 36), the majority (n = 25) of which were newly founded settlements. The permanently occupied habitation units included 1 platform-mound village (Maricopa Mound), 1 village without public architecture (GR-1175), and 18 hamlets that were clustered into 4 probable dispersed villages (the I, Y, U, and VV Groups)—or 3 dispersed villages, if the Y and VV Groups were integrated as 1 residential group. Four, or possibly 6, camps between the VV Group hamlets were clustered into a probable dispersed hamlet (FFFF Group). The average distance between the villages, the dispersed villages, and the dispersed hamlet was 2.8 km. Activities were more restricted to the habitation areas than before. Lastly, the former Gila Butte community plausibly became integrated into the Snaketown community during the Classic period. Although the settlement distribution was dispersed, the settlement pattern still could be characterized as segmented when examined in general across the entire canal system. The same settlement pattern was prevalent in the Late Classic period, except that 1–3 hamlets and 4 camps were abandoned (see Figure 5.6). That contributed to a slightly more clustered appearance of the hamlet groups (dispersed villages), especially among the VV and Y Groups and the camp group.

During the Classic period, Study Area 1 included only one "central site" with public architecture (Maricopa Platform Mound), and it was situated roughly 15.7 km west of Gila Butte. The closest platform-mound site (Lower Santan) was roughly 22 km to the east. These are far greater distances than the typical 5-km spacing cited by researchers for Classic period platform mounds (e.g., Fish and Fish 1991:163; Gregory and Nials 1985). Thus, although Maricopa Mound was a focal village, there is no basis by which to define a focal-village interval. Even if the inferred territory included the entire south-branch canal, it would only encompass the U Group (dispersed village) and three camps (excluding all other habitations along the system). Supposing the mound represented the focal village for the entire canal system; that would run counter to the pattern of focal-village communities observed throughout the Phoenix Basin. Hence, at first glance, the Classic period settlement pattern does not appear to conform to the focal-village model.

Table 5.5. Modified Site-Type Counts and Percentages for Inferred Communities in Study Area 1 in the Late Colonial Period, with Combined Canal and Activity Areas

Site Type	Snaketown	%	GR-1157C	%	Maricopa Road	%
Village	1	*1.9*	1	*3.8*	1	*2.9*
Hamlet	1	*1.9*	5	*19.2*	1	*2.9*
Camp	3	*5.6*	2	*7.7*	2	*5.9*
Activity/canal area	48	*88.9*	17	*65.4*	30	*88.2*
Roasting area	1	*1.9*	1	*3.8*	—	—
Total	54	*100.0*	26	*100.0*	34	*100.0*

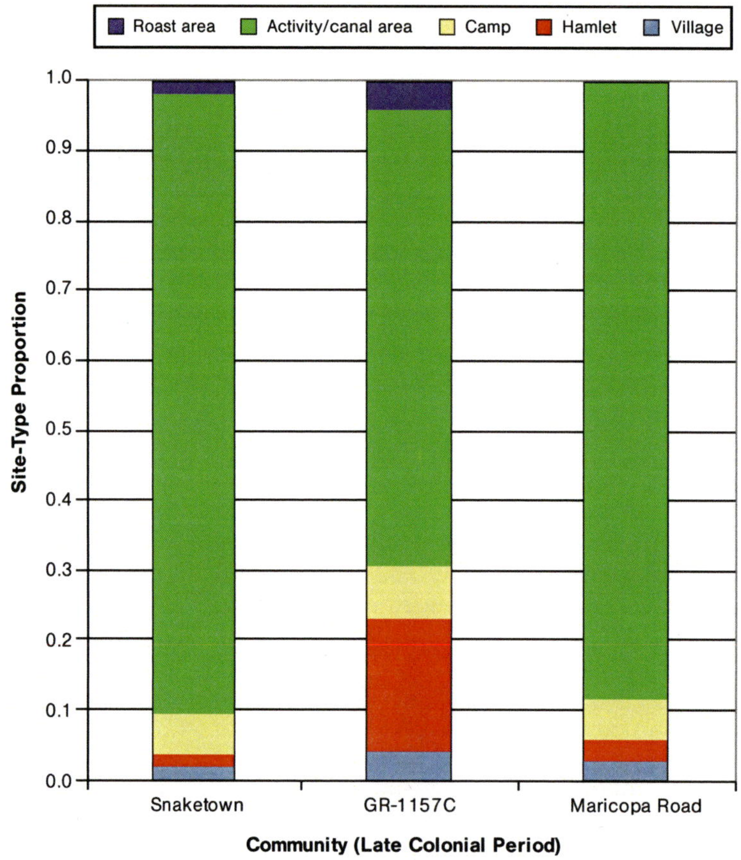

Figure 5.8. Bar chart of site-type proportions in the late Colonial period, by community.

Table 5.6. Modified Site-Type Counts and Percentages for Inferred Communities in the Sedentary Period, with Combined Canal and Activity Areas

Site Type	Snaketown	%	GR-1157C	%	Maricopa Road	%
Village	2	*2.9*	1	*4.3*	1	*2.2*
Hamlet	—	—	3	*13.0*	1	*2.2*
Camp	8	*11.6*	1	*4.3*	2	*4.4*
Activity/canal area	58	*84.1*	17	*73.9*	40	*88.9*
Roasting area	1	*1.4*	1	*4.3*	1	*2.2*
Total	69	*100.0*	23	*100.0*	45	*100.0*

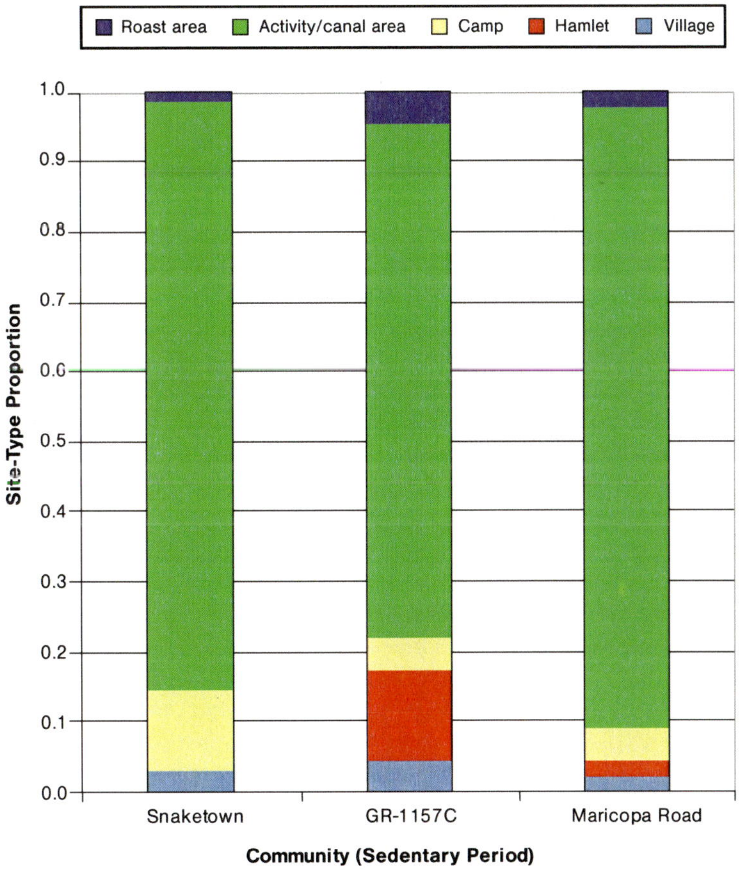

Figure 5.9. Bar chart of site-type proportions in the Sedentary period, by community.

Table 5.7. Modified Site-Type Counts and Percentages for Inferred Communities in the Early Classic Period, with Combined Canal and Activity Areas

Site Type	GR-1175	%	North Branch	%	South Branch	%
Village[a]	1	*1.8*	2	*13.3*	2	*8.3*
Hamlet[b]	3	*5.5*	—	*0.0*	—	*0.0*
Camp	9	*16.4*	1	*6.7*	4	*16.7*
Activity/canal area	42	*76.4*	12	*80.0*	18	*75.0*
Roasting area	—	*0.0*	—	*0.0*	—	*0.0*
Total	55	*100.0*	15	*100.0*	24	*100.0*

[a] Includes dispersed villages along the north and south branches.
[b] Includes a dispersed hamlet near GR-1175.

Nevertheless, the settlement pattern remained segmented, with three distinct clusters of habitation sites associated with the three main-canal branches. That continued the settlement trend from the Sedentary period, but with some key differences: the settlement distribution was more dispersed, only the south-branch cluster included a focal village, and the sites along the Gila Butte canal probably were associated with the sites along the upper part of the Snaketown canal. The settlements in the study area therefore appear to have remained organized in distinct communities associated with the three main-canal branches (see Figure 5.5). Only the south-branch community, with Maricopa Mound, though, was consistent with expectations for a focal-village community.

Table 5.7 provides the modified site-type counts and percentages of these three inferred Early Classic period communities, using the protocols described above. Using the column percentages shown in the table, Figure 5.10 displays the site-type proportions for each inferred community during the Early Classic period. A comparison of the Early Classic period site types in the three inferred communities indicated that the proportion of site types changed from the Sedentary period. There was still a village in two communities, but only one was a focal village (Maricopa Mound, along the south branch), whereas the other was simply a village, without public architecture (GR-1175, along the main canal). The north-branch community only included dispersed villages. Although the number of hamlets increased, most of them appear to have been grouped into three or four dispersed villages. There were more camps by proportion, a reflection of the more-dispersed settlement pattern. Also, the number of activity areas dropped along the north and south branches. No discrete roasting areas were documented, although roasting-pit features are known in some of the habitation areas (e.g., GR-1157, Loci DD and WW). The same pattern for the inferred communities characterized the Late Classic period, with minor differences (see Figure 5.6); those site-type proportions are not graphed here.

Interestingly, the Classic period pattern of community territories was similar to that of the pre-Classic period, and this reinforces the contention that the main-canal branches were key to the territorial extent of the communities. That remained the case, even though the settlement pattern was more dispersed, the Snaketown and Gila Butte canals had become consolidated, and only one of the inferred communities had a "true" focal village. It seems likely that the long-held and presumably productive, irrigated fields motivated many families and kinship groups to remain nearby (see Adler 1996). The fact that they remained in the same general territories suggests that the areas encompassed by the main and branch canals represented important organizational units for the Hohokam that endured through a major sociopolitical change during the Sedentary to Classic period transition.

Existence of a Canal-Wide Polity

Lastly, in those cases where multiple focal-village communities occurred along the canal system, it should be asked whether they could have been integrated into a larger polity. Three focal-village communities existed along the Snaketown canal system during the Colonial and Sedentary periods. What was the nature of the sociopolitical dynamics among these communities? As noted in Chapter 2, it might be assumed that these communities were integrated as a political entity, based on the fact that they shared a canal. I have argued that the sharing of a canal and the inherent need for irrigation management did not necessarily require the formation of an overarching political entity and could, instead, have been addressed through an irrigation organization, the authority for which could have been separate from the political entity (this is discussed further in Chapter 7). Some researchers have posited that interaction patterns discerned through evidence of economic exchange (e.g., of ceramics) can reveal the existence of a canal-wide polity (i.e., a linear community) (Abbott 2000; Abbott et al. 2006). Previous applications of this model in the lower Salt Valley have suggested that as organizational

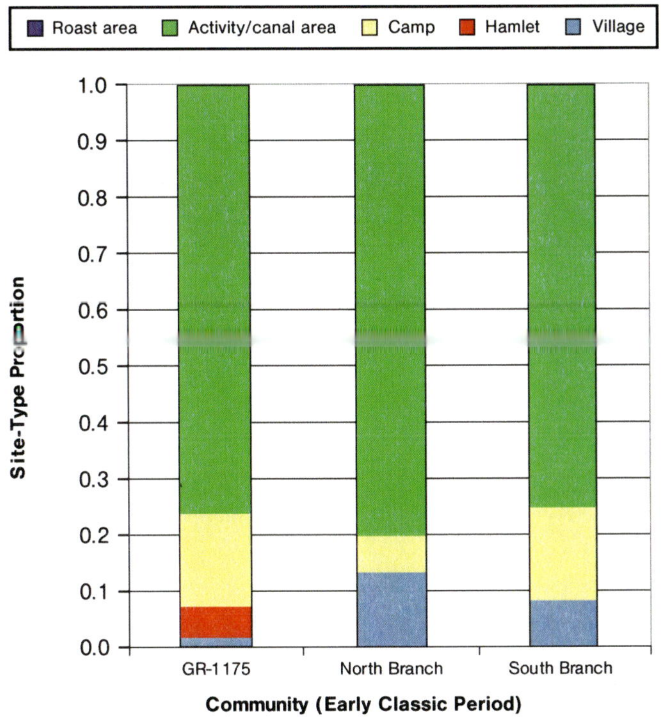

Figure 5.10. Bar chart of site-type proportions in the Early Classic period, by community.

nodes, focal-village sites were not as important as was the entire canal system. However, as noted in Chapter 2, that concept is somewhat problematic, and also, such exchange data are beyond the scope of this study.

Regardless of these conceptual problems, it is feasible that all three focal-village communities along the Snaketown canal system could have been part of a larger, canal-wide polity in the Colonial and Sedentary periods. Here, I approach the issue from the perspective that one village may have united all the communities into such a polity, by virtue of its being the preeminent or dominant settlement. Factors considered include village size, number and size of public architecture, village proximity to the heading, and which was the founding village. Snaketown was both the founding village and the largest village, with a sizable residential area and impressive public monuments (two ballcourts and three or four platform mounds), marking it as the preeminent village along the canal system (Ravesloot 2007). Features at Snaketown, such as the ballcourts, platform mounds, and large plaza, have been cited as principal integrative elements of pre-Classic period villages that would have attracted outlying populations for events such as ballgames, feasts, and market days (e.g., Abbott 2009; Gregory 1987; Wallace 2003; Wilcox and Sternberg 1983). The other two ballcourt villages along the system (the Maricopa Road site and GR-1157C) were smaller in size and had small ballcourts (there is still some question as to whether one of the GR-1157C courts actually was a ballcourt). GR-1206, which grew to village size in the Sedentary period, was relatively small and had no public architecture. These probably were daughter villages of Snaketown and thereby owed their loyalty to the founding village (see P. Fish and S. Fish 2007:41). One can easily envision the leaders of Snaketown using their higher status to influence the residents in these other settlements on various matters (see Crown 1987; Howard 2006; Rice 1998). The ceremonial and social dominance of Snaketown seems to be clear, and I would speculate that this probably translates into a leadership role for all three focal-village communities. This assumed superiority is suggestive of a multi-village polity but does not necessarily prove its existence. The situation is feasible, but I argue that the evidence of it is less convincing than the evidence of focal-village communities, at least in settlement-pattern terms. However, it is acknowledged that this issue cannot be fully addressed using settlement-pattern data alone. Further testing of the hypothesis is required, with other information, such as ceramic-exchange patterns.

A different situation ensued during the Classic period, when Maricopa Mound was the only focal village along the entire consolidated Gila Butte/Snaketown canal system. As argued above, the settlements along this canal system remained organized into three distinct communities that corresponded to the three main-canal branch segments. Only the south-branch-canal community represented a true focal-village community, with the Maricopa Mound village as its central site. Maricopa Mound was neither the largest nor the earliest village, although it could be considered the preeminent settlement, by virtue of its having a platform mound. As noted above, the notion that the mound represented the focal village for the entire canal system does not conform to the pattern for focal-village communities throughout the Phoenix Basin, because it was far removed from the canal heading, and the area of a community covering the entire canal system would have been much larger than that of any other irrigation-based focal-village community (see Crown 1987; Fish and Fish 1991; P. Fish and S. Fish 2007).

Despite these divergences from the model, it is feasible that Maricopa Mound indeed was the central site for the entire Gila Butte/Snaketown canal system. Most of the population along the canal system was living in two communities without a platform mound (the north-branch and GR-1175 communities). I suggest that we can assume that these people remained integrated in a ceremonial/ideological structure that we have defined for the Classic period Hohokam and that was centered on platform mounds (see Elson 1998; Gregory 1987; Wilcox 1991). Therefore, they may have looked to the leaders of Maricopa Mound for such matters and therefore may have been part of a canal-wide community. Again, this situation cannot be fully addressed using settlement-pattern data alone. This topic is addressed further in Chapter 7, in terms of its relationship to the organization of irrigation management.

Chapter 6

The Organization of Settlements along the Granite Knob, Santan, and Gila Butte Canal Systems

This chapter presents an analysis of the settlements and canals in Study Area 2, which includes the Granite Knob, Santan, and Gila Butte canal systems. The discussion addresses Research Goal 2, to describe and analyze settlements and evaluate settlement organization. Settlement and population trends are described, and the settlement pattern is defined as either segmented or non-segmented for each period, through an analysis of spatial, temporal, and functional data. The analysis then evaluates the settlement pattern in terms of community organization and examines possible signatures of inter-village dynamics. Study Area 2 includes 359 archaeological sites and loci within sites. Appendix C provides the site and locus data, including a summary of the settlement-analysis results (including information on the site-type designations and all habitation sites) and a description of the settlement trends through time. Appendix A and Chapter 4 describe the canal systems. The information in these appendixes and Chapter 4 forms the basis of the discussions in this chapter. The methods utilized in analyzing the Study Area 2 data were similar to those used for Study Area 1, as discussed in Chapter 5 (with some minor exceptions, as noted in Appendixes A and C).

Settlement Trends in Study Area 2

The settlement and population trends through time in Study Area 2, in relation to the canal systems and field areas, are summarized in this section. Appendix C provides a more detailed description of the settlement trends, with a focus on site function, accompanied by figures that display site function by time period in conjunction with the definition of habitation sites. This section draws from the appendix, focusing on the inferred community territories and habitation sites. The community-territory boundaries shown on the maps in this chapter are the same as those shown in Appendix C. The boundaries reflect the most practical configurations, based on application of the principles of the focal-community model and the boundary-definition criteria described in Chapter 2 (and addressed in Appendix C).

The discussion utilizes the information presented in the next three tables. Table 6.1 provides data on the number of focal villages, the spacing between focal villages and between all permanent habitations, and the general settlement distribution for the three canal systems. It also gives the average distances between the permanent habitations and the nearest canals and the average minimum and maximum distances to irrigated fields. Table 6.2 provides the total habitation-site area and total command area during each period for each canal system and the corresponding population estimates based on these measures. A range of population sizes is given, based on both habitation-site area and command area. These population sizes were used to compute the CAGR between periods (based on Hassan [1981:140]). Table 6.3 breaks down the population size by main-canal reach for each period, based on residential-site area for each canal reach. The trends in population are touched on in this chapter and addressed at greater length in Chapter 7.

Pioneer Period

During the Estrella/Sweetwater phase of the late Pioneer period, Upper Santan was initiated as a hamlet near the lower end of the Santan canal, followed by the founding of a settlement at Olberg, 5 km upstream, near the canal heading (Figure 6.1). Olberg could have begun as a camp and then been occupied permanently as a hamlet in the Snaketown phase. The settlement pattern probably was non-segmented at first, but it possibly became segmented with the addition of Olberg. The average distance to canals was 690 m, the minimum distance to the irrigated fields was 740 m, and the maximum distance was 2,900 m (see Table 6.1). Based on residential-site area, the population of both hamlets is estimated to have been between 184 and 367 people for the Estrella/Sweetwater phase and 198–396 people for the Snaketown phase. The canal system could have irrigated 421 ha in the late Pioneer period, which, if fully farmed, could have supported 1,053 people (see Table 6.2).

Table 6.1. Variables Measured for Settlement Distribution in Study Area 2 (Hypothesis 3)

Period	No. of Focal Villages	Average Distance between Focal Villages (km)	Average Distance between All Permanent Habitations (km)	Settlement Distribution	Average Distance to Canals (m)[a]	Average Minimum Distance to Fields (m)[a]	Average Maximum Distance to Fields (m)[a]
Granite Knob Canal		-	-	-	-	-	-
Late Pioneer (Snaketown)	—			nucleated	140	170	1,700
Colonial	1			nucleated	140	170	1,700
Sedentary	1		1.2	nucleated	195	225	1,100
Santan Canal System		-	-	-	-	-	-
Late Pioneer (Estrella/Sweetwater phase)	1		5.0	nucleated	690	740	2,900
Late Pioneer (Snaketown)	1		5.0	nucleated	690	740	2,900
Colonial	2	5.2	5.1	nucleated	250	317	3,767
Sedentary	2	5.2	5.1	nucleated	250	317	3,767
Granite Knob–Santan Canal System		-	-	-	-	-	-
Classic	2	5.2	1.4	dispersed	260	310	1,339
Gila Butte Canal System					-	-	-
Late Pioneer (Snaketown)	—			nucleated	300	360	4,400
Colonial	1		1.1[b]	nucleated	300	360	6,000
Sedentary	1		1.1[b]	nucleated	300	360	6,000
Classic (?)[c]	—		1.4	dispersed	233	100	3,800
Gila Butte–Snaketown Canal System (?)		-	-	-	-	-	-
Classic	1	13.2[d]	2.9	dispersed	205	200	2,200

[a] As measured from the center of each permanently occupied habitation site (villages and hamlets, including "dispersed").
[b] Assumes that GR-1206 is linked with the Gila Butte system and political community.
[c] These values assume that the Gila Butte system wasn't linked with the Snaketown system in terms of political organization.
[d] This is the distance between the Maricopa Platform Mound and GR-1175, a village without public architecture.

Table 6.2. Population Estimates for Study Area 2

Period	No. of Years	*Based on Habitation-Site Area* Total Habitation-Site Area (ha)	Population Size (@ 10 Persons/ha)	Population Size (@ 20 Persons/ha)	*Annual Growth Rate (%)*[a]	*Based on Command Area* Total Command Area (ha)	Population Size (@ 1 Person/ 0.4 ha)
Granite Knob Canal							
Late Pioneer (Estrella/ Sweetwater phase)	50	—	—	—		—	—
Late Pioneer (Snaketown)	50	2.00	20	40		100	250
Late Pioneer to early Colonial					*1.06*		
Early Colonial	100	5.73	57	115		100	250
Early to late Colonial					*0.46*		
Late Colonial	100	9.11	91	182		100	250
Late Colonial to Sedentary					*0.39*		
Sedentary	200	19.78	198	396		133	333
Sedentary to Early Classic					*0.34*		
Early Classic	150	33.08	331	662		133	333
Early to Late Classic					*–0.41*		
Late Classic	150	17.90	179	358		133	333
Santan Canal System							
Late Pioneer (Estrella/ Sweetwater phase)	50	18.35	184	367		421	1,053
Early to late Pioneer					*0.15*		
Late Pioneer (Snaketown)	50	19.82	198	396		421	1,053
Late Pioneer to early Colonial					*2.01*		
Early Colonial	100	145.27	1,453	2,905		1,193	2,983
Early to late Colonial					*0.05*		
Late Colonial	100	152.78	1,528	3,056		1,193	2,983
Late Colonial to Sedentary					*0.08*		
Sedentary	200	177.94	1,779	3,559		1,193	2,983
Sedentary to Early Classic					*–0.32*		
Early Classic	150	110.77	1,108	2,215		1,193	2,983
Early to Late Classic					*–0.08*		
Late Classic	150	98.86	989	1,977		1,193	2,983
Gila Butte Canal System							
Late Pioneer (Estrella/ Sweetwater phase)	50	—	—	—		—	—
Late Pioneer (Snaketown)	50	13.82	138	276		300	750
Late Pioneer to early Colonial					*0.74*		
Early Colonial	100	29.01	290	580		600	1,500
Early to late Colonial					*0.00*		
Late Colonial	100	29.01	290	580		600	1,500
Late Colonial to Sedentary					*0.10*		
Sedentary	200	35.49	355	710		680	1,700
Sedentary to Early Classic					*–0.67*		
Early Classic	150	12.94	129	259		680	1,700
Early to Late Classic					*–0.30*		
Late Classic	150	8.25	83	165		680	1,700

[a] The compound annual growth rate (CAGR) = $(p2/p1)^{1/n} - 1$, where p2 and p1 are the numbers of people at the end and beginning of the phase, respectively, and n is the number of years in the phase (see Hassan 1981:140).

Table 6.3. Population Estimates for Main-Canal Reaches in Study Area 2, Based on Residential-Site Area

Phase/Period	Granite Knob			Upper Santan/Olberg			Lower Santan			Gila Butte		
	Habitation-Site Area (ha)	Population Size (10 Persons/ha)	Population Size (20 Persons/ha)	Habitation-Site Area (ha)	Population Size (10 Persons/ha)	Population Size (20 Persons/ha)	Habitation-Site Area (ha)	Population Size (10 Persons/ha)	Population Size (20 Persons/ha)	Habitation-Site Area (ha)	Population Size (10 Persons/ha)	Population Size (20 Persons/ha)
Estrella/Sweetwater	—			18.35	184	367						
Late Pioneer	2.00	20	40	19.82	198	396				13.82	138	276
Early Colonial	5.73	57	115	60.40	604	1,208	84.87	849	1,697	29.01	290	580
Late Colonial	9.11	91	182	60.40	604	1,208	92.37	924	1,847	29.01	290	580
Sedentary	19.78	198	396	81.88	819	1,638	96.06	961	1,921	35.49	355	710
Early Classic	33.08	331	662	66.01	660	1,320	44.76	448	895	12.94	129	259
Late Classic	17.90	179	358	51.06	511	1,021	47.80	478	956	8.25	83	165

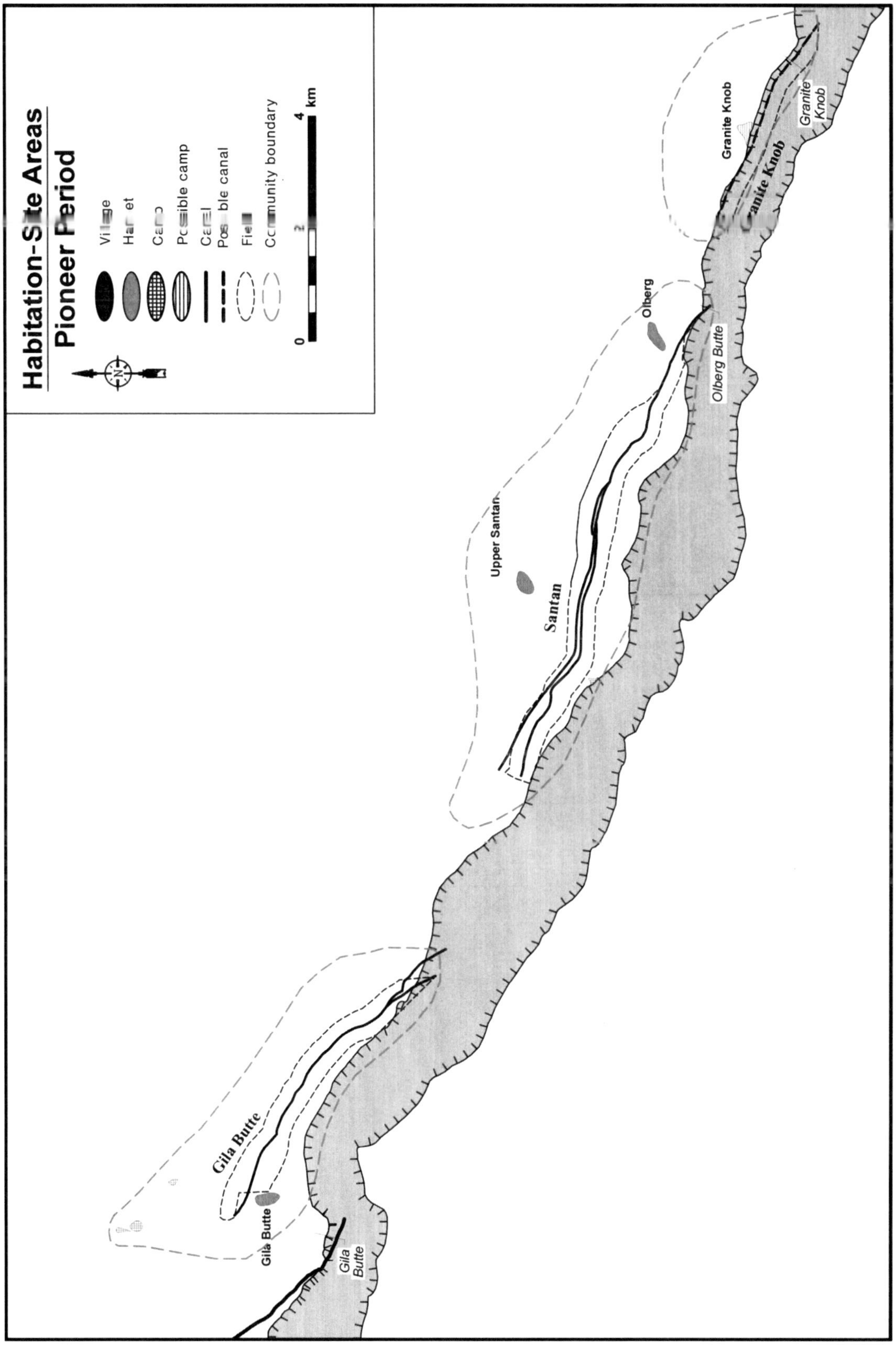

Figure 6.1. Map of the habitation sites, canals, and fields in Study Area 2 during the Pioneer period.

By the Snaketown phase, the Gila Butte site was founded as a hamlet at the end of the Gila Butte canal, and three camps to the north of the butte were used. The hamlet was 300 m from the canal and between 360 and 4,400 m from the irrigated fields (see Table 6.1). Population, based on residential area, was 138–276, and if the full command area of 300 ha was farmed, it could have supported 750 people (see Table 6.2). The Granite Knob site and Granite Knob canal possibly were built at this time, but the evidence is not conclusive. If the settlement was in place by this time, it probably was a camp with perhaps 20–40 people. The settlement pattern along both canals was non-segmented in structure.

Early Colonial Period

In the early Colonial period, the Santan and Gila Butte canal systems were built out to their full (or nearly full) extents, and the Granite Knob canal had certainly been built (Figure 6.2). The Santan canal system had two branch canals; the layout was very similar to the Snaketown canal system. The south-branch canal likely was connected with the Gila Butte canal during this period. Upper Santan and Olberg had grown to village size (Upper Santan had a ballcourt), and a new ballcourt village was founded 5.2 km down-canal, at Lower Santan, along with several camps. The settlement pattern became segmented (if it had not already become segmented in the late Pioneer period) among these three nucleated villages. The average distance to a canal was 250 m, a reduction from the previous period, and the average distance to fields was between 317 and 3,767 m (see Table 6.1). Although the settlements were closer to the nearest fields, the maximum distance increased from the previous period, a reflection of the more-extensive command area (1,193 ha) (see Table 6.2). The population rose steeply, to between 1,453 and 2,905 people, based on residential area. The population along the Lower Santan reach of the canal appears to have been higher than along the Upper Santan/Olberg reach (see Table 6.3). This population growth suggests that more people from outside the canal system moved in during the early Colonial period. The fully farmed command area could have supported 2,983 people, but even at that level, the population may have approached the carrying capacity of the irrigated fields.

The Gila Butte site grew to village size and probably added a ballcourt. A hamlet (GR-1206) was founded at the end of the extension of the Gila Butte canal, but the site may have been more closely associated with the Snaketown canal system. The settlement pattern appears to have remained non-segmented. The Gila Butte site was still 300 m from the canal and between 360 and 6,000 m from the irrigated fields (see Table 6.1). That relatively long distance to the farthest fields reflects the addition of new upstream fields along the main canal, the heading for which had been moved upstream to Diversion Point 2. The command area doubled to 600 ha, which could have supported 1,500 people (see Table 6.2).

Along the relatively short Granite Knob canal, Granite Knob village was founded, and it probably had a ballcourt. The settlement pattern was non-segmented, with all the population living in the village. The village was 140 m from the canal and between 170 and 1,700 m from the fields (see Table 6.1). The population was between 57 and 115 people, and the small command area of 100 ha could have supported 250 people (see Table 6.2). Despite the apparently small areas of irrigable land near Granite Knob village, its residents maintained extensive non-irrigated agricultural fields (with rock piles, terraces, check dams, and gridded gardens) along the alluvial fan of the Santan Mountains. Similarly, large non-irrigated fields were situated upslope from the Olberg, Upper Santan, and Lower Santan villages, but the residents of these villages also lived close to the extensive irrigated fields on the Holocene T-2 terrace. The community boundaries encompassed these non-irrigated fields.

Notably, the habitation sites along the Santan canal system were not split along the two canal branches like the sites along the Snaketown system, because the permanently occupied habitations in Study Area 2 (including those along the Granite Knob and Gila Butte canals) were situated above the floodplain, on the T-3 terrace or alluvial fan. However, the communities that were organized around the Upper Santan and Lower Santan ballcourt villages very well may have had claims to fields that were divided among the two branch canals. As shown in Figure 6.2, the Upper Santan community probably included the south-branch canal in its territory as well as the upper reach of the north-branch canal. The Lower Santan community probably only utilized the lower reach of the north-branch canal. Appendix C describes how the community boundaries were drawn, in accordance with the criteria outlined in Chapter 2.

Late Colonial and Sedentary Periods

The patterns continued in a similar manner for the late Colonial period (Figure 6.3). The settlement pattern remained segmented along the Santan system and non-segmented along the Gila Butte and Granite Knob systems. New additions included the expansion of Granite Knob village (with a second ballcourt) and the addition of two camps along the north branch of the Santan canal. Hence, the population sizes increased slightly along these two canals. With the growth along the Santan system, the population (1,528–3,056 people) possibly had reached the carrying capacity of the irrigation system (which could have supported up to 2,983 people) (see Table 6.2). That potential shortfall may have been lessened by the added productivity of the non-irrigated fields on the *bajada*, where farming was expanded

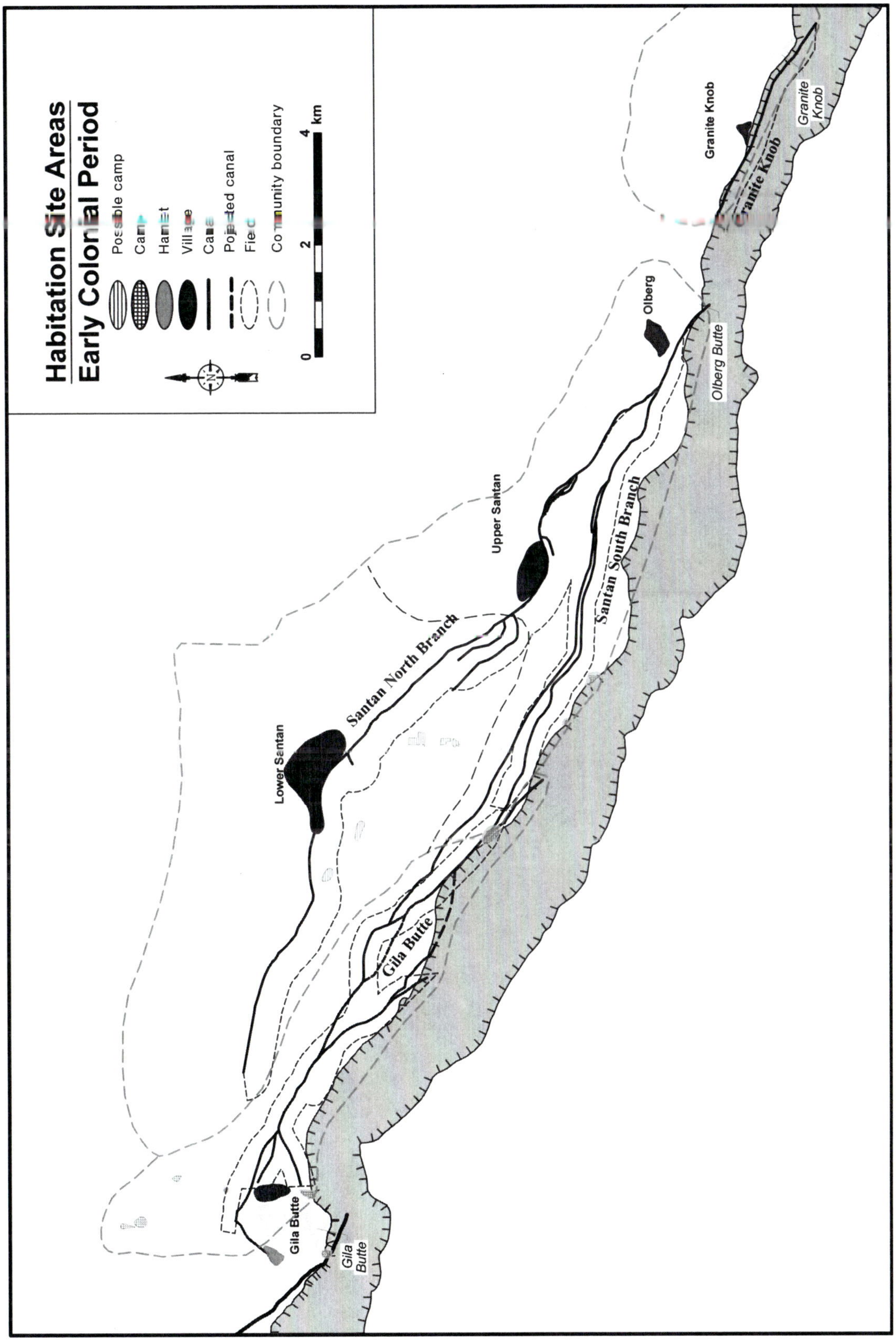

Figure 6.2. Map of the habitation sites, canals, and fields in Study Area 2 during the early Colonial period.

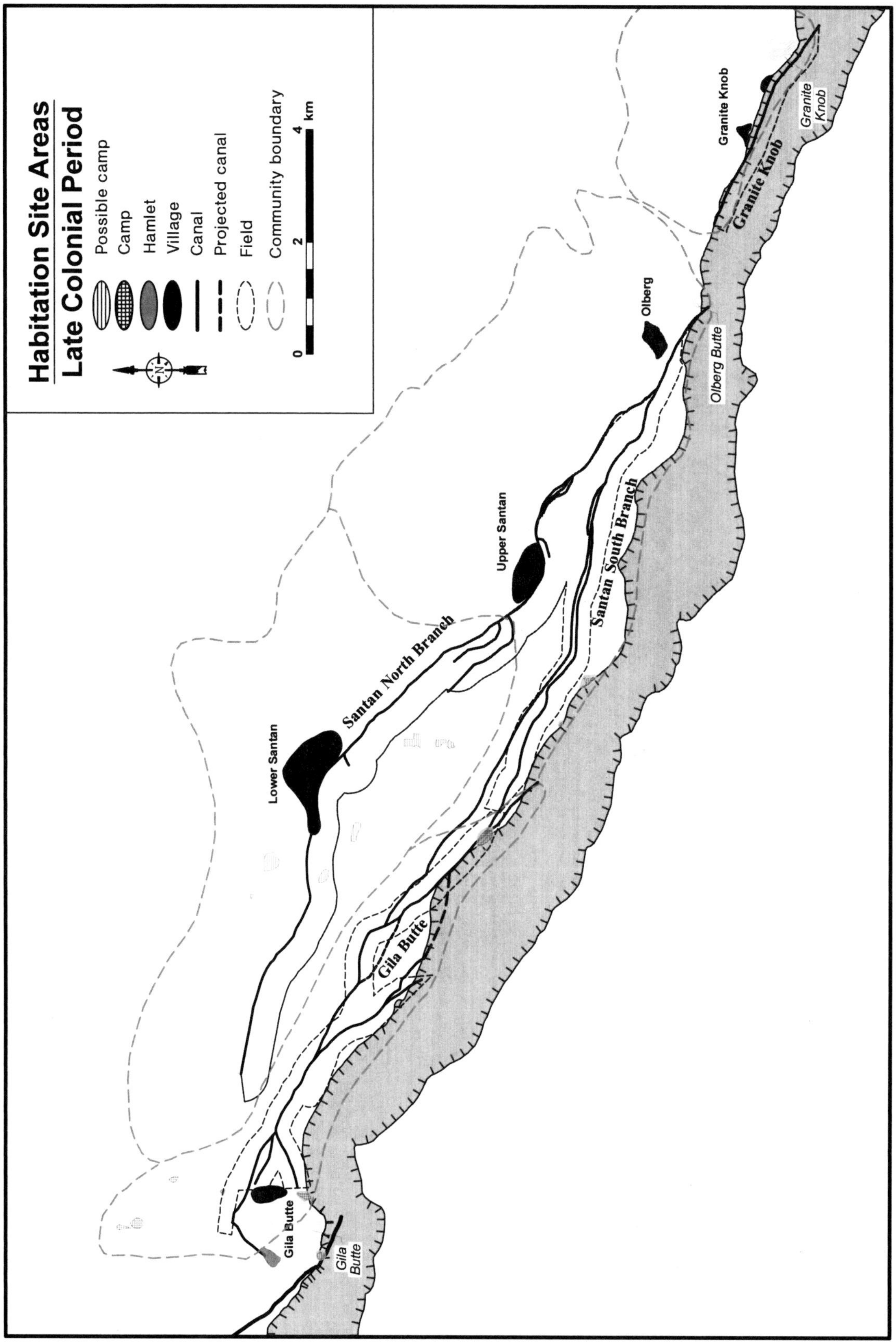

Figure 6.3. Map of the habitation sites, canals, and fields in Study Area 2 during the late Colonial period.

at this time. Also, the residents in the system may have relied on exchange relationships to buffer the risks of crop shortfalls (see Graybill et al. 2006:113). The distances between the habitations and the canals and fields remained the same.

In the Sedentary period, the population reached a peak of 2,332–4,162 people in Study Area 2 (Figure 6.4). The settlement pattern remained segmented along the Santan system and non-segmented along the Gila Butte system. People were living almost exclusively in the five nucleated villages, four of which (Granite Knob, Upper Santan, Lower Santan, and Gila Butte) were ballcourt villages. The exceptions were a small village on the western side of Gila Butte (GR-1206)—which may have been associated with the Snaketown canal—and a few hamlets established along the Granite Knob canal. The Granite Knob canal probably was extended and connected with the Santan canal at this time, and the Gila Butte canal was extended to connect with the Snaketown canal. Hence, the Granite Knob, Santan (south branch), Gila Butte, and Snaketown canals were joined by the Sedentary period, but each of the four original headings appears to have remained in operation. At 680 ha, the Gila Butte canal-system fields could have supported 1,700 people (see Table 6.2). With the consolidation of the Granite Knob and Santan canal systems in the Sedentary period, the boundary between the two inferred communities became much less distinct. The Granite Knob community could be considered another "main-canal-reach community" in the greater Granite Knob/Santan canal system. If so, then the settlement pattern would be considered segmented rather than non-segmented. Granite Knob village was situated 4.3 km upstream of Olberg, which is a shorter distance than the average 5.1 km between Olberg, Upper Santan, and Lower Santan. The combined command areas of the Granite Knob/Santan canals (1,326 ha) could have supported up to 3,316 people. The estimated population of the combined community, based on residential area, was 1,977–3,955 people, suggesting that the population had possibly reached or exceeded the carrying capacity of the irrigation system. Of course, that potential shortfall may have been lessened by the added productivity of the non-irrigated fields on the *bajada*.

The average distances to canals and fields remained at the same levels as in the Colonial period for the settlements along the Santan and Gila Butte canal systems. Along the Granite Knob canal, with the addition of several new hamlets, there was a decrease in the average distance to the nearest canal and the maximum distance to fields. The minimum distance to fields increased slightly, because the new hamlets were situated closer to the non-irrigated fields on the *bajada* than to the irrigated fields on the T-2 terrace.

Classic Period

In the Early Classic period, the settlement pattern changed to a more dispersed configuration with a dispersed population distribution, although the primary habitation-site locations remained the same along the Santan canal system (Figure 6.5). The 5 nucleated villages and 4 hamlets from the Sedentary period were replaced by 3 dispersed villages (2 with platform mounds) and 29 hamlets, and the number of camps declined by nearly half. The communities along the Santan canal system appear to have been organized around the 2 platform-mound villages at Upper Santan and Lower Santan. That continued the pattern from the Sedentary period, when the Santan focal-village communities were organized around the Upper Santan and Lower Santan ballcourt villages. The combined population of these two communities is estimated to have been between 1,108 and 2,215 (a 38 percent decline). Granite Knob village disintegrated and was replaced by a series of dispersed hamlets. The estimated population along the Granite Knob canal reach was 331–662 people (a 67 percent increase) (see Table 6.3). The Gila Butte site was abandoned and replaced by a hamlet (GR-776D) or possibly the new village (GR-1175) west of Gila Butte (which may have been more closely associated with the Snaketown canal). It is possible that the population that formerly lived at the Gila Butte site and GR-1206 drifted to the new village at GR-1175. The population along the Gila Butte canal was 129–259 people (a 64 percent decline) (see Table 6.3).

The inferred community territories also changed during the Early Classic period (see Figure 6.5). The former Granite Knob community probably was integrated with the Upper Santan community, if that integration had not already occurred in the Sedentary period. This conclusion is based on the lack of a focal village along the Granite Knob canal (which had been consolidated with the Santan canal) and the even distribution of hamlets between Granite Knob and Olberg Butte. The combined population decline for the consolidated Granite Knob/Upper Santan community was 27 percent (from 1,978 to 1,439 people, at 10 persons per hectare), even though the population along the Granite Knob reach increased (the significance of this is discussed in Chapter 7). Likewise, the former Gila Butte community probably was integrated with the Snaketown community (or possibly the Lower Santan community), because those canals had been consolidated, and only two hamlets and two camps remained along the Gila Butte segment of the canal. The uncertain association of the Gila Butte settlements is suggested by the dotted-line community outline in Figure 6.5. The combined population decline for the consolidated Gila Butte/Snaketown community was a staggering 44 percent (from 1,893 to 1,051 people, at 10 persons per hectare). No new field areas were built; so, the command areas and the estimated populations that could be supported by them remained the same as in the Sedentary period (although, as suggested in Chapters 4 and 5, the command area shrank along the Snaketown system, based on the decline in canal capacity).

Although the settlement distribution across Study Area 2 became dispersed in the Early Classic period, the settlement pattern still can be characterized as segmented when

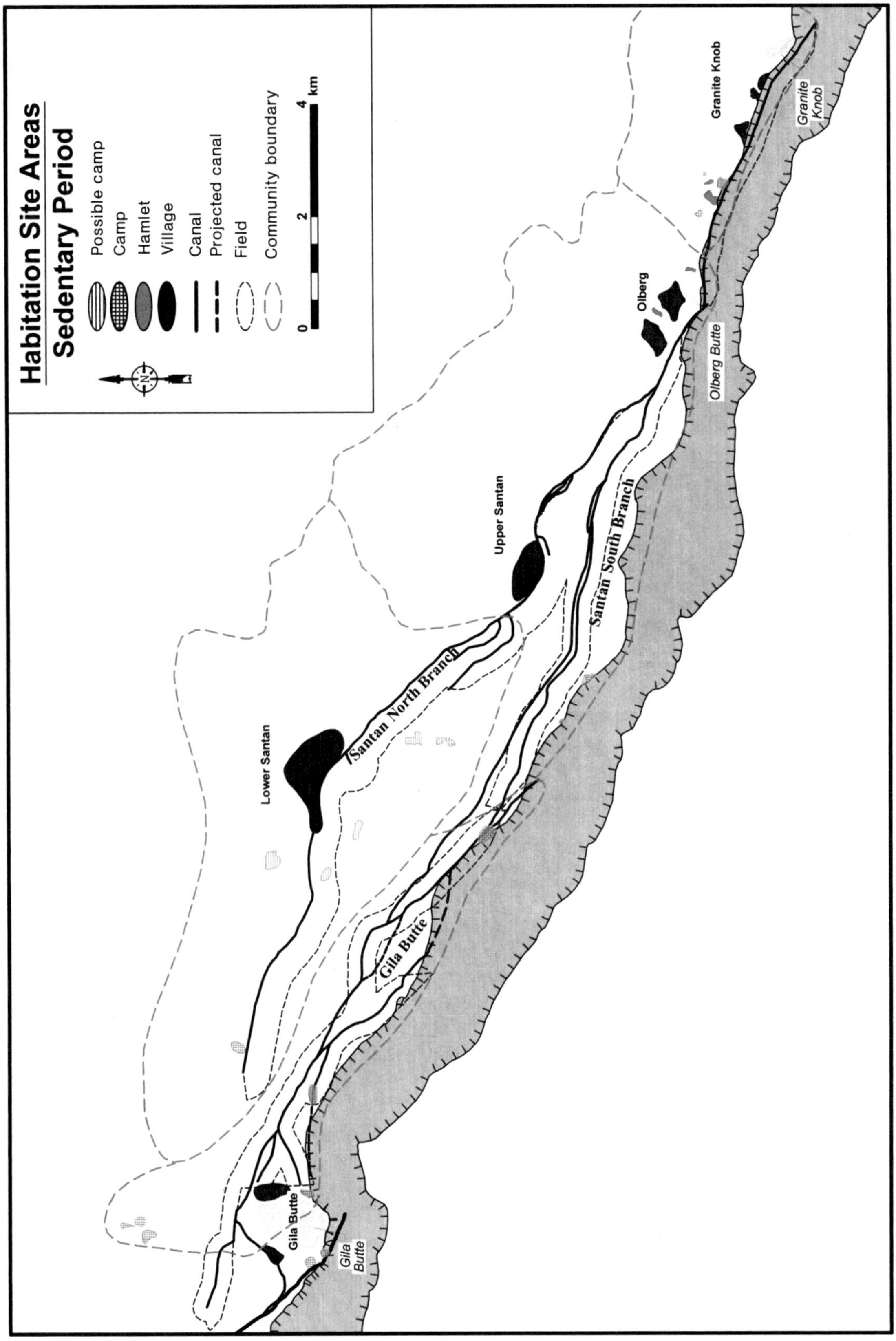

Figure 6.4. Map of the habitation sites, canals, and fields in Study Area 2 during the Sedentary period.

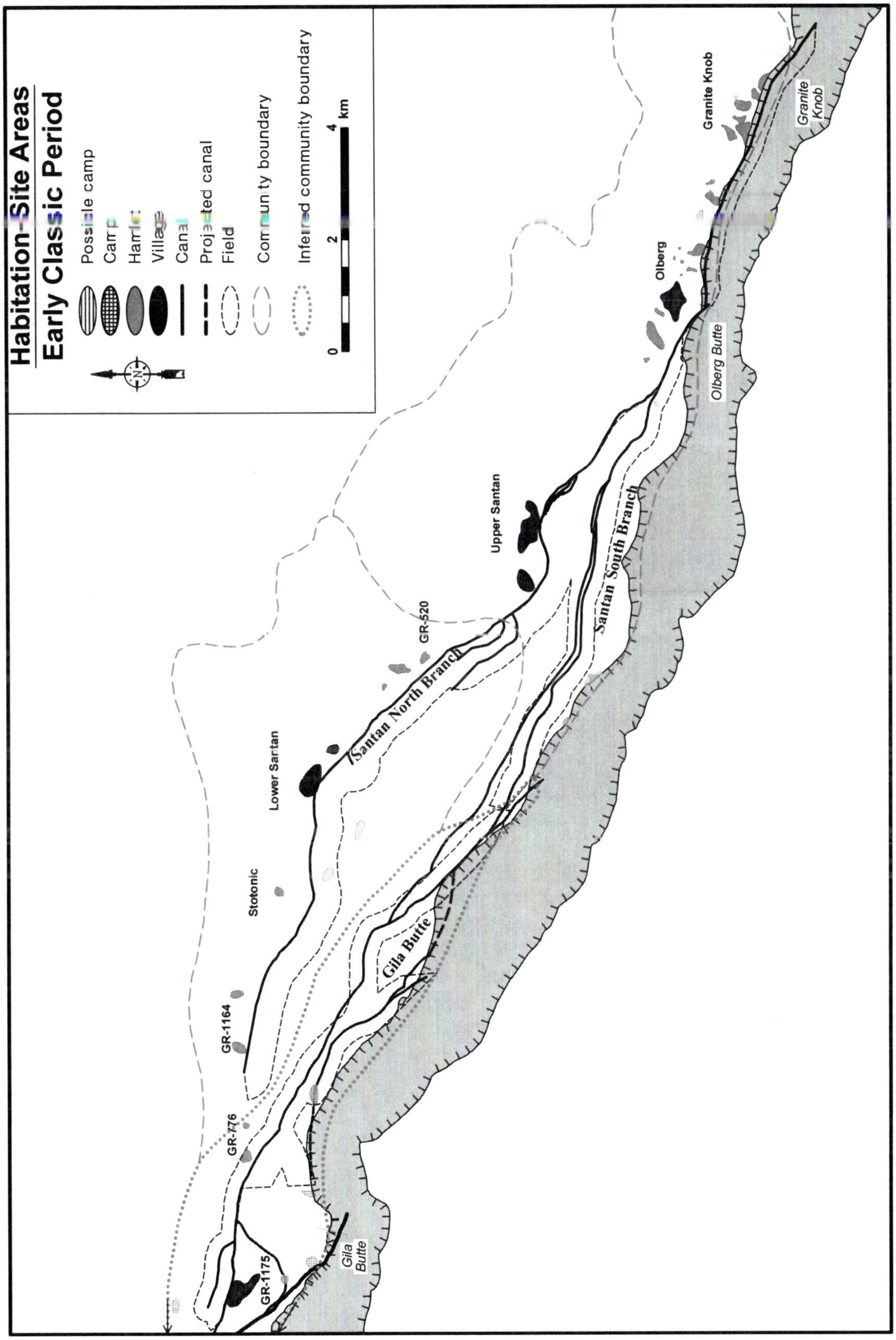

Figure 6.5. Map of the habitation sites, canals, and fields in Study Area 2 during the Early Classic period.

examined in general across the two consolidated canal systems. That is, there were essentially several clusters of permanently occupied habitation sites that coincided generally with the main-canal reaches, at Granite Knob, Olberg, Upper Santan, Lower Santan, and GR-1175. The Lower Santan segment was rather loosely clustered, but the sites still correlated to that main-canal reach. The absence of a primary settlement that clearly was linked with the Gila Butte canal and the appearance of the new settlement at GR-1175 (at the interface of the Gila Butte and Snaketown canal systems) further support the contention that the Gila Butte and Snaketown communities had become consolidated at this time.

With the new settlement and community configuration came a reduction in settlement spacing and the average distance to fields (see Table 6.1). Although the distance from habitations to the nearest canals in the combined Granite Knob/Santan community remained steady at 260 m, the average spacing of settlements reduced to 1.4 km, and the distance to fields reduced to between 310 and 1,339 m. If the Gila Butte community remained independent from the Snaketown or Santan community (which seems unlikely), the few habitations averaged 1.4 km apart, the distance to canals was 233 m, and the distance to fields was between 100 and 3,800 m. In the more-probable consolidated Gila Butte/Snaketown community, the average settlement spacing was 2.9 km, the average distance to canals was 205 m, and the distance to fields was between 200 and 2,200 m.

The same settlement pattern characterized the Late Classic period, except that eight of the hamlets along the Granite Knob canal reach and at Olberg and four camps around Gila Butte were abandoned at that time (Figure 6.6). Also, Upper Santan village contracted in size. That contributed to the slightly more-clustered appearance of these four habitation groups. These reductions resulted in an overall 19 percent decrease in population along the Granite Knob/Santan canal system, from 1,439 to 1,168 people (at a density of 10 persons per hectare). Some population reduction also occurred along the Gila Butte canal reach, from 129 to 83 people (at 10 persons per hectare) (see Table 6.3). The population of the combined Gila Butte/Snaketown canal system reduced by 19 percent, from 1,051 to 850 people (at 10 persons per hectare).

Settlement Organization in Study Area 2

The objective of this chapter is to examine the organization of settlements in Study Area 2. Through an analysis of spatial, temporal, and functional data, the settlement pattern is defined as either segmented or non-segmented for each period, and then it is evaluated in terms of community organization. The primary focus, in terms of organizational nodes, is at the level of the village and focal-village community. Where such communities are identified, they are examined to see whether they contained similar proportions of site types. Lastly, the possible signatures of intervillage dynamics, as reflected in the settlement pattern, are noted, especially where they are relevant to inferring the existence of a canal-wide political institution.

In general terms, the settlement pattern was non-segmented along all three canal systems at their initiation in the Pioneer period (again, it is unclear whether the Granite Knob canal and settlement were built at that time or not until the Colonial period). The Santan system was segmented in the Colonial to Sedentary periods, whereas the pattern along the Granite Knob and Gila Butte canal systems in those periods remained non-segmented. The Granite Knob community probably was integrated with the Upper Santan community in the Sedentary period, in which case the settlement pattern would have been segmented along the consolidated Granite Knob/Santan canal. The population distribution became much more dispersed in the Classic period, with the consolidation of the adjacent communities into the Granite Knob/Santan and Snaketown/Gila Butte communities. However, the settlement pattern remained segmented for both consolidated communities.

Pioneer Period

During the late Pioneer period, the habitations along the Santan and Gila Butte canal systems (and the Granite Knob canal system, if it was built by this time) were hamlets and lacked public architecture (see Figure 6.1). Therefore, they did not meet the principal criterion for a focal-village community. The settlement pattern was non-segmented for the systems during their initiation; so, each inferred political community was coterminous with the canal system at this time. With the founding of a hamlet at Olberg by the Snaketown phase, the settlement pattern might have become segmented along the Santan system. This is unclear, because the definition of "segmented" applies to two or more focal villages. These two hamlet-level settlements actually may have been integrated by one political structure. Also, that would have been the only segmented pattern in the study area during the Pioneer period. In concept, without a focal village, the Santan and Gila Butte canal systems (and possibly the Granite Knob canal system) cannot be classified as focal-village communities in this period. Feasibly, the settlements could be considered to have been organized as linear communities, with the caveats noted for this concept in Chapter 2.

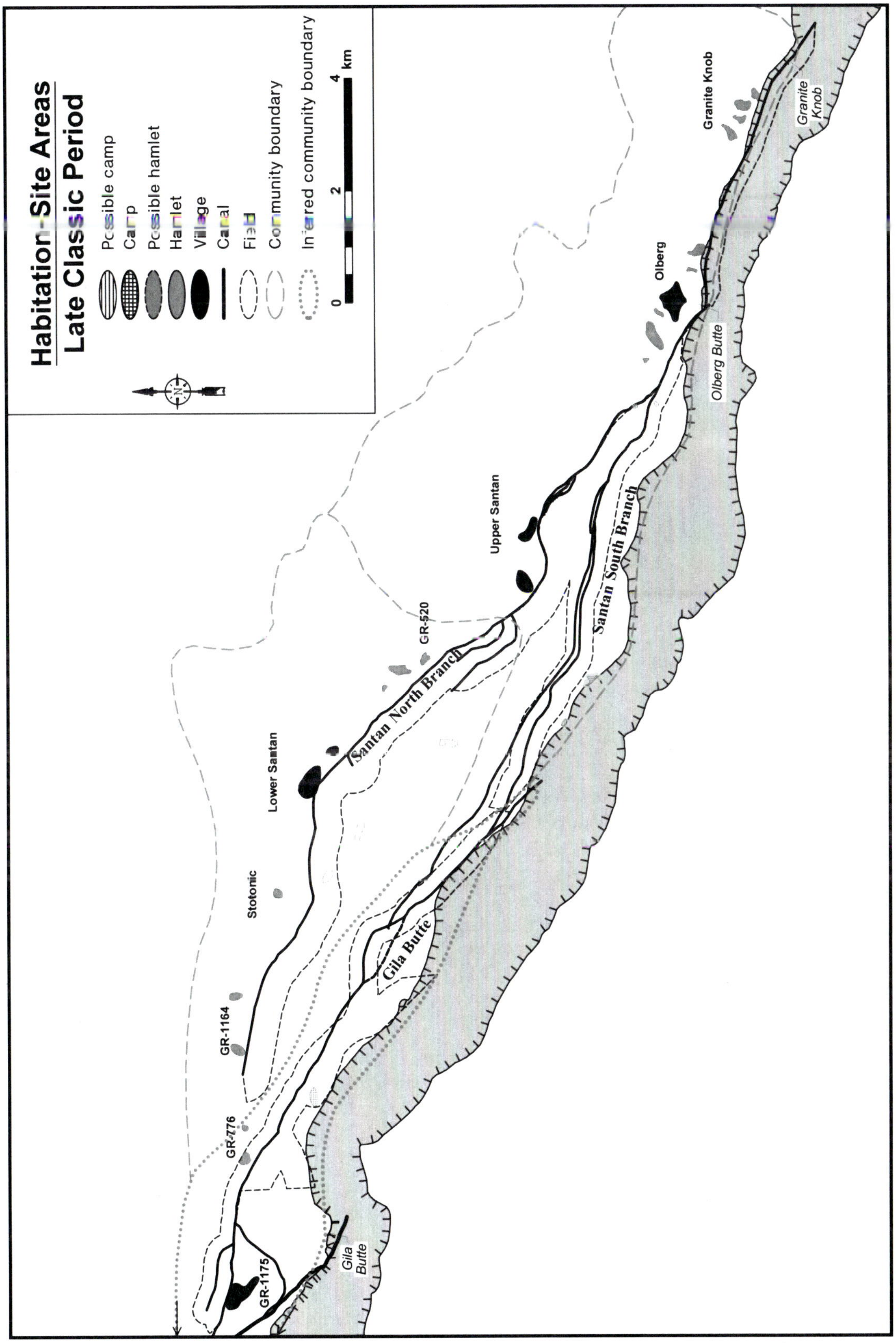

Figure 6.6. Map of the habitation sites, canals, and fields in Study Area 2 during the Late Classic period.

Table 6.4. Site-Type Counts and Percentages for Alternative Focal-Village Communities in Study Area 2 in the Early Colonial Period

Site Type	Upper Santan	%	Lower Santan	%	Gila Butte	%
Village	2	*5.6*	1	*1.8*	1	*1.7*
Camp	2	*5.6*	4	*7.0*	4	*6.7*
Activity/canal area	30	*83.3*	51	*89.5*	53	*88.3*
Roasting area	—	—	—	—	1	*1.7*
Rock-pile field	2	*5.6*	1	*1.8*	1	*1.7*
Total	36	*100.0*	57	*100.0*	60	*100.0*

Colonial to Sedentary periods

The inferred community organization changed in the early Colonial period, with the expansion of the Santan and Gila Butte canal systems (see Figure 6.2). The population along the Santan canal system was segmented and living in three nucleated villages, including two ballcourt villages (Upper Santan and Lower Santan) that were 5.2 km apart. The third village (Olberg) was 5 km upstream of Upper Santan and is assumed to have been part of the Upper Santan community. The Upper Santan/Olberg community essentially included the area within the original late Pioneer period territory, and the Lower Santan community encompassed the newly founded settlements, canals, and fields. Given the primacy of Upper Santan as the founding village, both Olberg and Lower Santan probably were "daughter villages" composed of both relatives and descendants of Upper Santan residents and possibly newly arrived immigrants. Along with the similar range of site types within the two territories, evidence indicates that these areas had developed into focal-village communities (this idea is tested below).

On the other hand, the Granite Knob and Gila Butte canal systems each included one ballcourt village at this time, and each is characterized by a non-segmented settlement pattern. There were few sites along the Granite Knob canal, and the village was quite small, suggesting that this inferred community was rather simple in organizational terms, compared to the rest of the study area. The Gila Butte community, though, included a full range of site types and appears to have been similar to the Santan focal-village communities. Along both the Granite Knob and Gila Butte canal systems, the political communities were essentially isomorphic with the canal systems under the focal-village-community or linear-community models (see Abbott et al. 2006:290; Gregory and Nials 1985:384).

To test these propositions, the site-type proportions in each inferred focal-village community were compared to each other. Table 6.4 provides the site-type counts and percentages for the Upper Santan, Lower Santan, and Gila Butte communities in the early Colonial period. Figure 6.7 presents bar graphs of the site-type proportions. The data suggest that the site-type proportions in the inferred community territories were quite similar to each other. The analysis supports the focal-village-community model for the two Santan communities. The site-type proportions along the Gila Butte canal system were similar to those in the Santan focal-village communities. The Gila Butte community thus was consistent with the focal-village-community model, but it feasibly could also be classified as a linear community. The Granite Knob community included too few sites to allow a robust analysis for any part of the Colonial period; so, it is not included in the table or chart.

Similar ranges of test results were obtained for the site-type proportions in these three inferred communities during the late Colonial and Sedentary periods (see Figures 6.3 and 6.4). One notable change in the Sedentary period was that the Granite Knob community probably could be considered another main-canal-reach community in the Granite Knob/Santan canal system after the consolidation of the two canals. By that time, the Granite Knob community included a full range of site types, like the Santan focal-village communities (Table 6.5; Figure 6.8). As can be seen, though, the site-type proportions were somewhat different, with greater percentages of hamlets and camps, which suggests a more-dispersed settlement pattern. Also, the Granite Knob community incorporated a higher proportion of rock-pile fields than the Santan communities did. That suggests that whereas the organization of the Granite Knob settlements was consistent with the focal-village-community model, the community composition differed from that of the other Santan communities. The differences most likely can be attributed to two major issues: (1) the Granite Knob community was independent during initial phases of development, and (2) the much smaller command area available for irrigated agriculture promoted a more-diversified subsistence-settlement strategy that included non-irrigation farms and a more-dispersed settlement pattern.

An important similarity to Study Area 1 is that the Colonial to Sedentary period focal-village communities in Study Area 2 had an elongated form that correlated to the main-canal reaches. The key to the territorial extent of the communities in both study areas during the Colonial

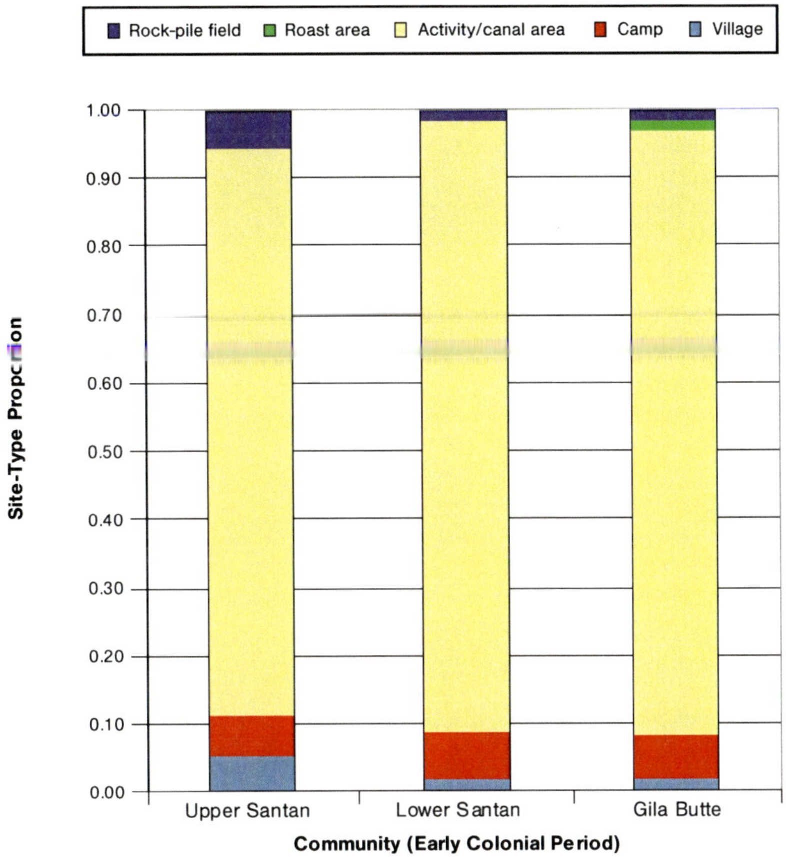

Figure 6.7. Bar chart of site-type proportions in the early Colonial period, by inferred community.

Table 6.5. Site-Type Counts and Percentages for Inferred Communities in Study Area 2 in the Sedentary Period

Site Type	Granite Knob	%	Upper Santan	%	Lower Santan	%	Gila Butte	%
Village	1	*5.9*	2	*4.7*	1	*1.5*	1	*1.9*
Hamlet	2	*11.8*	2	*4.7*	—	—	—	—
Camp	3	*17.6*	2	*4.7*	7	*10.4*	4	*7.7*
Activity/canal area	6	*35.3*	33	*76.7*	55	*82.1*	45	*86.5*
Roasting area	1	*5.9*	—	—	1	*1.5*	1	*1.9*
Rock-pile field	4	*23.5*	4	*9.3*	3	*4.5*	1	*1.9*
Total	17	*100.0*	43	*100.0*	67	*100.0*	52	*100.0*

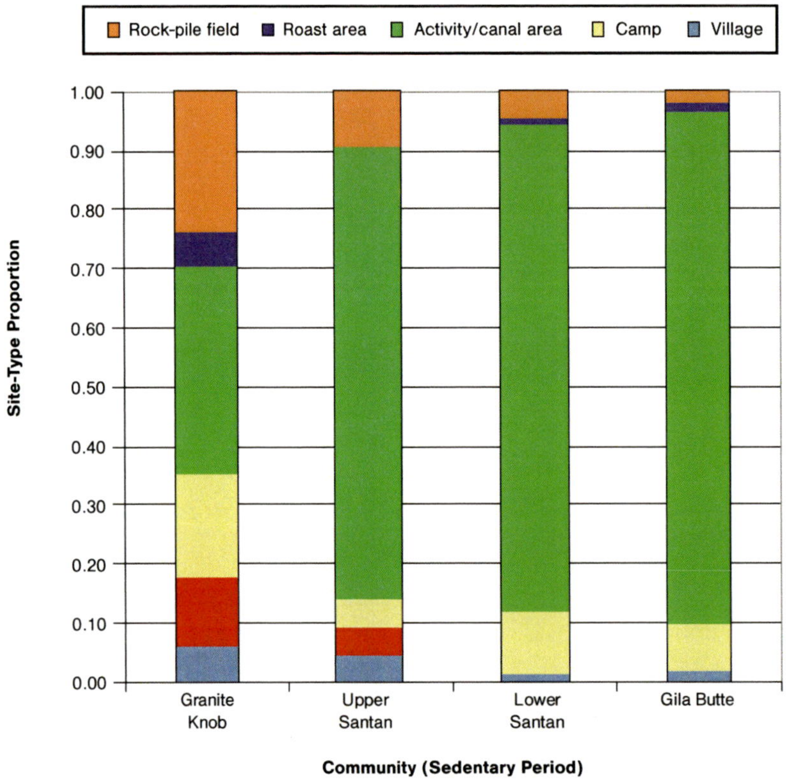

Figure 6.8. Bar chart of site-type proportions in the Sedentary period, by inferred community.

to Sedentary periods appears to have been the main-canal branches or main-canal reaches. The communities not only encompassed the main-canal-reach task groups and their constituent command areas but also included the focal villages. As is discussed further in Chapter 7, it is significant that two of the most important organizational nodes, as defined by Howard (2006), were included in each community territory.

Classic Period

The organization of settlements was more dispersed in the Classic period (see Figures 6.5 and 6.6). The Upper Santan and Lower Santan platform-mound villages still represented the central sites along the Granite Knob/Santan canal system, but they were more spread out and were characterized as dispersed villages. The number of hamlets increased sevenfold, a dramatic increase that contributed much to the dispersed nature of the settlement pattern. Although the settlement distribution was dispersed, it remained segmented when examined in general across the study area. Despite the less-clustered appearance of the settlements, the distribution and proportion of site types around these platform-mound villages appeared to conform to the focal-village-community model. That showed a continuity in community organization from the previous Colonial to Sedentary periods. One difference, as described above, was that the former Granite Knob community appeared to have integrated into the Upper Santan focal-village community. The proportions of site types between the two Santan focal-village communities were similar, but they had changed since the Sedentary period (the site-type proportions are not graphed here). The principal difference is that there were more hamlets by proportion, a reflection of the more-dispersed settlement pattern.

As described in Chapter 5, the former Gila Butte community probably was integrated into the Snaketown community (or the Lower Santan community) by this time. The settlements along the Gila Butte segment of the consolidated Gila Butte/Snaketown canal appear to have been incorporated into the community centered on the village at GR-1175. That village did not include a platform mound, which runs counter to the typical Classic period pattern for focal-village communities. Maricopa Mound represents the only central site along the Gila Butte/Snaketown system, but it was located at the tail end of the canal, roughly 16 km from the heading at Diversion Point 1 and nearly 26 km away from the Diversion Point 2 heading. So, it did not resemble a focal-village node for the entire system, as expected with the focal-village model. The pattern was atypical for the Phoenix Basin Hohokam, but Chapter 5 explains that the GR-1175 community was one of three communities along the consolidated system and that the south-branch community was the only "true" focal-village community.

In sum, the Classic period pattern of community territories in Study Area 2 was similar to the pre-Classic period pattern, and that reinforces the contention that the main-canal branches/reaches were key to the territorial extent of the communities. That remained the case, even though the settlement pattern was more dispersed, and the four canals were consolidated into two canal systems (Granite Knob/Santan and Gila Butte/Snaketown). That is similar to the pattern in Study Area 1 (as noted in Chapter 5). It seems likely that the long-held, and presumably productive, irrigated fields motivated many families and kinship groups to remain nearby (see Adler 1996). The fact that they remained in the same general territories suggests that the areas encompassed by the main and branch canals represented important organizational units for the Hohokam and endured through a major sociopolitical change during the Sedentary to Classic transition.

Existence of a Canal-Wide Polity

As examined for Study Area 1 in Chapter 5, I here consider what settlement patterns can tell us about sociopolitical dynamics among multiple focal-village communities along the canal systems in Study Area 2 and whether they could have been integrated into a larger polity. Two focal-village communities existed along the Santan canal system during the Colonial period, and possibly three existed during the Sedentary period. As noted in Chapter 2, I argued that the sharing of a canal and the inherent need for irrigation management did not necessarily require the formation of an overarching political entity and, instead, could have been addressed through an irrigation organization, the authority for which could have been separate from the political entity (this is discussed further in Chapter 7). I also contended that interaction patterns along a canal system, as discerned through evidence of economic exchange (e.g., of ceramics), may not be sufficient evidence to posit the existence of a canal-wide polity that bypassed the focal-village sites as the important organizational nodes (i.e., a linear community) (Abbott 2000; Abbott et al. 2006). Such exchange data are beyond the scope of this study; so, that model cannot be tested here.

Despite these theoretical issues, the Study Area 2 focal-village communities feasibly could have been part of a larger, canal-wide polity in the pre-Classic period. I assessed whether one village may have united all the communities into such a polity, by virtue of its being the preeminent settlement. Factors considered were village size, number and size of public architecture, village proximity to the heading, and which was the founding village. Upper Santan village was the founding "mother" settlement, yet Lower Santan village actually was larger in size upon its construction in the Colonial period. Each village had only one north–south-oriented ballcourt as public architecture. Olberg, the headgate village, was the smallest of the three villages and did not have public architecture. Most people were living along the Lower Santan reach (at the end of the north-branch canal); so, Lower Santan could have held sway over the others, based on size and population. But as the founding village, Upper Santan would have had first rights in various claims. Also, Olberg controlled the heading and was closest to the main-canal-bifurcation point. In all, these traits do not lend themselves to easy identification of a preeminent village in the Colonial period.

By the Sedentary period, the Granite Knob canal and its associated settlements appear to have been integrated as a possible third focal-village community along a consolidated Granite Knob/Santan canal system. Granite Knob village was considerably smaller than the other three villages, but it had two small north–south-oriented ballcourts, marking it as a third focal village. It possibly was perceived as the headgate village by this time, because it had the farthest-upstream intake that supplied the canal system. Again, I suggest (based on settlement pattern) that there was no clearly preeminent village in the Sedentary period.

In the Classic period, Study Area 2 included two consolidated canal systems. The unusual pattern of primary settlements along the Gila Butte/Snaketown canal system is discussed in Chapter 5. Two focal-village communities along the Granite Knob/Santan canal system were inferred, and they were centered on the platform-mound villages at Upper Santan and Lower Santan. The two platform mounds were nearly identical in size (roughly 2,000 m^3 in volume) (Ravesloot et al. forthcoming); so, neither clearly represents the preeminent mound. However, Upper Santan was the founding village and was larger in residential area and population by the Early Classic period. Also, recent work at Upper Santan documented a second, small platform mound (roughly 77 m^3 in volume) (Loendorf et al. 2007). These factors suggest that Upper Santan may have been the preeminent village in the Classic period, but it is unclear whether that translated into a leadership role for the entire canal system.

In sum, I would argue that there is no obvious basis for asserting that one village along the Santan canal system united all the communities into a canal-wide institution at any point in the sequence. This issue cannot be fully addressed using settlement-pattern data alone. Further testing of the hypothesis is required, using other data, such as ceramic-exchange patterns.

CHAPTER 7

Settlement Trends and the Signatures of Hohokam Irrigation Organizations

This chapter addresses Research Goal 3, to examine settlement organization and the canal systems in Study Area 1 (Snaketown canal system) and Study Area 2 (Granite Knob, Santan, and Gila Butte canal systems) in terms of their implications for the social organization of Hohokam irrigation management. First, I look more closely at the trends in settlement organization across the study area, the population dynamics, and the field-labor organization, as far as they are relevant to certain aspects of irrigation management. Second, I use the data accrued during the study to examine three aspects of Hohokam irrigation organizations: their internal structures, their external relationships with the local political systems, and the interrelationships among irrigation organizations.

Settlement Organization and Population Dynamics in the Study Area

The findings from Chapters 5 and 6 regarding settlement organization are reviewed here from the perspective of their implications for the organization of irrigation management (as discussed later in this chapter). Spatial, functional, and temporal data were used to establish whether the settlement pattern in each period was segmented or nonsegmented (Table 7.1). An evaluation was made of community organization, with a focus on organizational nodes at the levels of the village and the focal-village community.

Both study areas exhibited similar trends in settlement organization during the pre-Classic period. In the incipient stage of development in the Pioneer period, each of the canal systems included one primary settlement without public architecture. The settlement pattern was nonsegmented; so, the inferred political communities were coterminous with the canal systems. In concept, without a focal village, these inferred communities cannot be classified as focal-village communities. Feasibly, the settlements could have been organized as linear communities, with the caveats noted for that concept in Chapter 2. By the end of the Pioneer period, Snaketown had become a focal village, but the system still had a nonsegmented pattern. The political community essentially would have been isomorphic with the canal system under either the focal-village-community or the linear-community model. The Santan canal system added a second hamlet, possibly giving it a segmented pattern, but the inferred community had no focal villages and is not considered a focal-village community, per se.

During the Colonial to Sedentary periods, the settlement organization was segmented along the Snaketown and Santan canal systems and was consistent with expectations for the focal-village-community model. The settlement pattern was nonsegmented along the Gila Butte canal system; so, the inferred community was coterminous with the canal system. Although the site-type proportions along the Gila Butte canal system were similar to those in the Santan focal-village communities, it also could be classified as a linear community. The pattern along the Granite Knob canal system was nonsegmented in the Colonial period. With the probable consolidation of the Granite Knob and Santan canal systems in the Sedentary period, the Granite Knob settlements could be considered a focal-village community along that consolidated system. However, the proportion of site types differed from the Santan communities, reflecting a more-diversified subsistence-settlement strategy that included non-irrigation farms and a more-dispersed settlement pattern.

A significant settlement-pattern shift occurred during the Sedentary to Classic period transition in the study area. The three ballcourt villages were abandoned, and the population either moved away or settled in a series of smaller, dispersed habitations along the Snaketown canal system. The Snaketown and Gila Butte canal systems and their associated communities appear to have been consolidated at this time (see Ravesloot et al. forthcoming). Although there was a platform-mound village in the system, it was built in a new location, at the tail end of the south branch of the Snaketown canal. Despite the dispersed settlement distribution, the settlement pattern along the Gila Butte/Snaketown canal system remained segmented within three

Table 7.1. Settlement-Pattern Types for the Canal Systems

Canal System	Period						
	Early Pioneer	Late Pioneer	Early Colonial	Late Colonial	Sedentary	Early Classic	Late Classic
Snaketown	nonsegmented	nonsegmented	segmented	segmented	segmented		
Gila Butte		nonsegmented	nonsegmented	nonsegmented	nonsegmented		
Santan		nonsegmented/ segmented (?)[a]	segmented	segmented	segmented		
Granite Knob		nonsegmented/ segmented[b]	nonsegmented	nonsegmented	nonsegmented/ segmented[c]		
Gila Butte–Snaketown (consolidated)						segmented	segmented
Granite Knob–Santan (consolidated)					segmented	segmented	segmented

[a] The addition of a hamlet at Olberg might have resulted in a segmented pattern, but that is unclear.
[b] The Granite Knob canal might have been built as early as the Late Pioneer period, but that is unclear.
[c] The Granite Knob community probably was consolidated with the Upper Santan community in the Sedentary period; so, it is listed here both individually and as a consolidated community.

distinct clusters that were associated with the three main-canal branches. Only the south-branch community, with Maricopa Mound, though, is consistent with expectations for a focal-village community.

Similar settlement-pattern changes happened in parts of Study Area 2 during the Classic period, when the ballcourt villages at Gila Butte and Granite Knob were abandoned, and no platform mounds were built along their respective canal systems. The Sedentary period population in these two ballcourt villages probably "drifted" to the Classic period hamlets or to the GR-1175 village built in the vicinity. However, the Upper Santan and Lower Santan platform-mound villages remained the central sites along the Granite Knob/Santan canal system. Although the settlement distribution became dispersed across Study Area 2, the settlement pattern still was segmented across the two consolidated canal systems. The Upper Santan and Granite Knob communities appear to have been consolidated as one community at this time (see Ravesloot et al. forthcoming), and the Lower Santan community persisted toward the downstream end. In contrast to the Gila Butte/Snaketown community, the settlement organization along the Granite Knob/Santan canal system continued to be characterized as focal-village communities.

A number of other settlement trends revealed in Chapters 5 and 6 are worth summarizing here. These trends in the distribution of settlements and population in relation to the canals and fields are consistent with expectations for a population that placed great importance on canal-irrigation management (i.e., canal operation and maintenance) and on agricultural-field management (i.e., proximity for field access). In and of themselves, these trends are not surprising for the Hohokam, who were subsistence farmers practicing intensive agriculture. Also, other factors played a part in influencing these settlement trends, such as when the ballcourt villages were abandoned, at the end of the Sedentary period. However, I argue that these trends were important factors in the organization of agricultural labor as well as the development of the political organization along the canal systems in the study area. The trends, therefore, are also relevant to understanding the organization of irrigation management.

First, over time, the settlements moved closer or stayed close to the canals (see Tables 5.1 and 6.1). The analysis left little doubt that the settlements were structurally congruent with the canal systems during the entire Hohokam occupation sequence. In Study Area 1, for instance, at no time were the settlements located more than 400 m from the nearest canal, and that was during the Pioneer period, when Snaketown actually had a walk-in well inside the village (Figure 7.1). During subsequent periods, the habitation sites were situated an average of 100–200 m away from a canal. If the distances between the camps and the nearest canal also are included in these calculations, the average distance is approximately the same (although one camp, GR-1157DD, was located about 700 m from a canal). A similar trend was exhibited in Study Area 2. This close proximity would have facilitated canal-operation and maintenance activities.

Second, the decisions made by the Hohokam in locating new settlements support the notion that the settlement organization was closely linked with the canal systems:

a. Each founding village along the four canal systems was established at the end of a newly built canal, above the floodplain, to avoid the danger of flooding.

b. Three of the villages were situated to take advantage of premium canal headings at Granite Knob, Olberg Butte, and Gila Butte, which had bedrock "reefs" in the riverbed that created a more reliable surface water supply (Gregory 1991:177; Gregory and Nials 1985;

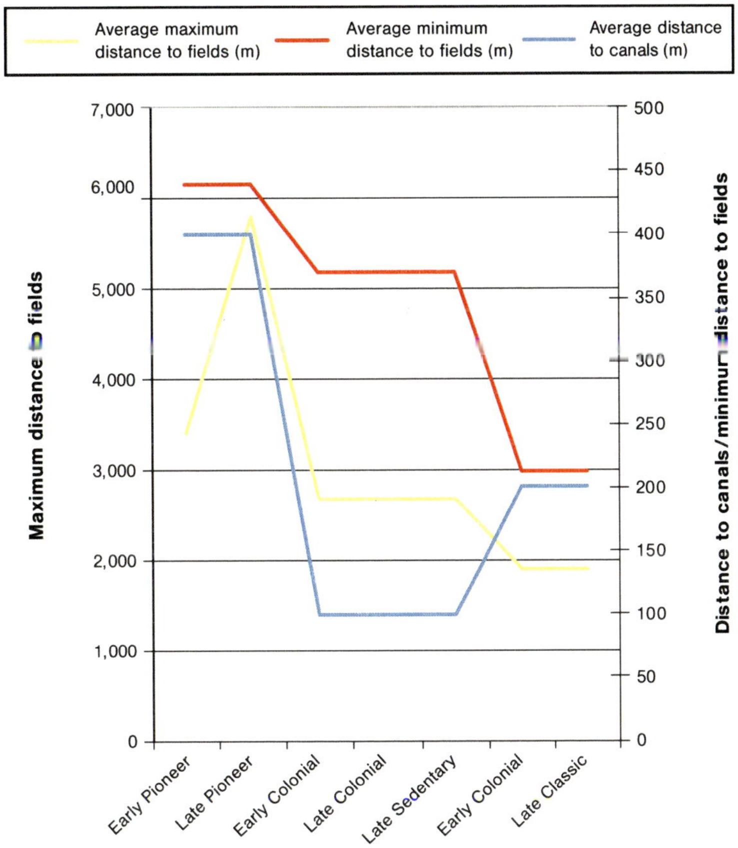

Figure 7.1. Graph of the distances between habitations and canals and the minimum and maximum distances to fields in Study Area 1.

Haury 1976). The Gila Butte canal heading at Diversion Point 2 also may have had a reliable surface flow, but it was not adjacent to a bedrock outcrop.

c. After the founding villages were established, new settlements built during the late Pioneer and early Colonial periods were located directly adjacent to the main canals or newly built canal extensions.

d. Shortly after the founding of each canal system, settlements were founded near the main-canal headings. In the late Pioneer period, these included GR-1184 along the Snaketown canal and Olberg along the Santan canal. In the Colonial period, they included GR-1206, GR-738A along the Gila Butte canal, and GR-157A along the Granite Knob canal. These settlements probably were established as maintenance or "guard" stations for the canal headings.

Third, over time, the habitation sites moved closer or stayed close to the agricultural fields (see Tables 5.1 and 6.1). In Study Area 1, the minimum distance throughout the Pioneer period was 440 m, and the maximum distance was 3,400 and 5,800 m, respectively, in the early and late Pioneer periods (see Figure 7.1). The latter distance may have been somewhat overestimated, since it is the distance from Snaketown to the tail end of the Pioneer Canal extension, near the camps at GR-1157C and GR-1157I. Thereafter, with the establishment of new villages and hamlets in the early Colonial period, residents were living between 370 and 2,700 m from the fields. These distances held through the late Colonial and Sedentary periods. The maximum distances are less if the camps are considered in the calculations. During the Classic period, with the shift to a more-dispersed settlement pattern, residents along the canal system were living even closer to their fields—between 213 and 1,900 m away. The temporal trend was that the settlements moved closer to the fields.

Fourth, the new settlements founded in the late Pioneer and early Colonial periods were established beyond a 3–4-km zone of distance from earlier primary settlements. In Study Area 1, GR-1157C and GR-1157I were founded as camps (and would later become a village and a dispersed village, respectively) at 4.5 and 6.5 km to the west of Snaketown, respectively. GR-1184 was established as a camp 6 km east of Snaketown, near the canal heading. In Study Area 2, Olberg was 5 km upstream of Upper Santan, and Granite Knob was 4.1 km upstream of Olberg. These two

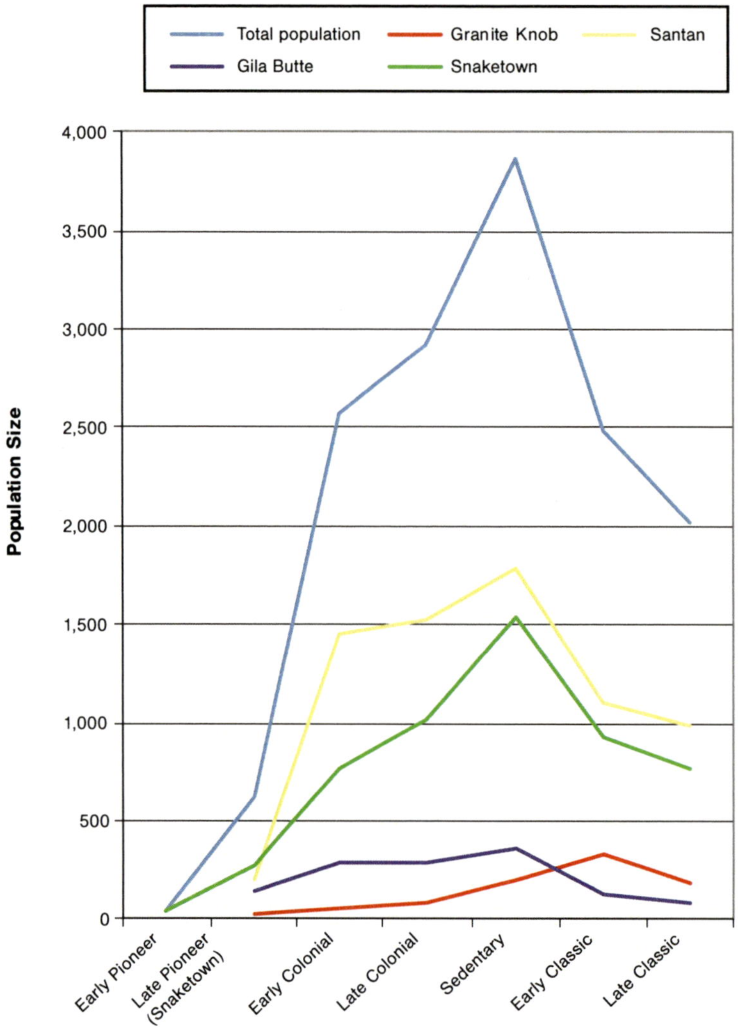

Figure 7.2. Graph of population size in the study area, by canal system, based on residential-site area (at a density of 10 persons/ha).

settlements may have been initiated as camps, and both developed into villages. Also, GR-738A was established as a camp 7.5 km east of the Gila Butte site, near the canal heading. These seasonally used settlements represent satellites of the permanently occupied villages (see Stone 1996). The Maricopa Road site was founded as a village 7.3 km west of Snaketown and 3.4 km away from GR-1157C. Lower Santan was founded in the early Colonial period as a village 5.2 km downstream from Upper Santan. These villages, and the other camps that developed into villages, probably represent daughter villages of the founding villages. These patterns conform to the expectations of the proximity-access principle (Chisholm 1979), which posits that land use in agrarian societies will develop with respect to optimal distances for agricultural travel. A primary motivation that leads to this behavior is related to improved efficiency in the organization of field labor (Chisholm 1979; Stone 1996).

Population Trends

The population-size data provide a unique opportunity to examine population growth and decline in the study area and to assess whether those changes might have been due to immigration/emigration or changes in fertility/mortality. This is the most-detailed and, I would argue, most-accurate analysis of Hohokam population trends in any part of the Phoenix Basin that has been presented to date. The estimated population size by period for Study Area 1 is given in Table 5.2; for Study Area 2, it is given in Table 6.2. The population trends over time for both study areas are depicted in Figure 7.2. The general trend in total population size is that it started from a very small level at the beginning of the Vahki phase of the early Pioneer period. Thereafter, population grew dramatically in the late Pioneer (1,260 percent) and early Colonial (311 percent) periods, grew by only 14 percent in the late Colonial

Table 7.2. Annual Population-Growth Rates for the Study Area, by Canal System

Time-Period Interval	No. of Years	*Annual Population-Growth Rate (%)*				
		Study Area	Granite Knob[a]	Santan[a]	Gila Butte[a]	Snaketown
Early to late Pioneer	100	*2.64*				1.78
Late Pioneer to early Colonial	100	*1.42*	1.06	2.16	0.74	1.06
Early to late Colonial	100	*0.13*	0.46	0.05	0.00	0.28
Late Colonial to Sedentary	200	*0.14*	0.39	0.08	0.10	0.21
Sedentary to Early Classic	150	*–0.29*	0.34	–0.32	–0.67	–0.34
Early to Late Classic	150	*–0.14*	–0.41	–0.08	–0.30	–0.12

[a] Early to late Pioneer period growth rates were not calculated for this canal, because it did not have an early Pioneer period occupation. The late Pioneer period population did factor into the growth-rate calculation for the entire study area, though.

period, grew by 32 percent and reached a maximum in the Sedentary period, declined back to early Colonial period levels in the Early Classic period (by 36 percent), and dropped again in the Late Classic period (by 19 percent). The population along each canal system followed a similar trend, with some variations, as evident in Figure 7.2.

To evaluate whether population change might have been due to immigration or emigration, I used the population size in each phase to compute the CAGR. The CAGR describes population change as a constant percentage each year. Table 7.2 lists the CAGR for each time period for the study area (taken from Tables 5.2 and 6.2). The framework for evaluating the growth rates was provided by Cowgill's (1975) examination of population change using worldwide regional-level data (which could cover up to tens of thousands of square kilometers). Cowgill (1975:511) concluded:

> Regional trends spanning a millennium or more show net population gains that are rarely more than what would have resulted from a steady rate of increase of 1 or 2 per 1,000 per year . . . [and that] are perhaps never over 3 per 1,000 per year . . . and rates of natural increase greater than about 6 or 7 per 1,000 per year—that is, increase due entirely to excess of fertility over mortality, apart from increase due to migration, have occurred only very briefly and locally, or during the rapid colonization of uninhabited or very weakly defended new territory.

As noted by Ingram (2008:148–149; see also Kintigh et al. 2004:440), who used a similar line of reasoning as is employed here, "Cowgill's regional-level population growth data may not be completely applicable to growth rates in a portion of a region . . . where internal mobility is also a possibility." Based on the trends identified by Cowgill (1975), both Ingram (2008:149) and Kintigh et al. (2004:443) inferred that immigration is implied at growth rates greater than 0.7 percent (7 per 1,000 per year). If the same assumptions are valid for the current study area, then immigration can be inferred from the growth rates between the early and late Pioneer periods (2.64 percent) and between the late Pioneer and early Colonial periods (1.42 percent). In the latter interval, the growth rate for each canal system also exceeded 0.7 percent, suggesting that immigration may have contributed to growth in each system.

In addition, I suggest that most or all of the founding population of Snaketown in the early Pioneer period (Vahki phase) were immigrants. This hypothesis cannot be evaluated according to growth rates, because the population size in the preceding Red Mountain phase (ca. A.D. 150–450) of the early Pioneer period is largely unknown for the middle Gila Valley. Evidence presented elsewhere suggests that the valley was used by mobile populations in the Late Archaic period, and it appears that nobody was living in sedentary settlements (Loendorf and Rice 2004). Speculatively, the population size within the study area would have fluctuated in a given year, but overall, it probably was very small during that time. Extensive archaeological investigations over the last 100 years have failed to reveal evidence of any sedentary populations living in the middle Gila Valley during the Late Archaic period or the Red Mountain phase. If the middle Gila Valley was largely unpopulated in the Red Mountain phase, then the area would have been open for colonization and the beginnings of irrigation agriculture. This view echoes the "empty niche" hypothesis of Haury (1976:352), even though it would appear that the area was not completely empty. Hence, the people who founded Snaketown probably were immigrants.

If so, where did the immigrants come from? In contrast to Haury's (1976:351–353) argument in favor of a Mexican origin, I would suggest that there were several possible source areas in much closer proximity to Snaketown. The most likely areas of origin are those locales where we now know farmers already were practicing canal irrigation, including the lower Salt Valley, the Tucson Basin, and other places in the Upper Sonoran Desert where evidence of early irrigation has been found. Semisedentary village life and canal irrigation has been documented for the Tucson Basin as early as 1250 B.C., during the Early Agricultural period (ca. 2,100 B.C.–A.D. 50) (Mabry 2008). Evidence of similar early irrigation-farming communities has been found along the upper Gila River near Kearny (Clark 2000) and in the Safford Valley (Clark, ed. 2004). Settlement and irrigation began in earnest in the lower Salt Valley during the Red Mountain phase (Ackerly and Henderson 1989; Cable and Doyel 1987; Henderson and Nials 2004). It seems feasible that some people in the farming communities in these possible source areas would have been "pulled" to the middle Gila Valley for the opportunity to settle a largely open area with excellent potential for irrigation farming. In this way, the Red Mountain phase settlers in the Salt Valley and the founders of Snaketown and Grewe (the forebears of the Hohokam cultural tradition) can be seen as immigrants, yet they probably originated from a Late Archaic/Early Agricultural period, San Pedro phase, Cochise base (Cable and Doyel 1987; Mabry 2008). Interestingly, the hypothesis that the Gila Valley was a relatively "late" site for irrigation has been supported by Pima oral traditions about the origins of irrigation during prehistoric times: the traditions specifically state that irrigation was first implemented in the Salt River Valley, and then the knowledge was passed to the people living in the Gila River Valley (Bahr et al. 1994).

Other areas in the Southwest, such as in the Rio Grande Valley in New Mexico, also experienced high population-growth rates in late prehistory that could be attributed to the rapid colonization of uninhabited or very weakly defended new territory (see Cameron 1995; Duff 1998). The population explosion in the Rio Grande Valley in the thirteenth century has been interpreted as colonization by immigrants. On the other hand, it is feasible that the growth rates in the study area between the early Pioneer and early Colonial periods may have been a result of natural increases in birth rates over death rates that occurred during the rapid colonization of uninhabited or very weakly defended new territory (see Cowgill 1975:511). Certainly, the study area appears to have been largely unpopulated and then rapidly colonized in these early periods. Annual growth rates at the levels seen in the study area have been known to occur in such situations, such as colonial Andover, Massachusetts, in the seventeenth and eighteenth centuries (Greven 1970). Thus, it may be premature to entirely dismiss the natural-growth argument. Although I would speculate that the population growth was due mostly to immigration, it might be best to view the population growth as a result of both immigration and natural increase.

The growth rates during the late Colonial and Sedentary periods for the study area, as well as for each canal system, were well within range of the growth rates typically expected from natural increases in birth rates over death rates in the absence of substantial migration. The Early Classic period witnessed a 0.29 percent decline, which was a marked change from the previous centuries of growth. That decline could have been due to an increase in death rates over birth rates, but it also may represent a period of emigration or population movement within the valley. The 0.67 percent decline along the Gila Butte canal, in particular, is sufficient to suggest that people were moving away from it. Of interest, however, is that the Granite Knob canal system actually added population during that interval. It is plausible that the increase was a result of people moving there from the downstream systems. The subsequent 0.14 percent decline in the study area during the Late Classic period was smaller than the decline during the Early Classic period, and it could have been due either to an increase in death rates over birth rates or to emigration/population movement. The latter process seems particularly applicable to the Granite Knob and Gila Butte canals, which witnessed relatively larger declines (0.41 and 0.30 percent, respectively).

The underlying reasons for the demographic declines in the Classic period were almost certainly linked to increase in periods of water scarcity as well as decrease of canal capacity in the four "tail-ender" study area canal systems (as described in Chapter 4). These factors would have resulted in greater uncertainty in crop success, possibly lower crop yields, and possible crop failures in some years. These conditions would have constituted "push" factors for people to leave those systems. If the population declines reflect either emigration or population movement, then where were people moving? I suggest that evidence from previous studies indicates that there were two primary destinations.

First, it appears that people were moving from the downstream systems to the upstream systems along the middle Gila River. Within the study area, the only canal system that appears to have been a recipient of the inferred population movement was the Granite Knob canal system during the Early Classic period. Farther upstream, the villages along the Casa Grande canal system expanded in number, size, and, by inference, population in the Classic period (Doelle 1995; Woodson and Rice 2002). A number of studies have documented the construction of new habitations during the Early Classic period in various areas along the Casa Grande canal system, both on the fringes of the Casa Grande village itself (e.g., Ambler 1961; Andresen 1985; Craig 2001; Darling 2009a, 2009b; Gladwin and Gladwin 1929; Rice et al. 2005) and in other locales upstream (e.g., Darling 2009c; Doyel 1974; Hart and Craig 2006; Sires 1983). The upstream canal systems with the higher river headings would have had fewer problems with water scarcity and crop failure. The population growth along the Casa Grande canal system and the concomitant rise in the sociopolitical prominence of its villages can be linked directly to its control of the highest heading on the middle Gila River and a large command area (Gregory 1994; Woodson 2010c). Although further demographic studies are needed for the left-bank Gila River canal systems, I suggest that this downstream-to-upstream population movement fully matches expectations for the situation along the middle Gila River at that time (Hunt and Ingram 2007).

Second, it is likely that some people from the middle Gila Valley (including in the study area) immigrated to the lower Salt Valley. Demographic studies have indicated that by the Classic period, the population in the lower Salt

Valley was significantly larger than in the middle Gila Valley (Cordell et al. 1994:121; Doelle 1995:218; Hill et al. 2004). This population imbalance is reflected generally in the changes in the number of sites with public architecture: during the pre-Classic period, there were 37 ballcourts at 28 sites in the lower Salt Valley, in comparison to 30 ballcourts in 19 settlements in the middle Gila Valley (Ravesloot et al. forthcoming; Wilcox and Sternberg 1983). During the Classic period, however, there were 52 platform mounds at 31 sites in the lower Salt Valley, compared to 14 platform mounds at 11 sites in the middle Gila Valley (Doelle et al. 1995:390). Also, population growth in the lower Salt Valley appears to have spiked in the Classic period, and that has been attributed partly to the arrival of immigrants (Abbott and Foster 2003; Wilcox et al. 1981:211). New arrivals were settling on the fringes of existing settlements, such as Pueblo Grande (Abbott and Foster 2003) and Mesa Grande (Howard 1987, 2006:227–230), and immigrants also may have helped to establish new settlements like Los Muertos (Haury 1945; Wilcox et al. 1981) and sites along the Lehi canal system (Howard 1987). Los Muertos must have been a particularly attractive locale, because it was close to the middle Gila River (only 15 km from Snaketown), located along a well-established travel route between the Gila and Salt Valleys, and situated in a zone of abundant agricultural land. These data, in conjunction with the population declines indicated by the current study, indicate that it is highly probable that people left the middle Gila Valley villages and moved to the lower Salt Valley villages.

These inferred population movements are consistent with behavior documented among the historical-period Gila River Pima (see Rea 1997; Russell 1975; Southworth 1919). When water shortages in the Gila River had a detrimental effect on subsistence farming, Akimel O'odham irrigators moved to where conditions were better. That includes when groups moved from the Casa Blanca area to the Gila Crossing District in the 1870s to build a series of completely new canal systems. Also, groups moved from the Gila Valley to parts of the lower Salt Valley, like Mesa and the area of the current-day Salt River Pima–Maricopa Indian Community. This historical-period pattern of population movement and reorganization appears to have been practiced by the Hohokam, as well, as indicated by the current study.

An important question that is raised by this situation is "Why would people continue farming and living along the downstream systems, especially the Snaketown canal system, if the problem of water scarcity was so great in the Classic period?" Although that question cannot be fully answered here, I offer several possible explanations that are not mutually exclusive. First, the degree of water scarcity experienced by the Snaketown irrigators may not have been as significant as proposed here. For instance, the significant population decline may have been adequate to match the new (lower) carrying capacity of the system in the Classic period, such that irrigators could still grow enough food with the reduced water supply to support the remaining residents. Through the consolidation of the Snaketown canal with the upstream canals, there might have been enough water supplied to irrigate sufficient field areas along the canal system. Also, through social, economic, or kinship ties with people in other areas, the Snaketown canal population may have been able to trade for, or otherwise acquire, food and other goods to buffer the shortfalls in any given year.

Second, there must have been strong pulls for some people to remain on their ancestral lands and continue farming their fields, which probably had been passed down through many generations. That might have been related to the kinds of behavioral patterns that seem contradictory in light of certain social and environmental conditions. For example, as posited by Hegmon et al. (2008), the Hohokam may have become enmeshed in a "rigidity trap" during the Classic period. In that scenario, during periods of social transformation, a "high degree of connectivity and the suppression of innovation prolong an increasingly rigid state, with the result that the eventual transformation is harsh" (Hegmon et al. 2008:313). These and other conditions within the settlement system suggest that the Gila Butte/Snaketown community was characterized by a more insular socioeconomic interaction sphere (see Abbott 2003). Since more people left all four of the study area canal systems in the Late Classic period, we might infer that water scarcity had become too problematic to sustain the populations living there. Yet it is clear that a smaller population remained along the systems until the end of the Hohokam occupation.

Finally, the demographic decline observed in the study area during the Classic period was consistent with the decline documented by Hill et al. (2004) throughout the Hohokam region and the rest of the southern Southwest. One difference is that the current study area does not include striking evidence that an influx of northern immigrants fled drought and social deterioration in the late 1200s, as was found by Hill et al. (2004) in valleys on the periphery of the Phoenix Basin (e.g., San Pedro and Safford Valleys and Tonto Basin). Hill et al. (2004:689) argued that in those areas, this demographic change led to a shift from a dispersed, extensive settlement/subsistence strategy to increased conflict, aggregation, and economic intensification. That shift led to diminished health and a transformation from population growth to decline. The ensuing, gradual population decline resulted in small, remnant groups who were unable to maintain viable communities. These small, terminal populations were ultimately unable to continue identifiable Hohokam cultural traditions and consequently disappeared from the archaeological record in southern Arizona.

In contrast, the subsistence base in the current study area already was highly intensified in the Early Classic period, as the canal-irrigation systems had reached their greatest extents. Also, the settlement pattern does not reflect a period of coalescence. Instead, the previous Sedentary period witnessed the largest villages and the most-nucleated settlement pattern, which shifted to a more-dispersed pattern of mostly smaller settlements in the Early Classic period. The only area along the middle Gila River that did witness coalescence was upstream from the study area, along the Casa Grande canal system, which held sway over the first canal heading on the river and the largest command area of the 13 Gila River canal systems (Woodson 2010b, 2010c). I would argue that the downstream-to-upstream population movement observed in the study area also operated throughout the middle Gila Valley and provided a significant influx of people to the Casa Grande canal system (see Woodson and Rice 2002). In addition, it is likely that groups of people living outside the valley may have settled along the upstream Gila River systems as the outlying Hohokam populations in the "periphery" zones contracted back to the Phoenix Basin.

Settlement Patterns and Field-Labor Organization

The aspects of Stone's (1996) model of agrarian settlement regarding pulls toward settlement dispersion and agglomeration are pertinent to the analysis of the settlement pattern and its relationship with agriculture. One way to examine that is to focus on the changes in settlement pattern in comparison to changes in land pressure between the Pioneer and Sedentary periods. Land pressure is characterized as the ratio of population to productive land. Since the study area encompasses all irrigated field areas and canals (as well as the non-irrigated dryland fields on the *bajada*) along this segment of the middle Gila River, land pressure can be characterized by the overall population density in the study area. First, there was clearly a significant growth of population in the early Pioneer period that may represent the migration of a sizable group of people into the middle Gila Valley. That migration, or population growth, was concurrent with the inception of irrigation, which was intensification. Second, there was significant population growth through the late Pioneer and early Colonial periods, which I argue also was related (at least in part) to immigration. There was growth to a lesser degree in the late Colonial and Sedentary periods, but that appears to have been related to natural growth rates. After the canal systems were expanded to their maximum extent in the early Colonial period, I would argue, the population density (and, hence, land pressure) along the canal systems rose from then until the Sedentary period, but without further intensification (unless they changed frequency of cropping, which cannot be seen archaeologically). An exception would be the addition of the dryland fields on the *bajada* of the Santan Mountains in the Colonial period, which can be construed as a different type of intensification. Third, by the Early Classic period, the population size and density within the study area dropped dramatically as a result of demographic decline (which, as described above, was a result of population movement upstream, emigration out of the valley, or population loss due to a decrease in fertility rates—or a combination of all three). A further, but slighter, decline in the Late Classic period suggests that people were still leaving the study area.

As far as settlement response, the population was mainly aggregated in villages during the Pioneer to Sedentary periods, indicating that there was a significant attraction/pull toward living in nucleated settlements. That suggests that the pull of agglomeration largely outweighed the pull toward settlement dispersal. I suggest that the settlement pattern partly followed the expectations for settlement dispersal, with the use of satellite settlements in the Pioneer to Sedentary periods (some of which developed into permanent habitations). Nearly all these satellites were established as seasonal settlements beyond a 3–4-km zone of distance from the earlier, primary settlements—a pattern that conforms to the expectations of the proximity-access principle (Chisholm 1979) and optimality for agricultural travel.

With the onset of the Early Classic period, the entire population in the study area was living in dispersed settlements. That change occurred during a major drop in population size and density within the study area that probably resulted from emigration or population movement. The only exception was that the population size increased along the Granite Knob canal, which was the farthest-upstream location in the study area. I would suggest that the population dispersal conforms to the expectations of Stone's (1996) model for an already intensified agricultural situation. The important change was the removal of the pull toward agglomeration, or population aggregation—the Hohokam in the study area clearly decided that living in nucleated settlements was not necessary anymore.

The depopulation of the Sedentary period nucleated villages and the change to a dispersed settlement pattern clearly was related to the sociopolitical and ideological changes that occurred over the Sedentary to Classic period transition. Many ballcourt villages throughout the Hohokam region were abandoned or largely depopulated, and the regional network represented by the ballcourt villages collapsed as populations contracted to the Phoenix Basin (see Abbott 2009; Abbott et al. 2007; Bayman 2001; Crown 1991; Doyel 1980, 1991b, 2000, 2007; Wilcox and Sternberg 1983). An important shift in Hohokam integrative ideology also occurred with the change from ballcourts and large, open plazas to walled compounds and elevated platform mounds. Hohokam "ritual became more centralized, with performers and observers of communal events becoming a more exclusive subset of the population" (Fish and Fish 2000b:162). At the same time, that change was coupled with continuity in the community pattern of territorial organization (Fish and Fish 2000a, 2000b). At the level of the residence, though, the pull toward coalescence around focal villages appears to have been lessened in the middle Gila Valley. As described previously, that transformation process took place during a period of increased water scarcity and significant population shifts within the study area.

In sum, the settlement system in the study area appears to have responded through time, in part, to adjust to land pressure and the needs for field-labor organization. The changes in the Classic period, though, could not have occurred without the important transformation in Hohokam society described above. The patterns appear to conform to the expectations of Stone's (1996) hypothesis that increases in land pressure will lead to settlement dispersal. At the same time, the settlements had moved closer together (settlement gravity) in the Classic period, which would have facilitated the pooling of labor forces for working on other farmers' fields. These relationships between settlements and the fields are not directly relevant to the organization of irrigation management for the canal system. However, I argue that the settlement trajectories that emerged as a result of those relationships would have had an indirect effect on irrigation organization. The concurrent settlement dispersal and settlement gravity in the Classic period would have facilitated tasks managed by the irrigation organization, such as operating and maintaining canals. The dispersed Classic period settlement system may have had something to do with being close to canals as well as to fields. In this way, the aspects of labor organization for fields and for canals would have been mutually reinforced by the settlement change. The irrigation organizations are discussed in the next section.

Hohokam Irrigation Organizations in the Middle Gila Valley

But what do these signatures of settlement organization tell us about the irrigation organizations? An irrigation organization is an institution that manages and assigns the roles and tasks associated with the construction and operation of a canal-irrigation system (Mabry 1996). The primary thrust of this study has been to examine settlement organization and the canal systems, together, in terms of their implications for the social organization of irrigation management. Three aspects of irrigation organizations are examined here. First, I discuss what the patterns observed in the settlements and canals tell us about the internal structures of the irrigation organizations. Next, I consider the external relationships of the irrigation organizations with the political institutions. Were the organizations that were responsible for irrigation management different from the political institutions, or were they the same? What type of irrigation organization managed each canal system? Lastly, I examine the interrelationships among irrigation organizations on separate canal systems, by considering the circumstances for cooperation between farmers in neighboring systems.

Internal Structures of the Irrigation Organizations

Elements of the internal structures of irrigation organizations addressed here include: (1) whether the organization had a unified (i.e., centralized) administrative authority, (2) whether the population was adequate to meet the labor requirements for canal maintenance, (3) task-group organization, and (4) the dynamics of inter-village relationships along multi-village canal systems and their effects on irrigation management. The framework for interpreting internal structure is provided by concepts about the relationships between settlement distribution along the canal systems, settlement decisions, and canal-labor organization (see Howard 2006; Hunt et al. 2005; Uphoff 1986). The discussion integrates information on the trends in settlement organization reviewed above and in previous chapters.

Centralized Administration

Cross-cultural studies of irrigation organizations have indicated that a canal system with a command area larger than 100 ha has a very high probability of having a unified, or concentrated, administrative authority structure (Hunt 1988a:347; see also Tang 1992; Uphoff 1986). These studies have also suggested that a system 1,000 ha or greater in size cannot be acephalous (see Hunt et al. 2005:449). From the beginning of the occupation sequence in the study area, during the Pioneer period, the command areas of the four canal systems were between 100 and 421 ha. Even at the incipient stages, these canal systems probably had unified administrative structures. By the early Colonial period, the command areas of the Snaketown and Santan canal systems had reached 1,492 and 1,193 ha, respectively. At those levels, the systems almost certainly had unified administrations. Their command areas remained at those levels through the Classic period, except that the significant reduction in capacity of the Snaketown canal in the Classic period probably prevented irrigation of the full area. The Gila Butte canal system reached 680 ha in the Classic period, which is still a sizable command area. The Granite Knob canal system only reached 133 ha (it could have been larger, but this could not be ascertained, because the river has scoured away the terrace with the former field areas). The latter two systems also probably had unified administrations, and they definitely did after they were consolidated with the other systems, by the Classic period.

Another element of the canal systems that may indicate unified administrative structure is the number of organizational levels (Howard 2006; Uphoff 1986). As discussed in Chapter 2, canal systems generally range between one level (simple system) and four levels (often at a state-level system) (see Figure 2.1). Generally, the complexity of irrigation management increases directly with the number of physical levels in a canal system. Whereas a one-level system might be able to function without a unified administration, it is likely that a two-level system (or greater) will require a controlling body (i.e., an irrigation organization) above the level of farmers, to organize water allocation, maintenance scheduling, and other tasks. By these criteria, the Snaketown canal system required a centralized administration by the late Pioneer period, and the Santan and Gila Butte canal systems required such administrative structures by the early Colonial period. Destruction of most of the Granite Knob canal system prevented determination of whether it rose above a one-level system. The current, incomplete data suggest that it might not have required centralized administration until it was consolidated with the Santan canal, in the Sedentary period.

Canal-Maintenance Imperatives

As part of this analysis, it is necessary to examine whether the population sizes were adequate to meet the canal-maintenance imperatives. Table 7.3 provides a comparison of population estimates for the four canal systems, using three methods: the first (population estimate) was based on habitation-site area (discussed in Chapters 5 and 6), the second (maintenance requirement) was based on the labor requirements for cleaning the main canal on an annual basis (discussed in Chapter 4), and the third (maintenance population) was an estimate of the population along each canal, calculated by multiplying the maintenance requirement value by 5 (see Chapter 4). As noted in Chapter 4, this 1:5 ratio was based on the assumption that a household included five persons, and one adult male from each household worked on canal-maintenance tasks. Minimum and maximum estimates are given for both methods: the site-area-based method assumes site densities of 10 persons per hectare (minimum) and 20 persons per hectare (maximum); the labor-based method assumes that the canal was cleaned in 2 weeks when it was one-quarter full of sediment (minimum) or in 1 week when it was three-quarters full of sediment (maximum). For cases in which the minimum population size, as determined by site area, was not as large as the estimated population size based on the minimum maintenance requirement (the value multiplied by 5), the numbers are underlined in the table.

In no case was there a lack of sufficient population to meet the minimum labor requirements for cleaning the main canals. That is true under the assumption that any and all of the people were available to help with the cleaning, regardless of gender or the proportion of a household required to meet the labor requirements. On the other hand, if we assume that the ratio of workers to total population was 1:5, then there were six cases in which the minimum population size (based on site area) was less than the estimated population size based on the minimum maintenance requirement (multiplied by 5). This means that cleaning the canal in those cases would have required more than one person from each household, assuming that each household included five people. That is, the ratio of workers to population would have been less than 1:5 if that population size accomplished the cleaning.

Two of the six cases were for the Snaketown Pioneer Canal, but that discrepancy was likely a result of uncertain measurements of the Pioneer Canal (see Chapter 4). In the other four cases, the populations would have had trouble cleaning the canal in a reasonable time if an average of one person out of a household of five persons worked. However, the workers in those cases feasibly could have enlisted help from neighboring canal systems to help with the task. In the case of the Gila Butte canal in the Classic period, that was nearly a certainty, since it had been consolidated with the Snaketown canal, which had more than enough people to spare the workers to help in cleaning the Gila Butte canal. To clean the Granite Knob canal in the Colonial period, the ratio of workers to population would have been 1:2 or 1:3.5, which seems unlikely and suggests either that they enlisted help from elsewhere or that the population estimate (based on site area) was too low. The adjacent Santan canal system had more than enough people to spare for the canal cleaning; so, the Granite Knob population could have enlisted their help to clean the canal in a reasonable time. An interesting question is what the Granite Knob irrigators offered in exchange for that labor (see the last section of this chapter).

In comparing the maximum population estimates based on site area and maintenance requirement (multiplied by 5), the maintenance-population estimate exceeded the site-area-population estimate in every case but the Snaketown canal in the Classic period. This indicates that the population sizes probably never were large enough to clean any of the main canals in 1 week when the canals were three-quarters full of sediment. That would have been true even if every person living along the canal was involved in the cleaning event. Even if the maximum maintenance-population estimate is calculated based on cleaning the canals in 2 weeks when the canals were three-quarters full (which would be one-half the maximum maintenance-population values in Table 7.3), the population sizes still were mostly insufficient to complete the job, except in seven cases (for the Granite Knob in the Early Classic period, the Santan canal in the Colonial and Sedentary periods, and the Snaketown canal in the Sedentary to Classic periods). I would suggest that this indicates that irrigators normally chose to clean the main canal before it was three-quarters full of sediment. Probably, that was because they did not

Table 7.3. Comparison of Population Estimates Based on Habitation-Site Area and Canal-Cleaning-Labor Requirements

Statistic, by Time Period	Canal System							
	Granite Knob		Santan		Gila Butte		Snaketown	
	Minimum	Maximum	Minimum	Maximum	Minimum	Maximum	Minimum	Maximum
Early Pioneer								
Population estimate							46	92
Maintenance requirements							45	424
Maintenance population							225	2,120
Late Pioneer								
Population estimate	20	40	198	396	138	276	269	538
Maintenance requirements	?	?	?	?	17	158	58	555
Maintenance population	?	?	?	?	85	790	290	2,775
Early Colonial								
Population estimate	57	115	1,453	2,905	290	580	770	1,540
Maintenance requirements	26	253	102	988	40	391	98	941
Maintenance population	130	1,265	510	4,940	200	1,955	490	4,705
Late Colonial								
Population estimate	91	182	1,528	3,056	290	580	1,014	2,029
Maintenance requirements	26	253	102	988	40	391	98	941
Maintenance population	130	1,265	510	4,940	200	1,955	490	4,705
Sedentary								
Population estimate	198	396	1,779	3,559	355	710	1,538	3,076
Maintenance requirements	27	270	102	988	42	398	86	825
Maintenance population	135	1,350	510	4,940	210	1,990	420	4,045
Early Classic								
Population estimate	331	662	1,108	2,215	129	259	922	1,844
Maintenance requirements	24	257	95	922	42	388	43	422
Maintenance population	120	1,285	475	4,610	210	1,940	190	1,800
Late Classic								
Population estimate	179	358	989	1,977	83	165	767	1,534
Maintenance requirements	24	257	95	922	42	388	43	422
Maintenance population	120	1,285	475	4,610	210	1,940	190	1,800

Note: Population estimate is based on habitation-site area (minimum @ 10 persons/ha, maximum @ 20 persons/ha). The maintenance requirement is the number of people required for cleaning the main canal (minimum for 2 weeks at 1/4 full, maximum for 1 week at 3/4 full). The maintenance population is the value in the "Maintenance requirement" cell multiplied by 5. Underlined numbers indicate that the minimum population size (based on the habitation-site area) was smaller than the maintenance-population size.

want the canal to fill up and reduce capacity below a certain level. Also, the irrigators would have been inclined to clean it before it was that full so that they could actually complete the task in a reasonable time, with a work crew that included roughly one male from each household.

In Chapter 4, I discuss the distances between the canal headings and the closest habitation sites as an indicator of how well situated irrigators were to deal with damage to the heading (i.e., how quickly they could identify a problem and mobilize to fix it) (see Table 4.8). In each of the canal systems, the longest distance between the heading and the nearest habitation was during the incipient phase of each system. That would have reduced the efficiency of managing the heading. Shortly after the initial phase of use, the residents along each system improved their ability to manage the heading, by establishing a habitation site nearby. These new habitations were founded as camps (except in the Santan canal system, in which it may have been a hamlet) and were beyond a 3–4-km zone of distance from the founding settlements, which conforms to expectations of the proximity-access principle (Chisholm 1979). The sites thus would have represented satellites of the primary settlement along each canal system (Stone 1996). The habitations remained camps in the Snaketown and Gila Butte canal systems, but they developed quickly into village-level settlements along the Santan and Granite

Knob canal systems. Through the Classic period, each system maintained at least one habitation in close proximity to the heading. In that way, such settlements probably served as maintenance or "guard" stations that were well positioned to manage the canal headings. In each of the three downstream systems, those stations also were situated near the connection points with the next upstream systems. The positions of those settlements would have aided irrigators in the daily and seasonal management tasks at those critical junctures in the canal system.

Lastly, in Chapter 4, I describe the reductions in canal capacity of all four canal systems in the Classic period and suggested several reasons for those reductions. Although it seems most likely that the reductions were due to water scarcity (which resulted from decreases in the water supply and high water demand), it was suggested that they also could have been related to less available labor to clean the canals. Table 7.3 indicates that only the Gila Butte canal in the Classic period lacked sufficient population to meet the minimum labor requirements. And because the Gila Butte and Snaketown communities appear to have been consolidated by that time, it is plausible that the labor deficiency was made up by the extra population along the Snaketown canal system. This observation further supports the notion that the declines in canal capacity were related to a decrease in the water supply from the river.

Task-Group Organization

Uphoff (1986:59–60) described how the physical elements of an irrigation system (i.e., main, branch, distribution, and lateral canals and water-control features) constitute levels of system control or levels of operation (see Figure 2.1). These levels of operation correspond to certain task groups that must cooperate in operating each segment of the system. Thus, the physical structure of a canal system reflects the social organization of the groups living along it (or vice versa). The premise is that the labor requirements for canal irrigation, and the ways in which that labor was organized, structured social relationships into sets of spatial blocs with their own unique sets of concerns.

Howard (2006:26–31) defined Hohokam task groups in relation to system elements through a review of ethnographic case studies of irrigation communities that closely resemble those of the Hohokam. The most basic system element was the field, and the social unit associated with it was the household. The next level up was the distribution canal, and Howard (2006:27) referred to the set of fields watered by it as a command area. That should not be confused with the more general usage of "command area" as the total area of fields irrigated by a canal system. Command-area groups were associated with the fields along a distribution canal, and they probably represent the most basic organizational unit, which frequently had a legal charter and was responsible for the organization of labor for operation and maintenance activities along the distribution canal (Howard 2006:104–107). This organizational unit is analogous to the *tramo* in Oaxaca (Downing 1974), and Howard (2006:160–161) suggested that it could have been equivalent to a "district" for the Akimel O'odham (see Castetter and Bell 1942:160).

Branch canals are divisions of main canals that service multiple distribution canals; the farmers receiving water from it compose branch-canal task groups. These can be seen as amalgamations of command-area task groups. The main canal is the highest level of a canal system, and the main-canal task group includes all individuals receiving water from it. Howard (2006:107) found that these two system levels were important in the organizational structures of the irrigation communities in his ethnographic case studies. Water scheduling, allocation, cleaning, and maintenance had to be coordinated at these levels (see Hunt et al. 2005:445–448). In terms of the social units that accomplished these tasks, though, Howard found that the responsibility often was organized at the level of the command-area task group(s) or the village.

Apart from the physical structure of the canal system, Howard (2006:29–30, 110) identified the village as a major organizational node that could crosscut the canal-system elements. Howard (2006:29–30) found that "villages can be administrative nodes for either entire irrigation systems when only one village is associated with the irrigation community or portions of irrigation systems when multiple villages are present." The village often is responsible for water scheduling, water allocation, and local conflict resolution (Howard 2006:287–88). When multiple villages are present and spatially integrated into the irrigation system, they can form multiple administrative nodes and create distinct organizational levels along bounded portions of the main canal.

In the current study area, the distribution of habitation sites and population in relation to the levels of the canal system can be used to evaluate the organization of task groups. Although the data lack the detail to examine the association between fields and households, the analysis found significant correlations between the branch- and main-canal levels and their related social groups. In the Pioneer period, the population size was small, and all residents were living at the primary settlements along the canals. The canal systems were relatively small but large enough to require an irrigation organization. People were living the farthest away from the canals and fields of any time. The inferred political communities were coterminous with the canal systems; so, the clearest association of those social groups was as main-canal task groups. No major task-group divisions in this period are apparent, except that the people living at Olberg and Upper Santan, along the Santan canal, may represent two divisions. Also, several command-area groups could have been included in each of the irrigation organizations.

Significant changes occurred in the early Colonial to Sedentary periods. In the early Colonial period, the canal systems were built out and used to their maximum (or nearly maximum) extents. The Santan canal was connected with the Gila Butte canal in the Colonial period. In the Sedentary period, the Granite Knob canal was connected with the Santan canal, and the Gila Butte canal was extended to connect with the Snaketown canal. Significant population growth occurred, reaching a maximum in the Sedentary period. The population was unevenly distributed across the canal systems: the majority were living along the Santan canal system, followed by the Snaketown, Gila Butte, and Granite Knob canal systems.

As we have seen, the early Colonial to Sedentary period settlements along the Santan and Snaketown canals were organized as focal-village communities. Those communities were aligned with either the main-canal branches (in the Snaketown system) or the main-canal reaches (in the Santan system), and they corresponded to branch-canal (or main-canal-reach) task groups. The communities along the Gila Butte and Granite Knob systems were aligned with the main canals (and could be characterized as either focal-village or linear communities) and corresponded to main-canal task groups. With the linking of the Santan and Granite Knob canals in the Sedentary period, the Granite Knob settlements might be characterized as a focal-village community, in which case that community could be seen as a main-canal-reach task group. Some correlations are evident between habitation areas (GR-1157, Loci C and M) and specific distribution canals in Study Area 1; so, some or all of those residents probably constituted command-area task groups. No such correlations are apparent in Study Area 2, probably as a result of either the lower detail in canal-system documentation or the fact that all the permanent habitations were located above the Holocene terrace (where the canals are located). The residents in both study areas lived within easy walking distance from the distribution canals.

By the Classic period, the settlement organization became more dispersed along the consolidated Gila Butte/Snaketown and Granite Knob/Santan canal systems. There were more habitations that were smaller and closer together, spaced at relatively short intervals. The more closely spaced and evenly distributed population along the canals would have facilitated cooperative behavior and tasks among members of the irrigation organization. Significant population declines occurred along the downstream systems in the Early Classic period, but the population rose along the Granite Knob canal. In the Late Classic period, though, the population dropped in all parts of the study area.

Despite the settlement-pattern shift and demographic decline in the Classic period, the population remained distributed along the branch canals or main-canal reaches in roughly the same areas and proportions as they were during the Sedentary period. The settlements along both consolidated canal systems continued to be organized in a segmented pattern. The settlements along the Granite Knob/Santan system continued to be organized into focal-village communities. Along the Gila Butte/Snaketown system, only the south-branch community (with Maricopa Mound) can be characterized as a focal-village community; the other segmented communities did not include focal villages. Hence, the Classic period population appears to have maintained their organization into branch-canal (or main-canal-reach) task groups. Lastly, some correlations are still evident between habitation areas (GR-1157, Loci C and M) and specific distribution canals in Study Area 1; so, some or all of those residents probably constituted command-area task groups. No such correlations are apparent in Study Area 2.

As noted in Chapters 5 and 6, the pattern of community territories in both study areas from the Colonial to Classic periods reinforces the contention that the main-canal branches (or reaches) were key to the territorial extent of the communities. The fact that they remained in the same general territories suggests that the areas encompassed by the main and branch canals represented important organizational units for the Hohokam that endured through a major sociopolitical change during the Sedentary to Classic transition.

Inter-Village Relationships and Irrigation Management

The ethnographic literature suggests that along canal systems with multiple villages, there is often one village with a preeminent status that holds a more important position in regard to irrigation management. That village often will take the lead in decisions about water allocation and in matters of conflict resolution. Along the Orbigo River canal systems in Spain, for instance, the chief administrative officer for the irrigation junta (a type of irrigation organization) "is from the 'founder' town, village or monastery, but is not one of the general village offices (like mayor)" (Hunt et al. 2005:449). The founder village held the right of leadership of the junta, which "met independently of local government and reported to local authorities" (Hunt et al. 2005:449). Howard (2006:82), in reviewing ethnographic case studies from Oaxaca (Downing 1974; Lees 1973), observed that the "villages at the headgates owned and controlled the water source and held a position of power within the irrigation community." Lees (1973) was not clear whether these were the founding villages.

Generally speaking, the "dominance of upstream over downstream in irrigation matters is as close to a natural law in human affairs" as any (Hunt 1988b:201). These dynamics of "head-ender vs. tail-ender" irrigators along a canal can be a source of much stress and conflict in regard to irrigation management, particularly in water allocation. The ability of head-end farmers to appropriate more than their allotted share of water can lead to inequities in the water supply to tail-enders. Tail-enders often are required to apply significant pressure to restrain the activities of those closer to the head (Hunt 1988b:201). That type of friction can be mediated by the monitoring and enforcement of water-allocation practices, which normally is the responsibility of the chief administrative officer, who is appointed by the irrigation organization. In addition, some mechanism for conflict resolution typically is integrated into an irrigation organization. The implementation of water-allocation principles and conflict-resolution mechanisms is perhaps the most important task for irrigation organizations (Mabry 1996:15).

Yet other social, economic, and political factors affect water-use behaviors and can either help or hinder the equity of water allocation. For instance, Ostrom (1993) found that the bargaining power of tail-enders is greater if their labor is needed to maintain the system. Such need for joint cooperation and joint labor can be an equalizing factor in inter-village relationships and negotiations (Howard 2006:217). In other cases, the tail-to-head distribution of water can lead to increased equity (Mabry 1996). Rice (1998) argued that the largest Hohokam settlements were at the tail ends, and in multi-village systems, they used coercion or threat of force to secure their water allocations. Clearly, tensions can exist among territorial communities sharing a canal, but the use of coercive force as an organizing principle has not been documented in the ethnographic literature (Howard 2006:206). The tail-ender/head-ender agreements could have been based on an exchange of goods or labor from the downstream users to the upstream users in return for an equitable distribution of water. A similar situation may occur in tail-ender/head-ender negotiations among irrigation organizations along canal systems sharing the same water source (this issue is discussed in the final section of this chapter).

These kinds of relationships are difficult to decipher in the archaeological record, but it is feasible to address some aspects. In his examination of Hohokam settlement hierarchy along Canal Systems 1 and 2 in the lower Salt Valley, Howard (1990, 2006:184) observed that the sites with the largest (and sometimes the greatest number of) public facilities were situated closest to the canal heading. Moreover, he suggested that the largest of those headgate sites (Mesa Grande and Pueblo Grande) correlated to the largest irrigation systems. Howard (2006:209) interpreted them as the preeminent sites with the most power as integrative and administrative nodes in the two systems. However, that was not generally the case for the middle Gila River, where the largest village along a canal system often was not the headward village (e.g., Casa Grande, Chee Nee, Santan, Snaketown, and Casa Blanca).

In Chapters 5 and 6, I examine the study area settlement patterns to assess what they might tell us about sociopolitical dynamics among multiple focal-village communities along the canal systems. The objective was to identify preeminent settlements and also whether multiple communities could have been integrated into a larger, canal-wide polity. Factors considered included village size, number and size of public architecture, village proximity to the heading, and which was the founding village. First, the only cases in which the largest village was the headward village were the two single-village systems in the pre-Classic period (Granite Knob and Gila Butte). The issue of inter-village dynamics is moot in those cases. Second, for the multi-village Snaketown and Santan systems in the pre-Classic period, the headward villages were neither the largest nor the founding villages, nor were they the sites with the largest public architecture. That prevented a straightforward identification of the preeminent sites.

In Study Area 1, Snaketown was both the largest and the founding village, with impressive public monuments, marking it as the preeminent village in the pre-Classic period. The ceremonial and social dominance of Snaketown seems to be clear, and this probably translated into a leadership role for all three focal-village communities along the system. Although this assumed superiority does not necessarily prove the existence of a multi-village polity, it suggests that might have been the case. By extension, it is likely that the irrigation leaders at Snaketown would have had a significant influence on matters of irrigation management.

In the Classic period, the settlements along the consolidated Gila Butte/Snaketown system remained organized into three distinct communities, but only the south-branch community (with Maricopa Mound) represented a true focal-village community. Maricopa Mound was neither the largest nor the earliest village, but it was the preeminent village, by virtue of its having a platform mound. This represents an unusual situation for Hohokam core-area irrigation systems, because the other two communities did not have a focal village. The residents of the entire system probably looked to Maricopa Mound for ceremonial/ideological matters, and in that way, it may have been part of a canal-wide community. However, the location of the mound at the tail end of the system may have presented problems for overseeing matters of irrigation management (this is discussed in the following section).

As for Study Area 2, there are no clearly preeminent villages along the Santan system in the pre-Classic period. With the consolidation of the Granite Knob/Santan system during the Classic period, Upper Santan exhibited some traits that suggest it could have been the preeminent village. Yet it is unclear whether that translated into a leadership role for the entire canal system. In sum, there is no obvious basis that one village along the Santan canal system united all the communities into a canal-wide institution during any point in the sequence. It is therefore not obvious which village would have had the most influence on irrigation-management issues. The issue cannot be fully addressed using settlement-pattern data alone. Further testing of the hypothesis is required, with other data, such as ceramic-exchange patterns.

Table 7.4. Inferred Irrigation-Organization Types

Canal System	Period						
	Early Pioneer	Late Pioneer	Early Colonial	Late Colonial	Sedentary	Early Classic	Late Classic
Snaketown	municipality	municipality	irrigation community	irrigation community	irrigation community		
Gila Butte		municipality	municipality	municipality	municipality		
Santan		municipal-ity/ irrigation community?[a]	irrigation community	irrigation community	irrigation community		
Granite Knob		*municipality*[b]	municipality	municipality	*municipality*[c]		
Gila Butte–Snaketown (consolidated)						irrigation community	irrigation community
Granite Knob–Santan (consolidated)					*irrigation community*[c]	irrigation community	irrigation community

[a] The system was managed initially as a municipality. If the settlement pattern became segmented after the founding of Olberg, the system might have been characterized as an irrigation community.
[b] The Granite Knob canal might have been built as early as the late Pioneer period, but this is unclear.
[c] The Granite Knob community probably was consolidated with the Upper Santan community in the Sedentary period; so, it is listed here both individually and as a consolidated community.

External Relationships to the Political Institutions

A primary goal of this research is to consider how the authority of an irrigation organization related to the political-system authority. An irrigation organization and a political institution may correlate to each other, but they may be mutually exclusive in any given case. In other words, was the irrigation system managed by a single-purpose entity (irrigation alone), or was it managed by an organization that was responsible for multiple administrative tasks (irrigation as well as political matters)? The answers to this question have a direct bearing on interpreting of the type of irrigation organization that managed a system. Unfortunately, this is a difficult issue to assess for the Hohokam, because the decision-making loci within these organizational units are not clearly reflected in the archaeological record. The approach taken in this study is therefore a simplified one and extends from the analysis of settlement organization. As described in Chapter 2, two basic situations are posited to have occurred in the study area:

1. If there was only one village with public architecture along a canal system, then the settlement pattern was nonsegmented (and contiguous with the canal system). In such a case, it is more plausible that the authority for the political institution also had authority over the decisions and activities within the irrigation organization (i.e., a municipality).

2. If there were two or more villages with public architecture along a canal system, then each focal village and its associated community would have had its own political institution/structure. The settlement pattern was segmented, and the authority for managing the irrigation organization along the canal system was independent of those political structures. In such a case, the inferred irrigation organization would be analogous to an irrigation community. One caveat is that multiple focal-village communities feasibly could have been integrated into a canal-wide polity, in which case the irrigation organization might be analogous to a municipality.

Based on this rationale, Table 7.4 indicates the inferred irrigation-organization types for the four canal systems in the study area. During the Pioneer period, the settlement pattern was nonsegmented along the Snaketown, Santan, and Gila Butte canal systems. So, each inferred political community was coterminous with the canal system. The population was relatively small, the canals were relatively short, and the number of task groups was low enough that the village administration units for each system could have overseen irrigation management. Therefore, the signatures of the Pioneer period irrigation organizations fit best with the expectations for a municipality. The possible exception was the Santan system, in which the addition of a hamlet at Olberg may have led to a segmented settlement pattern and possibly the system's being managed as an irrigation community.

From the early Colonial to Sedentary periods, the settlements along the Santan and Snaketown canal systems were segmented into focal-village communities. These communities were aligned with the main-canal reaches or branch canals and were commensurate to the branch-canal task groups. Because the focal villages represent the political centers of those communities, it is plausible that at that level, the authority for the political structure was the same as the authority for the irrigation organization (branch canal or main-canal-reach task group). That is, the political community as supervised by the ballcourt-village administration (e.g., a council) possibly had multiple management functions at that level of the system. In this way, the observed political communities conformed to a tenet of the focal-village model that assumes that the modular and territorial nature of Hohokam communities could have facilitated the administrative requirement of irrigation (e.g., Crown 1987; Fish and Fish 1991, 2000b). The distances between ballcourt villages (5.6 km for the Snaketown system and 5.1 km for the Santan system) correlate well to the average 5.5-km interval between ballcourts in the Phoenix Basin (Fish and Fish 1991:163).

Above these main-canal reaches, or branch canals, the entire Snaketown and Santan canal systems would have fallen under the supervision of the irrigation organization in the Colonial and Sedentary periods. In multi-village canal systems, "a different (and probably special-purpose) organization has to exist" above the village level, to manage the system (Hunt 1988a:347). Each village would negotiate "its own economic self-interest while recognizing the need to unite as a cooperative unit to build, maintain and operate the irrigation system" (Howard 2006:109). As described previously, there is no clear evidence of a system-wide, multi-village polity that administered political matters along the Santan system. The canal system therefore was managed by an irrigation organization with an independent authority structure. Inasmuch as that is found to be true, an irrigation community is the best model for the Colonial to Sedentary periods. Snaketown exhibited clear traits of preeminence that could be cited in support of a canal-wide polity, but that is not certain, and further testing of the hypothesis is needed. If that was the case, the irrigation organization might best be characterized as a municipality. However, I would argue that organization of the three separate focal-village communities for the purposes of irrigation management would fall more in line with expectations for an irrigation community.

Along the Gila Butte and Granite Knob systems, the settlement pattern was nonsegmented and isomorphic with the canal system in the Colonial to Sedentary periods. Although the inferred Gila Butte community shared some settlement-organization traits of a focal-village community, it might also have been a linear community. Presumably, the canal system was managed by a municipality. The same applies to the Granite Knob system in the Colonial period. It had a short canal that could easily have been managed by the village administration; hence, its irrigation organization likely was a municipality. By the Sedentary period, though, the Granite Knob canal was joined with the Santan canal, and its settlements had developed qualities that suggest it was part of a focal-village community. If its irrigation-management structure became integrated into the Santan canal-system institution, then it probably became part of the irrigation community in charge of the Granite Knob/Santan canal system.

In the Classic period, the parameters of the inferred irrigation organizations changed along the consolidated Granite Knob/Santan and Gila Butte/Snaketown canal systems: irrigation-management-complexity levels peaked, partly as a result of consolidating the canal systems; the river had downcut and widened and was witnessing prolonged low-flow periods; and water scarcity became a real problem. The settlement organization shifted to a dispersed mode, and the population declined in the study area (with a steep decline in Study Area 1). Despite these changes, the Classic period populations remained organized in a segmented pattern that would maintain the main-canal reach and branch-canal task-group organizations.

Yet the political communities along these consolidated systems were different in the Classic period. Here we encounter arguments that the regular, 5-km spacing of Hohokam platform mounds in the Phoenix Basin is a significant pattern that is related to the optimal distance for agricultural travel and the length of canal that could be maintained successfully by a single settlement (e.g., Crown 1987:154–155; Fish and Fish 1991:163; Gregory 1991; Gregory and Nials 1985; see Chisholm 1979). When this pattern in spacing is considered with the assumption that platform-mound sites occupied a seat of preeminence atop the settlement hierarchy, proponents have suggested that the mound sites played key roles in the organization and administration of labor for the canal systems. The platform mounds also were seen as loci of ceremonial and political authority, and that leads to the implication that an irrigation organization may be tied to other management institutions (e.g., ceremonial or political) (see Elson and Abbott 2000; Hunt et al. 2005:450), which is a corollary of the focal-village model.

On the one hand, the Classic period settlements along the Granite Knob/Santan canal system continued to be organized into focal-village communities centered on the Upper Santan and Lower Santan platform-mound sites. The communities were associated with the major main-canal reaches. The mound-spacing pattern meets the expectations of the 5-km-spacing model, suggesting that the leaders at the Upper Santan and Lower Santan mounds might have been more involved with irrigation management. Similar to the Sedentary period, when these central sites were ballcourt villages, the platform-mound authority structure probably served as the authority for the main-canal-reach task group. In this way, the mound-village authority likely had multiple management functions at that level of the system. There was no obvious preeminent settlement in the Classic period and no clear evidence of a system-wide, multi-village polity that would have administered political matters along the canal system. An irrigation community thus seems to be the best model for the irrigation organization of the entire Granite Knob/Santan system, for the same reasons as noted above for the Santan system in the Colonial to Sedentary periods.

On the other hand, although the settlements along the Gila Butte/Snaketown community were organized into three distinct communities, only the south-branch community (with Maricopa Mound) represented a "true" focal-village community. Maricopa Mound was the only platform mound along the system, and its placement does not conform to expectations of the model—it is situated roughly 16 km from the heading at Diversion Point 1, nearly 26 km away from the Diversion Point 2 heading, and 22 km from the nearest mound at Lower Santan. This situation suggests that something unusual was going on, in terms of irrigation management. Maricopa Mound may have served as the ceremonial center for the entire canal system, and it feasibly could have served to integrate a canal-wide community. However, if the mound leaders were overseeing irrigation matters, then it is confusing as to why the presumed symbol of Classic period Hohokam authority—the platform mound—was located at the tail end of a 16-km-long system during that time of environmental and agricultural stress. That would have been problematic for overseeing irrigation management for the entire canal system. The residents at the GR-1175 village would have been situated in the best position for dealing with irrigation management at the Diversion Point 1 heading and at the linkage points with the Gila Butte canal system, but the site did not have a platform mound. From a practical perspective, and keeping in mind the tenets of the 5-km-spacing model, the observed pattern in Study Area 1 suggests that the leaders of Maricopa Mound probably supervised irrigation management for the south-branch canal only. The other branches would have continued to be supervised by the residents of those branch-canal communities.

So, the Classic period irrigation organization probably remained a separate administrative authority over irrigation matters. As in previous time periods, the most plausible form of that organization would be an irrigation community rather than a municipality. If both the Santan and Snaketown systems were managed by irrigation communities, this further implies that the mound leaders did not necessarily have direct control over the means of agricultural production at the level of the canal system. This is particularly relevant because the platform-mound villages were not the headward villages that would have had direct control over the canal intakes. However, the mound leaders would have had more direct access to production at the branch-canal/main-canal-reach levels. This would be significant if platform mounds were initiated by the influence of effective leaders, or aggressive "aggrandizers," who used their accumulated wealth, influence, and probably religious authority to consolidate sociopolitical power (e.g., Doyel 2007; Earle et al. forthcoming). These leaders probably attained their positions by demonstrating effective skills of negotiation, alliance formation, and ideological manipulation that benefited the farmers along the canal system. They probably financed their positions through control over agricultural surpluses and an exclusive connection with ancestor spirits (Abbott 2000:209). Although the platform-mound leaders may not have had authority over entire irrigation communities, the last section of this chapter posits that the leaders possibly *did* have a role that was significant for inter-canal-system relations.

Interrelationships among Irrigation Organizations

The patterns in the study area provided some indications as to the nature of external relationships between the irrigation organizations for the canal systems and their neighboring canal systems. Howard (2006:214) observed that this level of organization "focuses on larger scale relationships, often relationships of power, between higher level organizations." These interrelationships might involve formal negotiations or larger-scale alliances of irrigation communities (Howard 2006:212). The decision to cooperate on a level external to the irrigation organization is directly related to the benefit of engaging in such a relationship. These benefits fall into three general categories: construction (and probably maintenance) of infrastructure, a higher level of conflict management, and communal resource management (Howard 2006:219). The data examined in this study are not amenable to the topic of conflict management, but they are suitable to address the other two categories.

As described earlier in this chapter, the number of people living along the canal systems would have been sufficient for canal maintenance activities. The only exceptions were for the Pioneer period Snaketown canal (but this probably was an artifact of insufficient data) and for the Gila Butte canal in the Classic period (but by then, it was consolidated with the Snaketown canal, where a surplus workforce could have supplied the additional labor). The analysis suggests that generally, there was no need for interaction between irrigators in these systems for the purpose of acquiring additional laborers for maintenance. Of course, there may have been unusual occasions, such as heavy damage caused by very-high-magnitude floods, when a larger labor force was required than in the typical instances calculated above.

Based on the findings of this study, the only factor that probably would have necessitated interaction between canal systems was maintaining an adequate water supply. Addressing this would be related to Howard's (2006) category of communal resource management. In the pre-Classic period, the four canal systems in the study area generally operated independently of each other. Specifically, this was the case for the Snaketown canal system between the early Pioneer and late Colonial periods, the Santan and Gila Butte systems in the Pioneer period, and the Granite Knob system in the Colonial period. The systems were not physically connected to other canal systems. The data presented in Chapter 3 suggests that although streamflow conditions in the late Pioneer period may have been undesirable for irrigation, the period from A.D. 800 to 1000 was characterized by consistently above-average river flow (Ravesloot et al. forthcoming, based on Graybill et al. 2006). Except in times of water scarcity, then, irrigators along each system would not have had reason to be concerned about irrigators in other systems (see Crown 1987:157). However, the four study area systems were "tail-ender" canal systems (numbered 7, 8, 10, and 11 in the sequence of heading position along the river); so, they were near the end of the order of systems that were diverting irrigation water from the river (Woodson 2010b). If there were times when these systems experienced water shortages, there feasibly could have been interactions with upstream systems, to negotiate for water allocation and scheduling.

In Chapter 4, I describe in detail how the streambed alterations and discharge changes that occurred along the Gila River during the Sedentary to Classic period transition and the context in which they occurred led to an increase in periods of water scarcity. The combination of a series of prolonged low-flow periods during the Early Classic period (A.D. 1160–1280) on the heels of a downcutting and widening event (between A.D. 1020 and 1160) would have presented a significant challenge for irrigators to maintain a reliable water supply in the canal systems. The detrimental conditions from the downcutting event would have lasted between 30 and 100 years. This may have required irrigators to move some of the canal intakes farther upstream, which could have infringed on the territory of upstream systems and necessitated agreements with those irrigators (see Hunt et al. 2005:449).

At the same time as these stream-channel and streamflow changes during the Late Sedentary and Early Classic periods, demand for irrigation water reached its highest level. All 13 of the middle Gila River systems were in operation by the Sedentary period (A.D. 950–1150), bringing the total length of canals in use and the total command area to the highest levels (Woodson 2010b). The total command area of these 13 systems is estimated to have been between 12,781 and 19,531 ha (see Chapter 3). All 13 systems remained in use during the Classic period. With demand at an all-time high and the onset of below-average-flow periods, the position of a canal heading on the river became very important to maintaining a sufficient water supply in the Classic period. The tail-ender positions of the study area canal systems would have increased the chances of water scarcity, especially during low seasonal flows (see Hunt and Ingram 2007). The capacity of the Snaketown canal was reduced during the Classic period, to the degree that it probably was insufficient to irrigate its inferred 1,492-ha command area, even with the additional water supplied by the Gila Butte canal. The heading at Diversion Point 1 possibly was abandoned in the Late Classic period. The capacity of the three main canals in Study Area 2 also diminished, but they probably were still adequate to irrigate their field areas.

These conditions support Howard's (2006) notion that water scarcity was a key factor in the sociopolitical changes of the Classic period Hohokam, and scarcity especially would have been an issue for the irrigation organizations. In Chapter 4, I discuss the range of options available to irrigators to cope with scarcity (increase water supply, place limits on demand, practice individual emigration, and shift allocation principles toward water monopolization) and the evidence of whether irrigators in the study area exercised those options. This study indicates that no new canal systems were built in the Classic period. Also, many people were moving away from the study area canal systems, most likely to areas with more-reliable water supplies, such as farther upstream along the Gila River or to the lower Salt Valley (see Wilcox et al. 1981; Woodson and Rice 2002). As noted earlier in this chapter, the same patterns have been documented among historical-period Pima irrigators who moved elsewhere when water shortages had a detrimental effect on farming (see Rea 1997; Russell 1975; Southworth 1919).

The most significant response by irrigators in the study area was that the downstream systems consolidated their main canals with the next upstream systems, to increase the water supply (see Ravesloot et al. forthcoming). Although the Santan system was connected with the Gila Butte system in the Colonial period, it was in the Sedentary period that links were made between the Granite Knob and Santan canals and between the Gila Butte and Snaketown canals. The importance of external interactions between the irrigation organizations in the Gila Butte and Santan systems was evident in the Colonial period. By the Sedentary period, external interactions must have existed between the Snaketown and Gila Butte canal systems and between the Granite Knob and Santan canal systems. These interactions became more crucial in the Early Classic period. The members of the downstream irrigation organizations had a clear motivation for cooperation in building an agreement with the upstream irrigation organizations for a supplemental water supply.

If so, what form of agreement would best describe these intersystem arrangements? Would there have been a kind of communal charter of authority for them (see Hunt et al. 2005)? Hunt et al. (2005:451) found no ethnographic basis for positing an intersystem or pan-valley cooperative institution for irrigation management in the lower Salt Valley, since such institutions have rarely occurred, even in the context of state societies. This includes cases documented in the Oaxaca Valley in Mexico (Lees 1973:109–110) and the Orbigo River in Spain (Guillet 1998). Lees (1973:110) concluded that "the sharing of a single water source does not inevitably lead to cooperation and the formation of supracommunity control systems, nor need such supracommunity systems of integration be linked directly to shared water resources." Hunt et al. (2005:449) observed that the 16 Orbigo systems "could operate independently of the others without the need for coordination." Any conflicts between systems were resolved either through state law and courts or through locally negotiated agreements. Bolin (1993) showed that in the Vilcanota Valley of highland Peru, irrigation organizations tend to remain autonomous, even where the state has decreed that irrigators must establish commissions at the level of an irrigation district.

Above, this study argued that there was no clear evidence of a political institution that integrated the entire population along the Snaketown or Santan canal system, although there was a case to be explored for Snaketown during the Colonial and Sedentary periods. The irrigation communities along these systems likely had independent administrative authority over irrigation matters from the early Colonial through Late Classic periods. It seems even more unlikely that an intersystem or valley-wide political institution or irrigation organization existed or was required, even in the situation of water scarcity and environmental and social stress. A major reason for this position is that the distances between all the canal systems were too long to allow for effective communication and coordination on issues like water allocation. Also, as this study shows, farmers in downstream systems could choose to "vote with their feet" and move elsewhere to seek better farming conditions if conditions became dire. In addition, the Hohokam do not appear to have developed other, valley-wide sociopolitical institutions, nor did they develop a state (Crown 1991; Fish and Fish 2000a, 2000b).

However, the clear linking of the study area canals through consolidation indicates that some type of intersystem agreement must have existed, at least in regard to water allocation. There have been several ethnographic examples of adjacent canal systems' being linked together, including for the historical-period Pima in Arizona (Southworth 1914–1915, 1919), at Órbigo in Spain (Guillet 1998), and in Bali (Jha 2002). Unfortunately, these accounts have offered little information on the nature of the intersystem agreements that would have facilitated the sharing of surplus water. Such agreements probably would have been in the form of locally negotiated agreements. Possible motivations for the upstream irrigators to link with the downstream systems would be to provide the surplus water in exchange for labor, some type of goods, better drainage, or simple altruistic behavior. However, there has to be surplus water in order to provide tailwater from the upstream to the downstream systems. Ravesloot et al. (forthcoming) observed that the incentive for the Santan irrigators to welcome the cooperation of downstream populations was to provide a larger labor pool for maintaining the Olberg heading and intake. I would speculate that the notion of an irrigation-community consortium is a plausible form of intersystem cooperation among the canal systems in the Classic period. As described by Hunt et al. (2005:441; see also Hunt 1988a), these forms of intersystem arrangements develop when a "number of contiguous irrigation systems organized as irrigation communities combine in a consortium to manage some of their affairs." Hunt et al. (2005) deemed such an arrangement plausible for Canal System 2 in the lower Salt Valley, as well.

Yet the typical constituency of an irrigation community consists of the users of the system: farmers. Officers are elected or appointed from within the group, and administrative matters revolve around the canal system. Negotiations with other irrigation communities possibly are not as easily undertaken by such officers, especially when a crisis in the water supply occurs. Here, then, is a plausible role for the platform mound leaders in regard to the level of canal-system management as it relates to adjacent canal systems. For the lower Salt Valley canal systems, Howard (2006:289) argued that an increase in water shortages during the Sedentary period "created a need for communal resource management that initiated a trajectory of social and political change. . . . The need to retain water rights established new relationships between irrigation communities based on negotiation." He further suggested that "the introduction of a new ideology linked to platform mound ceremonialism established new social and political relationships. . . . This new social order may have focused on the needs of communal resource management" (Howard 2006:289). The mound leaders thus may have played an important role in negotiations over water allocation. Abbott (2000) reached a similar conclusion for Canal System 2 in the Late Classic period, when ceramic exchange patterns indicated an expansion in the interaction between canal systems. Abbott (2000:206–210) suggested that irrigation and environmental stresses played a crucial role in changing the social order, in which aggressive individuals (or "aggrandizers") that probably lived on the tops of platform mounds negotiated alliances outside the system to provide sufficient water and other resources. In conclusion, I would suggest that the leaders associated with the Maricopa, Upper Santan, and Lower Santan platform mounds may have played a role in negotiating for water allocation or establishing alliances in the Classic period. Such negotiations would fall into the category of irrigation-management tasks that do not require daily oversight or the involvement of farmers at lower levels of the irrigation organization. In the case of Maricopa Mound, even though it appears to have been physically removed from involvement with the regular irrigation-management tasks, the leaders could have participated in these higher-level interactions with the upstream Santan system.

As a last topic, some researchers have suggested that the four study area canal systems may have been operated as a single consolidated canal system in the Classic period (e.g., Ravesloot 2007; Ravesloot et al. forthcoming; see Mitalsky 1935). They have posited that the canal system had only one heading, at either Olberg Butte or Granite Knob. This study shows that such a system would have included over 70 km of main canals, up to 3,500 ha of irrigated fields, and a population of between 2,000 and 4,000 people. The linear distance from a heading at

Granite Knob to the tail end would have been 40 km. A canal system of that magnitude would approach the lower end of the size range estimated for Canal System 2 in the lower Salt Valley (see Howard 1993). This proposition takes the notion of "interrelationships among irrigation organizations" to the extreme in suggesting that the four separate irrigation organizations were melded into one. Based on this study, it is clear that the four systems were linked together, but I argue that they were not operated as a single system. The hydraulic reconstructions of main-canal capacities indicate that each canal heading continued to be used, even after consolidation (see Appendix A). Also, I suggest that the separate irrigation organizations established during the pre-Classic period would have been reticent to relinquish their authority over their canal systems. Ethnographic cases cited above indicate the tendency for such institutions to maintain internal authority, even in the face of conflict or need.

CHAPTER 8

Conclusions

This study has examined the social organization of Hohokam irrigation management through an analysis of canal systems and settlements in the middle Gila River Valley during the Pioneer to Classic periods (ca. A.D. 450–1450). Two principal research questions guided the study: (1) "How was irrigation management organized by the Hohokam in the middle Gila Valley?" and (2) given the significant changes in Hohokam society during the Sedentary to Classic transition, "Did the organization of irrigation management change in the Classic period?" The study focused on the settlements and canals associated with the Snaketown canal system (Study Area 1) and the Granite Knob, Santan, and Gila Butte canal systems (Study Area 2). Three aspects of Hohokam irrigation organizations were examined, including their internal structures, their external relationships with the local political systems, and the interrelationships among irrigation organizations. To achieve this, the study had three research goals: (1) to describe and analyze canal systems and measure their irrigation-management complexity, (2) to describe and analyze settlements and evaluate settlement organization, and (3) to examine settlement organization and canal systems, together, in terms of their implications for the social organization of Hohokam irrigation management. This chapter reviews the substantive contributions of the study and discusses their relevance to Hohokam archaeology, southwestern archaeology, and beyond.

Significance of the Research

Social anthropologists have found that an irrigation organization has its own management structure that is not necessarily isomorphic with the general political system (Hunt 1988a; Hunt and Hunt 1976; Hunt et al. 2005; Kelly 1983). That is, an irrigation organization and a political institution may correlate to each other, but they may be mutually exclusive in any given case. The study examined four aspects of the internal structure of irrigation organizations. First, the four study area canal systems probably had unified (centralized) administrative structures from the earliest stages, or certainly by the early Colonial period. Second, the estimated population sizes along the canal systems were adequate to meet the minimum labor requirements for maintenance as represented by cleaning of the main canals. Third, a significant pattern in task-group organization was found at the branch-canal and main-canal levels of the canal systems. These represented important organizational units for the Hohokam that endured through a major sociopolitical change during the Sedentary to Classic transition. Fourth, as for the multi-village canal systems, there was no obvious preeminent village along the Santan system that could have had the most influence on irrigation-management issues. Along the Snaketown system, Snaketown appears to have been the preeminent village in the pre-Classic period and likely had a significant influence on matters of irrigation management. Maricopa Mound was preeminent in the Classic period and also could have been influential, but its unusual position at the tail end of a long canal system would have limited its involvement in irrigation management.

Regarding external relationships between the irrigation organizations and the political structures, this study concludes that the authority for the organizations responsible for managing the canal systems was not always the same as the authority for the political institutions that governed the people living along the systems. During the incipient phases of Hohokam occupation in the Pioneer period, the signatures of the irrigation organizations fit best with the expectations for a municipality. That is, the authority for the irrigation organizations probably was the same as the political authority. As an example, in a municipality, the village administration (e.g., a council) for the primary village along each canal system would oversee both political matters and irrigation-management issues (see Hunt et al. 2005:442).

The inferred irrigation organizations for the Gila Butte system in the Colonial to Sedentary periods and the Granite Knob system in the Colonial period continued to be consistent with municipalities. However, the patterns for the Snaketown and Santan canal systems in the Colonial to Sedentary periods (and probably the Granite Knob system in the Sedentary period) fit best with the model of irrigation communities. That is, the authorities for the organizations responsible for managing the canal systems were distinct from the authorities for the political institutions that governed the people living along the systems. During that time, the focal-village-community territories along the Snaketown and Santan canal systems corresponded to the parts of the canal system that were managed by the main- or branch-canal task groups. I argued that the political institutions represented by the focal-village communities may have managed these segments of the irrigation system. That is, the community organization as supervised through the ballcourt-village administration (e.g., a council) possibly had multiple management functions at this level of the canal system.

It would appear that by the Classic period, the consolidation of the canal systems was accompanied by the consolidation of the political communities. The settlements along the Granite Knob/Santan canal system continued to be organized into focal-village communities centered on the Upper Santan and Lower Santan platform-mound sites. In contrast, the settlements in the Gila Butte/Snaketown system were organized into three distinct communities, and only the south-branch community (with Maricopa Mound) represented a "true" focal-village community. For both systems, though, the irrigation-community model seems the best for characterizing the irrigation organizations; they were single-purpose management entities.

A significant implication of the canal systems' being managed by irrigation communities is that the political leaders at ballcourt and platform-mound villages did not necessarily have direct control over the means of agricultural production at the level of the canal system. Individuals and families probably owned and maintained the fields along the systems, based on patterns observed in ethnographic accounts of irrigation-farming societies (see Netting 1993). Yet some researchers (e.g., Doyel 2007; Earle et al. forthcoming) have argued that irrigated agricultural land represents the kind of concentrated, highly productive resource that would have been ideal for Hohokam elites seeking to control economic sources of political power (see Earle 1987:294, 1997:7, 12–13; Yoffee 1993:70). If so, then aspiring elites seeking to control irrigated land or produce as an economic source of power probably had to achieve that through means other than direct control. Doyel (2007:84, 88; also Earle et al. forthcoming) suggested that it was not the chiefs' management of irrigation but rather control over agricultural surpluses that financed emerging chiefdoms. That control may have been asserted by owning, or laying claim to, the best agricultural land or by the demands for "rent" or tribute. The notion of Hohokam "chiefdoms" is still being debated among researchers. However, it is plausible that leaders who achieved higher social and political status could have gained greater access to the sources of power, wealth, and labor that resulted in control of surpluses from the irrigation systems.

The pathway to the control of surpluses may have been more localized than the level of the canal system. I have suggested that during the Colonial through Classic periods, the ballcourt-village leaders within the focal-village communities may have managed both political and irrigation matters at the level of the branch canals or main-canal reaches. That might have provided a position through which the leaders could have asserted some control over surpluses. However, it is doubtful that they would have had control over entire canal systems, which would have placed limits on the accumulation of surpluses. On the other hand, the ballcourt-village leaders within the possible municipalities (i.e., Granite Knob in the Colonial period and possibly Gila Butte in the Colonial and Sedentary periods) might have been able to exert a level of control over surpluses, by virtue of their likely involvement in co-managing both political and irrigation matters. However, it is unclear whether these municipalities were long-lived, and in the case of Granite Knob, the command area probably was not large enough to generate surpluses.

A major finding of this study is that problems arising from water scarcity in the Late Sedentary and Early Classic periods forced a response by Hohokam populations. The responses are reflected in both the settlement patterns and the canal systems, including a decrease in main-canal capacities and the lack of new canal-system construction in the Classic period. Another key response was the movement of people away from downstream systems, as indicated by steep population declines. Segments of these downstream populations apparently moved to better-watered locales, either farther upstream along the Gila River or along the lower Salt River. An important adaptation to scarcity was to increase the water supply in downstream canals through the consolidation of canals, which, I argue, led to the need for external interactions between the irrigation organizations in adjacent canal systems. These interrelationships may have manifested in agreements or alliances for cooperation in water allocation, and possibly there was cause for labor exchange in critical times. The platform-mound leaders could have played important roles in water-allocation negotiations among adjacent canal systems—a situation that became more critical with the rise in water-scarcity problems. It is unclear whether these relationships were formal or informal and whether an actual institution was established to manage the intersystem relationships. Possibly, the inter-canal relationships were characterized as consortia of irrigation communities (see Hunt et al. 2005:441, 451). I would suggest that similar consortia may have been established during these periods in other groups of interconnected canal systems along the middle Gila River, such as the Casa Blanca and Sweetwater systems and the Grewe–Casa Grande and Blackwater systems (see Figure 1.2).

This study does not provide sufficient information to fully address the question of whether an arrangement like a consortium (or a larger type of management institution) was created at a valley-wide level, integrating all 13 middle Gila Valley canal systems, during these periods. Hunt et al. (2005:451) indicated that institutions at a valley level are rare, even in the context of a state, but that consortia of communally organized canal systems do occur and are effective. Although I suggest that consortia of communal irrigation organizations probably existed among adjacent, interconnected canal systems, I would speculate that a consortium or larger institution for the entire middle Gila Valley did not develop. A major reason for this position is that the distances between all the canal systems were too long to allow effective communication and coordination on issues like water allocation. In addition, the Hohokam do not appear to have developed other valley-wide sociopolitical institutions, nor did they develop a state (Crown 1991; Fish and Fish 2000a, 2000b).

Implications for Hohokam Archaeology

The results of this study have significant implications for Hohokam archaeology. First, this research has considerably increased our understanding of the four study area canal systems, including their layout, size (command area), capacity, and sequence of development; the timing of their consolidation; the labor requirements for cleaning the main canals; and their levels of irrigation-management complexity. Second, a dramatic change in settlement pattern and demography between the Sedentary and Classic periods has been clearly documented. This was exhibited by a shift to a more-dispersed pattern with smaller settlements, an overall demographic decline, and population movement from downstream to upstream locales. Despite these changes, the population remained distributed along the branch canals or main-canal reaches in roughly the same areas and proportions as they were during the Sedentary period. This suggests that the areas encompassed by the branch canals and main-canal reaches represented important organizational units for the Hohokam that endured through a major sociopolitical change during the Sedentary to Classic transition.

Third, the study traced settlement-pattern trends that were important factors in the organization of agricultural labor and in the development of the political organization in the study area. Because the subjects of the study were subsistence farmers, it is no surprise that these trends were consistent with expectations for a population that placed importance on both canal management (i.e., canal operation and maintenance) and agricultural-field management (i.e., proximity for field access). Yet the settlement trajectories that emerged as a result of the relationships between settlements and fields had indirect effects on irrigation organization. In this way, the aspects of labor organization for fields and canals would have been mutually reinforced by the settlement change.

Fourth, the study traced the formation and development of focal-village communities during the pre-Classic period along the Snaketown and Santan canal systems. The patterns in settlement organization along single-village canal systems could be interpreted as either focal-village communities or linear communities. The patterns along the multi-village systems, though, were consistent with the focal-village model, and they persisted into the Classic period, after consolidation of the canals. Yet an atypical pattern was noted along the Gila Butte/Snaketown system in the Classic period, in which two inferred communities did not include villages with public architecture. Further research is needed on this issue, using information different from settlement-pattern data.

Fifth, evidence presented herein suggests that irrigators were experiencing problems with water scarcity by the Classic period. The problem almost certainly was an impetus for irrigators to consolidate the canal systems and for some residents to move upstream along the Gila River or to the lower Salt Valley, and it may have been a key factor in the sociopolitical changes at the time. Sixth, these population movements indicate that mobility was an adaptive strategy exercised by the Hohokam in the face of poor ecological conditions. Although similar movements have been documented for historical-period Akimel O'odham populations under such conditions, the prehistoric situation reminds us that mobility was clearly was an option, despite the deep sedentism observed for the Phoenix Basin Hohokam.

This study also had an opportunity to address two other prominent issues explored in previous studies of Hohokam irrigation organization. First, was the Classic period an important hinge point in irrigation organization? Hohokam scholars have documented the major sociopolitical transformations that occurred during the Hohokam Sedentary to Classic period transition. It was posited that if Hohokam irrigation organizations and political institutions were linked (e.g., a single administrative organization was in charge of managing irrigation and other tasks), then an important shift in irrigation organization should have occurred during that transition. The current study traced the canal-system and settlement-pattern changes in the Classic period, as summarized above. In the Sedentary period, the canals appear to have been managed by irrigation communities, although the Gila Butte system may have been managed by a municipality. By the Classic period, the patterns for both consolidated systems appear to conform to expectations for irrigation communities. This conclusion suggests that a major change in irrigation organization did not occur in the Classic period, at least internally to the systems. However, the linking of the canal systems and the increased need for interaction and negotiation among them *did* alter the realm of interrelationships among irrigation organizations.

Second, the regular spacing between ballcourt and platform-mound settlements along canal systems is thought to have been partly related to the administrative requirements of irrigation (see Crown 1987; Fish and Fish 1991; Gregory 1991; Gregory and Nials 1985; Masse 1991). Hohokam researchers have suggested that the convergence of average distances between pre-Classic period ballcourts (5.5 km) and Classic period platform mounds (5 km) "is highly suggestive of continuity in a basic integrative unit size between the Sedentary and Classic periods" (Fish and Fish 1991:163). The current study supports this notion for the pre-Classic period along the Snaketown and Santan canal systems, for which the average spacing between ballcourt villages was 5.6 and 5.1 km, respectively. Situated at the level of the main-canal reaches and branch canals, the modular and territorial nature of these focal-village communities was well adapted to manage both political affairs and irrigation management within the community territory (see Crown 1987; Elson 1998; Elson and Abbott 2000; Fish and Fish 1991, 2000b; Hunt et al. 2005:450). The social units involved in managing these segments of the canal systems can be considered branch-canal task groups (see Howard 2006:26–29). At the level of management for the entire canal system, though, the irrigation organization operated at a higher level that probably had an independent authority structure.

In contrast, the Classic period pattern did not conform to the posited 5-km spacing along the consolidated Gila Butte/Snaketown system; the Maricopa Platform Mound site was situated nearly 16 km from the canal heading and 22 km from the nearest platform mound. It was suggested above that Maricopa Mound leaders may have dealt with irrigation management along the south-branch canal, but they may not have played a pivotal role in irrigation management for the entire canal system. The two platform-mound villages along the Santan system, though, were 5.2 km apart, conforming with the expectations of the hypothesis. Similar to the pre-Classic period pattern, that interval may have facilitated irrigation management along the main-canal reaches, but the entire canal system probably was managed as an irrigation community.

I would add a final, but important, caveat to the argument that the regular settlement spacing was related to irrigation-management requirements. All the canal systems along the middle Gila River were founded in the pre-Classic period, along with the establishment of one primary settlement, and each of them later became a ballcourt village. The addition of other settlements along a canal system seems to be part of the process of expanding the system and the fields and establishing satellites (or daughter villages) of the founding settlement. In many cases, these satellites developed into ballcourt villages. I have argued that the spacing of ballcourt settlements probably was established by settlement decisions that were more closely related to the proximity-access principle and the organization of agricultural labor (Chisholm 1979; Stone 1996). Farmers travel to and from their fields far more often than they go specifically to the canals. The fields are their private property and the sources of their subsistence; hence, they have every reason to seek ways to lessen the cost of that travel. In sum, any benefit that accrued to the efficiency of irrigation management as a result of settlement spacing was a secondary effect of the motivation to optimize distances for agricultural travel.

Redrawing the Map of the Middle Gila Valley Hohokam Canal Systems

An important contribution of this study is a detailed map of the entire Snaketown canal system. The new map builds from the earlier studies of canals in the Snaketown area, including those by Haury (1937, 1976) and Midvale (1935, 1972) (see Chapter 3). I examined aerial photographs and historical maps of the Gila Butte–Snaketown area to identify the array of linear features that could represent canal alignments. I then proceeded to a ground-truthing phase of the remaining linear features, based on field reconnaissance. The relict prehistoric canals frequently were marked on the surface by linear mounds or linear artifact scatters, or both. This, in combination with the relatively undisturbed landscape, facilitated the detailed reconstruction of the system layout (Woodson forthcoming).

Another important contribution of the research is that I was able to specifically define the irrigated field areas in the Snaketown canal system. That is important because it allows an assessment of the system size, or command area, the portion of land that was irrigated regularly under the system. Using field evidence, I was able to determine the ranges and average lengths of the Snaketown lateral canals. It turned out that these correlated well to the average lengths of laterals in early-historical-period Akimel O'odham canal systems and the lateral lengths inferred by Howard (2006:148) based on a detailed study of field sizes in a portion of Canal System 1 along the lower Salt River. This convergence supports the contention that the Hohokam in the lower Salt and middle Gila Valleys shared a common irrigation technology that resulted in similar adaptations in separate canal systems (see Woodson 2004).

Likewise, this study presents the most detailed reconstruction to date of the Gila Butte, Santan, and Granite Knob canal systems. The level of detail in the layout of these canal systems was not as high as the in the layout of the Snaketown system, because of the more-intensive agriculture and other developments that have characterized the Santan–Gila Butte area in historical-period and modern times. The Santan canal system is now far better delineated than in the past, a benefit of excavating over 50 canal segments and documenting numerous relict canal alignments on the surface (Woodson 2010b). Recent investigations identified the only known relict segment of the Granite Knob canal, which has helped confirm the existence and size of that canal, but the remainder of it has been washed away by historical-period flooding. Previous excavations and more-recent surveys have helped to define the Gila Butte canal system.

The effort of mapping the Snaketown, Gila Butte, Santan, and Granite Knob canal systems was part of a larger project that entailed redrawing the map of Hohokam canal systems in the middle Gila Valley (Woodson 2009, 2010b) (see Figure 1.2). The revised map was based on a study of irrigation conducted as part of the BOR-funded P-MIP (Woodson 2003). This has been facilitated by the data recovered during intensive archaeological surveys of large blocks of the middle Gila Valley landscape (Ravesloot and Waters 2004), examinations of aerial photographs, and detailed studies of the prehistoric canal systems (Woodson 2003, 2004, 2007, 2009, 2010b, forthcoming). The map also benefitted from data from over 200 excavated canal segments. As a result of this long-term study, there is now solid documentation of 13 canal systems and inferential support for 2 other systems along the middle Gila River.

Changing Views of Snaketown in a Larger Landscape

Because Snaketown holds a position of major significance for Hohokam and Southwest archaeology, some commentary is given here about how the current research has contributed to a better understanding of Snaketown in a larger context. Ravesloot (2007) recently presented a summary of the preliminary findings of the GRIC-CRMP surveys around Snaketown. This study has provided more details of these surveys, with considerably more elaboration on the growth and development of the settlement system and canal system from the early Pioneer to the Late Classic periods. The study supports the notion that Snaketown was founded in the Vahki phase of the early Pioneer period, around A.D. 450–650. The settlement was probably a hamlet at the time. Looking across the middle Gila Valley at that time, it would appear that Snaketown was one of the first sedentary, agriculture-based settlements founded along the river, along with the Grewe site (see Craig 2000, ed. 2001).

Of course, Snaketown did not exist in a vacuum. Other settlements in the vicinity were part of the social landscape and must be included in any consideration of community or irrigation organization. Many of these sites, especially the villages, have been known for some time, such as the Maricopa Road site, the Maricopa Platform Mound site, and the Gila Butte site. This study has taken these villages, along with Snaketown, and analyzed them in the larger context of the subsistence-settlement system. The analysis has resulted in an improved understanding of Hohokam community organization in the Snaketown area.

As for abandonment, there can be no doubt that Snaketown village "proper" was abandoned during the Sedentary period, probably at the end of the Middle Sedentary period, around A.D. 1070. Wilcox et al. (1981:210) suggested that ecological factors played a crucial role in the abandonment. They suggested that it had to do with the population's reaching the limits of the agricultural system, which also may have been affected by the amount of water available to the canal system. The decrease in water supply may have been due to an increase in droughts during the twelfth century, as well to increased usage by upstream irrigators. More-recent research has supported the contention that ecological problems contributed to the decision to abandon Snaketown. As described in Chapter 4, streamflow conditions were not optimal for irrigation during the time just prior to the abandonment (Graybill et al. 2006; Ravesloot et al. forthcoming). The downcutting and widening of the river would have presented major problems at the same time (Waters and Ravesloot 2001). Also, the Snaketown canal system was not situated well to compete for scarce irrigation water, because it was near the tail end of the reach of the Gila River, which was being tapped by numerous upstream irrigation systems (Woodson 2010b). The current study indicates that the capacity of the Snaketown canal system decreased significantly in the Early Classic period and again in the Late Classic period. The data suggest that the population declined by 41 percent in the Early Classic period and by 19 percent in Late Classic period (–0.34 and –0.12 annual growth rates, respectively).

In sum, although this study cannot add any information regarding the environmental conditions themselves, it does indicate that Snaketown residents were forced to contend with a series of environmental changes during the Sedentary to Classic period transition. The same conditions affected other Hohokam villages along the middle Gila River, especially those situated on the lower half of the river, where problems with water scarcity may have been significant for the canal systems (Woodson 2010b). Many other middle Gila Valley ballcourt villages were abandoned or depopulated at the same time as Snaketown (e.g., Los Canales, Poston, Grewe, Siphon, GR-311, Chee Nee, Granite Knob, Hospital site, Gila Butte site, Hidden Ruin, and Villa Buena). About half of these abandoned villages were located on canal systems in the lower half of the river, suggesting that water-scarcity problems may have been significant factors in the decision to abandon.

A few scholars have hypothesized that following the abandonment of Snaketown, the entire area along the Snaketown canal system also was abandoned and was not resettled until the Late Classic period (e.g., Gregory 1991:182–183;

Wilcox et al. 1981:210–212). Haury (1976:48, 355) observed that new Classic period settlements were built to the east and west of the abandoned Snaketown, but he concluded that these dated to the Late Classic period. Along with references to a lack of evidence that the Snaketown canal was used in the Early Classic period (Haury 1976:150), it seems that he insinuated that the Hohokam had also abandoned the Snaketown "hinterland." Wilcox et al. (1981:211) speculated that the Snaketown residents very likely could have moved and founded a new large village, such as Escalante, Adamsville, or Los Muertos. Wilcox et al. (1981:212), though, wisely recognized the need for more research on the chronology of these settlements. The current study and the recent surveys of the Snaketown area have made it clear that the area was *not* abandoned during the Early Classic period. Indeed, current evidence strongly indicates that the Hohokam continued to inhabit the area during both the Early and Late Classic periods. However, it also is certain that there was a substantial decrease in population in the Early Classic period, which probably indicates that people moved to other settlements upstream along the middle Gila River or to one of the new Classic period villages in the lower Salt Valley.

The nature of settlement along the Snaketown canal system clearly changed during the Classic period. The settlement pattern was characterized by smaller, more-numerous settlements dispersed along the canal system. Many of the new settlements probably were founded by residents who remained in the area after they abandoned the Sedentary period ballcourt villages. These people shifted, or even "drifted" (see Darling et al. 2004), to adjacent locales to found the new settlements. The rationale for this type of settlement behavior is unclear, but it would seem to symbolize a break with the past. Activities in the Classic period were more restricted to the loci of habitation, except for canals and fields. The current analysis also suggests that the trail corridors extending north toward the lower Salt Valley either ceased to be used or declined significantly in use. That may have been related to the collapse of the trade networks associated with the distribution of red-on-buff pottery and the ballcourt system (see Abbott 2009; Abbott et al. 2007; Doyel 1991b, 2007). In sum, many of the Classic period changes in the Snaketown canal system suggest that the community was characterized by a more-insular socioeconomic interaction sphere (see Abbott 2003). That new arrangement probably reflected an increase in the social distances between the separate social groups within individual settlements and between settlements (see Gregory 1994:186–187).

External Validity of Findings

It is worth considering the validity of my findings for Hohokam contexts external to the study area. Are the results applicable to other canal systems along the Gila River, and why? What about applicability to the lower Salt Valley systems, which were dendritic canal-system complexes along a river with a very different character? Do my patterns apply to "Hohokam," in general, or only to Gila River Hohokam? Other Hohokam canal systems occurred in the Phoenix Basin, in the lower Salt Valley and along Queen Creek; in the Tucson Basin; and in the Safford Basin.

Generally, the methodological approaches used for this study are applicable to any of the other middle Gila Valley canal systems, all of which shared a linear layout and were in the same size range as the study area systems. The same applies to the linear canal systems in the Tucson Basin, Safford Basin, and Queen Creek areas (canals in the Queen Creek area were considerably smaller than in most of the Gila Valley canal systems). The models employed in the current analysis of irrigation organization were based on those used by other researchers (Howard 1993, 2006; Hunt et al. 2005) and are grounded in well-developed anthropological models. These canal systems would have required an administrative authority in the form of an irrigation organization for canal operation and maintenance, water allocation, and conflict resolution. The exercise of analyzing irrigation organizations based on their internal structures, external relationships with political institutions, and interrelationships among irrigation organizations is one that can be fruitfully applied elsewhere.

The specific findings about the internal structures and external relationships of the irrigation organizations might be duplicated in these other systems, but these topics should be analyzed on a case-by-case basis. The patterns may not be applicable to all Hohokam contexts. The findings in the study area regarding canal-system consolidation, demographic decline, and population movement highlight the importance of interrelationships throughout the middle Gila Valley. There is a need to examine these issues in regard to the canals and settlements in the rest of the valley, to see whether they reflect trends that are similar to those in the current study area.

The middle Gila Valley canal systems are most often compared with the lower Salt Valley canal systems (see Howard 1990, 1993, 2006). The systems in both valleys have exhibited very similar trends in canal-system development. The most dramatic growth occurred during the late Pioneer period (Snaketown phase) and early Colonial period (Gila Butte phase). The administrative and maintenance requirements had already reached high levels by that time (see Howard 1993:314). Relative stability in the systems was reached by the late Colonial period (Santa Cruz phase) or, at latest, by the Sedentary period (Sacaton phase). No new canal systems seem to have been added to either valley in the Classic period (see Howard 1993:316).

However, there are some important differences between the valleys. The practice of consolidating or joining adjacent canal systems observed for the middle Gila Valley canals does not appear to have been widespread in the lower Salt Valley (although Nicholas and Neitzel [1984] suggested that Canal System 1 became "interconnected" in the Classic period). The dendritic canal-system complexes in the lower Salt Valley included multiple main canals, especially Canal Systems 1 and 2, which were quite different from the linear-layout middle Gila Valley systems. Therefore, each main canal in the lower Salt Valley may have had its own irrigation organization (Hunt et al. 2005). Likewise, the command areas of Canal Systems 1 and 2 were significantly larger than those of the middle Gila Valley systems. The estimated annual discharge of the Salt River is nearly four times the volume of the middle Gila River.

A comparison of settlement and population trends in the middle Gila and lower Salt Valleys also reveals both similarities and differences. The lower Salt Valley was settled during the Red Mountain phase, earlier than the settlement of the middle Gila Valley, where irrigation-based settlements began in the Vahki phase. As noted in Chapter 7, the early settlers in the middle Gila Valley may have originated in the Salt River area. This scenario actually is supported by Pima oral traditions on the origin of irrigation (Bahr et al. 1994), which have stated that irrigation first was learned by farmers in the Salt Valley who then taught the technique to farmers in the Gila Valley. Other possible source areas for the middle Gila Valley pioneer settlers are the Tucson Basin and other Upper Sonoran Desert areas where irrigation farming already had been established.

Thereafter, the explosive population growth in the late Pioneer and Colonial periods in the middle Gila Valley was similar to the growth inferred for the lower Salt Valley (Howard 1990, 1993:314; Ingram 2008). Ingram (2008) examined Hohokam population-growth patterns (using changes in house counts as a proxy for growth rates) in Canal System 2 in the lower Salt Valley and their correlation to Salt River streamflow-discharge variation (see Nials et al. 1989; Graybill et al. 2006) between A.D. 775 and 1450. Ingram (2008:150) documented the highest growth rates in Canal System 2 during the Gila Butte (0.65 percent) and Santa Cruz (1.3 percent) phases. The latter rate differs from the current study's findings for the Santa Cruz phase, which was the smallest growth rate found in the study area. For the Sacaton phase, the flat growth of 0 percent found by Ingram (2008) resembled that for the current study area (0.14 percent), as did the decline in the subsequent Soho phase (0.15 percent in Canal System 2 and 0.29 percent in the current study area). Ingram (2008) found another spike in growth (0.47 percent) in Canal System 2 during the final interval of Hohokam occupation, in the Civano phase, which contrasted with the further decline (0.14 percent) in the current study area.

These periods of growth and decline are attributed to somewhat different causes in each valley. Contrary to expectations, Ingram (2008) found that population-growth rates in the lower Salt Valley generally increased as floods, droughts, and discharge variability increased. He proposed that the growth rates were the results of substantial immigration and emigration that were strongly related to agricultural conditions for canal farmers in the lower Salt Valley and for non-canal farmers outside the valley. Ingram (2008:158) highlighted how a "motivator of this movement may have been regional precipitation patterns affecting agricultural conditions for non-canal farmers in addition to the streamflow conditions along the lower Salt River valley." Agricultural conditions for non-canal farmers outside the Salt River canal systems "were likely directly related to precipitation conditions" (Ingram 2008:158). That is, when rainfall was sufficient, non-canal farmers were able to subsist on non-irrigation farming (with hunting and gathering). In contrast, when drought conditions prevailed, "perennial water sources such as the Salt River would have been a major attraction" for non-canal farmers to immigrate to (Ingram 2008:158). Another "pull" factor for farmers outside the valley was the demand for labor to repair canal infrastructure that was damaged after floods.

As described in Chapter 7, I suggest that growth rates between the early Pioneer and early Colonial periods in the middle Gila Valley support the contention that immigration took place. People in the farming communities in the lower Salt Valley or the upper Gila Valley would have been "pulled" to the middle Gila Valley for the opportunity to settle a largely open area with excellent potential for irrigation farming. Growth rates during the late Colonial and Sedentary periods for the study area were well within the range typically expected from natural increases in birth rates over death rates. The declines in the Early Classic period were sufficient to suggest that people were moving away, except in the Granite Knob system, which added population. Population declined in all parts of the study area in the Late Classic period. The underlying reasons for the demographic declines in the Classic period were almost certainly linked with periods of water scarcity. The population trends indicate that there were differences among the canal systems in terms of the "pushes" and "pulls" that attracted or repulsed people from them. I argue that these were related to the ability to maintain an adequate water supply, which was dependent upon (1) position of the heading along the river and (2) reliability of the heading (bedrock reef). It is likely that people were moving from the downstream systems to the upstream systems.

The advent of the Classic period saw the abandonment of, or population decline along, canal systems in the downstream portions of both valleys. This pertains to those canals in the far-western end of the lower Salt Valley, like Cashion, and farther downstream, along the lower Gila River, such as Gila Bend (Howard 1993:317). It is likely that these demographic declines resulted from the rising levels of water scarcity, which created more-intense water shortages for the downstream canal systems. This would have created a significant "push" for downstream irrigators to move upstream to canal systems with more-reliable water supplies. Similar intrabasin population movement has been argued for Canal System 2 and Pueblo Grande (Abbott and Foster 2003). The current study has provided the basis to infer population movements from downstream to upstream locations, as well as immigration to the lower Salt Valley. The construction of the largest platform mounds in both valleys occurred in the farthest-upstream systems (Casa Grande in the Gila Valley and Mesa Grande in the Salt Valley). Population movement between canal systems along the middle Gila River may have been as important a factor as immigration/emigration into and out of the valley.

Recently, however, Howard (2006:247–251) argued that the construction of canals, mounds, and sites continued in tail-ender systems in the central portion of the lower Salt Valley. This suggests that water shortages were not causing system decline or abandonment but, rather, success in maintenance and growth of canal infrastructure. He argued that this supports the hypothesis that some form of valley-wide communal resource management was in place among the Salt River irrigation systems, to ensure equitable water sharing/allocation. Howard saw that need for communal resource management as arising from the fact that the population exceeded the threshold of available water and the ability of irrigation agriculture to provide adequate subsistence—that is, agricultural success as measured not by annual yields but by the amount of storage accrued (Howard 2006:239). That threshold was passed when the Lehi system was built, in the Late Sedentary period. Yet the overall greater volume of discharge of the Salt River may have allowed the villages in that area to continue to prosper in the Classic period, in contrast to the downstream canals in middle Gila Valley. In contrast to that finding, Ackerly (1982) examined the spatial distributions of canal systems and population centers, particularly in relation to alluvial soils, and concluded that there is little support for the existence of regulatory mechanisms for water allocation.

Another difference from the lower Salt Valley is that the middle Gila Valley did not fully experience the same process of coalescence (i.e., unification and aggregation) in the Classic period (see Hill et al. 2004). That was reflected generally in the very low occurrence of large, aggregated Classic period sites and a much lower number of platform mounds in the middle Gila Valley. The only part of the middle Gila Valley with such manifestations was the Casa Grande canal system, which was the farthest-upstream system with the greatest number of platform mounds (six) and the only "big house." I have argued that the rise of Casa Grande and its associated villages was related to its control of the first heading along the middle Gila River and a large expanse of productive agricultural land during a time of growing water scarcity (Woodson 2010c). These conditions of scarcity, in tandem with the much smaller discharge of the river and available farmland (see Graybill et al. 2006; Woodson 2004), may have been sufficiently different from conditions in the lower Salt Valley to have prevented the development of the same kind of aggregated villages and numerous platform mounds.

Relevance for Southwest Archaeology and Beyond

Some aspects of this research have broader relevance to both Hohokam and Southwest archaeology. The primary contribution is the explication of settlement organization through the use of a detailed, systematic site-function model (Wells et al. 2003, 2004). In this regard, the study also has more general significance for settlement-pattern studies. Most settlement-pattern analysis relies heavily or exclusively on spatial data, which are prone to divergent interpretations about interaction patterns. The site-function approach employed in this study helps to avoid some of those problems and provides a more robust picture of the prehistoric landscape. A second important contribution is the technique used for estimating population size. Estimating Hohokam population size has proven to be a difficult endeavor with widely varying results (e.g., Craig 2000, 2001a; Dean et al. 1994:70–71; Fish and Fish 1991). The level of detail of the current data allows a more rigorous approach to population and has revealed important trends in population growth and decline. Three estimates are provided, based on (1) residential-site area in habitation sites, (2) the size of irrigated lands (or command area) for each canal system, and (3) the number of people required for cleaning the main canal on an annual basis. A third contribution is the method developed for defining the command area of the canal systems, thanks in part to the excellent surface preservation of most of the Snaketown canal system. Fourth, the study has provided a well-defined approach to estimating labor requirements for canal maintenance.

Another aspect of the study relevant to Southwest studies is the examination of how the Hohokam adapted to the streamflow and landscape changes that affected much of southern Arizona during the Sedentary to Classic period transition (see Graybill et al. 2006; Huckleberry 1993, 1995; Nials et al. 1989; Waters and Ravesloot 2000, 2001). These deteriorating conditions, in tandem with population growth, resulted in rising water-scarcity problems, which presented a challenge for irrigators' efforts to maintain a reliable water supply in the canal systems, especially the downstream systems. They responded by consolidating canals, while some segments of the population moved away from downstream canal systems. The previous chapters describe this in more detail.

Lastly, the study has contributed a perspective on the sociopolitical complexity of prehistoric southwestern societies. Much study and speculation have been promulgated about the identity and role of Hohokam leaders at ballcourt and platform-mound villages, especially in regard to the topic of sociopolitical complexity (e.g., Abbott 2000, 2003; Doyel 2007; Earle et al. forthcoming; Elson 1998; Redman 1991; Wilcox 1991). As noted above, the relationship between the political leadership and the principal means of irrigation-agricultural production is not entirely clear. The study results suggest that the leaders probably were involved in matters of irrigation management at the levels of the focal-village communities (i.e., branch canals/ main-canal reaches). Therefore, they probably had means of control over agricultural production and surpluses at those levels of the system, but they did not necessarily have the ability to exert control over entire canal systems.

The results of this study also speak to questions important to comparative irrigation studies. The Hohokam, with their large irrigation systems, were included in some of the debates among the anthropological community over Wittfogel's (1955, 1957) hydraulic hypothesis, which proposes that large-scale irrigation in arid regions requires mass labor efforts that must be directed by a centralized authority, which, in turn, leads to greater political integration (Mitchell 1973:532). By extension, irrigation is seen as a prime mover in the rise of states in arid or semiarid environments. The concept of "centralization" as used by Wittfogel and Steward has to do with the total society. Some scholars have cited the Hohokam as an example of a hydraulic society that would have required a central managerial authority (e.g., Steward 1955:71–72). Although some (e.g., Gregory and Nials 1985) have argued that large Classic period platform-mound sites represent evidence of a managerial elite, the construction of large scale canal systems was accomplished long before the appearance of such mounds. Other Hohokam researchers (e.g., Haury 1976; Woodbury 1961:556) have contended that clear archaeological evidence of a central managerial authority is lacking for the Hohokam. Moreover, the recent assessments of Hohokam sociopolitical organization have argued that there is no evidence that the Hohokam had a state (e.g., Abbott 2000:222; Crown 1991; Fish and Fish 2000b). These points fall in line with those of cross-cultural irrigation studies that have demonstrated that large-scale canal systems do not necessarily require centralized control by a state or central government (e.g., Hunt 1988a; Leach 1961; Millon 1962; Mitchell 1973). In addition, other studies have identified the rise of states with no apparent use of canal irrigation (e.g., the Maya) and the rise of states before the use of large-scale irrigation (e.g., the Ur III Dynasty in Mesopotamia).

However, the current study offers another perspective on the apparent enigma of the Hohokam case. Mitchell (1973:533; see also Lees 1973) argued that critiques of the hydraulic hypothesis "can be obviated by reformulating it: it is not irrigation itself, but the centralized coordination of irrigation activities that has important social consequences. It is the synergistic action of irrigation and its centralized coordination that results in greater political integration." Managing the Hohokam canal systems along the middle Gila River (including construction, operation and maintenance, allocation, and dispute resolution) clearly required the coordinated efforts of skilled engineers and many laborers. The same conclusion has been reached for the canal systems in the lower Salt Valley (Abbott 2000:221–223; Howard 1990, 2006). I have argued that the management of the middle Gila Valley canal systems required centralized authorities from their beginnings, or certainly by the Colonial period. However, these centralized, administrative authority structures were in the form of irrigation organizations (see Kelly 1983; also see Hunt 1988a), not centralized political institutions, and certainly not a state. Although the authorities for these irrigation organizations may have been the same as the authorities for the political organizations in the early phases of irrigation, the two management spheres seem to have diverged as population size and sociopolitical complexity increased in the Colonial and Sedentary periods. It is feasible, then, that the "synergistic action of irrigation and its centralized coordination" (Mitchell 1973:533) resulted in greater political integration for the Hohokam. Hence, the cases studied here could be cited as support for a "modified" hydraulic hypothesis, albeit a hypothesis of a different kind from the one envisioned by Wittfogel (1955, 1957).

In addition, the analytical framework of the study successfully applies the ethnographic concept that the internal authority structure of an irrigation organization must be examined separately from its external relationship to the political system (Kelly 1983; also Hunt 1988a). This strategy promotes a more nuanced understanding of the various levels of social organization. Another contribution of the current study is the level of detail presented for the physical structure and sequence of the development of indigenous, prehistoric canal systems and their associated settlements. Few systems reported by ethnographers or archaeologists have been documented in such detail, and this study provides a basis for evaluation of some elements of irrigation social organization. This approach echoes another recent effort by Howard (2006) for the Hohokam canal systems in the lower Salt River Valley, in which he demonstrated the connection between the physical structure of the canal system and the organization of the social groups that operated the system. Lastly, the study results suggest that locally managed irrigation systems have a long history in North America, extending back at least 1,500 years in the middle Gila Valley. And it speaks to the persistence and adaptability of local, community-based irrigation organizations that have flourished around the world (see Mabry 1996; Tang 1992; Uphoff 1986).

References Cited

Abbott, D. R.

1983 A Technological Assessment of Ceramic Variation in the Salt-Gila Aqueduct Area: Toward a Comprehensive Documentation of Hohokam Ceramics. In *Material Culture*, edited by L. S. Teague and P. L. Crown, pp. 3–118. Hohokam Archaeology along the Salt-Gila Aqueduct, Central Arizona Project, vol. 8. Archaeological Series No. 150. Arizona State Museum, University of Arizona, Tucson.

2000 *Ceramics and Community Organization among the Hohokam*. University of Arizona Press, Tucson.

2009 Extensive and Long-Term Specialization: Hohokam Ceramic Production in the Phoenix Basin, Arizona. *American Antiquity* 74:531–557.

Abbott, D. R. (editor)

2001 *Ceramic Studies*. Material Culture, pt. 1. The Grewe Archaeological Research Project, vol. 2. Anthropological Papers No. 99-1. Northland Research, Flagstaff, Arizona.

2003 *Centuries of Decline during the Hohokam Classic Period*. University of Arizona Press, Tucson.

Abbott, D. R., and M. S. Foster

2003 Site Structure, Chronology, and Population. In *Centuries of Decline during the Hohokam Classic Period*, edited by D. R. Abbott, pp. 24–47. University of Arizona Press, Tucson.

Abbott, D. R., S. E. Ingram, and B. G. Kober

2006 Hohokam Exchange and Early Classic Period Organization in Central Arizona: Focal Villages or Linear Communities? *Journal of Field Archaeology* 31:285–305.

Abbott, D. R., A. M. Smith, and E. Gallaga

2007 Ballcourts and Ceramics: The Case for Hohokam Marketplaces in the Arizona Desert. *American Antiquity* 72:461–484.

Ackerly, N. W.

1982 Irrigation, Water Allocation Strategies, and the Hohokam Collapse. *The Kiva* 47:91–106.

1991 Constructing Analog Models of Hohokam Irrigation Using Historic Documents. In *Prehistoric Irrigation in Arizona: Symposium 1988*, edited by C. D. Breternitz, pp. 41–60. Publications in Archaeology No. 17. Soil Systems, Phoenix.

Ackerly, N. W., and T. K. Henderson (editors)

1989 *Prehistoric Agricultural Activities on the Lehi-Mesa Terrace: Perspectives on Hohokam Irrigation Cycles*. Northland Research, Flagstaff, Arizona.

Ackerly, N. W., J. B. Howard, and R. H. McGuire

1987 *La Ciudad Canals: A Study of Hohokam Irrigation Systems at the Community Level*. Anthropological Field Studies No. 17. Office of Cultural Resource Management, Arizona State University, Tempe.

Adams, Robert McC.

1966 *The Evolution of Urban Society: Early Mesopotamia and Prehistoric Mexico*. Aldine, Chicago.

Adler, M. A.

1996 Land Tenure, Archaeology, and the Ancestral Pueblo Social Landscape. *Journal of Anthropological Archaeology* 15:337–371.

Ambler, J. R.

1961 Archaeological Survey and Excavations at Casa Grande National Monument, Arizona. Unpublished Master's thesis, Department of Anthropology, University of Arizona, Tucson.

Andresen, J. M.
1985 Pottery and Architecture at Compound F, Casa Grande Ruins National Monument, Arizona. In *Proceedings of the 1983 Hohokam Symposium*, pt. 2, edited by A. E. Dittert, Jr., and D. E. Dove, pp. 595–640. Occasional Paper No. 2. Arizona Archaeological Society, Phoenix Chapter, Phoenix.

1987 Frank Midvale and the Casa Grande Canal. *The Kiva* 52:229–235.

Bahr, D., J. Smith, W. S. Allison, and J. Hayden
1994 *The Short Swift Time of Gods on Earth: The Hohokam Chronicles*. University of California Press, Berkeley.

Bandelier, A. F.
1892 *Final Report of Investigations among the Indians of the Southwestern United States, Carried on Mainly in the Years 1880 to 1885*, pt. 2. Papers of the Archaeological Institute of America, American Series No. 4. J. Wilson and Son and Cambridge University Press, Cambridge, England.

Bayman, J. M.
2001 The Hohokam of Southwest North America. *Journal of World Prehistory* 15:257–311.

Bohrer, V. L.
1970 Ethnobotanical Aspects of Snaketown, a Hohokam Village in Southern Arizona. *American Antiquity* 35:413–430.

Bolin, P.
1993 Levels of Autonomy in the Organization of Irrigation in the Highlands of Peru. In *Irrigation at High Altitudes: The Social Organization of Water Control Systems in the Andes*, edited by W. P. Mitchell and D. Guillet, pp. 141–166. Society for Latin American Anthropology and American Anthropological Association, Arlington, Virginia.

Boserup, E.
1965 *The Conditions of Agricultural Growth: The Economics of Agrarian Change under Population Pressure*. Aldine, New York.

Brooks, D., and R. G. Vivian
1978 *An Archaeological Investigation of the Queen Creek Floodway Project*. 2nd ed. Archaeological Series No. 66. Arizona State Museum, University of Arizona, Tucson.

Brown, P., and A. Podolefsky
1976 Population Density, Agricultural Intensity, Land Tenure and Group Size in the New Guinea Highlands. *Ethnology* 15:211–238.

Bunge, W.
1962 *Theoretical Geography*. C. W. K. Gleerup, Lund, Sweden.

Burt, E. S.
2007 *Results of Archaeological Testing at Three Proposed Home Sites on Allotted Lands, Gila River Indian Community, Pinal and Maricopa Counties, Arizona*. Technical Report No. 2007-05. Cultural Resource Management Program, Gila River Indian Community, Sacaton, Arizona.

Burton, M. L., and D. R. White
1984 Sexual Division of Labor in Agriculture. *American Anthropologist* 86:568–583.

Cable, J. S., and D. E. Doyel
1987 Pioneer Period Village Structure and Settlement Pattern in the Phoenix Basin. In *The Hohokam Village: Site Structure and Organization*, edited by D. E. Doyel, pp. 21–70. American Association for the Advancement of Science, Glenwood Springs, Colorado.

Cameron, C. M.
1995 Migration and the Movement of Southwestern Peoples. *Journal of Anthropological Archaeology* 14:104–124.

Cantley, G. J.
1991 Archaeology of a Rockpile Field in the Santan Mountains, Arizona. Unpublished Master's thesis, Department of Anthropology, Arizona State University, Tempe.

Castetter, E. F., and W. H. Bell
1942 *Pima and Papago Indian Agriculture*. University of New Mexico Press, Albuquerque.

Chisholm, M.
1979 *Rural Settlement and Land Use: An Essay on Location*. 3rd ed. Hutchinson University Library, London.

Chow, V. T.
1959 *Open Channel Hydraulics*. Civil Engineering Series. McGraw-Hill, New York.

Clark, C. P. (compiler)
2000 *Archaeological Investigations at AZ V:13:201 (ASM), Town of Kearny, Pinal County, Arizona.* Cultural Resources Report No. 114. Archaeological Consulting Services, Tempe, Arizona.

Clark, J. J. (editor)
2004 *Ancient Farmers of the Safford Basin: Archaeology of the U.S. 70 Safford-to-Thatcher Project.* Anthropological Papers No. 39. Center for Desert Archaeology, Tucson, Arizona.

Clark, T. C.
2004 A Study of Small-Scale Irrigation Agriculturalists. In *Hohokam Farming on the Salt River Floodplain: Refining Models and Analytical Methods*, edited by T. K. Henderson, pp. 153–165. Anthropological Papers No. 43. Center for Desert Archaeology, Tucson, Arizona. Anthropological Papers No. 10. Pueblo Grande Museum, Phoenix.

Cordell, L. S., D. E. Doyel, and K. W. Kintigh
1994 Processes of Aggregation in the Prehistoric Southwest. In *Themes in Southwest Prehistory*, edited by G. J. Gumerman, pp. 109–133. School of American Research Press, Santa Fe, New Mexico.

Cordell, L. S., and F. Plog
1979 Escaping the Confines of Normative Thought: A Reevaluation of Puebloan Prehistory. *American Antiquity* 44:405–429.

Coward, E. W., Jr.
1979 Principles of Social Organization in an Indigenous Irrigation System. *Human Organization* 38:2–36.

Coward, E. W., Jr. (editor)
1979 *Irrigation and Agricultural Development in Asia: Perspectives from the Social Sciences.* Cornell University Press, Ithaca, New York.

Cowgill, G. L.
1975 On Causes and Consequences of Ancient and Modern Population Changes. *American Anthropologist* 77:505–573.

Craig, D. B.
1995 The Social Consequences of Irrigation Agriculture: A Perspective from Meddler Point. In *The Roosevelt Community Development Study: New Perspectives on Tonto Basin Prehistory*, edited by M. D. Elson, M. T. Stark, and D. A. Gregory, pp. 227–249. Anthropological Papers No. 15. Center for Desert Archaeology, Tucson, Arizona.

2000 The Demographic Implications of Architectural Change at the Grewe Site. In *The Hohokam Village Revisited*, edited by D. E. Doyel, S. K. Fish, and P. R. Fish, pp. 139–166. Southwestern and Rocky Mountain Division of the American Association for the Advancement of Science, Fort Collins, Colorado.

2001a The Demographic Implications of Architectural Change at Grewe. In *Synthesis*, edited by D. B. Craig, pp. 37–49. The Grewe Archaeological Research Project, vol. 3. Anthropological Papers No. 99-1. Northland Research, Tempe, Arizona.

2001b Summary and Conclusions. In *Synthesis*, edited by D. B. Craig, pp. 141–147. The Grewe Archaeological Research Project, vol. 3. Anthropological Papers No. 99-1. Northland Research, Tempe, Arizona.

Craig, D. B. (editor)
2001 *Project Background and Feature Descriptions.* The Grewe Archaeological Research Project, vol. 1. Anthropological Papers No. 99-1. Northland Research, Tempe, Arizona.

Crawford, S.
1988 *Mayordomo: Chronicle of an* Acequia *in Northern New Mexico.* Doubleday, New York.

Crown, P. L.
1987 Classic Period Hohokam Settlement and Land Use in the Casa Grande Ruins Area, Arizona. *Journal of Field Archaeology* 14:147–162.

1991 The Hohokam: Current Views of Prehistory and the Regional System. In *Chaco and Hohokam: Prehistoric Regional Systems in the American Southwest*, edited by P. L. Crown and W. J. Judge, pp. 135–157. School of American Research Press, Santa Fe, New Mexico.

Crown, P. L., and W. J. Judge (editors)
1991 *Chaco and Hohokam: Prehistoric Regional Systems in the American Southwest.* School of American Research Press, Santa Fe, New Mexico.

Cummings, B.
1926 Ancient Canals of the Casa Grande. *Progressive Arizona* 3(5):9–10.

D'Altroy, T., and T. K. Earle
1985 Staple Finance, Wealth Finance, and Storage in the Inca Political Economy. *Current Anthropology* 26:187–206.

Darling, J. A.
2009a *Preliminary Report on Archaeological Data Testing at AZ AA:2:66 (ASM), the Vahki Village Site, along the Pima Lateral Canal, Pima-Maricopa Irrigation Project, Coolidge, AZ.* Letter report. On file, Cultural Resource Management Program, Gila River Indian Community, Sacaton, Arizona.

2009b *Preliminary Report on Archaeological Data Testing at AZ AA:2:222 (ASM) along the Pima Lateral Canal, Pima-Maricopa Irrigation Project, Coolidge, AZ.* Letter report. On file, Cultural Resource Management Program, Gila River Indian Community, Sacaton, Arizona.

2009c *Preliminary Report on National Register of Historic Places Eligibility Testing at AZ AA:2:143, AA:2:144, and AA:3:229 (ASM) along the Pima Lateral Canal, Pima-Maricopa Irrigation Project, Coolidge, AZ.* Letter report. On file, Cultural Resource Management Program, Gila River Indian Community, Sacaton, Arizona.

Darling, J. A., J. C. Ravesloot, and M. R. Waters
2004 Village Drift and Riverine Settlement: Modeling Akimel O'odham Land Use. *American Anthropologist* 106:282–295.

Dart, A.
1986 Sediment Accumulation along Hohokam Canals. *The Kiva* 51:63–84.

Dean, J. S.
1988 A Model of Anasazi Behavioral Adaptation. In *The Anasazi in a Changing Environment*, edited by G. J. Gumerman, pp. 25–44. Cambridge University Press, Cambridge, England.

1991 Thoughts on Hohokam Chronology. In *Exploring the Hohokam: Prehistoric Desert Peoples of the American Southwest*, edited by G. J. Gumerman, pp. 61–149. New World Studies Series No. 1. Amerind Foundation, Dragoon, Arizona, and University of New Mexico Press, Albuquerque.

Dean, J. S., W. H. Doelle, and J. D. Orcutt
1994 Adaptive Stress, Environment, and Demography. In *Themes in Southwest Prehistory*, edited by G. J. Gumerman, pp. 53–86. School of American Research Press, Santa Fe, New Mexico.

DeJong, D. H.
2009 *Stealing the Gila: The Pima Agricultural Economy and Water Deprivation, 1848–1921.* University of Arizona Press, Tucson.

Doelle, W. H.
1995 Tonto Basin Demography in a Regional Perspective. In *The Roosevelt Community Development Study: New Perspectives on Tonto Basin Prehistory*, edited by M. D. Elson, M. T. Stark, and D. A. Gregory, pp. 201–226. Anthropological Papers No. 15. Center for Desert Archaeology, Tucson, Arizona.

Doelle, W. H., D. A. Gregory, and H. D. Wallace
1995 Classic Period Platform Mound Systems in Southern Arizona. In *The Roosevelt Community Development Study: New Perspectives on Tonto Basin Prehistory*, edited by M. D. Elson, M. T. Stark, and D. A. Gregory, pp. 385–440. Anthropological Papers No. 15. Center for Desert Archaeology, Tucson, Arizona.

Doolittle, W. E., and J. A. Neely (editors)
2004 *The Safford Valley Grids: Prehistoric Cultivation in the Southern Arizona Desert.* Anthropological Papers No. 70. University of Arizona Press, Tucson.

Downing, T.
1974 Irrigation and Moisture-Sensitive Periods: A Zapotec Case. In *Irrigation's Impact on Society*, edited by T. Downing and M. Gibson, pp. 113–122. Anthropological Papers No. 25. University of Arizona Press, Tucson.

Downing, T., and M. Gibson (editors)
1974 *Irrigation's Impact on Society.* Anthropological Papers No. 25. University of Arizona Press, Tucson.

Doyel, D. E.

1974 *Excavations in the Escalante Ruin Group, Southern Arizona.* Archaeological Series No. 37. Arizona State Museum, University of Arizona, Tucson.

1980 Hohokam Social Organization and the Sedentary to Classic Period Transition. In *Current Issues in Hohokam Prehistory: Proceedings of a Symposium*, edited by D. E. Doyel and F. Plog, pp. 23–40. Anthropological Research Papers No. 23. Arizona State University, Tempe.

1981 *Late Hohokam Prehistory in Southern Arizona.* Contributions to Archaeology No. 2. Gila Press, Scottsdale, Arizona.

1991a Hohokam Cultural Evolution in the Phoenix Basin. In *Exploring the Hohokam: Prehistoric Desert Peoples of the American Southwest*, edited by G. J. Gumerman, pp. 231–278. New World Studies Series No. 1. Amerind Foundation, Dragoon, Arizona, and University of New Mexico Press, Albuquerque.

1991b Hohokam Exchange and Interaction. In *Chaco and Hohokam: Prehistoric Regional Systems in the American Southwest*, edited by P. L. Crown and W. J. Judge, pp. 225–252. School of American Research Press, Santa Fe, New Mexico.

2000 The Santan Phase in the Phoenix Basin. In *The Hohokam Village Revisited*, edited by D. E. Doyel, S. K. Fish, and P. R. Fish, pp. 221–244. American Association for the Advancement of Science, Southwestern and Rocky Mountain Division, Fort Collins, Colorado.

2007 Irrigation, Production, and Power in Phoenix Basin Hohokam Society. In *The Hohokam Millennium*, edited by S. K. Fish and P. R. Fish, pp. 83–90. School for Advanced Research Press, Santa Fe, New Mexico.

Doyel, D. E. (editor)

1987 *The Hohokam Village: Site Structure and Organization.* American Association for the Advancement of Science, Glenwood Springs, Colorado.

Duff, A. I.

1998 The Process of Migration in the Late Prehistoric Southwest. In *Migration and Reorganization: The Pueblo IV Period in the American Southwest*, edited by K. A. Spielmann, pp. 31–52. Anthropological Research Papers No. 51. Arizona State University, Tempe.

Earle, T. K.

1987 Chiefdoms in Archaeological and Ethnohistorical Perspective. *Annual Reviews in Anthropology* 16:279–308.

1997 *How Chiefs Come To Power: The Political Economy in Prehistory.* Stanford University Press, Stanford, California.

Earle, T. K., D. Doyel, and J. Ravesloot

forthcoming Political Economy of the Hohokam: A Consideration. In *Hohokam Trajectories in World Perspective*, edited by P. R. Fish and S. K. Fish. New World Series. Amerind Foundation, Dragoon, Arizona.

Elson, M. D.

1998 *Expanding the View of Hohokam Platform Mounds: An Ethnographic Perspective.* Anthropological Papers No. 63. University of Arizona, Tucson.

Elson, M. D., and D. R. Abbott

2000 Organizational Variability in Platform Mound-Building Groups of the American Southwest. In *Alternative Leadership Strategies in the American Southwest*, edited by B. L. Mills, pp. 117–135. University of Arizona Press, Tucson.

Ely, L. L.

1997 Response of Extreme Floods in the Southwestern United States to Climatic Variations in the Late Holocene. *Geomorphology* 19:175–201.

Erasmus, C. J.

1956 Culture Structure and Process: The Occurrence and Disappearance of Reciprocal Farm Labor. *Southwestern Journal of Anthropology* 12:444–469.

1965 Monument Building: Some Field Experiments. *Southwestern Journal of Anthropology* 21:277–301.

Ezell, P. H.

1961 *The Hispanic Acculturation of the Gila River Pimas.* American Anthropologist series, vol. 63, no. 5, pt. 2. Memoir 90. American Anthropological Association, Menasha, Wisconsin.

Fernea, R.

1970 *Shaykh and Effendi: Changing Patterns of Authority among the El Shabana of Southern Iraq.* Harvard University Press, Cambridge, Massachusetts.

Fertelmes, C. M., and C. Loendorf
2010 *Archaeological Testing at Seven Cultural Properties for Proposed Agricultural Development, Gila River Indian Community, Pinal County, Arizona.* Technical Report No. 2009-23. Cultural Resource Management Program, Gila River Indian Community, Sacaton, Arizona.

Fewkes, J. W.
1913 Casa Grande, Arizona. In *Twenty-Eighth Annual Report of the Bureau of American Ethnology, 1906–1907*, pp. 25–179. Smithsonian Institution, Washington, D.C.

Fish, P. R., and S. K. Fish
1991 Hohokam Political and Social Organization. In *Exploring the Hohokam: Prehistoric Desert Peoples of the American Southwest*, edited by G. J. Gumerman, pp. 151–175. New World Studies Series 2. Amerind Foundation, Dragoon, Arizona, and University of New Mexico Press, Albuquerque.

2007 Community, Territory, and Polity. In *The Hohokam Millennium*, edited by S. K. Fish and P. R. Fish, pp. 39–47. School for Advanced Research Press, Santa Fe, New Mexico.

Fish, S. K., and P. R. Fish
2000a Civic-Territorial Organization and the Roots of Hohokam Complexity. In *The Hohokam Village Revisited*, edited by D. E. Doyel, S. K. Fish, and P. R. Fish, pp. 373–390. Southwestern and Rocky Mountain Division of the American Association for the Advancement of Science, Fort Collins, Colorado.

2000b The Institutional Contexts of Hohokam Complexity and Inequality. In *Alternative Leadership Strategies in the American Southwest*, edited by B. L. Mills, pp. 154–167. University of Arizona Press, Tucson.

2007 The Hohokam Millennium. In *The Hohokam Millennium*, edited by S. K. Fish and P. R. Fish, pp. 1–11. School for Advanced Research Press, Santa Fe, New Mexico.

Fish, S. K., P. R. Fish, and J. Madsen
1992 *The Marana Community in the Hohokam World.* Anthropological Papers No. 56. University of Arizona Press, Tucson.

Gladwin, H. S.
1948 *Excavations at Snaketown IV: Review and Conclusions.* Medallion Papers No. 38. Gila Pueblo, Globe, Arizona.

Gladwin, H. S., E. W. Haury, E. B. Sayles, and N. Gladwin
1937 *Excavations at Snaketown: Material Culture.* Medallion Papers No. 25. Gila Pueblo, Globe, Arizona.

Gladwin, W., and H. S. Gladwin
1929 *The Red-on-buff Culture of the Gila Basin.* Medallion Papers No. 3. Gila Pueblo, Globe, Arizona.

Glassow, M. A.
1977 Population Aggregation and Systemic Change: Examples from the American Southwest. In *Explanation of Prehistoric Change*, edited by J. N. Hill, pp. 185–214. University of New Mexico Press, Albuquerque.

Glick, T. F.
1970 *Irrigation and Society in Medieval Valencia.* Belknap Press/Harvard University Press, Cambridge, Massachusetts.

Graybill, D. A., D. A. Gregory, G. S. Funkhouser, and F. L. Nials
2006 Long-Term Streamflow Reconstructions, River Channel Morphology, and Aboriginal Irrigation Systems along the Salt and Gila Rivers. In *Environmental Change and Human Adaptation in the Ancient Southwest*, edited by D. E. Doyel and J. S. Dean, pp. 69–123. University of Utah Press, Salt Lake City.

Gregory, D. A.
1987 The Morphology of Platform Mounds and the Structure of Classic Period Hohokam Sites. In *The Hohokam Village: Site Structure and Organization*, edited by D. E. Doyel, pp. 183–210. American Association for the Advancement of Science, Glenwood Springs, Colorado.

1991 Form and Variation in Hohokam Settlement Patterns. In *Chaco and Hohokam: Prehistoric Regional Systems in the American Southwest*, edited by P. L. Crown and W. J. Judge, pp. 159–194. School of American Research Press, Santa Fe, New Mexico.

1994 Prehistoric Irrigation Communities in the Blackwater Area. In *The History of Human Settlement in the Blackwater Area*, by D. A. Gregory and G. A. Huckleberry, pp. 145–190. An Archaeological Survey of the Blackwater Area, vol. 1. Cultural Resources Report No. 86. Archaeological Consulting Services, Tempe, Arizona.

Gregory, D. A., and D. L. Douglas
1994 *Site Descriptions and Related Data.* An Archaeological Survey of the Blackwater Area, vol. 2. Cultural Resources Report No. 86. Archaeological Consulting Services, Tempe, Arizona.

Gregory, D. A., and G. A. Huckleberry
1994 *The History of Human Settlement in the Blackwater Area.* An Archaeological Survey of the Blackwater Area, vol. 1. Cultural Resources Report No. 86. Archaeological Consulting Services, Tempe, Arizona.

Gregory, D. A., and F. L. Nials
1985 Observations Concerning the Distribution of Classic Period Hohokam Platform Mounds. In *Proceedings of the 1983 Hohokam Symposium*, pt. 1, edited by A. E. Dittert, Jr., and D. E. Dove, pp. 373–388. Occasional Paper No. 2. Arizona Archaeological Society, Phoenix Chapter, Phoenix.

Greven, P. J., Jr.
1970 *Four Generations: Population, Land, and Family in Colonial Andover, Massachusetts.* Cornell University Press, Ithaca, New York.

Guillet, D.
1998 Rethinking Legal Pluralism: Local Law and State Law in the Evolution of Water Property Rights in Northwestern Spain. *Comparative Studies in Society and History* 40:42–70.

Gumerman, G. J. (editor)
1991 *Exploring the Hohokam: Prehistoric Desert Peoples of the American Southwest.* New World Studies Series No. 1. Amerind Foundation, Dragoon, Arizona, and University of New Mexico Press, Albuquerque.

Hackenberg, R. A.
1974 *Aboriginal Land Use and Occupancy of the Pima-Maricopa Indians.* 2 vols. Garland, New York.

Hart, D. R., and D. B. Craig
2006 *Archaeological Investigations along the Santan Expansion Project Pipeline Corridor from Gilbert to Coolidge, Maricopa and Pinal Counties, Arizona: Investigations at AZ U:10:2(ASM), AZ U:10:175(ASM), AZ U:10:176(ASM), AZ U:15:248(ASM), AZ U:14:54(ASM), AZ U:14:361(ASM), AZ U:14:74(ASM), and AZ AA:2:131(ASM).* Technical Report No. 05-48. Northland Research, Tempe, Arizona.

Hassan, F. A.
1981 *Demographic Archaeology.* Academic Press, New York.

Haury, E. W.
1937 The Snaketown Canal. In *Excavations at Snaketown: Material Culture*, by H. S. Gladwin, E. W. Haury, E. B. Sayles, and N. Gladwin, pp. 50–58. Medallion Papers No. 25. Gila Pueblo, Globe, Arizona.

1945 *The Excavation of Los Muertos and Neighboring Ruins: The Hemenway Expedition.* Papers, vol. 24, no. 1. Peabody Museum of American Archaeology and Ethnology, Harvard University, Cambridge, Massachusetts.

1976 *The Hohokam: Desert Farmers and Craftsmen, Excavations at Snaketown 1964–65.* University of Arizona Press, Tucson.

Hegmon, M., M. A. Peeples, A. P. Kinzig, S. Kulow, C. M. Meegan, and M. C. Nelson
2008 Social Transformation and Its Human Costs in the Prehispanic U.S. Southwest. *American Anthropologist* 100:313–324.

Henderson, T. K.
2001 Chronology. In *Project Background and Feature Descriptions*, edited by D. B. Craig, pp. 163–207. The Grewe Archaeological Research Project, vol. 1. Anthropological Papers No. 99-1. Northland Research, Tempe, Arizona.

Henderson, T. K., and F. L. Nials
2004 The Sky Harbor Project Canals. In *Hohokam Farming on the Salt River Floodplain: Refining Models and Analytical Methods*, edited by T. K. Henderson, pp. 125–152. Anthropological Papers No. 43. Center for Desert Archaeology, Tucson, Arizona. Anthropological Papers No. 10. Pueblo Grande Museum, Phoenix.

Hill, J. B, J. J. Clark, W. H. Doelle, and P. D. Lyons
2004 Prehistoric Demography in the Southwest: Migration, Coalescence, and Hohokam Population Decline. *American Antiquity* 69:689–716.

Hill, W. W.
1936 Notes on Pima Land Law and Tenure. *American Anthropologist* 38:586–589.

Howard, J. B.
1987 The Lehi Canal System: Organization of a Classic Period Irrigation Community. In *The Hohokam Village: Site Structure and Organization*, edited by D. E. Doyel, pp. 211–221. American Association for the Advancement of Science, Glenwood Springs, Colorado.

1990 Paleohydraulics: Techniques for Modeling the Operation and Growth of Prehistoric Canal Systems. Unpublished Master's thesis, Department of Anthropology, Arizona State University, Tempe.

1993 A Paleohydraulic Approach to Examining Agricultural Intensification in Hohokam Irrigation Systems. In *Economic Aspects of Water Management in the Prehispanic New World*, edited by V. L. Scarborough and B. L. Isaac, pp. 261–322. Research in Economic Anthropology, Supplement No. 7. JAI Press, Greenwich, Connecticut.

2006 Hohokam Irrigation Communities: A Study of Internal Structure, External Relationships and Sociopolitical Complexity. Unpublished Ph.D. dissertation, School of Human Evolution and Social Change, Arizona State University, Tempe.

Howard, J. B., and G. E. Rice
1982 *The Archaeological Monitoring of Reach 1, Roosevelt Water Conservation District Floodway, Pinal County, Arizona*. Report No. 59. Office of Cultural Resource Management, Department of Anthropology, Arizona State University, Tempe.

Huckleberry, G. A.
1992 Soil Evidence of Hohokam Irrigation in the Salt River Valley, Arizona. *Kiva* 57:237–249.

1993 Late-Holocene Stream Dynamics on the Middle Gila River, Pinal County, Arizona. Unpublished Ph.D. dissertation, Department of Geosciences, University of Arizona, Tucson.

1995 Archaeological Implications of Late-Holocene Channel Changes on the Middle Gila River, Arizona. *Geoarchaeology: An International Journal* 10:159–182.

Hunt, R. C.
1988a Size and the Structure of Authority in Canal Irrigation Systems. *Journal of Anthropological Research* 44:335–355.

1988b Hydraulic Management in Southern Mesopotamia in Sumerian Times. In *Irrigation and Cultivation in Mesopotamia*, pt. 1, edited by J. N. Postgate and M. A. Powell, pp. 189–206. Bulletin on Sumerian Agriculture 4. Sumerian Agriculture Group, Cambridge University, Cambridge, England.

1989 Appropriate Social Organization? Water Users Associations in Bureaucratic Canal Irrigation Systems. *Human Organization* 48:79–90.

2000 Labor Productivity and Agricultural Development: Boserup Revisited. *Human Ecology* 28:251–277.

Hunt, R. C., D. Guillet, D. R. Abbott, J. M. Bayman, P. R. Fish, S. K. Fish, K. W. Kintigh, and J. A. Neely
2005 Plausible Ethnographic Analogies for the Social Organization of Hohokam Canal Irrigation. *American Antiquity* 70:433–456.

Hunt, R. C., and E. Hunt
1976 Canal Irrigation and Local Social Organization. *Current Anthropology* 17:389–411.

Hunt, R. C., and S. E. Ingram
2007 Double-Cropping Maize on the Middle Gila River: Intra-Annual River Regime and Canal Management in the Classic Period. Paper presented at the Arizona Archaeological Council symposium, Going with the Flow: Current Research in Prehistoric Irrigation Technology, Mesa, Arizona.

2010 Traditional Maize Production in the Southwest: Irrigation along the Middle Gila River. Manuscript in possession of the authors.

Ingram, S. E.
2008 Streamflow and Population Change in the Lower Salt River Valley of Central Arizona, ca. A.D. 775 to 1450. *American Antiquity* 73:136–165.

Ives, R. I. (editor and translator)
1939 *Sedelmayr's Relación of 1746*. Bureau of American Ethnology Bulletin 123, pp. 99–117; Anthropological Papers No. 9. Smithsonian Institution, U.S. Government Printing Office, Washington, D.C.

Jacobs, D. R., C. Garraty, and M. K. Woodson
2010 *An Archaeological Survey of the Santan Mountain Canal Alignment, Pima-Maricopa Irrigation Project, Gila River Indian Community, Arizona*. Pima-Maricopa Irrigation Project Report No. 4. Cultural Resource Management Program, Gila River Indian Community, Sacaton, Arizona.

Jha, N.
2002 The Bifurcate Subak: The Social Organization of a Balinese Irrigation Community. Unpublished Ph.D. dissertation, Brandeis University.

Johnson, A. E.
1964 Archaeological Excavations in Hohokam Sites of Southern Arizona. *American Antiquity* 30:145–161.

Johnson, G. A.
1982 Organizational Structure and Scalar Stress. In *Theory and Explanation in Archaeology: The Southampton Conference*, edited by C. Renfrew, M. J. Rowlands, and B. A. Segraves, pp. 389–421. Academic Press, New York.

1989 Dynamics of Southwestern Prehistory: Far Outside—Looking In. In *Dynamics of Southwest Prehistory*, edited by L. S. Cordell and G. J. Gumerman, pp. 371–389. Smithsonian Institution Press, Washington, D.C.

Johnson, W. W., Jr., P. D. Camp, and J. D. Preston
1998 *Soil Survey of the Gila River Indian Reservation, Arizona, Parts of Maricopa and Pinal Counties*. U.S. Department of Agriculture, Natural Resources Conservation Service, Washington, D.C.

Kelly, W. W.
1983 Concepts in the Anthropological Study of Irrigation. *American Anthropologist* 85:880–886.

Kintigh, K. W.
1994 Chaco, Community Architecture, and Cibolan Aggregation. In *The Ancient Southwestern Community: Models for the Study of Prehistoric Social Organization*, edited by W. H. Wills and R. D. Leonard, pp. 131–140. University of New Mexico Press, Albuquerque.

Kintigh, K. W., D. M. Glowacki, and D. L. Huntley
2004 Long-Term Settlement History and the Emergence of Towns in the Zuni Area. *American Antiquity* 69:432–456.

Kowalewski, S., P. R. Fish, H. D. Wallace, D. B. Craig, and J. C. Ravesloot
forthcoming Hohokam Demography. In *Hohokam Trajectories in World Perspective*, edited by P. R. Fish and S. K. Fish. New World Series. Amerind Foundation, Dragoon, Arizona.

Lansing, J. S.
1991 *Priests and Programmers: Technologies of Power in the Engineered Landscape of Bali*. Princeton University Press, Princeton, New Jersey.

Larson, A.
1926 *Map of Prehistoric Canal System, Gila Valley*. On file, Arizona State Museum, University of Arizona, Tucson.

Leach, E. R.
1961 *Pul Eliya: A Village in Ceylon*. Cambridge University Press, Cambridge, England.

Lees, S. H.
1973 *Sociopolitical Aspects of Canal Irrigation in the Valley of Oaxaca*. Memoirs, no. 5. Museum of Anthropology, University of Michigan, Ann Arbor.

Lewis, H. T.
1991 *Ilocano Irrigation: The Corporate Resolution*. Asian Studies at Hawaii No. 37. University of Hawaii Press, Honolulu.

Loendorf, C., and G. E. Rice
2004 *Projectile Point Typology, Gila River Indian Community, Arizona*. Anthropological Research Papers No. 2. Cultural Resource Management Program, Gila River Indian Community, Sacaton, Arizona.

Loendorf, C., M. K. Woodson, J. A. Darling, D. Burden, B. G. Randolph, and R. Barfield
2007 *A Preliminary Report on the Results of Phase I Data Recovery Investigations of Cultural Resources in Santan Reaches ST-IB, ST-IC, and ST-FP of the Pima-Maricopa Irrigation Project, Gila River Indian Community, Pinal County, Arizona.* Pima-Maricopa Irrigation Project Technical Report No. 2006-03. Cultural Resource Management Program, Gila River Indian Community, Sacaton, Arizona.

Loendorf, C., M. K. Woodson, G. E. Rice, and J. A. Darling
2009 *Revised Treatment Plan for Cultural Resources in Santan Reaches ST-IB, ST-IC, and ST-FP of the Pima-Maricopa Irrigation Project, Gila River Indian Community, Pinal County, Arizona.* Pima-Maricopa Irrigation Project Technical Report No. 2006-04. Cultural Resource Management Program, Gila River Indian Community, Sacaton, Arizona.

Mabry, J. B.
1996 The Ethnology of Local Irrigation. In *Canals and Communities*, edited by J. B. Mabry, pp. 3–30. University of Arizona Press, Tucson.

Mabry, J. B. (editor)
2008 *Las Capas: Early Irrigation and Sedentism in a Southwestern Floodplain.* Anthropological Papers No. 28. Center for Desert Archaeology, Tucson, Arizona.

Mabry, J. B., J. P. Holmlund, F. L. Nials, and M. R. Palacios-Fest
2008 Modeling Canal Characteristics and Trends. In *Las Capas: Early Irrigation and Sedentism in a Southwestern Floodplain*, edited by J. B. Mabry, pp. 267–282. Anthropological Papers No. 28. Center for Desert Archaeology, Tucson, Arizona.

Masse, W. B.
1981 Prehistoric Irrigation Systems in the Salt River Valley, Arizona. *Science* 214(23):408–415.

1991 The Quest for Subsistence Sufficiency and Civilization in the Sonoran Desert. In *Chaco and Hohokam: Prehistoric Regional Systems in the American Southwest*, edited by P. L. Crown and W. J. Judge, pp. 195–223. Advanced Seminar series. School of American Research Press, Santa Fe, New Mexico.

McGuire, R. H.
1980 The Mesoamerican Connection in the Southwest. *The Kiva* 46:3–38.

McGuire, R. H., and A. V. Howard
1987 The Structure and Organization of Hohokam Shell Exchange. *The Kiva* 52:113–146.

Meskimons, J. R.
1955 *Map Showing First Complete Survey of Indian Irrigation on Pima and Maricopa Reservation.* Reprinted. U.S. Department of the Interior Bureau of Indian Affairs, Phoenix Area Office, Phoenix. Originally published 1904.

Midvale, F.
1935 *A General Map of the Central Pima Country on the Gila.* Prepared for the Arizona Geography course. On file, Cultural Resource Management Program, Gila River Indian Community, Sacaton.

1946 *The Prehistoric Canals and Ruins of the Casa Grande–Florence Area of the Gila River in Southern Arizona.* Map. On file, Frank Midvale Collection, Arizona Collection, Hayden Library, Arizona State University, Tempe.

1963 The Prehistoric Irrigation of the Casa Grande Ruins Area of the Gila River in Southern Arizona. Unpublished map. On file (No. 225), Frank Midvale Collection, Arizona Collection, Hayden Library, Arizona State University, Tempe.

1965 Prehistoric Irrigation of the Casa Grande Ruins Area. *The Kiva* 30:82–86.

1972 Frank Midvale Papers, 1865–1972, Bulk 1930–1972. Frank Midvale Collection, Arizona Collection, Hayden Library, Arizona State University, Tempe.

Miles, W. D.
2009 *Investigation of a Cutbank Exposure of the Prehistoric Granite Knob Canal in GR-146 on the Gila River Indian Community.* Letter report. Pima-Maricopa Irrigation Project Technical Report No. 2009-02. Cultural Resource Management Program, Gila River Indian Community, Sacaton, Arizona.

Miles, W. D., M. K. Woodson, and F. Landreth
2008 *Annual Report on Cultural Resources Tasks Conducted in Fiscal Year 2007 under the Programmatic Agreement Regarding Approval of Essential Services Construction in an Underground Utility Corridor on the Gila River Indian Community, Arizona.* Technical Report No. 2007-10. Cultural Resource Management Program, Gila River Indian Community, Sacaton, Arizona.

Miles, W. D., D. K. Wright, and M. K. Woodson
2008 Hohokam Irrigated Fields near Upper Santan Village on the Gila River. Poster presented at the Arizona Archaeological Council conference, Advances in Hohokam Archaeology (organized by D. B. Craig and T. W. Bostwick), Phoenix.

Millon, R.
1962 Variations in Social Responses to the Practice of Irrigated Agriculture. In *Civilizations in Desert Lands*, edited by R. B. Woodbury, pp. 56–88. Anthropological Papers No. 62. University of Utah, Salt Lake City.

Mitalsky, F. (F. Midvale)
1935 A General Map of the Central Pima Country on the Gila. Prepared for the Arizona Geography Course. On file, Cultural Resource Management Program, Gila River Indian Community, Sacaton.

Mitchell, W. P.
1973 The Hydraulic Hypothesis: A Reappraisal. *Current Anthropology* 14:532–534.

1976 Irrigation and Community in the Central Peruvian Highlands. *American Anthropologist* 78:25–44.

Morgan, D., and M. K. Woodson
2004 *National Register of Historic Places Eligibility Assessment of Nine Sites in the Proposed Blackwater Reservoir (BW-RS) and Two Sites along Main-Stem Canal Reaches BW-IB and BW-IIA of the Pima-Maricopa Irrigation Project, Pinal County, Arizona.* Pima-Maricopa Irrigation Project Technical Report No. 2004-03. Cultural Resource Management Program, Gila River Indian Community, Sacaton, Arizona.

Motsinger, T. N.
1993 *Archaeological Investigations at the Gila Butte Site: Hohokam Irrigation and Economic Systems along the Gila River, Arizona.* Archaeological Report No. 93-84. SWCA Environmental Consultants, Phoenix.

Neily, R. B., M. Brodbeck, and K. S. Wigglesworth
1999 *An Archaeological Survey of the Santan Canal Reaches and Adjoining Areas in the Santan Management Area, Pima-Maricopa Irrigation Project (P-MIP), Gila River Indian Community, Arizona.* Pima-Maricopa Irrigation Project Report No. 2. Cultural Resource Management Program, Gila River Indian Community, Sacaton, Arizona.

Neily, R. B., B. G. Randolph, S. R. James, and M. Brodbeck
2000 *An Archaeological Assessment of the Southwestern Portion of the Santan Management Area, Pima-Maricopa Irrigation Project (P-MIP), Gila River Indian Community, Arizona.* Pima-Maricopa Irrigation Project Report No. 10. Cultural Resource Management Program, Gila River Indian Community, Sacaton, Arizona.

Nelson, R. S.
1986 Pochtecas and Prestige: Mesoamerican Artifacts in Hohokam Sites. In *Ripples in the Chichimec Sea: New Considerations of Southwestern-Mesoamerican Interactions*, edited by F. J. Mathien and R. H. McGuire, pp. 154–182. Southern Illinois University Press, Carbondale.

Netting, R. M.
1993 *Smallholders, Householders: Farm Families and the Ecology of Intensive, Sustainable Agriculture.* Stanford University Press, Stanford, California.

Nials, F. L., D. A. Gregory, and D. A. Graybill
1989 Salt River Streamflow and Hohokam Irrigation Systems. In *The 1982–1984 Excavations at Las Colinas: Environment and Subsistence*, by D. A. Graybill, D. A. Gregory, F. L. Nials, S. K. Fish, R. E. Gasser, C. H. Miksicek, and C. R. Szuter, pp. 59–76. Archaeological Series No. 162, vol. 5. Arizona State Museum, University of Arizona, Tucson.

Nicholas, L. M.
1981 Irrigation and Sociopolitical Development in the Salt River Valley, Arizona: An Examination of Three Prehistoric Canal Systems. Unpublished Master's thesis, Department of Anthropology, Arizona State University, Tempe.

Nicholas, L. M., and G. M. Feinman
1989 A Regional Perspective on Hohokam Irrigation in the Lower Salt River Valley, Arizona. In *The Sociopolitical Structure of Prehistoric Southwestern Societies*, edited by S. Upham, K. Lightfoot, and R. Jewett, pp. 199–235. Westview Press, Boulder, Colorado.

Nicholas, L. M., and J. Neitzel
1984 Canal Irrigation and Sociopolitical Organization in the Lower Salt River Valley: A Diachronic Analysis. In *Prehistoric Agricultural Strategies in the Southwest*, edited by S. K. Fish and P. R. Fish, pp. 161–178. Anthropological Research Papers No. 33. Arizona State University, Tempe.

Olberg, C. R.
1919 San Carlos Irrigation Project. In *Hearings before the Committee on Indian Affairs, House of Representatives, Sixty-Sixth Congress, First Session, on the Condition of Various Tribes of Indians*, vol. 2, Appendix A, pp. 5–102. U.S. Government Printing Office, Washington, D.C.

Ostrom, E.
1993 Constituting Social Capital and Collective Action. Paper presented at the Heterogeneity and Collection Action Workshop in Political Theory and Policy Analysis, Indiana University, Bloomington.

Phillips, B. G., and D. B. Craig
2001 Canals. In *Project Background and Feature Descriptions*, edited by D. B. Craig, pp. 146–162. The Grewe Archaeological Research Project, vol. 1. Anthropological Research Papers No. 99-1. Northland Research, Tempe, Arizona.

Purcell, D. E., L. S. Cummings, K. Puseman, and T. E. Montoux
1997 Hohokam Non-Irrigation Agriculture in the Middle and Upper Gila Valley. In *The Eastern Mining Area Project Coolidge to Hayden Segment Data Recovery: Hohokam Agriculture in the Middle and Upper Gila River Valley of Pinal County, Arizona*, edited by D. E. Purcell, pp. 5.1–5.44. Archaeological Report No. 97-47. Draft. SWCA Environmental Consultants, Flagstaff, Arizona.

Rafferty, K.
1982 Sociopolitical Organization in the Desert Southwest: The Hohokam of the Gila Butte Region, South-Central Arizona. Unpublished Ph.D. dissertation, State University of New York, Stony Brook.

Ravesloot, J. C.
2007 Changing Views of Snaketown in a Larger Landscape. In *The Hohokam Millennium*, edited by S. K. Fish and P. R. Fish, pp. 91–98. School for Advanced Research Press, Santa Fe, New Mexico.

Ravesloot, J. C., J. A. Darling, and M. R. Waters
2009 Hohokam and Pima-Maricopa Irrigation Agriculturalists: Maladaptive or Resilient Societies? In *The Archaeology of Environmental Change: Socionatural Legacies of Degradation and Resilience*, edited by C. T. Fischer, J. B. Hill, and G. M. Feinman, pp. 232–245. University of Arizona Press, Tucson.

Ravesloot, J. C., and A. Lascaux (editors)
1993 *The Maricopa Road Site: A Pre-Classic Hohokam Village, AZ T:16:13 (ASU), Pinal County, Arizona*. Anthropological Field Studies No. 28. Department of Anthropology, Arizona State University, Tempe.

Ravesloot, J. C., G. E. Rice, and M. K. Woodson
forthcoming The Growth and Consolidation of Settlement Complexes and Irrigation Communities on the Middle Gila. In *Hohokam Trajectories in World Perspective*, edited by P. R. Fish and S. K. Fish. New World Series. Amerind Foundation, Dragoon, Arizona.

Ravesloot, J. C., and M. R. Waters
2004 Geoarchaeology and Archaeological Site Patterning on the Middle Gila River, Arizona. *Journal of Field Archaeology* 29:203–214.

Ravesloot, J. C., M. K. Woodson, and M. J. Boley (editors)
2007 *Testing and Data Recovery, SFPP, LP, East Line Expansion Project, Arizona Portion: Cochise, Pima, Pinal, and Maricopa Counties*. Technical Report No. 2007-04. William Self Associates, Tucson, Arizona.

Rea, A.
1997 *At the Desert's Green Edge: An Ethnobotany of the Gila River Pima.* University of Arizona Press, Tucson.

Redman, C. L.
1991 The Comparative Context of Social Complexity. In *Chaco and Hohokam: Prehistoric Regional Systems in the American Southwest*, edited by P. L. Crown and W. J. Judge, pp. 277–292. School of American Research Press, Santa Fe, New Mexico.

1999 *Human Impact on Ancient Environments.* University of Arizona Press, Tucson.

Rice, G. E.
1998 War and Water: An Ecological Perspective on Hohokam Irrigation. *Kiva* 63:263–301.

2000 Hohokam and Salado Segmentary Organization: The Evidence from the Roosevelt Platform Mound Study. In *Salado*, edited by J. S. Dean, pp. 143–166. University of New Mexico Press, Albuquerque.

2001 *The Role of Field Houses and Farmsteads in Hohokam Settlement Systems.* Pima-Maricopa Irrigation Project Technical Report No. 2001-10. Cultural Resource Management Program, Gila River Indian Community, Sacaton, Arizona.

Rice, G. E., R. Greenspan, and K. Peterson
2005 *The Archaeological Test of AZ AA:2:239 (ASM) and AZ AA:2:240 (ASM) in the City of Coolidge, Pinal County, Arizona.* Technical Report No. 05-19. Rio Salado Archaeology, Tempe, Arizona.

Rice, G. E., and J. C. Ravesloot
2002 Hohokam Public Architecture and Settlement Systems on the Middle Gila River. Paper presented in the symposium, Visible Archaeology on the Gila River Indian Reservation, at the 67th Annual Meeting of the Society for American Archaeology, Denver.

Rice, G. E., D. Wilcox, K. Rafferty, and J. Schoenwetter
1979 *An Archaeological Test of Sites in the Gila Butte–Santan Region, South-Central Arizona.* Anthropological Research Papers No. 18. Department of Anthropology, Arizona State University, Tempe.

Richards, P.
1978 Spatial Organisation and Social Change in West Africa—Notes for Historians and Anthropologists. In *The Spatial Organisation of Culture*, edited by I. Hodder, pp. 271–289. University of Pittsburgh Press, Pittsburgh.

Rodrigues, T. L., M. K. Woodson, C. Loendorf, and D. Burden
2003 *National Register of Historic Places Eligibility Testing at Five Sites along the P-MIP Main Stem Canal Alignment in the Santan Management Area, Pima-Maricopa Irrigation Project, Gila River Indian Community, Pinal County, Arizona.* Pima-Maricopa Irrigation Project Technical Report No. 2003-04. Cultural Resource Management Program, Gila River Indian Community, Sacaton, Arizona.

Russell, F.
1975 *The Pima Indians, Twenty-Sixth Annual Report of the Bureau of American Ethnology, 1904–1905.* Reprinted. University of Arizona Press, Tucson. Originally published 1908, Smithsonian Institution, Washington, D.C.

Scarborough, V. L.
2003 *The Flow of Power: Ancient Water Systems and Landscapes.* School of American Research Press, Santa Fe, New Mexico.

Schiffer, M. B.
1982 Hohokam Chronology: An Essay on History and Method. In *Hohokam and Patayan: Prehistory of Southwestern Arizona*, edited by R. H. McGuire and M. B. Schiffer, pp. 299–344. Academic Press, New York.

1987 *Formation Processes of the Archaeological Record.* University of New Mexico Press, Albuquerque.

Schroeder, A. H.
1966 Partial Diffusion from Mexico into the Southwest after A.D. 600. *American Antiquity* 31:683–704.

Sellars, W., and R. H. Hill
1974 *Arizona Climate.* University of Arizona Press, Tucson.

Seymour, D. J., and M. B. Schiffer
1987 A Preliminary Analysis of Pithouse Assemblages from Snaketown, Arizona. In *Method and Theory for Activity Area Research: An Ethnoarchaeological Approach*, edited by S. Kent, pp. 549–603. Columbia University Press, New York.

Sheridan, T. E.
1996 *La Gente Es Muy Perra*: Conflict and Cooperation over Irrigation Water in Cucurpe, Sonora, Mexico. In *Canals and Communities*, edited by J. B. Mabry, pp. 33–52. University of Arizona Press, Tucson.

Sires, E. W., Jr.
1983 Archaeological Investigations at Las Fosas (AZ U:15:19): A Classic Period Settlement on the Gila River. In *Habitation Sites along the Gila River*, edited by L. S. Teague and P. L. Crown, pp. 493–658. Hohokam Archaeology along the Salt-Gila Aqueduct, Central Arizona Project, vol. 6. Archaeological Series No. 150. Arizona State Museum, University of Arizona, Tucson.

Smith, P. E. L.
1972 Land-Use, Settlement Patterns and Subsistence Agriculture: A Demographic Perspective. In *Man, Settlement, and Urbanism*, edited by P. J. Ucko, R. Tringham, and G. W. Dimbleby, pp. 409–425. Schenkman, Cambridge, Massachusetts.

Southworth, C. H.
1914–1915 *Gila River Survey, Pinal County, Arizona*. Map. U.S. Department of the Interior, U.S. Indian Service Irrigation, Washington, D.C. On file, Cultural Resource Management Program, Gila River Indian Community, Sacaton, Arizona.

1919 The History of Irrigation along the Gila River. In *Hearings before the Committee on Indian Affairs, House of Representatives, Sixty-Sixth Congress, First Session, on the Condition of Various Tribes of Indians*, vol. 2, Appendix A, pp. 103–225. U.S. Government Printing Office, Washington, D.C.

Stein, G.
1994 Economy, Ritual, and Power in 'Ubaid period Mesopotamia. In *Chiefdoms and Early States in the Near East: The Organizational Dynamics of Complexity*, edited by G. Stein and M. S. Rothman, pp. 35–46. Monographs in World Archaeology No. 18. Prehistory Press, Madison, Wisconsin.

Steward, J. H.
1949 Cultural Causality and Law. *American Anthropologist* 51:1–27.

1955 Some Implications of the Symposium. In *Irrigation Civilizations: A Comparative Study*, edited by J. H. Steward, pp. 58–78. Social Sciences Monograph No. 1. Pan American Union, Washington, D.C.

Stone, G. D.
1996 *Settlement Ecology: The Social and Spatial Organization of Kofyar Agriculture*. University of Arizona Press, Tucson.

Stone, G. D., R. M. Netting, and M. P. Stone
1990 Seasonality, Labor Scheduling and Agricultural Intensification in the Nigerian Savanna. *American Anthropologist* 92:7–24.

Swarthout, J. E., and L. Blank-Roper
1984 *Studies of Small Prehistoric Sites in the Gila Butte–Santan Area*. Report No. 61. Office of Cultural Resource Management, Department of Anthropology, Arizona State University, Tempe.

Tang, S. Y.
1992 *Institutions for Collective Action: Self-Governance in Irrigation*. ICS Press, San Francisco, California.

Turner, B. L., II, and W. E. Doolittle
1978 The Concept and Measure of Agricultural Intensity. *Professional Geographer* 30:297–301.

Turner, R. M., and D. E. Brown
1994 Sonoran Desertscrub. In *Biotic Communities: Southwestern United States and Northwestern Mexico*, edited by D. E. Brown, pp. 181–221. University of Utah Press, Salt Lake City.

Underhill, R.
1939 *Social Organization of the Papago Indians*. Columbia University Press, New York.

Unknown
1974 *The White Man's Friend*. On file, Special Collections, University of Arizona Library, Tucson.

Uphoff, N.
1986 *Improving International Irrigation Management with Farmer Participation: Getting the Process Right*. Westview Press, Boulder, Colorado.

U.S. Department of the Interior Bureau of Reclamation
1951 *Irrigation Advisor's Guide.* U.S. Department of the Interior Bureau of Reclamation, U.S. Government Printing Office, Washington, D.C.

Wallace, H. D.
2001 Time Seriation and Typological Refinement of the Middle Gila Buffware Sequence: Snaketown through Soho Phases. In *Ceramic Studies*, edited by David R. Abbott, pp. 177–262. The Grewe Archaeological Research Project, vol. 2, pt. 1. Anthropological Papers 99-1. Northland Research, Tempe, Arizona.

2004 Update to the Middle Gila Buff Ware Ceramic Sequence. In *Hohokam Farming on the Salt River Floodplain: Refining Models and Analytical Methods*, edited by T. K. Henderson, pp. 45–124. Anthropological Papers No. 42. Center for Desert Archaeology, Tucson, Arizona.

Wallace, H. D. (editor)
2003 *Roots of Sedentism: Archaeological Investigations at Valencia Vieja, a Founding Village in the Tucson Basin in Southern Arizona.* Anthropological Papers No. 29. Center for Desert Archaeology, Tucson, Arizona.

Wallace, H. D., J. D. Heidke, and W. H. Doelle
1995 Hohokam Origins. *Kiva* 60:575–618.

Walsh-Anduze, M.
1993 The Gila Butte Site: Inference and Evidence for Hohokam Ceramic Production. Paper presented at the 66th Pecos Conference, Springerville, Arizona.

Waters, M. R.
1992 *Principles of Geoarchaeology: A North American Perspective.* University of Arizona Press, Tucson.

1996 *Surficial Geologic Map of the Gila River Indian Community.* Pima-Maricopa Irrigation Project Technical Report No. 96-1. Cultural Resource Management Program, Gila River Indian Community, Sacaton, Arizona.

Waters, M. R., and J. C. Ravesloot
2000 Late Quaternary Geology of the Middle Gila River, Gila River Indian Reservation, Arizona. *Quaternary Research* 54:49–57.

2001 Landscape Change and the Cultural Evolution of the Hohokam along the Middle Gila River and Other River Valleys in Southern Arizona. *American Antiquity* 66:285–299.

2003 Disaster or Catastrophe: Human Adaptation to High- and Low-Frequency Landscape Processes—A Reply to Ensor, Ensor, and De Vries. *American Antiquity* 68:400–405.

Wells, E. C., and R. L. Greenspan
2002 *A Cultural Resources Assessment of the Lone Butte Management Area, Pima-Maricopa Irrigation Project, Gila River Indian Community, Arizona.* Pima-Maricopa Irrigation Project Technical Report No. 12. Cultural Resource Management Program, Gila River Indian Community, Sacaton, Arizona.

Wells, E. C., J. C. Ravesloot, and M. K. Woodson
2005 Landscape between Villages: A Test of the Model Using Hohokam Excavation Data. Poster presented at the 70th Annual Meeting of the Society for American Archaeology, Salt Lake City.

Wells, E. C., G. E. Rice, and J. C. Ravesloot
2003 *Toward Understanding the Use, Management and Meaning of Landscapes between Villages on the Gila River Indian Community.* Pima-Maricopa Irrigation Project Technical Report No. 2003-06. Cultural Resource Management Program, Gila River Indian Community, Sacaton, Arizona.

2004 Peopling Landscapes between Villages in the Middle Gila River Valley of Central Arizona. *American Antiquity* 69:627–652.

Wilcox, D. R.
1986 A Historical Analysis of the Problem of Southwestern-Mesoamerican Connections. In *Ripples in the Chichimec Sea: New Considerations of Southwestern-Mesoamerican Interactions*, edited by F. J. Mathien and R. H. McGuire, pp. 9–44. Southern Illinois University Press, Carbondale.

1987 The Evolution of Hohokam Ceremonial Systems. In *Astronomy and Ceremony in the Prehistoric Southwest*, edited by J. Carlson and W. J. Judge, pp. 149–168. Papers, no. 2. Maxwell Museum of Anthropology, Albuquerque, New Mexico.

1991 Hohokam Social Complexity. In *Chaco and Hohokam: Prehistoric Regional Systems in the American Southwest*, edited by P. L. Crown and W. J. Judge, pp. 253–275. School of American Research Press, Santa Fe, New Mexico.

Wilcox, D. R., T. R. McGuire, and C. Sternberg

1981 *Snaketown Revisited: A Partial Cultural Resource Survey, Analysis of Site Structure, and an Ethnohistoric Study of the Proposed Hohokam-Pima National Monument.* Archaeological Series No. 155. Arizona State Museum, University of Arizona, Tucson.

Wilcox, D. R., and L. O. Shenk

1977 *The Architecture of the Casa Grande and Its Interpretation.* Archaeological Series No. 115. Arizona State Museum, University of Arizona, Tucson.

Wilcox, D. R., and C. Sternberg

1983 *Hohokam Ballcourts and Their Interpretation.* Archaeological Series No. 160. Arizona State Museum, University of Arizona, Tucson.

Wilson, J. P.

1999 *Peoples of the Middle Gila: A Documentary History of the Pimas and Maricopas, 1500s–1945.* On file, Cultural Resource Management Program, Gila River Indian Community, Sacaton, Arizona.

Wittfogel, K. A.

1955 Developmental Aspects of Hydraulic Civilizations. In *Irrigation Civilizations: A Comparative Study*, edited by J. H. Steward, pp. 43–52. Social Sciences Monograph No. 1. Pan American Union, Washington, D.C.

1957 *Oriental Despotism: A Comparative Study of Total Power.* Yale University Press, New Haven, Connecticut.

Wood, D. G.

1972 *Recorded Archaeological Sites on the Gila River Indian Reservation: Phase III.* Archaeological Series No. 16. Arizona State Museum, University of Arizona, Tucson.

Woodbury, R. B.

1961 A Reappraisal of Hohokam Irrigation. *American Anthropologist* 63:550–560.

1976 West Fork. In *The Hohokam: Desert Farmers and Craftsmen, Excavations at Snaketown 1964–1965*, by E. W. Haury, pp. 141–142. University of Arizona Press, Tucson.

Woodbury, R. B., and J. O. Ressler

1962 Effects of Environmental and Cultural Limitations upon Hohokam Agriculture, Southern Arizona. In *Civilizations in Desert Lands*, edited by R. B. Woodbury, pp. 41–53. Anthropological Papers No. 62. University of Utah, Salt Lake City.

Woodson, M. K.

2003 *A Research Design for the Study of Prehistoric and Historic Irrigation Systems in the Middle Gila Valley, Arizona.* Pima-Maricopa Irrigation Project Technical Report No. 2003-10. Cultural Resource Management Program, Gila River Indian Community, Sacaton, Arizona.

2004 Constraints and Capacities of Hohokam Canal Systems in the Salt and Gila River Valleys, South-Central Arizona. Paper presented at the 1st Annual Archaeological Sciences of the Americas symposium, University of Arizona, Tucson.

2006 *National Register of Historic Places Eligibility Assessment of GR-436 along Reach ST-IB of the Pima-Maricopa Irrigation Project Main-Stem Canal, Santan Management Area, Gila River Indian Community, Pinal County, Arizona.* Pima-Maricopa Irrigation Project Technical Report No. 2006-06. Cultural Resource Management Program, Gila River Indian Community, Sacaton, Arizona.

2007 Hohokam and Akimel O'odham Canal Irrigation Systems. In *Testing and Data Recovery, SFPP, LP, East Line Expansion Project, Arizona Portion: Cochise, Pima, Pinal, and Maricopa Counties*, edited by J. C. Ravesloot, M. K. Woodson, and M. J. Boley, pp. 21.1–21.38. Technical Report No. 2007-04. William Self Associates, Tucson, Arizona.

2009 *Map of Prehistoric Hohokam Canal Systems in the Middle Gila Valley.* 3rd ed. Cultural Resource Management Program, Gila River Indian Community, Sacaton, Arizona.

2010a The Social Organization of Hohokam Irrigation in the Middle Gila River Valley, Arizona. Unpublished Ph.D. dissertation, School of Human Evolution and Social Change, Arizona State University, Tempe.

2010b Re-Drawing the Map of the Hohokam Canals in the Middle Gila River Valley. *Journal of Arizona Archaeology* 1(1):5–19.

2010c Hohokam Canal Systems along the Middle Gila River. *Archaeology Southwest* 23(4):9.

forthcoming Building and Cleaning the Snaketown Canal: Hohokam Labor Requirements and Work Force Sizes in the Middle Gila River Valley. Manuscript accepted for publication in *Water History*, expected 2015.

Woodson, M. K. (editor)

2002 *Archaeological Investigations at the Sweetwater Site on the Gila River Indian Community.* Technical Report No. 2002-14. Cultural Resource Management Program, Gila River Indian Community, Sacaton, Arizona.

Woodson, M. K., and G. A. Huckleberry

2002 Prehistoric Canal Irrigation in Arizona. In *Prehistoric Water Utilization and Technology in Arizona: Background for Historic Contexts, A Component of the Arizona Historic Preservation Plan*, by M. S. Foster, M. K. Woodson, and G. A. Huckleberry, pp. 91–138. Arizona State Parks, Phoenix.

Woodson, M. K., and J. C. Ravesloot

2005 New Insights on Hohokam Canal Irrigation Systems on the Middle Gila River, Arizona. Poster presented at the 70th Annual Meeting of the Society for American Archaeology, Salt Lake City.

Woodson, M. Kyle, Jonathan A. Sandor, Colleen Strawhacker, and Wesley D. Miles

2015 Hohokam Canal Irrigation and the Formation of Irragric Anthrosols in the Middle Gila River Valley, Arizona, USA. *Geoarchaeology: An International Journal* 30:271–290. DOI http://dx.doi.org/10.1002/gea.21513.

Woodson, M. K., and G. E. Rice

2002 The Hegemony of the Casa Grande Platform Mound Community. Paper presented in the symposium, Visible Archaeology on the Gila River Indian Reservation, at the 67th Annual Meeting of the Society for American Archaeology, Denver.

Wright, D. K, and M. R. Waters

2010 *Results of Geomorphic Test Excavations along the Middle Gila River within the Gila River Indian Community, Arizona.* Pima-Maricopa Irrigation Project Report No. 11. Cultural Resource Management Program, Gila River Indian Community, Sacaton, Arizona.

Yoffee, N.

1993 Too Many Chiefs? (or, Safe Texts for the 90s). In *Archaeological Theory: Who Sets the Agenda?* edited by A. Sherratt and N. Yoffee, pp. 60–74. Cambridge University Press, Cambridge, England.

Appendix A

Additional Data on Canal Systems

This appendix provides additional data on the canal systems described in Chapter 4: the Snaketown canal system (Study Area 1) and the Granite Knob, Santan, and Gila Butte canal systems (Study Area 2). This information includes a summary of the methods used in canal-system documentation and basic descriptive data for the systems. Also included is a discussion of how the locations and sizes of the irrigated fields were determined in the system reconstruction.

Methods of Canal-System Documentation

The methods used in documenting the canal systems are described here, including mapping the canal systems, determining the ages of canals, estimating canal-system size (command area), and defining irrigated field areas.

Mapping the Canal Systems

The identification and mapping of canals in the Snaketown canal system constituted the primary fieldwork for the project. My research has resulted in a detailed map of the entire Snaketown canal system. The new map builds from the earlier studies of canals in the Snaketown area that were described previously in this study. However, the survey of linear features between Gila Butte and Maricopa Road (Gila River Indian Community–Cultural Resource Management Program [GRIC-CRMP] site files; Neily et al. 2000) did not evaluate all the linear features in the study area, and the overall results had not been analyzed in detail. I found that there were some gaps in the data that required further assessment. In particular, a systematic effort had not been made to determine which features were definitely (or probably) prehistoric canal alignments. At the onset of my research, I re-evaluated the linear-feature-survey results.

As part of my re-evaluation, I first examined several different aerial photographs (dated 1936, 1986, 1994, and 2005) and historical maps of the Gila Butte–Snaketown area, to narrow the array of linear features that could represent canal alignments. In this way, I was able to eliminate those features that clearly represented historical-period and modern features (roads, ditches, and utility corridors). I then proceeded to a phase of ground-truthing of the remaining linear features, based on field reconnaissance. I applied a set of criteria for deciding which linear features represented prehistoric canal alignments based on previous experience with and study of the surficial expressions of canals in the middle Gila Valley (Woodson 2007, 2009; Woodson and Huckleberry 2002), as well as the guidelines of prior researchers, such as Frank Midvale (see Andresen 1987). An important finding of these studies was that relict prehistoric canals are frequently marked on the surface by linear mounds or linear artifact scatters or both (Figure A.1). Previous researchers, such as Odd Halseth, Frank Midvale, and Allen Dart (1986), also have noted this characteristic of prehistoric canal alignments. That correspondence has been confirmed through the excavation of backhoe trenches across these linear features in numerous locations in the middle Gila Valley (e.g., Loendorf et al. 2007; Miles et al. 2008; Woodson 2007). In addition, my assessment of the linear artifact scatters/mounds in the Snaketown canal system indicated that the canal segments excavated by Haury (1937, 1976) correspond to the same surface linear features documented here.

Because these linear artifact scatters so closely match the alignments of relict prehistoric canals, it is worth considering the cultural and natural processes that contributed to the formation of the canals (Schiffer 1987; Waters 1992; Woodson and Huckleberry 2002). These formation processes can be grouped into those that occurred during the use-life of the canal (including construction and operation) and those that occurred after abandonment of the canal (Figure A.2). The initial formation phase of a canal is its construction, when sediments and other materials are excavated along the alignment of the irrigation feature (see Figure A.2a). The dirt, or spoil, removed during the excavation is deposited alongside the canal channel, which

Figure A.1. Photograph of a linear earthen mound and artifact scatter marking the course of the north branch of the prehistoric Snaketown canal to the west of Maricopa Road (State Route 347), in GR-815, Locus B, view to the north-northwest (*Note*: the width of the lighter-soil-color area is about 60 m).

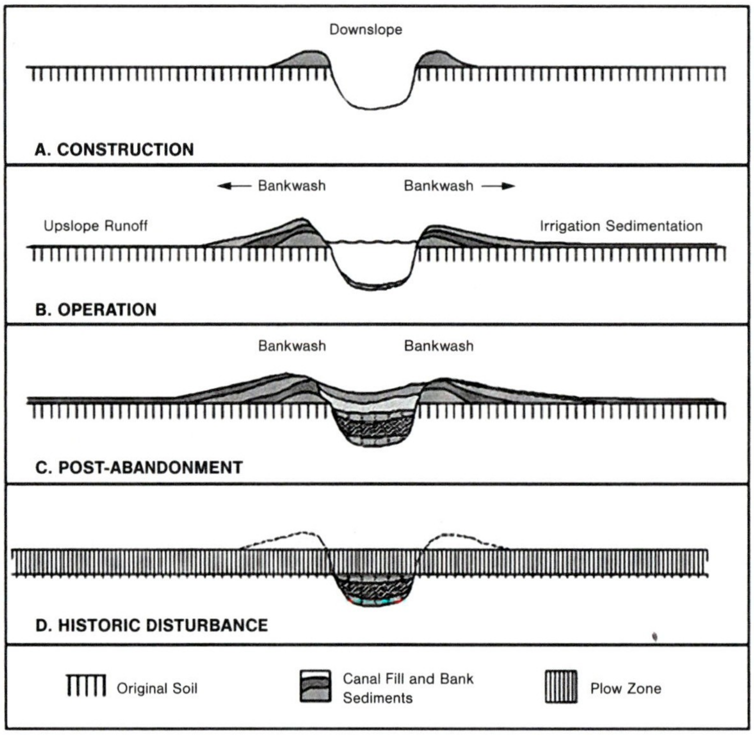

Figure A.2. Schematic representation of the formation processes of a prehistoric canal (after Huckleberry 1992:239, Figure 1).

creates one or two embankments (also called berms, banks, or levees) that parallel the channel. The operation phase of a canal includes the period of time when the feature is used to divert and deliver water to agricultural fields, reservoirs, or other water-utilization features (see Figure A.2b). Canal-channel morphology can be transformed by both natural actions (e.g., natural hydraulic adjustment) and cultural actions, such as maintenance (e.g., cleaning) and remodeling.

During the operation phase, a range of activities takes place along canals and can result in the breakage of pots and the accumulation of sherds and other artifacts (Robert C. Hunt, personal communication 2007). For instance, canals probably were the major sources of water for drinking, cooking, and washing for the people living along them. Canals also would have been used as transportation corridors to and from fields and villages. Riparian environments develop along canals that are used for a long time, providing trees, shade, and cool, moist air. Such places would have been attractive to people for resting or taking a break during work in the fields. Another possibility is that sherds and other artifacts got dumped in the canals. That was more common near habitation areas, but it did not appear that canals were used as the main refuse heaps, as were trash mounds and middens.

Once a canal ceases to be used for water diversion and delivery, it can be altered by a series of postabandonment processes (see Figure A.2c). First, abandoned canals continued to be used for some cultural activities, such as footpaths for transportation, and in some cases, they were reused as cemeteries (Ravesloot et al. 2007). Mourners may have interred the deceased within or near defunct canals because they were elevated above the zone of flood inundation. Most abandoned canals become slowly eroded or buried, or both, by natural surficial processes. The canals become filled mostly with alluvial sediments, primarily from surface runoff, but also possibly from aeolian and colluvial sediments as well as human-emplaced deposits. Canals located outside floodplains on relatively stable geomorphic surfaces may persist several centuries after abandonment. Finally, relict canals can be further modified by historical-period or modern disturbances, such as land leveling and plowing for agricultural purposes (see Figure A.2d). In areas where historical-period disturbances have not modified or destroyed them, relict canals can appear on the surface as linear earthen mounds, and frequently, they will have associated artifact scatters. The artifacts that remain along relict canals attest to the previous activities that occurred there, as described above. In areas where erosion has been more active, a linear mound may have been partially or completely effaced, leaving only a linear artifact scatter.

As an interesting note, Odd Halseth, City of Phoenix archaeologist in the early 1930s, examined some of the prehistoric canals in the middle Gila Valley as part of a project, directed by Neil Judd, to identify prehistoric canals using aerial photography. Halseth recounted that many of the canals in the Gila Valley were apparent as "trails of artifacts" (Todd Bostwick, Pueblo Grande Archaeologist, in a public presentation on November 17, 2005). Midvale (1965:83), based on his field studies of prehistoric canals, also recognized that "[s]ometimes only a path of stone tools and other broken litter marks the course of the canal across the desert." One of Midvale's 10 canal types, in terms of their states of preservation, was described as "a wide path of ancient litter and debris [that often] shows the [canal] alignment extending across the desert" (Andresen 1987:234). Because the GRIC includes large, undeveloped areas along the river terraces, it may be one of the last places in the Phoenix Basin where prehistoric canals can be seen as artifact "trails."

Other Aspects of Canals

The methods of measuring the time period and size of a canal system require some explanation. Establishing the ages of canals is always difficult, and several methods have been used for the middle Gila Valley canals (see Ackerly et al. 1987; Woodson 2003). For a canal that has only been mapped on the surface, age is estimated based on temporally diagnostic ceramics recovered from surface collections along the canal alignment, the ages of sites situated along the canal (based on surface collections and other diagnostic site criteria), and stratigraphic relationships to other canals, sites, and features. For an excavated canal, age is most commonly based on diagnostic ceramics recovered from the canal fill (from trench exposures and hand-excavated test units). Interpreting age based on ceramic samples is problematic, and the analyst must consider formation processes that were responsible for the deposition of the ceramics. Stratigraphic relationships can provide good relative-dating sequences. To date, only a handful of radiocarbon dates are available for the middle Gila Valley canals (e.g., Ravesloot et al. 2007; Waters and Ravesloot 2000), no archaeomagnetic dates are known, and only two optically stimulated luminescence dates have been processed from canals. Absolute dates are available for some contexts that are superimposed on canals, providing indirect ages. In sum, use-life typically can be defined at the level of time period (i.e., a 100–200-year interval) or periods, especially for main and distributary canals. A slightly more refined date (a 50–100-year range) is possible in situations where stratigraphic relationships exist between canals.

Past approaches to estimating system sizes of Hohokam canal systems also have been problematic (Hunt et al. 2005:440–441). Size is measured as command area, defined as the area of fields under the physical system that was irrigated regularly, or at least once. Notably, *command area* is different from *irrigable land*, which is the maximum extent that could receive irrigation water. Hohokam archaeologists have used measurements of main-canal lengths and cross-sectional areas to estimate system size, but those estimates do not necessarily equate to the actual area of the fields irrigated by the system (i.e., command area). During a previous study (Woodson 2004), I determined that the range of irrigable lands (the maximum amount of land downslope from a main canal that potentially could be irrigated in a canal system) for the 13 middle Gila Valley canal systems with good documentation ranged from 236 ha (Granite Knob) to 6,315 ha (Snaketown). The total maximum irrigable area, based on topography, for all 13 systems was 34,233 ha. More recently, I calculated two revised irrigable areas by assuming that the lateral canals, which were the direct supply of water to the fields, were either 254 or 500 m in length (Woodson 2010b). The 254-m length was determined based on research reported in this study. If the laterals were 500 m long, the range was from 186 ha (Granite Knob) to 3,607 ha (Grewe-Casa Grande), for a total of 19,531 ha for the 13 systems. If the laterals were 254 m long, the range was 133–2,374 ha, for a total of 12,449 ha for the 13 systems. The actual command area of the 13 systems was somewhere between the two amounts but was probably closer to the lower end.

The actual sizes, or command areas, of these systems may have been smaller, because entire irrigable areas (corrected or not) may not have been farmed at the same time. However, historical accounts have indicated that the Gila River Pima and Euroamerican farmers in the Salt and Gila Valleys did not employ a fallow system but, rather, practiced a system of continuous cultivation (e.g., Castetter and Bell 1942:172; Ezell 1961; Hackenberg 1974; Southworth 1919). Hence, the corrected irrigable area tentatively was used in this study as an estimation of size for Hohokam canal systems. A detailed set of survey maps of Gila River Pima canals and fields, drawn by C. H. Southworth in 1914–1915, though, shows a patchwork of cultivated and uncultivated fields in many canal systems. It is not clear why some fields were uncultivated (e.g., abandoned or fallow), but it could have been because it was a difficult time for the Pimas as a result of water shortages and other social factors. If so, then this suggests that the Pimas, and possibly the Hohokam, farmed only portions of all irrigable areas during times of stress and/or water scarcity. Further study of this and other ethnographic cases may provide the basis for a more rigorous method of estimating the sizes of prehistoric canal systems.

During the fieldwork for this study, it became clear that other observations could be used to more specifically define the irrigated field area of the Snaketown canal system. First, the field-survey data allowed the identification of many areas along the main and distribution canals and evidence of lateral canals extending from them, into adjacent areas. The areas along the laterals are inferred to have been irrigated fields. Second, I assessed the lengths of lateral canals as mapped for a set of canal systems used historically by the Akimel O'odham along the middle Gila River (Southworth 1914–1915). I suggest that the range of these lengths is a useful analog because of the similarities in the environments, water sources, and layouts of historical-period and prehistoric canal systems. The range provides a comparative basis for evaluating the probable range of prehistoric lateral-canal lengths. Third, previous research (Dart 1986; Huckleberry 1992) on the effects of irrigation on soils has shown that linear zones along prehistoric canals can correlate to soil phases/types on soil maps produced by the Natural Resources Conservation Service (NRCS) (Johnson et al. 1998). I evaluated the correspondence between soil types and the canals and inferred field areas by using AutoCAD to overlay the mapped canals on the soil map. By considering all four sources of data, I argue, I can identify, with a high probability, the locations of the prehistoric irrigated fields, which probably correspond to the command area of the Snaketown canal system.

Snaketown Canal System

The primary fieldwork for the project consisted of the identification and mapping of canals in the Snaketown canal system. A map of all the canals in this system is presented in Figure A.3. It is worth reiterating that the mapping process was greatly facilitated by the recognition that alignments of buried prehistoric canals are frequently marked on the surface by linear mounds or linear artifact scatters, or both. The undeveloped and relatively undisturbed terrain along the Snaketown canal system is another factor that allowed the assembly of such a detailed map.

Table A.1 provides an inventory of the canal types, listed by canal or segment number (correlating to Figure A.3), and the canal lengths that were documented in the Snaketown canal system. The primary heading of the main canal was located at the foot of Gila Butte (Diversion Point 1). The main canal divided into two branch canals at the West Fork, which was roughly midway along the linear extent of the canal. The two main canals are designated Canal 1 and Canal 2. Canal 1 includes the main canal, from the heading at Diversion Point 1 to the West Fork and along the extent of the north-branch canal. Canal 2 includes the south-branch canal, from the West Fork to its terminus. The main canals are divided into segments defined between junctions with other canals (usually a turnout point along the main canal). Distribution and lateral canals are numbered in sequence from upstream to downstream, as they diverged from a main or distribution canal (in a few cases of canals added later in the study, the sequence does not apply). Hence, the first canal to diverge from Canal 1 is designated 1-1; the first canal to turn out of Canal 2 is designated 2-1. More digits are used to designate a canal at a second or third level of divergence from the main canal; for example, Canal 1-15-3 is a lateral canal that turns out of distribution canal no. 1-15.

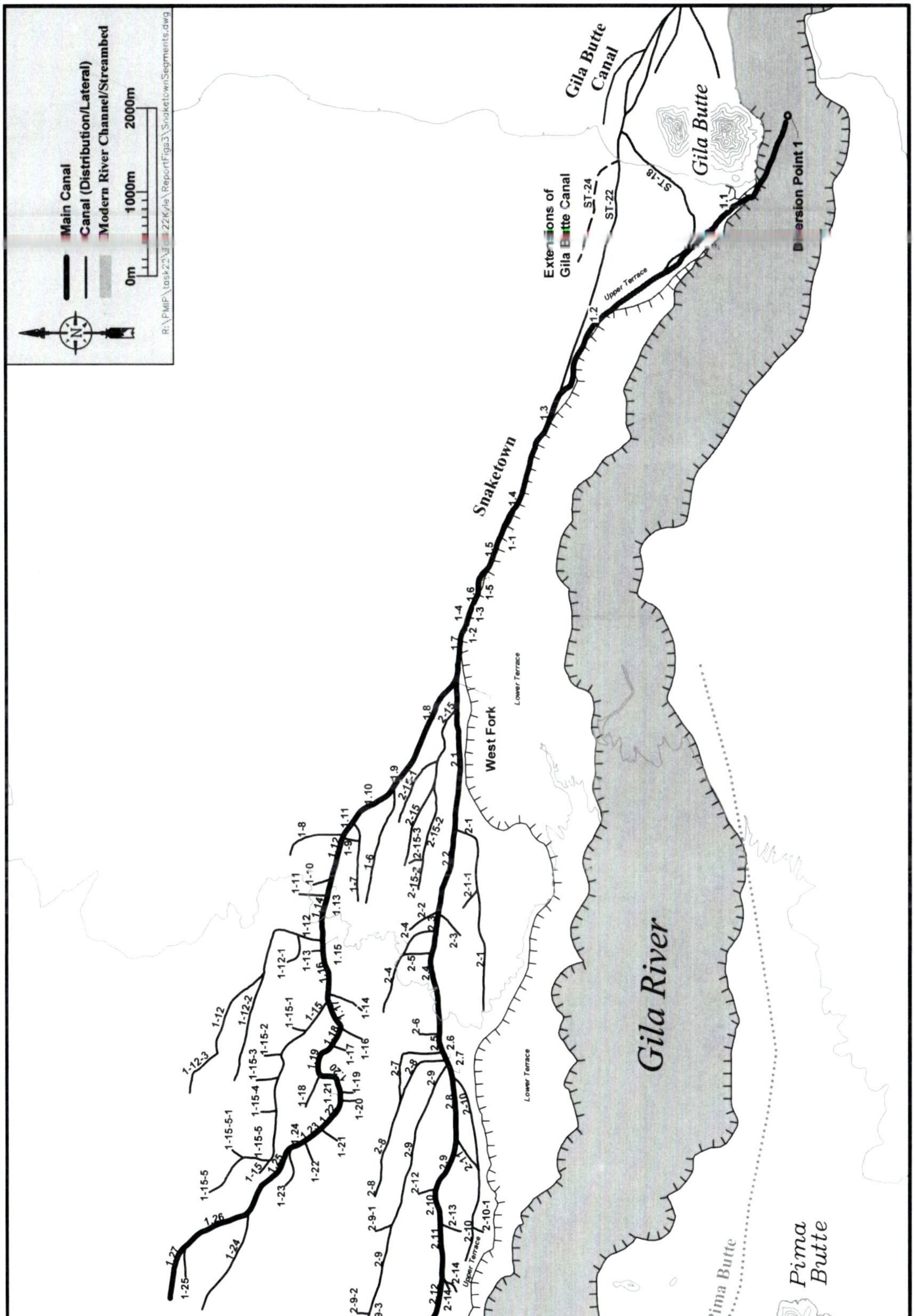

Figure A.3. Map of the Snaketown canal system, indicating canal and segment numbers.

Table A.1. Canal Types, Segments, and Lengths in the Snaketown Canal System

Canal Type	Canal/Segment No.	Length (m)	Comments
Main Canal 1			
Main	1.01	2,490	From Division Point 1 to the junction with ST-18
Main	1.02	1,961	From the junction with ST-18 to the junction with ST-22
Main	1.03	900	From the junction with ST-22 to CT 14
Main	1.04	1,007	From CT 14 to CT 12
Main	1.05	463	From CT 12 to Diversion Area (CT 8)
Main	1.06	650	From Diversion Area to Canal 5 intersection (CT 18)
Main	1.07	658	From CT 18 to West Fork, which is the branch point in the main canal
Main/branch	1.08	1,362	
Main/branch	1.09	158	
Main/branch	1.10	681	Extends through the GR-1157Y habitation
Main/branch	1.11	164	
Main/branch	1.12	559	
Main/branch	1.13	203	
Main/branch	1.14	549	
Main/branch	1.15	121	
Main/branch	1.16	607	Ends at the Locus I branch (Canal 1-15 turnout)
Main/branch	1.17	361	
Main/branch	1.18	245	
Main/branch	1.19	427	Part of the "S" curve in the canal
Main/branch	1.20	367	Part of the "S" curve in the canal
Main/branch	1.21	102	Part of the "S" curve in the canal
Main/branch	1.22	425	
Main/branch	1.23	253	
Main/branch	1.24	161	Ends at the Canal 1-23 turnout (to GR-948A)
Main/branch	1.25	954	
Main/branch	1.26	865	
Main/branch	1.27	684	End of Canal 1
Total, Canal 1		**17,378**	
Main Canal 2			
Main/branch	2.01	1,815	
Main/branch	2.02	1,013	Ends at the Locus FF Lateral 2-2 turnout
Main/branch	2.03	228	
Main/branch	2.04	1,252	
Main/branch	2.05	219	
Main/branch	2.06	142	Ends at the Locus S branch (Canal 2-9 turnout)
Main/branch	2.07	173	
Main/branch	2.08	734	
Main/branch	2.09	668	
Main/branch	2.10	408	
Main/branch	2.11	628	
Main	2.12	803	End of Canal 2; adjacent to Maricopa Platform Mound
Total, Canal 2		**8,083**	
Distribution Canals (n = 13, maybe 11)			

Canal Type	Canal/Segment No.	Length (m)	Comments
Distribution	1-6	1,448	GR-1157NN
Distribution	1-7	966	GR-1157MM
Distribution	1-12	2,298	Extends through the GR-1157C village; may have been for domestic use
Distribution	1-12-2	1,341	Branch of Canal 1-12; extends through the GR-1157C village
Distribution	1-15	2,361	Good canal; follows the N branch of GR-1157I
Distribution	1-24	1,323	Possible canal; late Colonial to Classic period only
Distribution	2-1	2,344	Southernmost canal in the canal system
Distribution	2-4	1,275	Extends through the GR-1157M habitation
Distribution	2-8	2,037	Extends through GR-1157Q
Distribution	2-9	3,679	Extends through GR-1157S, GR-957, and GR-951
Distribution	2-10	2,293	Possible canal in GR-1157, Loci V, X, and Z; least clear in Loci X and Z; lowest confidence of all distribution canals
Distribution	2-15	2,022	Extends through GR-1157, Loci CCC, BBB, LL, OO
Distribution	2-15-2	1,302	Branch of Canal 2-15
Total, distribution canals		**24,687**	
Lateral Canals (n = 45)			
Lateral	1-1	243	Lateral identified by Haury (1976:128); evident on the surface in GR-1157GGG; might be a distribution canal
Lateral	1-2	78	Pioneer period lateral (Haury 1976:136–137)
Lateral	1-3	73	Probable Pioneer period lateral (Haury 1976:134)
Lateral	1-4	85	Probable Pioneer period lateral (Haury 1976:134); extends north onto the upper terrace (possibly for domestic water supply?)
Lateral	1-5	639	Corresponds to Haury's "Lateral Canal," which actually might be a distribution canal
Lateral	1-8	772	Extends by the GR-1157BB habitation and possibly to Locus QQ; this could be a distribution canal
Lateral	1-9	192	May tie into the GR-1157MM distribution canal 1-7
Lateral	1-10	231	LB-28
Lateral	1-11	341	LB-16
Lateral	1-12-1	408	
Lateral	1-12-3	620	Possible canal at the tail end of distribution Canal 1-12; could be part of Canal 1-12
Lateral	1-13	132	First part of LB-32
Lateral	1-14	464	Extends between habitation areas in Locus I—West and Locus I—Central
Lateral	1-15-1	161	Extends north of 1-15
Lateral	1-15-2	201	Extends north of 1-15
Lateral	1-15-3	265	Extends north of 1-15
Lateral	1-15-4	182	Extends north of 1-15
Lateral	1-15-5	915	Longest lateral; it could be a distribution canal (i.e., an extension of 1-15)
Lateral	1-15-5-1	160	
Lateral	1-16	280	
Lateral	1-17	176	
Lateral	1-18	418	
Lateral	1-19	152	

continued on next page

Canal Type	Canal/Segment No.	Length (m)	Comments
Lateral	1-20	175	
Lateral	1-21	243	Possible canal
Lateral	1-22	248	Possible canal
Lateral	1-23	502	Probable canal extends to the small habitation in GR-948A; could have been a distribution canal or used for domestic water
Lateral	1-25	381	Extends through GR-819
Lateral	2-1-1	270	Extends through GR-1157, Loci KK and JJ
Lateral	2-2	412	
Lateral	2-3	372	Extends through GR-1157FF; it might be longer and could be a distribution canal
Lateral	2-5	360	This might be an upper segment of a distribution canal that combined with the lower half of 2-4
Lateral	2-6	241	Possible canal
Lateral	2-7	675	Could be a distribution canal
Lateral	2-9-1	210	GR-957D
Lateral	2-9-2	147	GR-951A
Lateral	2-9-3	105	GR-951B
Lateral	2-9-4	94	GR-951B
Lateral	2-10-1	143	
Lateral	2-11	467	Possible canal; might be the upper segment of distribution Canal 2-10
Lateral	2-12	218	Possible canal
Lateral	2-13	272	By GR-674E
Lateral	2-14	411	Might be a feeder/inlet to the Maricopa Mound reservoir; length includes split canal
Lateral	2-15-1	600	Possible lateral between Loci BBB and SS, length uncertain
Lateral	2-15-3	177	Possible canal
Total, lateral canals		**13,911**	

Note: Italicized lengths indicate lower confidence in the identification of the canals.

Total length of recorded canals	**64,139 m (64.14 km)**
Canal 1 to West Fork	8,128 m (8.13 km)
West Fork to the end of Canal 1	9,250 m (9.25 km)
Total length, Canal 1	17,378 m (17.38 km)
Total length, Canal 2	8,083 m (8.08 km)
Total length, Canals 1 and 2	25,461 m (25.46 km)

In all, over 64 km of main, distribution, and lateral canals have been documented in the Snaketown canal system, of which 25.5 km are main canals. The main canal (Canal 1) measures 8.1 km long from its primary heading at the foot of Gila Butte (Diversion Point 1) to its branch point at the West Fork. From there, the north main-canal branch (Canal 1) extends another 9.3 km, and the south main-canal branch (Canal 2) extends 8.1 km. In addition to defining the full lengths of the branch canals, I documented 13 distribution canals and 45 lateral canals. Six distribution canals were identified along Canal 1, and 7 distribution canals are situated along Canal 2. The distribution canals range in length between 966 and 3,679 m, with an average length of 1,899 m. However, 2 of the canals (1-12-1 and 2-15-2) are actually branches of two other distribution canals, and 2 are considered possible canals (1-24 and 2-10) because of a lower confidence in identification. Of the 45 lateral canals, 29 laterals are along Canal 1, and 16 are along Canal 2. The laterals range between 73 and 915 m in length, with an average length of 312 m. Notably, 7 of the laterals are considered "possible" canals because of a lower confidence in their identification (1-12-3, 1-21, 1-22, 2-6, 2-11, 2-12, and 2-15-3). Also, 6 of the longer lateral canals could have functioned as distribution canals rather than laterals (1-5, 1-8, 1-15-5, 1-23, 2-7, and 2-15-1).

Importantly, the canals mapped here represent all of the linear alignments that were detectable at the ground surface and judged to be probable canal alignments. My confidence in whether all the canals of a given type (main, branch, distribution, or lateral) were found is highest for the main/branch canals, moderate to high for the distribution canals, and lowest for the lateral canals. That is because the visibility of these features was directly related to their size and the intensity and length of their use. The model of the formation processes of canals presented in Chapter 3 provided the basis for this reasoning. I argue that the full extents of the main/branch canals have now been documented, and probably all of the distribution canals have been identified along the system. It is certain that more lateral canals were used, but they lack visibility as surface archaeological features.

The layout of the Snaketown canal system as mapped here is very different from what has been shown on previous maps (Haury 1937, 1976 [see Figure 3.5, this report]; Midvale 1935 [see Figure 3.4, this report], 1972). The part of the system mapped by Haury (1937:50, 1976:122) matches the corresponding part of the current map fairly well, but his maps did not conclusively identify the main-canal heading, nor did they trace the full extent of the branch, distribution, and lateral canals. The current map builds from these earlier studies, with modifications and additions based on the results of more recent projects, such as surveys conducted by the GRIC-CRMP in conjunction with the Pima-Maricopa Irrigation Project (P-MIP), including the tracing of linear earthen mounds and other alignments, many of which appear to represent relict canals (Neily et al. 2000; Wells and Greenspan 2002; Woodson 2009). Also, excavations conducted near Gila Butte documented numerous canal segments that were part of the Gila Butte canal system and some that may have been part of the Snaketown canal system (Burt 2007; Howard and Rice 1982; Motsinger 1993; Rice et al. 1979; Swarthout and Blank-Roper 1984 [see Figure 3.6, this report]). The new map also benefited from the examination of aerial photos for traces of linear features that could be canals, followed by ground-truthing of these features. As a result, the current map is more expansive and more detailed than the earlier maps. Most of the details that have been added are along the two branch canals, downstream from the West Fork. That is, the current map traces the full extent of the branch canals, identifies the probable distribution canals, and maps all the probable and possible lateral canals that could be detected on the ground surface. In addition, the current map identifies the primary heading on the river, at the foot of Gila Butte (Diversion Point 1), and defines the interface between the Snaketown canal system and the tail end of the Gila Butte canal system. The relationship between these two canal systems is discussed later in this appendix.

Prior to completion of the current map of the Snaketown canal system, a previous map version was published by GRIC-CRMP researchers (Ravesloot 2007; Ravesloot et al. forthcoming; Woodson and Ravesloot 2005); it is shown in Figure 3.7. Although this previous map is more detailed than the Midvale and Haury maps, it lacks the details of the canal system that were determined during the current research. There are two important differences between the current map and the previous GRIC-CRMP map, in that the previous map (1) depicts the north branch of the main canal as extending westward to Hidden Ruin (roughly 6 km west of the end of the north branch canal as shown on the current map) and (2) shows a separate main canal that exclusively served Hidden Ruin and headed downstream from the Snaketown canal. The latter "Hidden Ruin Canal" was inferred primarily based on a linear feature visible in aerial photographs, on the upper terrace (Wells and Greenspan 2002); however, it was not checked on the ground to confirm whether it was a canal. The current research involved a detailed ground-truthing survey of these previously mapped canal segments extending to Hidden Ruin. Importantly, I found little to no evidence on the ground of either canal segment; the north-branch canal did not appear to extend to Hidden Ruin, and the Hidden Ruin Canal did not exist in the previously mapped location. Adjacent areas on the lower terrace also were examined for evidence of Hidden Ruin Canal, but no linear features or artifact scatters could be found in those areas. It is worth noting that a major study on the opposite side of the river from Hidden Ruin documented an extensive canal system (the Riverbend canal system) that may have been used by the inhabitants of Hidden Ruin (Woodson 2007).

Issues in Mapping the Canal system

Several aspects of the Snaketown canal system had to be addressed to achieve a complete reconstruction, including some previously unresolved issues. These included the location of the heading of the main canal, whether the canal system was used to irrigate fields on the lower terrace, and the locations and sizes of the irrigated fields.

Canal-System Heading

The question of where the Snaketown canal system headed on the Gila River has been the subject of much discussion and speculation. Four diversion points have been proposed for the main-canal heading (from west to east): Diversion Point 1 (at the foot of Gila Butte), Diversion Point 2, Olberg Butte, and Granite Knob (Figure A.4). During the two excavations at Snaketown, the farthest-upstream extent of the main canal was traced to about 3 km northwest of the possible heading at the foot of Gila Butte (see Figure 3.5).

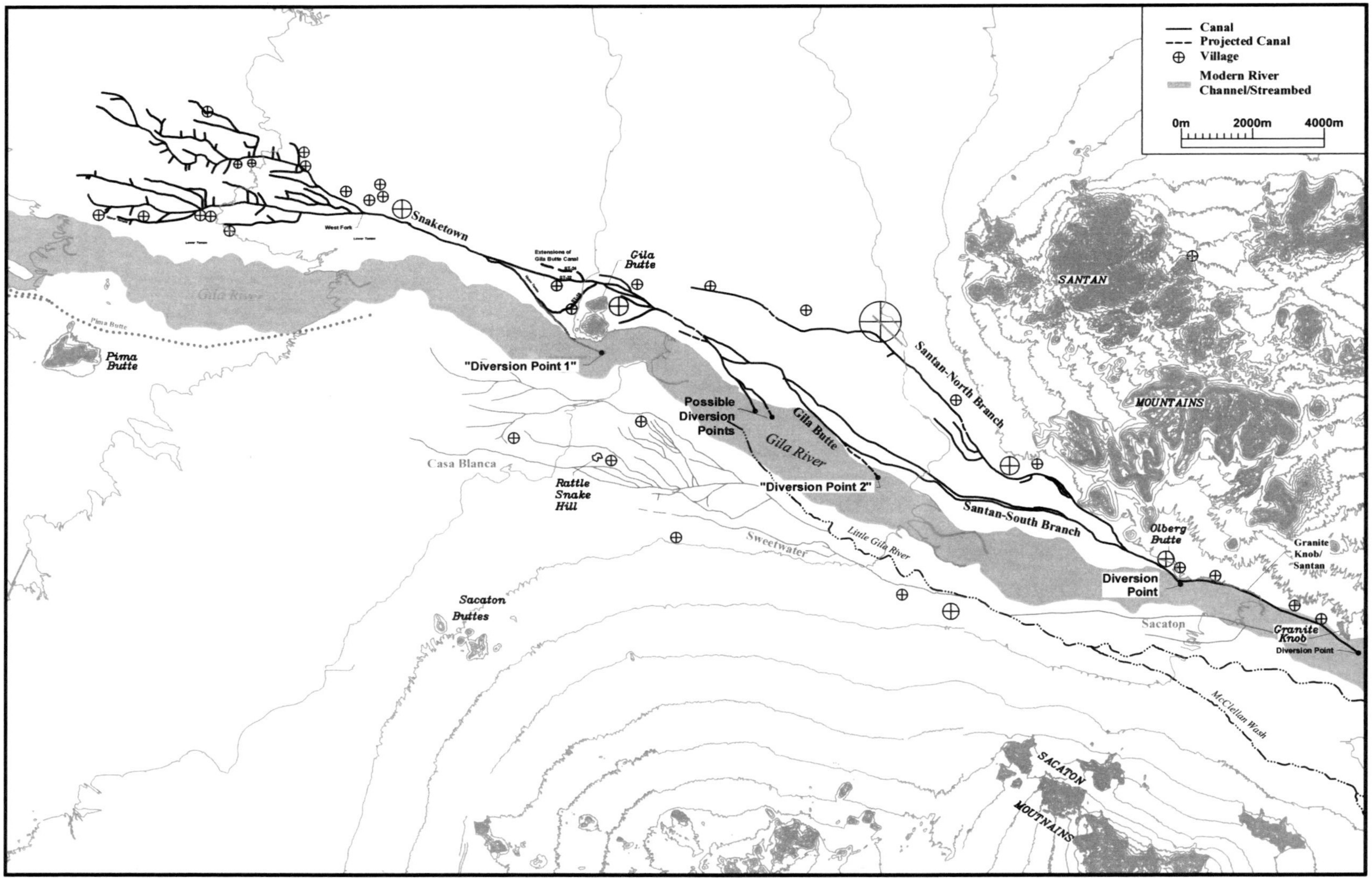

Figure A.4. Map showing the possible river headings for the canal systems in the study area and the connection points between them.

Haury (1937) initially thought the canal headed at the foot of Gila Butte, where historical-period Pima canals, including the Sratuka Ditch, headed at one time. Haury (1976) later referred to this heading as "Diversion Point 1." However, in 1937, he concluded that this heading was not feasible, based on readings from his surveyor's instrument. He instead suggested that the canal headed about 5 miles (8 km) east of Gila Butte, in the location of a relict canal segment that was inferred to be prehistoric in age. Haury (1976) later referred to this heading as "Diversion Point 2." This relict segment was mapped by Southworth (1914–1915) and, though not clearly labeled on his map, it probably was the former course of the historical-period Lower Santan canal, built about 1879.[1] Later, Haury (1976:123) revised his position somewhat, indicating that both Diversion Points 1 and 2 were possible locations of the canal heading. He also suggested that Diversion Point 1 may have been used during the pre-Classic period, and Diversion Point 2, during the Classic period. Haury (1976:123) decided that Diversion Point 1 was a feasible heading, since "[t]he terrain would permit this because in the first 2 km west of Gila Butte the upper-lower terrace configuration is lost and a gentle slope exists." He suggested that the relict segment of the historical-period Sratuka Ditch, mapped by Southworth (1914–1915), could have been the headward segment of the prehistoric Snaketown canal.

Excavations conducted on the northeastern side of Gila Butte, near the modern East Maricopa Floodway (EMF), documented several prehistoric canals that provided further information on whether the Snaketown canal could have headed at Diversion Point 2 (see Figures 3.6 and A.4). Investigations by Arizona State University (ASU) resulted in the documentation of two main-canal alignments of the "Gila Butte Canal," AZ U:13:120 (ASM); the alignments were designated the Southern and Northern Canal Groups (Howard and Rice 1982; Rice et al. 1979; Swarthout and Blank-Roper 1984). The three canals in the Southern Canal Group dated to the pre-Classic period, and the two canals in the Northern Canal Group dated to the Classic period. Swarthout and Blank-Roper (1984) suggested that in the Southern Canal Group, the two earliest canals (Features 3 and 2) were contemporaneous with and similar in morphology to the two earliest canals in the Snaketown canal system (Canals 1 and 2), respectively. ASU Feature 3 dated to the late Pioneer/early Colonial period, and ASU Feature 2 dated to the late Colonial–Sedentary period. Swarthout and Blank-Roper (1984:204) surmised that these similarities supported the contention that the ASU canals (Features 2 and 3) and the Snaketown canal (Canals 1 and 2) were segments of the same canal that headed at Diversion Point 2 in the pre-Classic period. The significance of this, they observed, is that the occupants of Snaketown and the Gila Butte site would have had to share the water in the canal. As noted below, current evidence does not support this scenario, because of the different hydraulic characteristics of these pairs of canals and because Snaketown Canal 1 was built during the Vahki phase of the early Pioneer period, predating the construction of the Gila Butte canal. Swarthout and Blank-Roper (1984) did not speculate on the relationship between the Classic period canals in the Northern Canal Group and those in the Snaketown canal system.

A subsequent excavation by SWCA Environmental Consultants, Inc. (SWCA), along the western edge of the EMF, identified five canals (Motsinger 1993) that this author has determined are situated along the trajectory of ASU's Northern Canal Group (see Figure 3.6). One feature was a large, broad canal (SWCA Feature 5) that investigators concluded was a Classic period main canal that traveled past Gila Butte to connect with the Snaketown canal. The feature is, by far, the largest canal exposed in either the Snaketown or Gila Butte system, and its inferred area (maximum of 7.04 m^2 but likely closer to 4.40 m^2) is larger than that of the largest channel in the Snaketown main canal (Colonial period) and much larger than that of the Classic period channel (1.44 m^2; see the following section for descriptions of the canal hydraulics of the Gila Butte and Snaketown canals). Because of its status as an "outlier" and because only one cross section of the feature was exposed, it is possible that Feature 5 represents an anomalous part of a smaller canal or another feature, such as a reservoir or settling basin. In addition, extensive test excavations by ASU in their Northern Canal Group immediately east of SWCA Feature 5 did not identify such a large canal feature dating to the Classic period (Swarthout and Blank-Roper 1984). However, two overlapping canals (SWCA Features 6 and 8) documented by Motsinger (1993) appear to correlate to a pair of smaller, overlapping Classic period canals recorded by ASU (ASU Features 1 and 2) (Swarthout and Blank-Roper 1984). These latter, Classic period canals excavated in the Gila Butte area do not appear to have had adequate capacity to irrigate fields as far west as the Maricopa Platform Mound site, but they could have been "feeder" canals or "waste ditches" used to augment the water supply in the Snaketown canal. On the other hand, these canals may have been used only to supply fields on the eastern side of Gila Butte. These issues are discussed further below.

The picture of how and when canals may have been extended around the northern side of Gila Butte to connect with the Snaketown canal, and the locations of the headings of both canal systems, was made clearer by recent archaeological studies by the GRIC-CRMP. First, survey on the southwestern side of Gila Butte revealed sites and linear features arrayed along the inferred alignment of the Snaketown canal that would have headed at Diversion Point 1 (GRIC-CRMP project files, linear-alignment survey; Woodson 2014). Survey data revealed that the relict Sratuka Ditch (recorded as LB-26 during the linear-alignment survey) almost certainly was a prehistoric canal alignment and probably was the headward segment of the Snaketown canal (as suggested by Haury

[1976:123]) (see Figure 3.5). Diagnostic ceramics found along the first 5.4 km of this alignment dated to between the late Pioneer and Classic periods, suggesting that the alignment was used throughout the Hohokam sequence. Yet this section of the canal and the artifact scatters along it only had sparse Late Classic period ceramics, which could suggest that the heading at Diversion Point 1 was no longer functional by that time. These survey data also support the contentions that the Pioneer Canal headed at Diversion Point 1 and that the late Pioneer period canal found by ASU near the Gila Butte site (Feature 3) (Swarthout and Blank-Roper 1984) was a separate canal that headed farther upstream, at Diversion Point 2.

Second, linear earthen-mound alignments (predominantly with Sedentary and Classic period ceramics) extending around the northern side of Gila Butte appear to be extensions of canals in the Gila Butte canal system (Neily et al. 2000; Woodson 2014) (see Figures A.3 and A.4). Two of these alignments connect with the Snaketown canal to the west of Gila Butte, and they probably were used to augment the water supply in the Snaketown system beginning in the Sedentary period. The first canal alignment (ST-18) curves around Gila Butte, extends through GR-1207 and GR-1206, and appears to have been connected to the Snaketown canal during the Sedentary and Early Classic periods, and possibly during the Late Classic period. This canal probably operated as a kind of "waste ditch" from the Gila Butte canal system that supplemented the water in the Snaketown canal (whose primary water source was the heading at Diversion Point 1). It is recognized here that a previous study (Motsinger 1993) surmised that the pre-Classic period Gila Butte canal did not extend to the north and west of Gila Butte. That conclusion was based on the lack of evidence of a canal of that age in a long, east–west-oriented backhoe trench excavated on the northeastern side of Gila Butte. However, it is argued here that the current evidence suggests that a pre-Classic canal did actually extend through this area. Perhaps the previous excavation did not identify the canal because it had been disturbed by slope wash and erosion from Gila Butte or because the obtuse angle at which the trench would have cut the canal prevented its clear identification. Notably, SWCA recorded a midden (Feature 2) in the approximate location where the canal may have crossed the trench, suggesting that Feature 2 actually may have been a canal. The second canal alignment (ST-22, extending through GR-1175) that connected with the Snaketown canal probably was built in the Classic period, and it correlates roughly to the previously mapped course of the "Classic period" Snaketown canal (see Midvale 1972; Motsinger 1993). Neither canal alignment (ST-18 or ST-22) had surface artifacts dating to earlier than the Sedentary period, suggesting that no earlier canals extended around the northern side of the butte to connect with the Snaketown canal.

Third, both of these canals (ST-18 and ST-22) were extensions of the canal alignment that appears to have headed on the river at Diversion Point 2 for at least part of its use-life. Recent survey (Neily et al. 2000) has documented linear artifact scatters and earthen mounds (recorded as GR-1220, GR-1222, and GR-1187) that I argue are situated along the relict Gila Butte canal alignment. GR-1220 and GR-1222 are linear sites found along the same relict canal segment that Southworth (1914–1915) mapped and referred to as the historical-period Lower Santan canal. Recent excavations at GR-1220 revealed that a buried prehistoric main canal is present there, and an overlapping historical-period canal appears to correlate to Southworth's Lower Santan canal (GRIC-CRMP Project 2006.36, Task 2 [home-sites testing]). This Gila Butte canal is inferred to have headed at Diversion Point 2, and from the point where it extends from the edge of the modern floodplain to the point where it connects with the Snaketown canal is roughly 15 km (along extension ST-22). This canal alignment correlates to the canal recorded near Gila Butte as AZ U:13:120 (ASM). The angle at which this canal departs the floodplain suggests that it extended into the former river channel near Diversion Point 2.

However, the Gila Butte canal may not have always had its heading at that point. First, when it was first built, in the late Pioneer period, the canal may have headed on the river closer to Gila Butte (at the "possible diversion points" shown on Figure A.4). This possibility is supported by the finding of Snaketown Red-on-buff ceramics along this inferred segment of the canal during survey (Neily et al. 2000) and the excavation of a similar-age canal segment (Burt 2007), as well as by the lack of Snaketown Red-on-buff ceramics from survey and excavation along the segment that headed at Diversion Point 2 (at GR-1220 and GR-1222) (GRIC-CRMP Project 2006.36, Task 2; Neily et al. 2000). Second, some researchers (e.g., Midvale 1935, 1972; Ravesloot and Waters 2004; Ravesloot et al. forthcoming) have posited that the best headgate for canals in the Gila Butte–Snaketown area was farther upstream, at Olberg Butte, the location of the inferred heading for the prehistoric Santan canal. In that scenario, the Classic period Gila Butte canal system headed there. Because the Santan canal system already was in place by that time, the canal that would have extended to the Gila Butte area actually would have been the south branch of the Santan canal (see Figure A.4). The resulting "Gila Butte–Santan Canal" would have been roughly 24 km long from Olberg Butte to the junction with the Snaketown canal.

The last possible scenario to consider here is a heading at Granite Knob, a bedrock outcrop roughly 5.5 km upstream from Olberg Butte. A recent investigation of a cutbank exposure of the relict segment of the Granite Knob/Santan canal suggested that it was much larger than necessary for irrigating the area between Granite Knob and Olberg Butte, but it was not large enough to have been the only water supply for the Santan canal and its fields (Miles 2009). Therefore, the Santan canal probably headed at Olberg Butte, and the tail end of the Granite Knob canal was joined to the Santan canal to provide supplemental water.

It is important to note here that the relationship of the Gila Butte canal to the Snaketown canal during the Classic period, especially the Late Classic period, is not entirely clear. On the one hand, the extensions of the Gila Butte canal noted above (ST-18 and ST-22) appear to have been just that—extensions of an independent canal system that provided additional water to the Snaketown canal. Hence, it is not correct to think of these extensions as "the" Classic period Snaketown canal. Survey data from the Sedentary and Early Classic periods suggest that the original heading at Diversion Point 1 was still functioning as the principal water source for the Snaketown canal. On the other hand, surveyed areas along the Snaketown canal, between its Diversion Point 1 heading and its intersection with ST-22, revealed a lack or very low quantities of Late Classic period diagnostic ceramics (i.e., Salado polychromes), which may suggest that the heading at Diversion Point 1 was no longer functional by that time. If that was the case, then the water in the Snaketown canal system was supplied exclusively by the Gila Butte canal. Hence, the actual heading for the Snaketown canal system would have been either at Diversion Point 2 or at Olberg Butte during the Late Classic period. From Diversion Point 2, the Gila Butte canal would have extended roughly 15 km to its intersection with the Snaketown Canal. From Olberg Butte, the Gila Butte–Santan Canal would have extended 24 km to the Snaketown main canal. Because the Santan canal divided into two branches 2 km from the Olberg Butte heading, the Gila Butte–Santan Canal (which represents the south branch) would actually have been 22 km long from the branch point of the Santan canal to the Snaketown canal. From there, it was another 11.7 km to the end of the south branch of the Snaketown canal (33.7 km total) or 12.9 km to the end of the north-branch canal (34.9 km total). Although other farmers probably still irrigated fields along the upper part of this canal to the east of Gila Butte, it would be remarkable if the Snaketown farmers were using a canal of this length to supply all the water to the Snaketown canal system and fields.

Hydraulic Analysis of Excavated Canal Segments

An analysis of the cross-sectional areas of excavated Classic period main-canal segments in the study area canal systems provided further insight into the relationships between these canal systems and the location of the Classic period heading of the Snaketown canal (Table A.2). These canal segments include the Snaketown main canal (at Canal Trench [CT] 14) (Haury 1976), the canals excavated near Gila Butte by ASU (Swarthout and Blank-Roper 1984) and SWCA (Motsinger 1993), and seven canal segments (at GR-146, GR-442, GR-1086, GR-640, GR-1210, and GR-1220) situated along the inferred alignments of the Granite Knob, Gila Butte, and Santan canals (Fertelmes and Loendorf 2010; GRIC-CRMP Project 2006.36, Task 2; Loendorf et al. 2007; Miles 2009; Rodrigues et al. 2003; Wright and Waters 2010). The analysis assumes that the area of a main canal would reduce longitudinally from the head to the tail of the canal (Howard 1990, 1993). The regression formula for cross-sectional area by Howard (1990, 1993) is used in this analysis.[2]

Figure A.5 is a chart plotting the regression curves of cross-sectional area for each of the four main canals in relation to their inferred headings, or diversion points. The calibration points used in the regression formula for each main canal were GR-146 (Granite Knob canal), GR-442 (Santan canal), GR-1220 (Gila Butte canal), and CT 14 (Snaketown canal). The unlabeled points in the figure are inferred canal areas that were "retrodicted" using the regression formula. The upper-left-hand points along the curve for each main canal are the inferred areas at the canal headings. The curves and data points are shown in relation to their distances from the Granite Knob canal heading, such that the left side of the graph is the farthest-upstream point.

As described in Chapter 4, the tail ends of the three upstream canals (Granite Knob, Santan, and Gila Butte) had been connected with the adjacent downstream canals (Santan, Gila Butte, and Snaketown) by the Sedentary period. Thus, in Figure A.5, the end points of the curves for the three upstream canals represent the junction of a canal with the next downstream canal. In that way, the tail ends of the three upstream canals each operated as a kind of "waste ditch" that conveyed excess water (or, potentially, water that was scheduled for allocation) to the next adjacent downstream canal. Clearly, the upstream canals were supplying some water to the adjacent downstream canals by the Classic period. The main point that is indicated in the graph is that the cross-sectional areas at the tail ends of the three upstream canals are not as large as the canal areas in the adjacent downstream canals at the linking points. This suggests that the three upstream canals were not large enough to be the sole suppliers of water for the three adjacent downstream canals in the Classic period. That pattern also pertains to the regression curves of main-canal areas for the pre-Classic period (these data are not shown here).

The graph also illustrates how the area of the large feature recorded by SWCA (Feature 5) as a canal is an outlier point, compared with the regression curves for the Gila Butte and Snaketown canals. Although the SWCA Feature 5 point appears to be above the point for the Snaketown canal heading, this is misleading, because SWCA Feature 5 is on the northern side of Gila Butte and adjacent to ASU Feature 2. The SWCA feature is therefore associated with the Gila Butte canal. The analysis does not support a link between SWCA Feature 5 and any of the other canals along the Gila Butte canal alignment (whether it headed at Diversion Point 2 or Olberg Butte). This further supports the interpretation of SWCA Feature 5 as a reservoir, a settling basin, or an anomalous part of a smaller canal.

Table A.2. Cross-Sectional Areas of Classic Period Canals Excavated in the Granite Knob, Santan, Gila Butte, and Snaketown Canal Systems

Site/Locus No.	Feature No.	Cross-Sectional Area (m²)	Distance From Granite Knob Division Point (km)	Distance from Olberg Butte Division Point (km)	Distance from Division Point 2 (km)	Distance from Division Point 1/ Gila Butte (km)
Granite Knob Canal (Heading = Granite Knob)						
Heading	[inferred point]	4.17	—			
GR-146	1 (upper channel)	2.16	3.00			
[GR-442]	[inferred point at the junction with Santan Canal]	1.35	6.00	0.80		
Santan Canal (Heading = Olberg Butte)—South Branch (to Gila Butte Canal)						
Heading	[inferred point]	4.33	5.20			
GR-442	25	3.60	6.00	0.80		
GR-445D	8 (upper channel)	2.89	7.70	2.50		
GR-1086	1 (upper channel)	2.13	10.00	4.80		
GR-640	Feature 6 (upper channel)	2.05	10.40	5.20		
GR-1210	Feature 3 (lower channel)	1.64	12.80	7.60		
[End of south branch]	[inferred point]	1.19	16.50	11.30		
Gila Butte Canal (Heading = Diversion Point 2)						
Heading	[inferred point]	3.86	14.60	9.40		
GR-1220	Feature 1.01	2.16	17.20	12.00	2.90	
[Inferred point]	[inferred point]	1.64	19.20	14.00	4.90	
U:13:120 (ASM)/ASU Northern Group	ASU Feature 2 (1984)—lower channel	1.03	23.20	18.00	8.60	
U:13:120 (ASM)	SWCA Feature 5 (1993)—corrected dimensions	*4.40*	23.30	18.10	8.70	
[End of canal at junction]	[inferred point]	0.70	27.30	22.10	12.70	
Snaketown Canal (Heading = Diversion Point 1/Gila Butte)						
Heading	[inferred point]	3.75	22.85	17.65	8.25	
[Inferred point]	[inferred point]	2.18	25.35	20.15	10.75	2.50
GR-1157BBBB (CT 14)	main canal (second-lowest channel)	1.44	28.20	23.00	11.50	5.35
Diversion Area	main canal	1.17	29.74	24.54	13.04	6.89

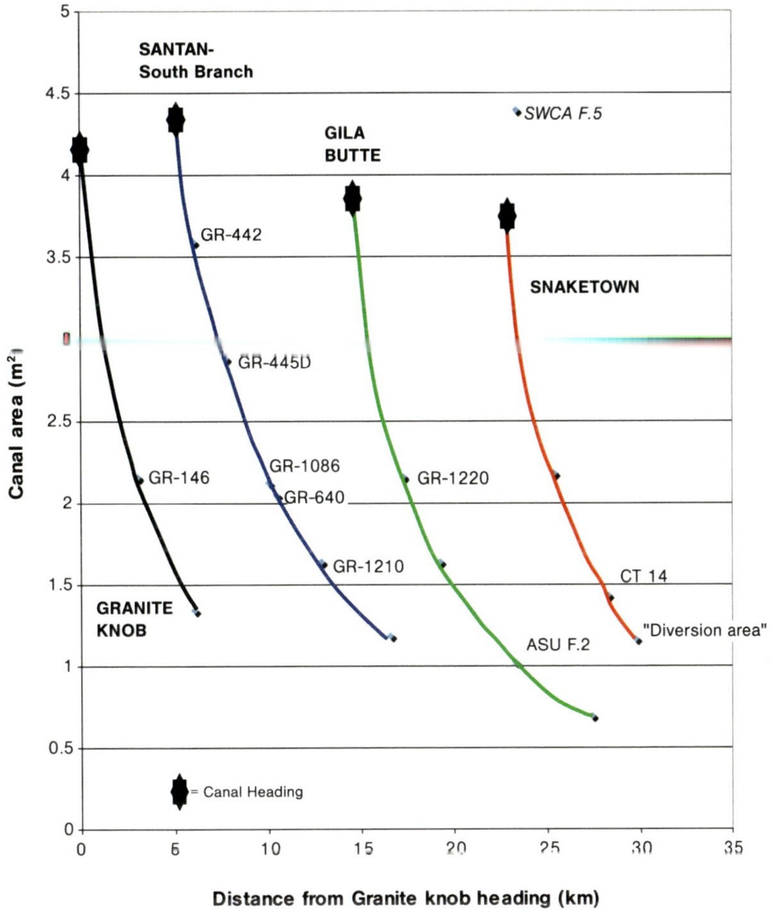

Figure A.5. Graph showing regression curves for a cross-sectional area of the four main canals during the Classic period, in relation to the distance from the Granite Knob heading.

In sum, the weight of evidence indicates that the main canals in the Snaketown, Gila Butte, and Santan canal systems each maintained separate headings during most of their use-lives. The same situation pertained to the Granite Knob canal, as well. Despite that, it is clear that these canal systems were linked to each other during the Colonial and Sedentary periods. The only possible exceptions that should be noted were in the Late Classic period for the Snaketown and Granite Knob canals. Polychrome ceramics appeared to be absent from the surface of the relict segment of the Snaketown canal, near its heading, and also on the surface of the only known relict segment of the Granite Knob canal. This suggests that Diversion Point 1 and the Granite Knob headings might have fallen into disuse at that time. If that was the case, then the Snaketown and Gila Butte canal systems truly would have been a consolidated system with one heading (probably at Diversion Point 2), and the Granite Knob canal was not used through the end of the Classic period.

Irrigation on the Lower Terrace

Another question is whether the Hohokam irrigated fields on the lower terrace as well as the upper terrace. Haury (1937:53, 1976:121–122) seemed convinced that they did. Based on the extensive historical-period cultivation of the lower terrace by the Pimas, Haury (1937:53) stated that "the main fields of the Hohokam were on the rich alluvial plain of the lower terrace in the vicinity of Snaketown, while auxiliary fields west of Snaketown undoubtedly were cultivated on the upper terrace." Later, he stated that "Hohokam cultivation was certainly there [on the lower terrace] too, but they also mastered upper terrace tillage" (Haury 1976:121). Yet no archaeological evidence supports that contention, because "all obvious traces of Hohokam use of the same acreage" (Haury 1976:121) on the lower terrace have been erased by Pima agricultural activity and periodic flooding. Some reconnaissance was conducted on the lower terrace, but "diligent searching failed to reveal any concentrations of pre-1400 Hohokam pottery. If such evidence is present, it is buried under silt, but our machine-dug trenches failed to produce any subsurface indications either of old cultivated land surfaces or of buried cultural vestiges."

Interestingly, Haury did provide examples from the 1964–1965 excavations that supported the contention that fields were irrigated on the lower terrace. First, the Pioneer Canal (Canal 1) included at least one lateral canal turnout, and possibly two, that would have led to fields on the lower terrace (Haury 1976:136–137) (see laterals 1-2-1-4 in Figure A.3). Second, a "lateral" canal was identified that turned out of the main canal at the "diversion area" where the upper and lower terraces were merged together (Haury 1976:125–128). That canal (designated 1-5 in Figure A.3) parallels the main canal on its downslope side for 640 m and probably rejoins the main canal in the Pioneer Canal area. Although no field lateral turnouts were found along the canal (during the limited testing along its length), its course and context suggest that laterals probably diverged from it, to supply irrigation water to fields on the lower terrace. If so, then the canal would be more accurately defined as a distribution canal. Third, another probable lateral canal was found during testing several hundred meters east of the diversion area; it also parallels the main canal on the downslope side (Haury 1976:128) (designated 1-1 in Figure A.3). Hence, although no obvious evidence of prehistoric canals or fields has been found on the lower terrace, it is clear that at least part of the lower terrace was irrigated from the main Snaketown canal, where it traversed the lower edge of the upper terrace. That would have been more easily accomplished within the roughly 7-km-long zone between the foot of Gila Butte and Snaketown itself, where several portions of the upper and lower terraces are merged together. Farther west of Snaketown, the drop from the upper to the lower terrace becomes much steeper and would have been extremely difficult to do.

Haury never depicted any possible Hohokam canals on the lower terrace on his maps of the Snaketown canal system (see Figure 3.5). Although it was not clearly stated, he assumed either that they were there or that the Snaketown canal could have irrigated the fields by itself. As noted above, canals were definitely turned out from the main Snaketown canal and led to the lower terrace. Perhaps that was sufficient to supply water to the fields on the lower terrace. On maps dating to 1935 and 1972, Frank Midvale, apparently taking the suggestion from Haury that the Hohokam had irrigated fields on the lower terrace, showed a prehistoric canal following the alignment of the historical-period Snaketown canal on the lower terrace (see Figure 3.4). However, no solid archaeological evidence of this proposed prehistoric canal has been documented. Although the lower terrace between Gila Butte and Snaketown has not been fully surveyed, no prehistoric sites have been recorded in the area, with the exception of the linear feature (LB-26) noted above, which marks the course of the main Snaketown canal. Therefore, it would appear that overbank flooding of the Gila River and historical-period Pima farming have either covered or erased the surface evidence of prehistoric use of the lower terrace.

Irrigated Field Areas

An important aspect of the research is that I was able to specifically define the irrigated field areas in the Snaketown canal system. That is significant because it allowed for an assessment of the system size, or command area, which is the portion of land under the system that was irrigated regularly (Hunt 1988a:344). Understanding command area allows for the estimation of agricultural productivity as well as population size. As a beginning point, if one were to assume that all of the land situated downslope from the Snaketown main canals could be irrigated, that area would total 6,315 ha. This is strictly a theoretical maximum amount of land that could be farmed, irrespective of the capacity of the canal system and the length to which lateral canals could feasibly have been built out. It also does not consider the presence of habitations and other objects, such as washes, that would not have been under cultivation. As described below, the command area of the Snaketown canal system was significantly smaller than the total area of land that theoretically could have been irrigated. I applied several criteria to estimate the command area.

First, I assumed that irrigated fields would be located along lateral canals that would have been the direct sources of water. The research resulted in the identification of 45 lateral canals, which are depicted in Figure A.3 and listed in Table A.1. The areas along these laterals were inferred to have been irrigated fields. As noted above, it is certain that more than 45 lateral canals (and, hence, more fields) were used during prehistoric times, but they are not all visible as archaeological features. There are many areas along the main and distribution canals where it could be inferred that other lateral canals once existed, though. If a solid basis could be found for that inference, I reasoned that I could identify all the potential irrigated fields and calculate the command area of the Snaketown canal system. Beginning with the known laterals, I brought several other lines of evidence to bear on this issue, as discussed here.

Because the size of the irrigated fields is partly dependent on the lengths of the lateral canals, I examined the recorded lateral lengths in more detail. In previous studies (e.g., Ravesloot et al. forthcoming; Woodson 2004), lateral canals in the Snaketown canal system were assumed to measure between 800 and 1,000 m in length, based on the observed spacing between branch canals and the distribution of activity areas thought to be associated with irrigated fields. As found in the current study, the 45 laterals range between 73 and 915 m long, with an average length of 309 m (Table A.3, top). For this exercise, I modified the list to exclude 16 laterals: the 7 "possible" canals (i.e., canals with lower confidence in identification: 1-12-3, 1-21, 1-22, 2-6,

Table A.3. Lateral-Canal Lengths in the Prehistoric Snaketown Canal System and Historical-Period Canal Systems Used as Analogs

Statistic	Length (m)	Comments
Prehistoric Snaketown Lateral Canals		
Total	13,911	(all 45 laterals)
Minimum	73	254 feet
Maximum	915	3,003 feet
Mean	309	1,031 feet
Standard deviation	196	
Prehistoric Snaketown Lateral Canals, Revised		
Total	7,359	(29 laterals; excludes 7 possible canals, 3 shortest laterals, and 6 possible distribution canals)
Minimum	94	
Maximum	464	
Mean	254	
Standard deviation	110	
Historical-Period Bapchil Canal Laterals		
Minimum	91	(300 feet)
Maximum	458	(1,500 feet)
Rough average	213	(700 feet)
Historical-Period Stotonick Canal Laterals		
Minimum	152	(500 feet)
Maximum	579	(1,900 feet)
Rough average	350	(1,150 feet)
Historical-Period Santan (Indian) Canal Laterals		
Minimum	152	(500 feet)
Maximum	1,188	(3,900 feet)
Rough average	700	(2,300 feet)

2-11, 2-12, and 2-15-3), 6 longer canals that could have functioned as distribution canals rather than laterals (1-5, 1-8, 1-15-5, 1-23, 2-7, and 2-15-1), and the 3 shortest laterals (1-2, 1-3, 1-4; these probably were longer than was documented by Haury [1976], because only the excavated lengths are known). The revised list of 29 laterals resulted in a range of 94–464 m in length, with an average length of 254 m (see Table A.3). Thus, the recorded laterals with high confidence in their lengths all were considerably less than 800 m long and averaged around 254 m long. Notably, the range and average length correlated well to the lateral lengths inferred by Howard (2006:148) based on a detailed study of field sizes in a portion of Canal System 1, along the lower Salt River. He found that field lengths (and, by extension, lateral lengths) varied between 150 and 380 m, with a mean of 238 m. If correct, both studies support the contention that the Hohokam in the lower Salt and middle Gila Valleys shared a common irrigation technology that resulted in similar adaptations in separate canal systems (see Woodson 2004).

To provide a comparative basis for evaluating these lateral-canal lengths, I examined the lengths of laterals in three historical-period Akimel O'odham canal systems along the middle Gila River. I suggest that the historical-period lateral lengths are a useful analog, because of their similarities to the prehistoric canal systems in terms of environment, water source, topography, irrigation technology, and canal-system layout. The results for the historical-period Bapchil, Stotonick, and Santan Indian canals were based on the Southworth (1914–1915) Gila River survey maps (see Table A.3). The average length of these historical-period laterals was less than 800 m—much less, in the cases of the Bapchil canal (213 m) and the Stotonick canal (350 m). I consider these two canals to be better analogs for the prehistoric canals, because they are two of the oldest historical-period canals along the middle Gila River (Southworth 1919; see Woodson 2003). Both canals predate 1850 and probably were built as early as 1744, when Father Sedelmayer recorded the first observations of irrigation canals along the middle Gila River (Ezell 1961:36; Ives 1939). Although Sedelmayer did not indicate where he saw canals, he most likely made his observation in the Casa Blanca area, which is in the core territory of the Akimel O'odham. The Santan Indian Canal was finished in 1883 and actually was surveyed by instrument, with the assistance of Rev. C. H. Cook; so, it may not be as appropriate for comparison with the prehistoric canals. Thus, the range of lateral-canal lengths for the Bapchil and Stotonick canals is 91–579 m, with average lengths of 213 and 350 m, respectively. This correlates well to the range and average length of the Snaketown laterals (the revised list) and the Canal System 1 laterals noted above.

Thus, using a lateral-canal length of 254 m, the locations and sizes of the irrigated field areas along the prehistoric Snaketown canal system could be mapped, by applying a 254-m-wide buffer along each side of the main and distribution canals (Figure A.6). The boundaries of the irrigated field areas took into account (and omitted) the areas that would not have been irrigated, such as habitations, washes, dunes, and topographic obstacles, like the terrace edges. In addition, where a field area overlapped with an adjacent field area, they were simply combined in the area of overlap. The area that could be irrigated on the lower terrace was identified based on the zone along the main canal where a lateral could feasibly be turned out onto the lower terrace. This correlated to the downslope side of the main canal between Locus RRRR on the east and the midpoint of Locus DDD on the west. In sum, a total of 1,492 ha could have been farmed along the system within these field areas. For comparison, if the lateral canals measured 500 m long, then a maximum of 2,660 ha could have been farmed along the system. If the laterals were 1,000 m long, then 3,667 ha could have been irrigated. As noted above, if all the land downslope from the main canals theoretically could have been irrigated (which would have been impossible, in a practical sense), it would have encompassed 6,315 ha. Hence, the lengths of the lateral canals are very important factors to consider in estimating the command area of a canal system.

The command area of 1,492 ha can be subdivided into smaller irrigated field areas based on logistical considerations of irrigation technology (Table A.4; see Figure A.6). That is, since fields were supplied with water directly from lateral canals, and the laterals extended from main or distribution canals, a given part of the field areas could be watered only by certain distribution canals or main-canal segments. Table A.4 provides the sizes of the 20 individual field areas identified using this method, along with the corresponding main- or distribution-canal numbers. As indicated in the table and explained in the following section ("developmental sequence"), not all 20 field areas were irrigated during the Pioneer period.

To further test the validity of the inferred irrigated field areas, I crosschecked the field areas against two other pertinent data sources. First, I evaluated the correspondence between soil phases shown on the 1998 NRCS soil map (Johnson et al. 1998) and the inferred field areas and canal alignments. Irrigation agriculture results in physical and chemical impacts to soils (Ackerly et al. 1987). Soil data has been used by some researchers to examine aspects of prehistoric Hohokam canal irrigation (Dart 1986; Huckleberry 1992). Dart (1986) studied the association between soil phases mapped by the NRCS as narrow bands, or "ribbons," and prehistoric Hohokam canal alignments along Queen Creek and in a portion of the lower Salt Valley. His premise was that sediments transported by canals and deposited along them over long periods of time resulted in the formation of soil-phase ribbons that are often distinct from surrounding soil phases. Dart (1986:74) found that only "about 14 percent of the total canal length in the study area coincide[d] precisely with soil ribbons as a direct result of canal sediment deposition." This low correlation rate might have resulted because prehistoric irrigation signatures in soil were too subtle to be recognized by soil scientists when they created soil-survey maps, or because the soil data used to create the maps might have lacked sufficient resolution to identify prehistoric irrigation patterns (see Huckleberry 1992:244). Where correlations did exist between canals and soil-phase ribbons, the strongest associations occurred within the first 4 km (along Queen Creek) to 10 km (along lower Salt River) of canals from their intakes. Dart (1986:75) suggested that this is probably because most of the sediment carried in canals dropped out at locations relatively close to the river. The soil-phase ribbons with the strongest associations with canals were those with coarser textures, mostly represented by sandy loams. The associations may not be as clear or strong in active floodplains or other Holocene settings as they are in older, more stable geological landforms.

Huckleberry (1992) emphasized the more general and expansive impacts to soil due to irrigation, including the deposition of sediments in field areas as well as along the canals, which was emphasized by Dart (1986). The deposition of fine-textured alluvium (sands, silts, and clays) physically modifies soils into cohesive, fine-textured surface horizons that tend to be resistant to many postdepositional processes, such as plowing. Also, the thickness of irrigation sediment is related to cumulative irrigation history (Huckleberry 1992:245). Although a paucity of soil evidence of prolonged prehistoric irrigation in the lower Salt River Valley has been gathered, he suggested that further study may reveal those signatures.

Figure A.7 shows the Snaketown canal system and its inferred field areas plotted on the NRCS map. There are very few soil-phase ribbons within or near the canal system. Two ribbons of the Glenbar silt loam (No. 17) occur on the lower terrace, just downslope from the upper-terrace edge. Two ribbons of the Casa Grande complex (No. 7) are visible in the western half of the system: one at the upper-terrace edge and the other marking the alignment of the wash that divides the north and south main-canal branches in the western part of the system. Another narrow section of the Casa Grande complex occurs on the northern side of Gila Butte, within the tail end of the Gila Butte canal system, but the section appears too wide to be considered a ribbon, based on the

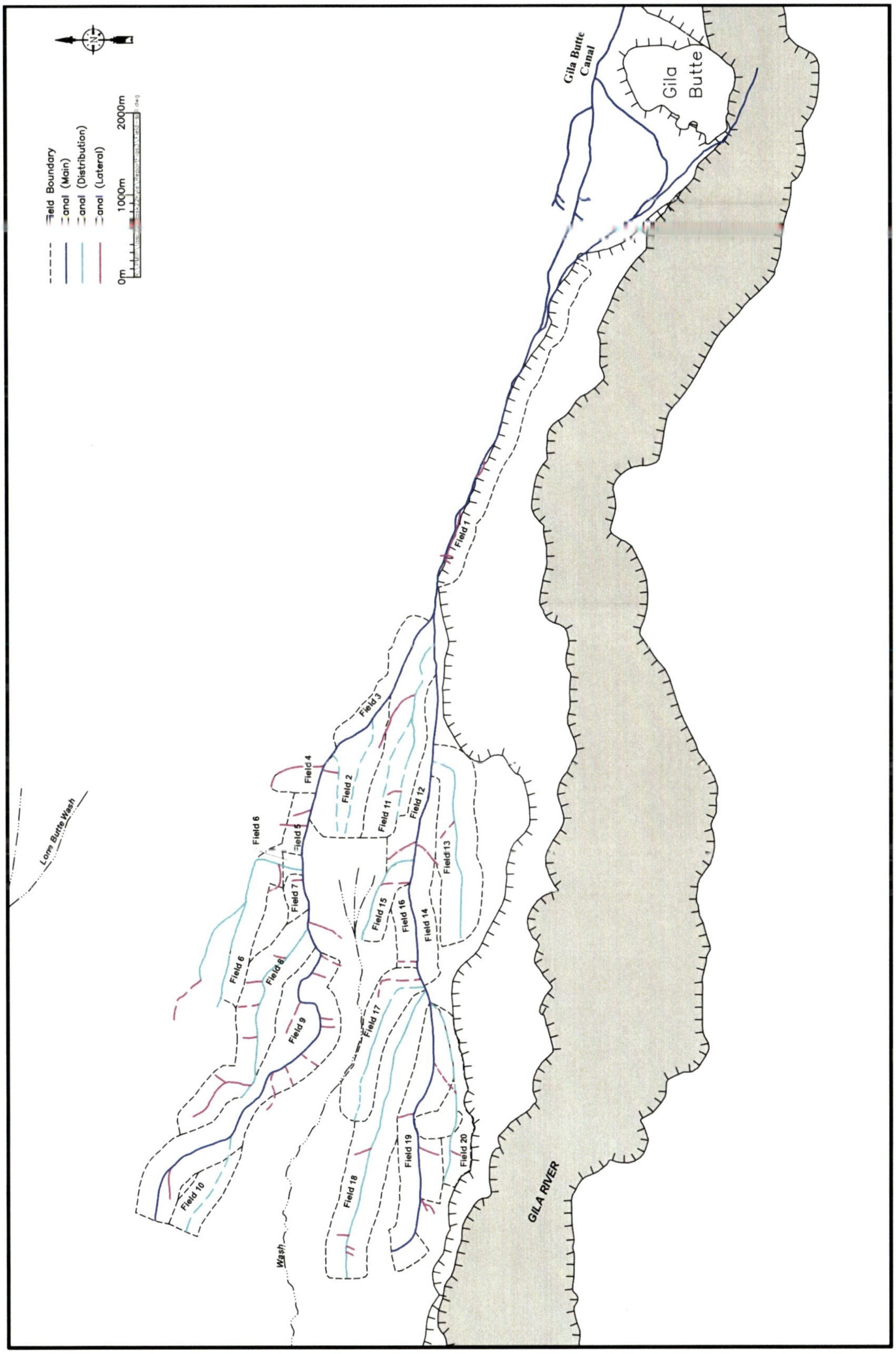

Figure A.6. Map of the Snaketown canal system, showing the inferred irrigated field areas.

Table A.4. Irrigated Field Areas along the Snaketown Canal System

Period	Field-Area No.	Area (ha)	Area in Tatai Silt Loam (ha)	Area in Shontik-Redun Sandy Loam (ha)	Associated Canal No. (Canal Type)	Comments
Early Pioneer	1	109.0	0.0	0.0	1 (main)	on lower terrace
Late Pioneer	1	109.0	0.0	0.0	1 (main)	on lower terrace
	2	72.0	37.14		1 (main)	
	3	37.7	29.42	0.13	1 (main)	
	4	89.6	59.43	20.92	1 (main)	
Total		*308.4*	*126.0*	*21.0*		74% of field area on upper terrace is within loamy soil units
Colonial to Classic	1	109.0	0.0	0.0	1 (main)	on lower terrace
	2	85.4	79.57	5.80	1, north branch (main)	along Canal 1
	3	37.7	29.42	0.13	1, north branch (main)	along Canal 1
	4	16.6	0.0	6.39	1-8 (lateral)	along Canal 1
	5	20.0	1.77	14.82	1, north branch (main)	along Canal 1
	6	59.0	35.09	10.44	1-12 (distribution)	along Canal 1
	7	12.7	12.70	0.0	1, north branch (main)	along Canal 1
	8	128.3	99.67	0.0	1-15 (distribution)	along Canal 1
	9	207.1	190.17	5.84	1, north branch (main)	along Canal 1
	10	38.5	36.08	2.44	1-24 (distribution)	along Canal 1
	11	114.0	113.99	0.0	2-15 (distribution)	along Canal 2
	12	43.9	43.86	0.0	2, south branch (main)	along Canal 2
	13	114.5	113.96	0.0	2-1 (distribution)	along Canal 2
	14	57.4	51.84	0.0	2, south branch (main)	along Canal 2
	15	25.2	25.05	0.0	2-4 (distribution)	along Canal 2
	16	23.7	23.18	0.0	2, south branch (main)	along Canal 2
	17	75.7	53.61	0.0	2-8 (distribution)	along Canal 2
	18	157.5	61.39	94.56	2-9 (distribution)	along Canal 2
	19	127.6	45.59	71.47	2, south branch (main)	along Canal 2
	20	38.7	13.31	21.13	2-10 (distribution)	along Canal 2
Total		*1,492.3*	*1,030.2*	*233.0*		75% of field area on the upper terrace is within silt loam; 91% is within loamy soil units

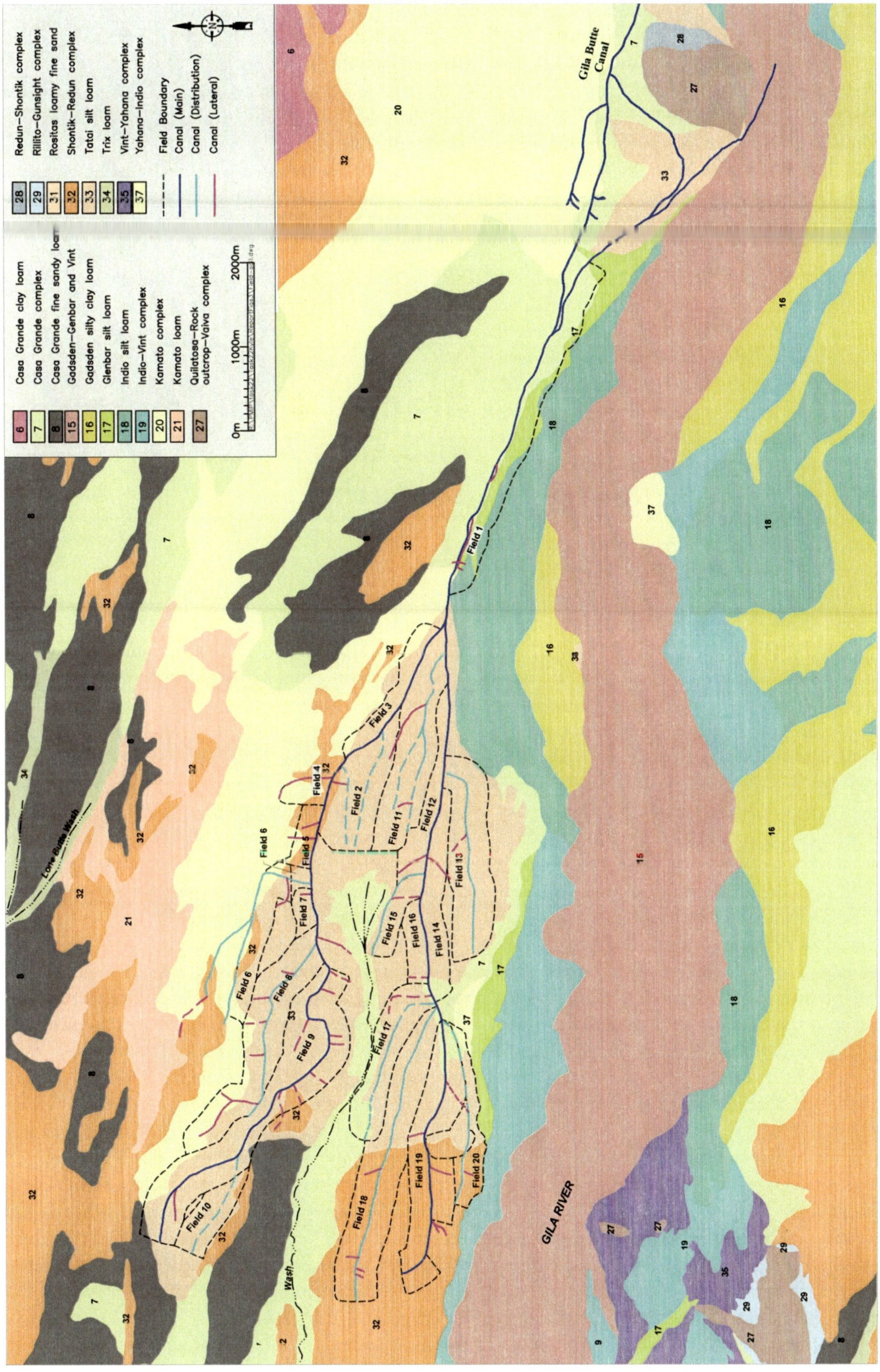

Figure A.7. Map of the Snaketown canal system overlaid onto a 1998 NRCS soil map, showing the correspondences between soil phases, canal alignments, and inferred irrigated field areas.

criteria from Dart (1986). Finally, three ribbons of the Shontik-Redun complex (No. 32) occur along the north main-canal branch in the western half of the system. Overall, none of these soil-phase ribbons is closely correlated to any of the Snaketown canal alignments. Indeed, the only correlations are two short sections of the main-canal branches (defined by Segments 1.11–1.14 and Segments 2.5–2.8) and three very short sections of two distribution canals (1-12 and 1-12-2) in the western half of the canal system. The lack of correlation is surprising, because the system is situated on an older, more stable landform, and the main and distribution canals are so clearly visible on the ground surface. In addition, the upper half of the main canal (especially Segments 1.3–1.7) is clearly demarcated by extensive spoil piles—the context in which, Dart (1986) argued, the strongest association between soil phases and canals should occur. As an explanation for the apparent discrepancy, I would echo Huckleberry (1992:244) by stating that the soil data used to create the soil map in this area probably suffered from problems related to low resolution.

On the other hand, a close correspondence was found between the inferred field areas in the western half of the canal system (i.e., the fields downstream from the West Fork, on the upper terrace) and a large area mapped as the Tatai silt loam (No. 33) (see Figure A.7). This correlation is remarkable: 75 percent of these western field areas occur in that silt loam unit (see Table A.4). The fact that the soil phases surrounding this silt loam are coarser, sandy loams suggests that the Tatai silt loam might have formed as a result of the deposition of fine-textured sediments during a long period of prehistoric irrigation (Woodson et al. 2015; see Huckleberry 1992). Woodson and others (2015) examined this issue in more detail. Also, the Shontik-Redun complex (No. 32) corresponds to some peripheral field areas at the western ends of the south- and north-branch canals. However, the latter correlations are less impressive than the Tatai silt loam correlations, and there are numerous other sections of the Shontik-Redun complex in surrounding areas. Lastly, the inferred field areas on the lower (Holocene) terrace (in the upper half of the system) correspond partly to the Glenbar silt loam (No. 17) and the Indio silt loam (No. 18). However, the correspondence between soil units and field areas is less clear on the lower terrace than on the upper terrace, because the lower terrace is on the floodplain and has been subjected to modifications from active geological processes since prehistoric times.

A similar correlation is evident between these western field areas and the Class 1 soils (the best soils for irrigation) that were mapped in the late 1990s, during a land-classification study. The study, conducted by the P-MIP, involved extensive, systematic soil auguring across the GRIC, to identify and certify all lands according to their suitability for irrigation. The Class 1 soils in the Snaketown area on the upper terrace conformed closely to the Tatai silt loam mapped by the NRCS. I suggest that this correlation provides yet further support for the inferred prehistoric field areas and for the contention that the soils in this area exhibit evidence of modification by prehistoric irrigation. Notably, the remaining field areas under the Snaketown canal system were classified as Class 2 soils, the next best for irrigation.

By considering all sources of data, I argue, I have identified with a high probability the locations of the prehistoric irrigated fields along the Snaketown canal system. The total area of these fields of 1,492 ha probably corresponds closely to the size, or command area, of the Snaketown canal system. The field areas in the western half of the system also correlated closely to the Tatai silt loam soil unit on the NRCS soil map, the Class 1 soils identified by P-MIP, and the linear zones on the 1936 aerial photographs.

Granite Knob, Santan, and Gila Butte Canal Systems

Study Area 2 encompasses the Granite Knob, Santan, and Gila Butte canal systems (Figure A.8). The Santan and Gila Butte systems are situated directly upstream from the Snaketown canal system, on the right bank of the river, with the Santan system heading farthest upstream, at Olberg Butte (or possibly Granite Knob), and the Gila Butte system heading at Diversion Point 2. The Granite Knob canal headed at Granite Knob, upstream from the Santan canal system, and is included in this analysis because it probably was consolidated with the Santan canal system during most of its use-life. Addressing these systems is particularly relevant because each system is linked with the next successive system.

The level of detail in the layout of these canal systems is not as high as that of the Snaketown system, because of the more intensive agriculture and development that have characterized the Santan–Gila Butte area in historical-period and modern times. One reason for this is that the land traversed by the prehistoric systems is mostly on the Holocene T-2 terrace, which remains the preferred locale for irrigation agriculture even today. The Snaketown system, in contrast, is largely on the Pleistocene T-3 terrace, which was not farmed in historical-period or modern times. Because the Santan–Gila Butte area has been heavily modified, it is more difficult to identify prehistoric canals there.

Table A.5 is an inventory of the canal types, listed by canal or segment number (correlating to Figure A.8), and the lengths of individual canals that were documented in the three systems. Table A.6 provides a summary of the irrigated field areas. Figure A.8 depicts the canal systems, with the segment numbers and inferred field areas, and also includes locations of the major habitation sites in Study

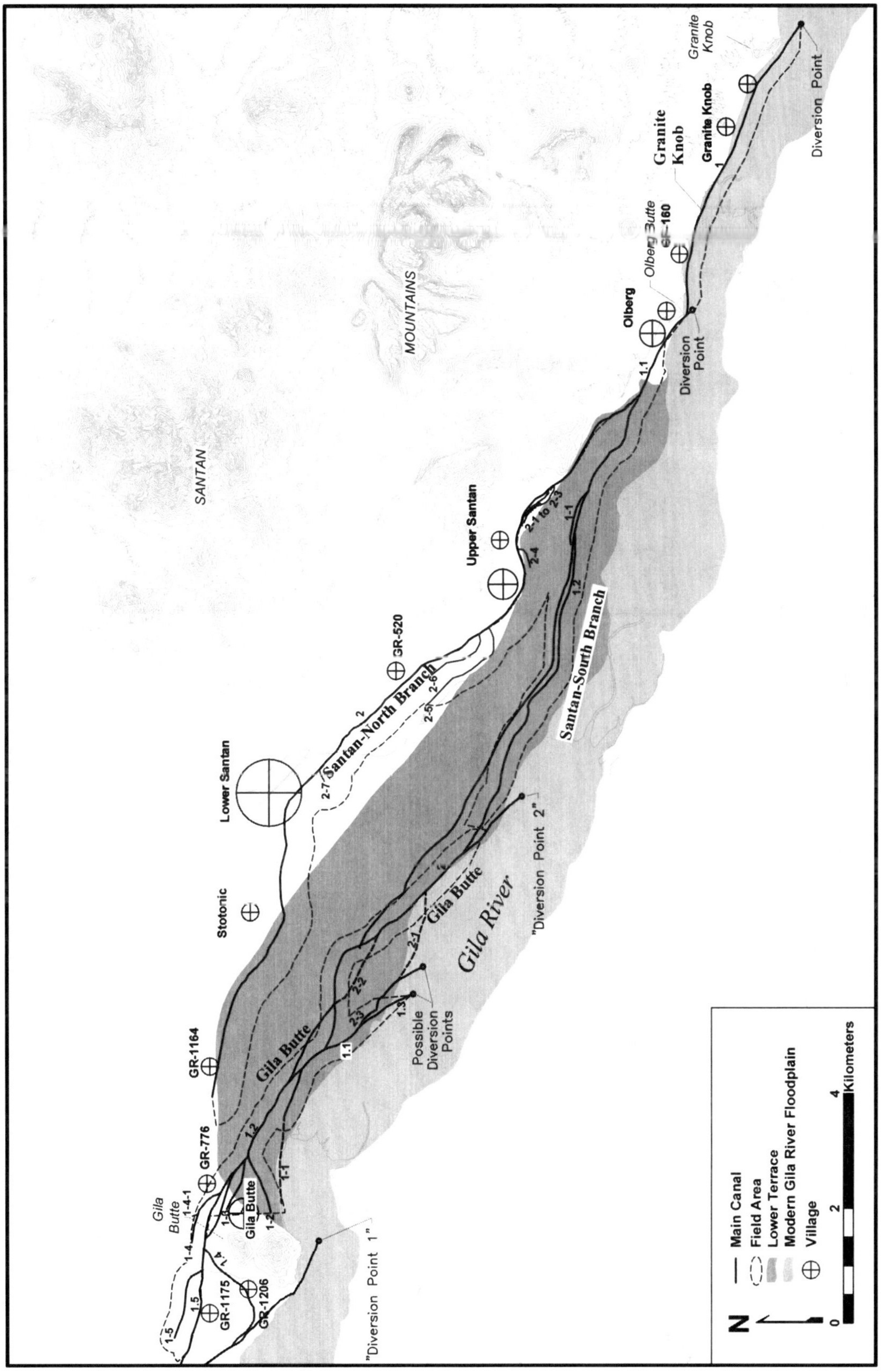

Figure A.8. Map showing the canal-segment numbers and inferred irrigated field areas along the Granite Knob, Santan, and Gila Butte canal systems.

Table A.5. Canal Types, Segments, and Lengths in the Granite Knob, Santan, and Gila Butte Canal Systems

Canal Type	Canal/Segment No.	Length (m)	Comments
<u>Granite Knob Canal</u>			
Main	1	5,500	from Granite Knob heading to the junction with the Santan canal near Olberg Butte
Total length of recorded canals		5,500	in the Granite Knob canal system
<u>Santan Canal System</u>			
Main	1.1	2,000	Olberg Butte heading to the branch point in the main canal
Main/branch	1.2	9,300	south branch—branch point to the junction with the Gila Butte canal
Main/branch	2	15,300	north branch—branch point to the end of the canal
Total, main and branch canals		**26,600**	
Pioneer period main-canal length		**9,300**	Olberg Butte to most of the way along the south branch canal
Colonial to Classic period main-canal length		**26,600**	Olberg Butte heading and both canal branches
Distribution canals			
Distribution	1-1	*800*	GR-640 Feature 4
Distribution	2-1	1,000	GR-441G Feature 378
Distribution	2-2	800	GR-441G Feature 696
Distribution	2-3	*500*	GR-441G Feature 366
Distribution	2-4	*800*	GR-441C Feature 254?
Distribution	2-5	*2,100*	GR-441K Feature 1158
Distribution	2-6	*1,500*	GR-441K Feature 2
Distribution	2-7	*800*	GR-522S, linear feature on the aerial photograph
Total, distribution canals		**3,100**	
Lateral canals			
Lateral	2-1-1	70	turns out of GR-441G Feature 696
Lateral	2-1-2	60	turns out of GR-441G Feature 696
Lateral	2-1-3	50	turns out of GR-441G Feature 696
Lateral	2-1-4	40	turns out of GR-441G Feature 696
Lateral	2-1-5	50	turns out of GR-441G Feature 696
Total, lateral canals		**270**	
Total length of recorded canals		**29,970**	in the Santan canal system
<u>Gila Butte Canal System</u>			
Main	1.1	3,100	from the possible Pioneer period heading to the junction with Canal 2, but might be a main-branch canal
Main	1.2	3,300	from the junction of Canals 1.1 and 2 to the ST-18 junction
Main	1.3	*1,000*	possible headward canal segment from a possible Pioneer period heading to Canal 1.1
Main	1.4	2,300	ST-18, Colonial period extension (1.1 km), Sedentary to Classic period extension (1.2 km)
Main	1.5	3,400	ST-22, Classic period extension
Main	2	6,500	from Diversion Point 2 to the junction with the end of Canal 1.1

Canal Type	Canal/Segment No.	Length (m)	Comments
Main/branch? (or distribution)	1-1	*2,500*	from Canal 1.1 to ASU Feature 5 (Howard 1982), Sedentary and possible Early Classic period, possibly a main-branch canal
Total, main canals		**22,100**	
Pioneer period main-canal length		**6,400**	from the possible Pioneer period heading, if the heading was at Diversion Point 2; length = 9.3 km
Colonial period main-canal length		**10,400**	Diversion Point 2 to GR-1206, along ST-18
Sedentary period main-canal length		**11,600**	Diversion Point 2 to the Snaketown canal, along ST-18
Classic period main-canal length		**15,000**	Diversion Point 2 to the Snaketown canal; includes ST-18 and ST-22; length is 12.7 km if only ST-22 is counted
Distribution canals			
Distribution	1-2	1,100	ASU Feature 2 (Howard 1982), Colonial to Sedentary period
Distribution	1-3	1,000	ASU Feature 7 (Howard 1982), Colonial to Sedentary period
Distribution	1-4	*800*	SWCA Feature 7 (Mostinger 1993), Classic period
Distribution	1-5	1,350	ST-24, Sedentary to Classic period canal
Distribution?	2-1	*1,400*	inferred canal between Canals 2 and 1.1
Distribution?	2-2	*1,400*	linear feature on an aerial photograph marking a possible route for Canal 2
Distribution?	2-3	*955*	possible canal between Canals 2 and 1.1
Total, distribution canals		**3,150**	
Lateral canals			
Lateral	1-4-1	*150*	SWCA Feature 1 (Mostinger 1993), late Sedentary to Classic period
Lateral	1-5-1	*110*	at the tail end of ST-24/Canal 1-5
Lateral	1-5-2	*150*	at the tail end of ST-24/Canal 1-5
Lateral	1-6	*120*	possible feeder off ST-22 to reservoirs in GR-1175
Lateral	1-7	*110*	possible lateral off ST-22
Total, lateral canals		**640**	
Total length of recorded canals		**25,890**	in the Gila Butte canal system

Note: Italicized lengths indicate lower confidence in the identification of the canals.

Table A.6. Irrigated Field Areas along the Granite Knob, Santan, and Gila Butte Canal Systems

Period	Field-Area No.	Area (ha)	Associated Canal No. (Canal Type)	Comments
Granite Knob Canal				
Pioneer (?)	1	*100*	1 (main)	canal may not have been built yet
Colonial to Classic	1	*133*	1 (main)	
Santan Canal System				
Late Pioneer	1	*50*	1.1 (main)	
	2	*371*	1.2 (main)	south main-canal branch
Total		*421*		
Colonial to Classic	1	50	1.1 (main)	
	2	371	1.2 (main branch)	south main-canal branch
	3	772	2 (main branch)	north main-canal branch, using 500-m-long laterals on the downslope
Total		*1,193*		
Gila Butte Canal System				
Late Pioneer	1	*300*	1.1, 1.2, 1.3 (main)	extends from the lower to the upper terrace
Colonial	1	250	1.1, 1.2 (main)	extends from the lower to the upper terrace
	2	280	2 (main)	from Diversion Point 2
	3	0	1.4 (main)	part of the ST-18 extension
	4	70	1-1, 1-2 (distributions)	
Total		*600*		
Sedentary	1	250	1.1, 1.2 (main)	extends from the lower to the upper terrace
	2	280	2 (main)	from Diversion Point 2
	3	0	1.4 (main)	ST-18 extension
	4	70	1-1, 1-2 (distributions)	
	5	30	1-5 (distribution)	ST-24
Total		*630*		
Classic	1	250	1.1, 1.2 (main)	extends from the lower to the upper terrace
	2	280	2 (main)	from Diversion Point 2
	3	0	1.4 (main)	ST-18 extension
	4	70	1-1, 1-2 (distributions)	
	5	80	1.5 (main), 1-5 (distribution)	ST-22 and ST-24
Total		*680*		

Note: Italicized numbers are estimates.

Area 2. One modification was made in the procedure for estimating the irrigated field areas (see previous section for description) along the Santan canal system. Along the north-branch canal, a 500-m length was used for the lateral canals, instead of the 254-m length used for the other lateral canals in the system, because it was apparent from recent archaeological investigations that more distribution canals existed downslope from the north-branch canal than had been previously known. Combined with the extent of artifact scatters downslope from the north-branch canal, it seems that the irrigated fields probably extended beyond the 254-m-long zone that was used in the original analysis.

The Santan canal system is now far better delineated than in the past, a benefit of excavating over 50 canal segments and documenting numerous relict canal alignments on the surface (Woodson 2010b). One issue that has needed resolution is whether the system headed at Olberg Butte or farther upstream, at Granite Knob (see Figure A.8). That issue also was discussed above (in the Canal-System Heading section). Historical-period flooding scoured away most of the terrace where the canal would have existed between those points. However, early maps (Larson 1926; Midvale 1946, 1963) indicate that a canal headed at Granite Knob (see Figure 3.3). Recent work documented the only known relict segment of that canal, which is visible on the ground surface (Gregory 1994; Miles 2009). It was thought to have been either a headward segment of the Santan canal or an independent canal, or both, if they were consolidated at some point (Gregory 1994). If it was independent, it would have been atypically short (5.5 km) for a main canal on the middle Gila River. Placing the Santan canal heading at Granite Knob makes more sense from a settlement-pattern perspective, given the proximity of the Granite Knob and Olberg villages (4 km apart), and it would have provided a farther-upstream heading at a bedrock outcrop. A recent investigation of a cutbank exposure of the relict segment of the Granite Knob canal suggested that it was much larger than necessary for irrigating the area between Granite Knob and Olberg Butte but probably not large enough to have been the only water supply for the Santan canal and its fields (Miles 2009; see previous section above). Therefore, the Santan canal probably headed at Olberg Butte, and the end of the Granite Knob canal was joined to the Santan canal to provide supplemental water. The timing of that consolidation is unclear, but available evidence suggests that it was done by the Sedentary period (see Chapter 4).

The main Santan canal, including both its branches, measures 26.6 km long (32.1 km, if it headed at Granite Knob) and is the second longest on the middle Gila River. The main canal divides into two branches roughly 2 km from the inferred heading at Olberg Butte; the north branch courses 15.3 km by the villages of Upper Santan and Lower Santan, and the south branch extends 9.3 km toward Gila Butte. Several distribution and lateral canals, canal turnouts (or gates), and large reservoirs have been documented along the north-branch canal. Reservoirs in Lower Santan village were filled by water diverted from washes on the *bajada* (Loendorf et al. 2007), similar to others at the Olberg and Granite Knob villages (see Gregory 1994). A reservoir at Upper Santan village appears to have been filled from both washes and the Santan canal. In one area near Upper Santan, a series of irrigated fields was identified along the north-branch canal (Miles et al. 2008). The fields are evident as rectangular areas between distribution and lateral canals and were defined based on the occurrence of anthropogenic sediments, which contrasted with the natural soil. That contrast was particularly clear because of the excellent preservation of the fields and their location at the distal end of an alluvial fan. The layout conforms well to the canal-field-system model outlined by Howard (2006).

The Gila Butte canal headed at Diversion Point 2 (see Haury 1976), located about 9 km downstream from Olberg Butte. This canal probably was built in the Snaketown phase and initially extended to the Gila Butte site (Swarthout and Blank-Roper 1984) (see Chapter 4). As described above (in the Canal-System Heading section), this first canal may have headed about 5 km closer to Gila Butte (see location labeled as a "possible diversion point" in Figure A.8). In the early Colonial period, the canal was extended to a settlement on the northwestern side of Gila Butte, and by the Sedentary period, it was connected with the Snaketown canal (Woodson 2010b, 2014). Excavations near Gila Butte revealed segments of both the pre-Classic and Classic period main canals in the Gila Butte system (Brooks and Vivian 1978; Motsinger 1993; Swarthout and Blank-Roper 1984) (see Figure 3.6). Recent work (Fertelmes and Loendorf 2010; GRIC-CRMP site files, GR-738 and GR-1220) has indicated that the south branch of the Santan canal connected with the Gila Butte canal about 3 km below the latter canal's heading. The two canals may have been connected as early as the early Colonial period and definitely by the Sedentary period, but the precise timing is unclear. Hence, the Santan (south branch), Gila Butte, and Snaketown canals were joined by the Sedentary period, but it appears that each of the three original headings remained in operation.

About 80 percent of field areas that were irrigated by the three canal systems in Study Area 2 are located on the lower (T-2) terrace (see Figure A.8). All the land irrigated by the Granite Knob canal throughout its use-life would have been on the lower terrace (which has been scoured away by flooding since prehistoric times). Only the last 4 km of the Gila Butte canal is on the upper terrace (the portion north and northeast of Gila Butte), which would account for roughly 100 ha of field areas that could have been farmed in that zone. Within the Santan canal system, roughly 40 percent of the field areas (about 309 out of 772 ha) along the north-branch canal are situated on the upper terrace. The lower terrace in Study Area 2 is dominated by the Gadsden silty clay loam, as classified by the NRCS (Johnson et al. 1998). The portions of the irrigated field areas on the upper terrace, along the Santan and Gila Butte canal systems, are on soils classified as the Casa Grande complex.

The locations of the irrigated field areas in Study Area 2 contrast with those along the Snaketown canal system. First, about 80 percent of the irrigated fields along the three canal systems in Study Area 2 are on the lower terrace, compared to less than 10 percent of the fields in the Snaketown system. The fields and canals on the upper terrace would have been better protected from river flooding than those on the lower terrace. Hence, the Snaketown fields (and canals) were less vulnerable to the adverse effects that might result from flooding than were the Study Area 2 fields (which were mostly on the lower terrace). Second, the Snaketown fields are situated mostly on the Tatai silt loam, whereas the Study Area 2 fields are situated mostly on the Gadsden silty clay loam (Johnson et al. 1998). I argued above that the Tatai silt loam probably formed as a result of modification by prehistoric irrigation, and it is highly doubtful that the Gadsden silty clay loam in Study Area 2 was formed by the same process, because it is on the lower terrace, which is on the floodplain, and has been subjected to modifications from active geological processes (i.e., overbank flooding and sediment aggradation) since prehistoric times.

Third, it is possible that, in terms of agricultural potential, one of these soil types might have had better crop-growing characteristics. For instance, the Tatai silt loam is a better-draining soil than the Gadsden silty clay loam. Perhaps it would have been more productive and advantageous for the Hohokam to grow crops in one soil area as opposed to the other. As noted above, a recent soil study by the P-MIP classified the majority of land within the Tatai silt loam as Class 1 soils (the best soils for irrigation) and designated the remaining Snaketown field areas Class 2 soils. The same study classified the majority of the Gadsden silty clay loam in Study Area 2 as Class 2 soils. Based on the P-MIP soil study, it would appear that the field areas along all four canal systems had good-quality agricultural soils (at least under modern-day conditions). Yet it is possible that the conditions during prehistoric times were different, and thus the soil quality, for agricultural purposes, also may have been different. Although this subject is outside the purview of this study, comparing the two soil types would be an interesting topic for further research.

---

[1] The Lower Santan canal should not be confused with the Santan Indian Canal, which headed at Olberg Butte and was completed about 1883. Regarding the Lower Santan canal, Southworth (1919:134) stated that "this ditch not long after its construction was used simply as an extension to the Santan Indian Canal." That is, the Lower Santan canal was combined with the Santan Indian Canal when the latter canal was completed in 1883.

[2] The maximum capacity (discharge) of an excavated main canal can be retrodicted at its inferred heading using regression modeling (Howard 1993). Ideally, a unique regression formula should be calculated for each prehistoric canal system based on analog data from historical-period gravity-fed canal systems traversing the same landscape. The regression formula of cross-section reduction established by Howard (1993:287) to retrodict discharge at the head of the canal is $y^\wedge = z(\log(x+1)) + (y \text{ intercept})$, where z is the multiplicative constant (slope). Howard calculated a slope of −2.215 for Canal System 2 using known points along the historical-period Appropriator's Canal as an analog model. The same formula can be applied to discharge reduction. I determined the z values for each canal system in the study area by conducting a regression analysis of the cross-sectional areas of known excavated segments along each main canal. The z values were as follows: Granite Knob Canal, −1.65 for the Colonial and Sedentary periods and −1.45 for the Classic period; Santan Canal, −1.65 for the Colonial and Sedentary periods and −1.25 for the Classic period; Gila Butte Canal, −1.25 for the Pioneer and Classic periods and −1.75 for the Colonial and Sedentary periods; and Snaketown Canal, −1.65 for the Pioneer to Sedentary periods and −1.25 for the Classic period. The values were found to vary in correspondence to the topographic slope (used as a proxy for the gradient) of the canal system.

Appendix B

Settlements in Study Area 1

This appendix provides additional data on the settlements in Study Area 1 described in Chapter 5. The primary focus of the study is Study Area 1, encompassing the Snaketown canal system and its environs, because it has had the most detailed documentation of the canals and settlements in the middle Gila Valley (Figure B.1). The appendix provides a brief description of the methods used in settlement documentation (including the definition of site function and habitation sites), a summary of the settlement-analysis results, and a description of the settlement trends through time.

Methods of Settlement Documentation

This section describes the methods used for assessing site function, defining habitation sites, and assigning time period designations for the settlements. These methods were used for both Study Areas 1 and 2.

Site Function

The site- and locus-function designations are based on an approach developed by Wells et al. (2003, 2004) in a study of the landscapes between Hohokam villages on the Gila River Indian Community (GRIC). Wells et al. (2003, 2004) evaluated the function of sites classified as "artifact scatters containing multiple artifact types" as part of a project that used predictive modeling to characterize the range of archaeological deposits situated between villages. A specific goal was to develop a method to break down the site type, "artifact scatter (containing multiple artifact types)," into more behaviorally meaningful categories, because the function of these site types is ambiguous because of a lack of surface features. Surface-artifact-assemblage data from known habitation sites and nonresidential activity areas were characterized using quantitative measures of artifact density and diversity to distinguish residential sites from nonresidential sites. Four functional categories were defined on the basis of these measures (Figure B.2): habitations (i.e., villages and hamlets), camps (i.e., farmsteads and field houses), multiple activity areas (i.e., nonresidential activity areas with diverse assemblages), and single activity areas (i.e., nonresidential activity areas with specialized assemblages).

Similar density and diversity measures were then calculated for sites classified as "artifact scatters." These measures were compared against the baseline measures in a two-step procedure, dividing sites first on the basis of artifact density and then by artifact-assemblage diversity. Each artifact scatter then was assigned to one of the functional categories based on the best fit (see Figure B.2). Some artifact scatters were assigned to one of two intermediate categories, possible habitations or multiple activity areas and possible camps or single activity areas. These sites represent scatters with artifact densities that fall in the range between those of habitation middens and those of nonresidential activity areas, but the diversity measures provided enough data to speculate on the categories to which the scatters might belong. Together, the density and diversity measures allowed Wells et al. (2003, 2004) to categorize 794 artifact scatters into six functional groups.

Because a significant number of sites on the GRIC (roughly 70 percent) recorded by the GRIC Cultural Resource Management Program (GRIC-CRMP) have been classified as artifact scatters, this method can serve as a useful tool in generating hypotheses of site function (Wells et al. 2003, 2004). Such hypotheses, of course, need to be tested against subsurface data recovered by excavation. Tests of the site-function-classification model have been conducted during recent test-excavation projects conducted by the GRIC-CRMP (Morgan and Woodson 2004; Rodrigues et al. 2003; Wells et al. 2005). Overall, these tests indicate that the model is successful or partially successful in accurately predicting site function in 83 percent of cases (Wells et al. 2005). Excavation was particularly effective in clarifying the function of sites assigned to the two intermediate categories, suggesting that excavation may be necessary to ascertain classification in such cases.

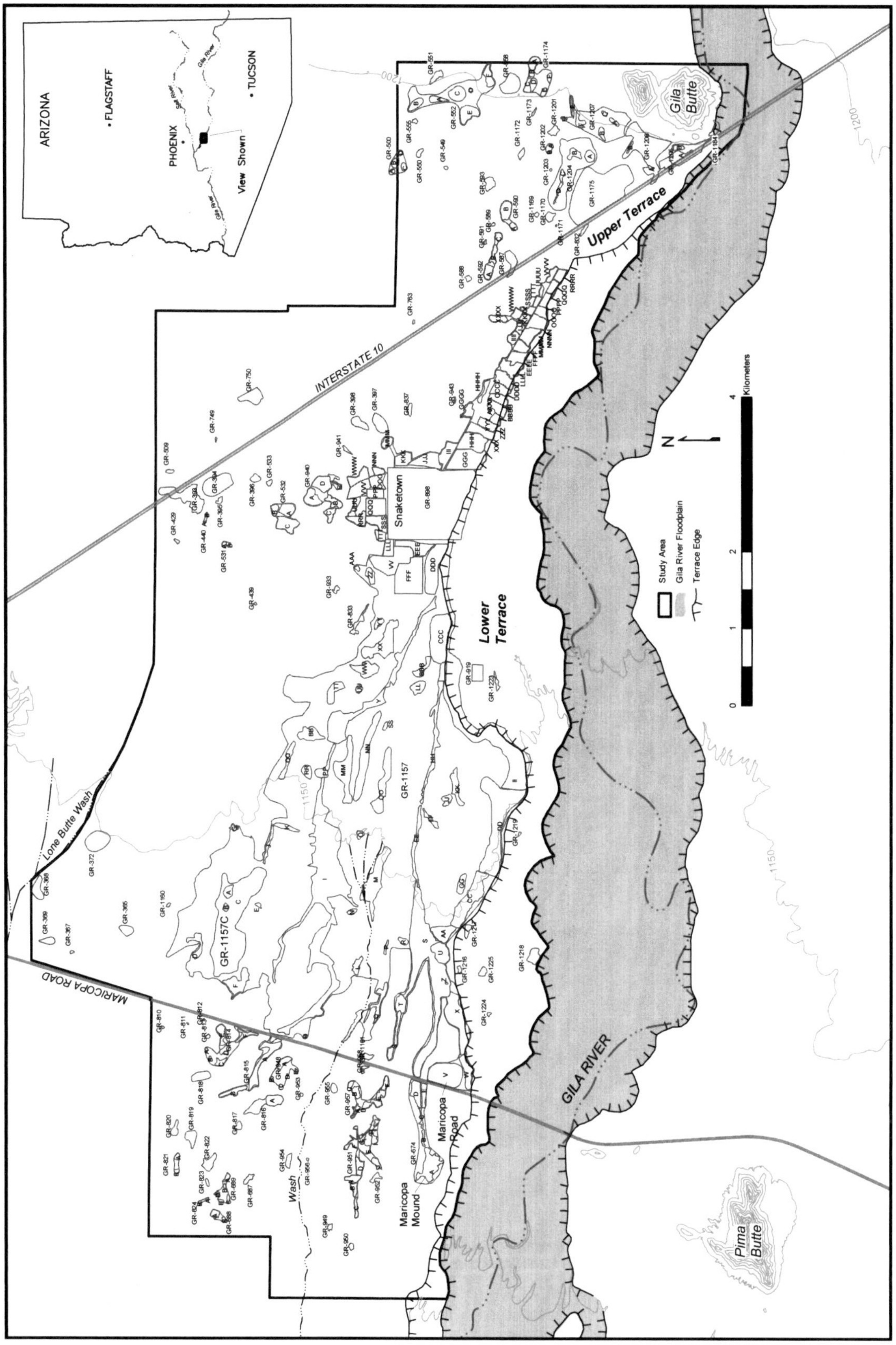

Figure B.1. Map of GR-1157 and other sites in Study Area 1 that encompassed the Snaketown canal system.

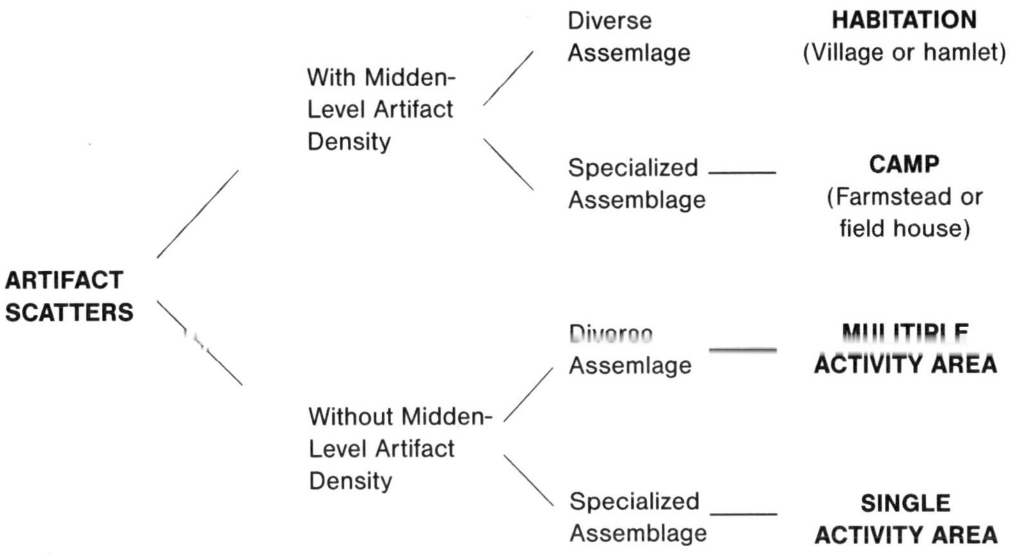

Figure B.2. Subcategories of the site type, artifact scatter, based on density and diversity characteristics (from Wells et al. 2003).

The test results also highlight the need to consider the depositional context of a site when evaluating the initial site-function assignment. For instance, surface-artifact density (and possibly diversity) can be affected differentially in aggrading vs. eroding contexts, as well as in disturbed areas, such as plowed agricultural fields. By considering these factors, a researcher can better evaluate the functional category assigned by the model.

During the current project, I re-evaluated the site-function designations for all sites and loci in the study area by considering site context as well as additional criteria. This was necessary because the original site-function study had evaluated the cases at a general level, based on artifact assemblages and basic information recorded during the site surveys. As a result, information such as depositional context was not integrated into assignment of functional categories to the sites and loci in the study area. For example, canal alignments were not recognized during the initial surveys at many sites and loci. As described above, a major contribution of the current research is the identification of the numerous canal alignments in the Snaketown canal system that are evident on the ground surface. In other cases, the number of surface features, feature types, feature arrangements, and the context and size of a site or locus were important to the assessment of function. In such cases, the original site-function designation was revised based on my assessment. For instance, habitation sites were classified as either *village*, *hamlet*, or *camp* in the revised assessment of site function. Also, the function of some sites and loci appeared to have changed over time or exhibited evidence of multiple functions at the same time. The categories for *single activity area* and *multiple activity area* are combined into one category, *activity area*, for this study. However, two specialized types of activity areas, *canal areas* and *roasting areas*, were recognizable during survey, based on the occurrence of canal alignments (see explanation in section above) and roasting pits. The canal areas are sites/loci defined primarily by the presence of a canal alignment, but they also can include agricultural fields and activity areas related to agricultural pursuits. These situations are accounted for in Chapters 5 and 6.

Lastly, a few additional site-function designations are used to identify site types not classified as artifact scatters based on surveys. These include *rock-pile field*, *rock art*, and *trail*. The type *rock-pile field* includes sites defined by the presence of non-irrigation agricultural features, such as rock piles, but also can include check dams, grid (or bordered) gardens, and terraces.

Habitation Sites

A specific focus of the assessment of site types through time was the analysis of habitation sites, or settlements. Three habitation-site types were defined in the study area: *villages* (including village with public architecture), *hamlets*, and *camps* (farmsteads and field houses). These habitation types were defined based on the settlement types defined by Gregory (1991:162–163):

- *Villages*, the largest and most complex units in the settlement hierarchy, are defined as settlements inferred to have more than 100 people; occupation was continuous and year-round over a relatively long period of time, such as a phase or longer; they usually have facilities, like ballcourts, that are often absent from hamlets and always absent from other types.

- *Hamlets* represent relatively smaller population aggregates, never having reached the theoretical 100-person threshold, yet they were continuously occupied on a year-round basis and often had occupations similar in duration to villages.

- *Farmsteads* were established primarily for the purpose of agricultural and related subsistence pursuits and are most often occupied by a single social group. Occupied seasonally, perhaps for a few seasons, or as repeated seasonal locus of residence for small social groups with continuing ties to one or more larger settlements. Functionally, they are extensions of villages and hamlets.

- *Field houses* are individual structures and associated facilities established solely for the purpose of tending agricultural fields.

For the purposes of this analysis, farmsteads and field houses are combined into one type (camps), because it is difficult to differentiate those two types on the basis of surface evidence. Functionally, though, they served similar purposes as seasonal residences, albeit on different scales (Rice 2001). Hamlets and villages are both permanent residences and are distinguished from each other primarily on the basis of size (area), since area can be used as a proxy for relative population size (Kowalewski et al. forthcoming). However, factors other than size are considered in differentiating between villages and hamlets, such as the occurrence of public architecture (only found at villages); the number, types, arrangement, and density of surface features (e.g., trash mounds and structural mounds); and the apparent length and intensity of occupation, as suggested by artifact content, diversity, and density. Most of the villages and hamlets could be differentiated through application of these criteria; the exceptions are described in Chapters 5 and 6.

Scrutiny also was given to the area covered by each habitation. The actual portions of the sites/loci that were used for habitation does not usually correspond to entire areas of the particular sites/loci as they were defined during archaeological survey. As part of the habitation-site analysis, I designated specific boundaries around the portions of these sites and loci that appeared to represent the zones of habitation as indicated by surface evidence (augmented by excavation evidence, in some instances). In the cases of villages and hamlets, the boundaries encircled clusters of surface features, such as trash mounds, structural mounds, compounds, public architecture (ballcourts and platform mounds), roasting pits, cemeteries, and artifact concentrations. At some settlements, the areas that were occupied changed through time, and these are noted, where possible. The camps, on the other hand, were identified first, based on the site-function model, and then boundaries were drawn around the portions of those sites and loci that appear to have been the foci of the camps. Some camps include trash mounds or structural mounds, but others are represented only by one or more artifact concentrations. In a few cases, camps are identified on the basis of previous excavations. It should also be noted that in some cases, the habitation-site boundaries include parts of two loci (e.g., a hamlet that includes parts of GR-1157, Loci CC and DD); conversely, some loci include more than one habitation site each (e.g., GR-1157, Locus I [GR-1157I], includes three separate hamlets).

Time-Period Assignments

The time period for each site/locus is coded as follows. Each site/locus was assigned to one or more of these time periods: Pioneer (Vahki, Estrella/Sweetwater, and Snaketown phases), early Colonial (Gila Butte phase), late Colonial (Santa Cruz phase), Sedentary (Sacaton phase), Early Classic (Soho phase), and Late Classic (Civano phase). The evaluation of whether a site/locus was occupied or used during a given time period was based primarily on the presence or absence of temporally diagnostic ceramics, including the red-on-buff pottery types in the traditional Hohokam buff ware sequence (Haury 1976) and Roosevelt Red Ware (Gila and Tonto Polychromes, indicating a Late Classic period age). The refined buff ware typology outlined by Wallace (2001, 2004) was not applied in the current ceramic analyses, which were conducted by GRIC-CRMP laboratory staff. This omission presented some challenges to interpreting Sedentary period patterns, since the refined typology allowed analysts to split the period into Early, Middle, and Late subphases based on subtypes of Sacaton Red-on-buff. So, the current study cannot fully apply a finer-grained evaluation for the Sedentary period. Smudged plain and red wares also were considered in assessing some sites/loci as dating to the Classic period; however, I only considered smudged wares in the absence of other Classic period diagnostics and only when the smudged wares were present in relatively large quantities. I took this stance because some smudged wares were produced in the Sedentary period (see Abbott 1983, 2001; Henderson 2001:165–166), and I didn't want to skew the time-period assignments based on smudged wares. Also, the GRIC-CRMP analysis guidelines for identifying red wares and smudged wares appear to be less specific than other Hohokam ceramic analysts have been, resulting in overly broad typological definitions for these types. Architectural features also were considered in assigning time period, such as compounds or surface adobe structural areas, ballcourts, and the platform mound (at GR-674).

The relative dominance of a time period was determined for each site/locus based on a rank-order system in which 10 is the most dominant, 20 is the next most dominant, and so on, through 60. A code of 60 indicates that diagnostic ceramic types for that period constitute 5 percent or less of the total number of prehistoric diagnostic

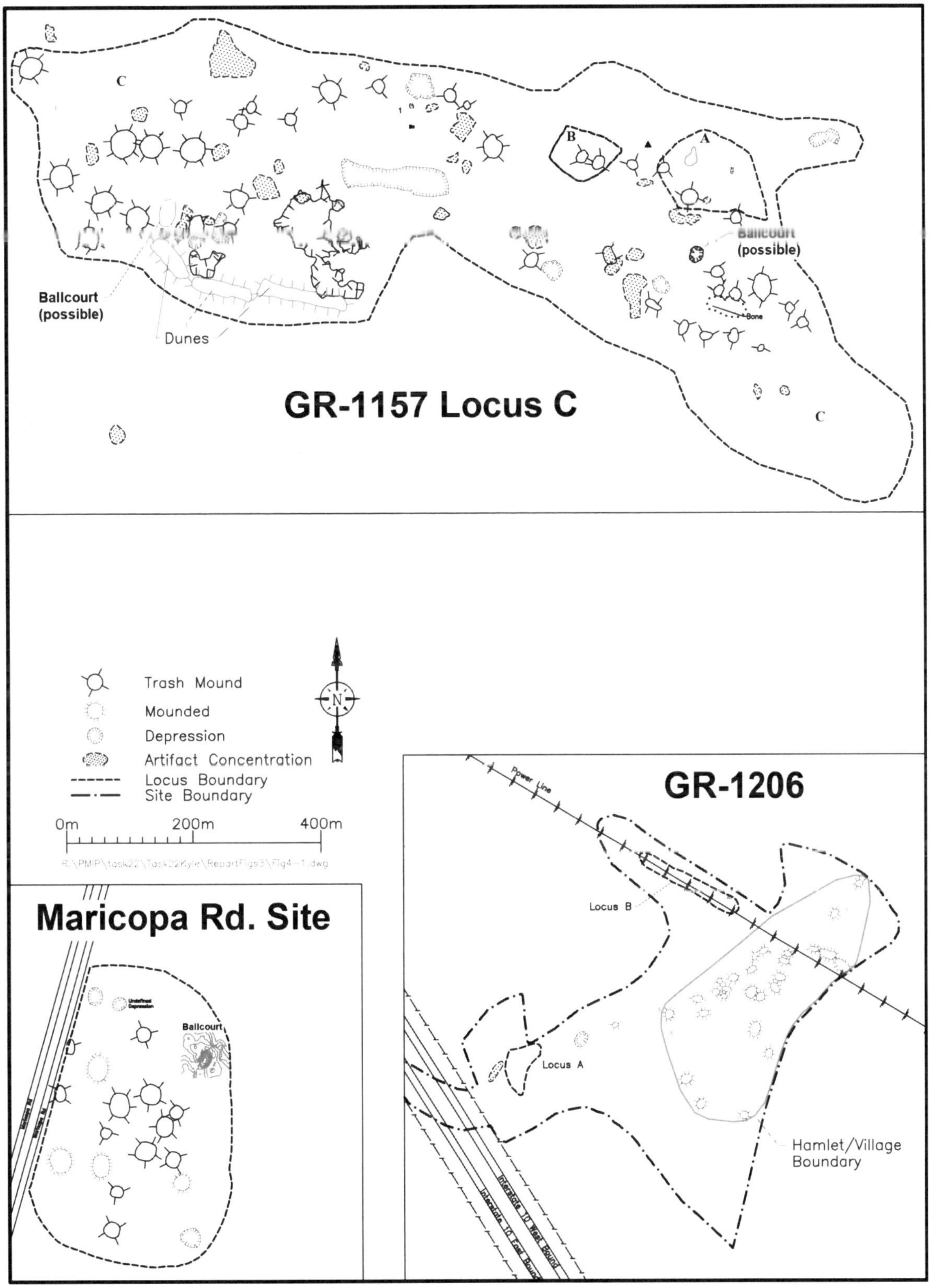

Figure B.3. Maps of pre-Classic period village sites: GR-1157C, the Maricopa Road site (GR-1157V), and GR-1206.

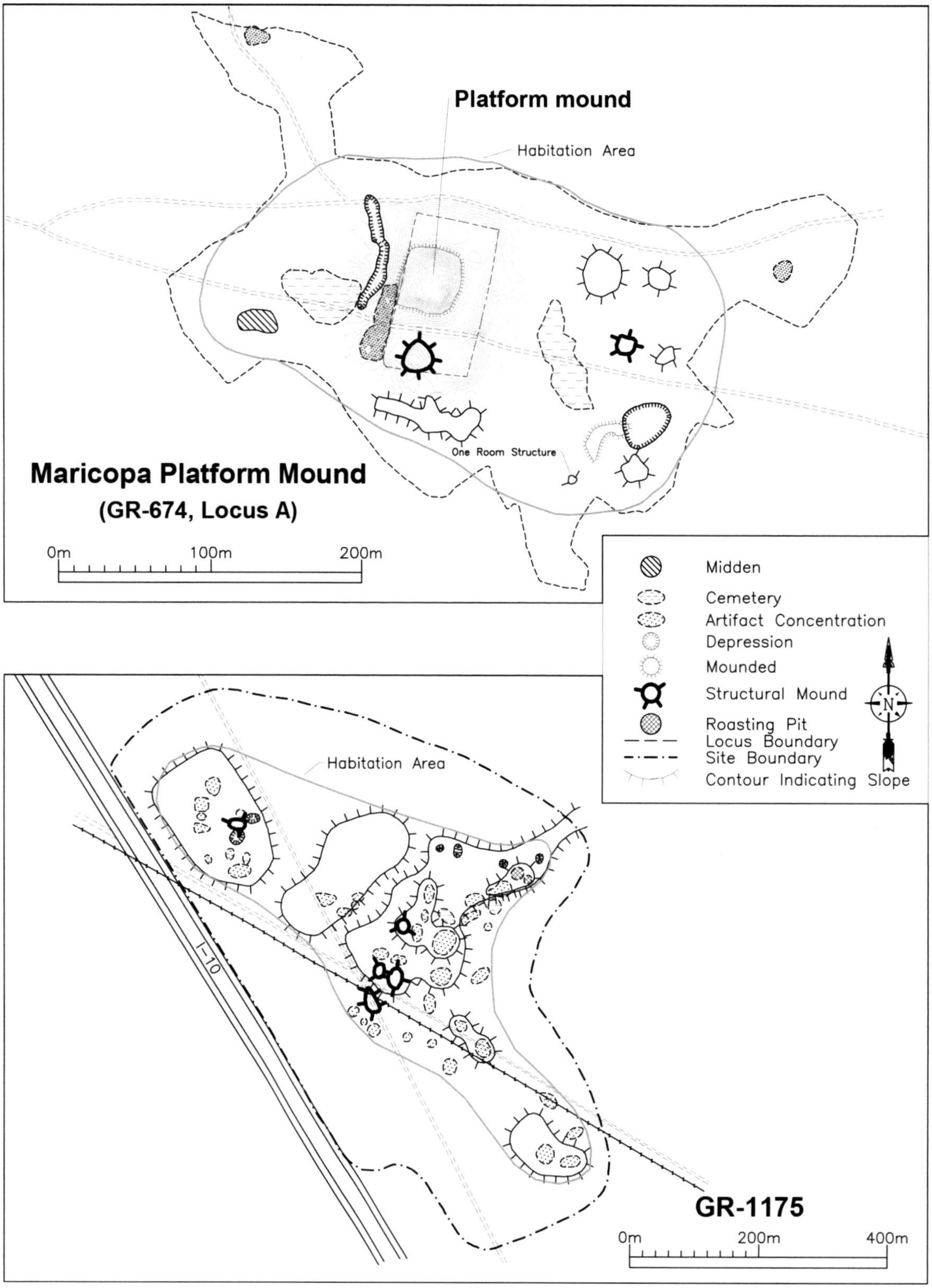

Figure B.4. Maps of Classic period village sites: Maricopa Platform Mound (GR-674A) and GR-1175.

Table B.2. Counts of Primary Site Types per Time Period along the Snaketown Canal System

Site Type	Period					
	Pioneer	Early Colonial	Late Colonial	Sedentary	Early Classic	Late Classic
Village	—	7[a]	7[a]	8[a]	2	2
Hamlet	1	3[b]	4[b]	2[b]	15[c]	13[c]
Possible hamlet	—	—	—	—	—	3
Camp	3[d]	8[e]	7[e]	8[e]	14[f]	11[f]
Possible camp	1	2[g]	2[g]	12[h, i]	4[i]	—
Canal area	8	54	49	53	32	47
Activity area	28	92	60	82	17	27
Roasting area	—	4	3	4	—	2
Total	41	170	132	169	84	105

[a] Loci A, B, and C at GR-1157 are part of one village; three loci compose the Snaketown village (for an actual total of three villages in the Colonial period and four in the Sedentary period).

[b] GR-1157I includes three separate hamlets (for an actual total of five hamlets in the early Colonial period, six in the late Colonial period, and four in the Sedentary period).

[c] GR-1157I includes 3 hamlets, and GR-1157VV includes 2 hamlets (for an actual total of 18 hamlets in the Early Classic period and 17 in the Late Classic period).

[d] Together, Loci C and F at GR-1157, together, represent one camp (for an actual total of two camps in the Pioneer period).

[e] GR-1157F may be part of the GR-1157C village.

[f] Together, Loci KKKK and WWWW at GR-1157, together, represent 1 possible camp (for an actual total of 13 in the Early Classic period and 10 in the Late Classic period).

[g] Together, Loci TTTT and UUUU at GR-1157 represent one possible camp (for an actual total of one).

[h] Loci Y, BB, TT, WW, XX, and LLL at GR-1157 may not have been camps in the Sedentary period.

[i] Loci TTTT/UUUU and QQQQ/RRRR at GR-1157 represent 2 possible camps (for an actual total of 10 in the Sedentary period and 2 in the Early Classic period).

More specific identifications now have been made for canals and habitation sites in the study area. Also, the function of some sites/loci appear to have changed over time or exhibited evidence of multiple functions. These situations are accounted for in the "Revised Site Type" columns in Table B.1. The site-type codes utilized in the current study include *village, hamlet, camp, activity area, canal area, roasting area,* and *trail.* The methods used in defining and measuring the site variables are described above. Again, the relative dominance of a time period (or "intensity of occupation") for each site/locus is coded according to a rank-order system in which 10 is most dominant, 20 is next most dominant, and so on, through 60.

Table B.2 lists the numbers of occurrences of the primary site types in each time period. The general trends are worth noting, including a sharp fourfold increase in the total count from the Pioneer to early Colonial periods, followed by a 22 percent decline in the late Colonial period and a 28 percent increase to a peak in the Sedentary period. A 50 percent decrease occurred in the Early Classic period, followed by a 25 percent increase in the Late Classic period. The large increase in the early Colonial indicates a surge in intensity of use and, as will be seen below, almost certainly an increase in population. The drop during the late Colonial period could reflect an actual decrease in intensity of use, although the primary category that registered this drop was *activity area.* Activity areas have lower densities and diversities of artifacts than the other site-type categories; so, there usually are fewer temporally diagnostic ceramics in activity areas. A caveat that might explain the lower counts for the late Colonial period is the lower rate of identifying diagnostic ceramics that date exclusively to that period (Santa Cruz Red-on-buff). For instance, analysts find it relatively easy to identify Gila Butte Red-on-buff (because of the presence of incising), the early Colonial period buff ware type, in contrast to identifying Santa Cruz Red-on-buff. Also, it is sometimes difficult to distinguish between Santa Cruz and Sacaton Red-on-buff. Both situations may lead to suppressed counts of late Colonial period sites. This might make more sense, especially since the counts for the Sedentary period are nearly the same as those for the early Colonial period. The late Colonial period problem in dating sites also was noted by Gregory and Huckleberry (1994) in their analysis of upstream settlements at Olberg, Granite Knob, and Chee Nee villages.

The 50 percent drop in counts in the Early Classic period almost certainly indicates a major drop in intensity of use and probably population. A caveat should be noted here, too, because sites of this age normally are dated based on the presence of Casa Grande Red-on-buff (as well as Tanque Verde Red-on-brown). Yet the overall proportion of the Early Classic period Hohokam ceramic inventory represented by buff and brown wares was lower than in the Sedentary period (Henderson 2001); so, the chance is lower for recovering these types on survey. Red wares, especially smudged red wares, and smudged plain wares also were produced by the Hohokam, primarily in the Classic period. However, these types occurred in both the Early and Late Classic periods as well as in the Sedentary period, in lower proportions. These red and plain ware types therefore cannot be used to confidently date a site to the Early Classic period. As a result, the number of sites from the Early Classic period probably is skewed downward, but the error range represented by that skew cannot account for the 50 percent decrease.

Regarding the habitation-site types (village, hamlet, possible hamlet, camp, and possible camp), several caveats apply to the numbers given in the table. As noted in Chapter 2, the boundaries of some habitation sites include parts of two loci (e.g., a hamlet that includes parts of GR-1157, Loci CC and DD); conversely, some loci include more than one habitation site within them (e.g., GR-1157I includes three separate hamlets). The footnotes provided in Table B.2 identify where these situations made a difference in the "actual" number of a certain habitation type for a given time period, as opposed to a simple count of the number of sites/loci designated as that habitation type. The actual number of habitations per time period will be more relevant to the discussion later in this chapter.

Habitation Sites

Table B.3 provides summary information for the 49 habitation sites identified along the Snaketown canal system. For each habitation, the table lists the site/locus, relevant remarks (including corresponding Arizona State Museum [ASM] site numbers), and area (in square meters and hectares), and it indicates the phases during which the site was occupied. The table groups the habitations into five sections (for ease of organization and reference): Snaketown, GR-1157C, GR-1157I, GR-1157 (other loci), and other settlements along Snaketown canal.

As noted in Chapter 2, farmsteads and field houses were combined into one type (camps). Hamlets and villages are both permanent residences and were distinguished from each other primarily on the basis of size (area), but other factors were considered, such as the occurrence of public architecture (only found at villages); the number, types, arrangement, and density of surface features (e.g., trash mounds and structural mounds); and the apparent length and intensity of occupation, as suggested by artifact content, diversity, and density. Based on that approach, the villages were larger than 10 ha (with two exceptions), and the hamlets were about 5 ha or smaller. The Maricopa Platform Mound site (5.5 ha) and GR-1206 (7.3 ha) were the smallest villages in the study area. Notably, the camps were about 3 ha or smaller, with a few exceptions. Three settlements (GR-1157, Loci WW, XX, and Y) that were about 4–5 ha in area were inferred to have begun as camps in the Sedentary period before developing into hamlets; however, these sites actually may have been initiated as hamlets in the Late Sedentary period. This is uncertain because of the lack of chronological detail during the Sedentary period, as a result of not integrating the revised buff ware typology into the analysis (see Chapter 2). Also, the village at GR-1157C is inferred to have begun as a camp during the Snaketown phase, when it is estimated to have measured about 8 ha.

Another issue regarding the hamlet-village distinction is that a group of hamlets situated close to each other could be considered large enough to be a village. That is relevant to four groups of hamlets in the study area: GR-1157, Loci I, M, and N ("I Group"); GR-1157, Loci U, AA, and CC ("U Group"); GR-1157, Loci Y, BB, TT, UU, WW, and XX ("Y Group"); and GR-1157, Loci VV, ZZ, and LLL ("VV Group"). The I Group was persistent from the late Pioneer through Late Classic periods (in some combination of Loci I, M, and N), and the latter three groups were present only during the Classic period. Notably, Locus VV includes the Classic period compound sites AZ U:13:22 (ASM) and AZ U:13:24 (ASM), which were studied by Haury (1976). Each group was visually discernible as a cluster of settlements, but the hamlets within them varied in their proximity to one another. Each of the four hamlets in the VV Group was 50 m or less apart from the next-closest hamlet in the group. This spatial propinquity not only would have resulted in the regular interaction between the residents of the hamlets but also probably reflects the sociopolitical closeness of the residents. The VV Group therefore may be best viewed collectively as a village. On the other hand, the hamlets within the I, Y, and U Groups were separated by more than 100 m. Although this is not a great distance, it is not clear whether the residents within these groups interacted on a daily basis or would have considered themselves to be part of a village (albeit a dispersed one), or both. Regardless, the fact that these groups existed in these configurations for long periods suggests that they do represent permanent residences that collectively were larger than hamlets. None of the three groups contains public architecture; hence, they were not "primary" settlements. In the discussions below, these three groups are viewed as dispersed villages and are considered to be correlates to "villages without public architecture" in the Hohokam settlement hierarchy (see Gregory 1991, 1994; Wilcox 1991). This settlement-grouping situation also applies to one group of camps in the upper end of the canal system (GR-1157, Loci FFFF, IIII, KKKK, and MMMM—referred to as the "FFFF Group") that appears to represent a dispersed hamlet from the Classic period.

Lastly, in Table B.3, some habitation sites are designated "camp/hamlet," one is "hamlet/possible hamlet," and one is "hamlet/village." These designations are used to indicate settlements that each began as one habitation type and developed into another type; the period in which the change occurred is noted in the Remarks column for each. In sum,

Table B.3. Habitation Sites along the Snaketown Canal System

Site/Locus	Settlement Type	Remarks[a]	Area (m²)	Area (ha)	Phase						
					Vahki	Snaketown	Gila Butte	Santa Cruz	Sacaton	Soho	Civano
Snaketown											
Snaketown	hamlet	Vahki	46,057.9	4.61	X						
Snaketown	village	Snaketown	160,682.0	16.07		X					
Snaketown	village (with ballcourt)	Gila Butte	255,663.0	25.57			X				
Snaketown	village (with ballcourt)	Santa Cruz	401,897.4	40.19				X			
Snaketown	village (with ballcourts)	Sacaton	683,453.1	68.35					X		
GR-1157C											
C–F	camp	Snaketown	81,703.3	8.17		X					
C	village (with possible ballcourts)	Gila Butte, western part	85,707.2	8.57			X				
C	village (with possible ballcourts)	Gila Butte, eastern part	19,355.2	1.94			X				
C	village (with possible ballcourts)	Santa Cruz, western part	127,843.1	12.78				X			
C	village (with possible ballcourts)	Santa Cruz, eastern part	73,166.4	7.32				X			
A, B, C	village (with possible ballcourts)	Sacaton	401,468.3	40.15					X		
GR-1157I											
I—East	camp	early phase of I—East	26,752.5	2.68		X					
I—East	hamlet	Gila Butte–Sacaton	58,899.7	5.89			X	X	X		
I—East	hamlet	Soho-Civano	42,657.2	4.27						X	X
I—Central	hamlet	U:13:20	31,924.2	3.19			X	X	X	X	X
I—West	hamlet	U:13:18	10,494.7	1.05			X	X	X	X	
GR-1157 (Other Loci)											
AA	hamlet		13,947.6	1.39						X	X
AAA	possible hamlet	part of a hamlet in Loci ZZ and VV—north?	3,362.1	0.34							X
AAAA—north and BBBB	camp	U:13:222 (in part)	19,031.4	1.90			X	X	X		

continued on next page

Site/Locus	Settlement Type	Remarks[a]	Area (m²)	Area (ha)	Phase						
					Vahki	Snaketown	Gila Butte	Santa Cruz	Sacaton	Soho	Civano
AAAA—south	camp	U:13:222 (in part)	4,884.4	0.49						X	X
BB	camp/hamlet	possible camp = Sacaton phase	21,142.7	2.11					X	X	X
CC	hamlet		13,975.6	1.40						X	X
CC–DD	hamlet		41,891.8	4.19						X	X
CCC	camp		8,607.4	0.86						X	X
DD	camp	2 roasting pits	18,101.7	1.81			X	X	X	X	X
DDDD	camp	U:13:222 (in part)	4,620.9	0.46			X		X	X	
FFF	hamlet	U:13:21	24,463.9	2.45						X	X
FFFF	camp		7,083.2	0.71						X	X
II—East	camp		13,565.8	1.36			X	X	X	X	X
IIII	possible camp/ camp	possible camp in the Sacaton phase; camp in the Classic period; U:13:2?	13,342.5	1.33					X	X	X
K	camp		3,820.0	0.38							X
KKKK–WWWW	camp		8,602.5	0.86						X	X
LLL	camp/hamlet	camp in the Sacaton phase	11,331.3	1.13					X	X	X
M	hamlet		16,866.2	1.69			X	X	X		
MMMM	possible camp/ camp	possible camp in the Sacaton phase; camp in the Classic period	3,689.8	0.37					X	X	X
N	hamlet	U:13:19?	6,831.5	0.68				X			X
PP	camp		12,304.7	1.23			X	X	X		
QQQQ–RRRR	possible camp	U:13:221 (in part)	12,715.1	1.27					X	X	
RR	camp		13,519.7	1.35			X	X			
TT	camp/hamlet	possible camp in the Sacaton phase	20,431.6	2.04					X	X	X
TTTT–UUUU	possible camp	U:13:221 (in part)	10,379.6	1.04			X	X	X	X	
U	hamlet		29,186.6	2.92						X	X
UU	hamlet/possible hamlet	possible hamlet in the Civano phase	7,726.5	0.77						X	X

Site/Locus	Settlement Type	Remarks[a]	Area (m²)	Area (ha)	Phase						
					Vahki	Snaketown	Gila Butte	Santa Cruz	Sacaton	Soho	Civano
V	village (with ballcourt)	Maricopa Road site, T:16:13 (ASU)	111,940.6	3.72			X	X	X		
VV—North	hamlet	U:13:24	33,286.9	5.25						X	X
VV—South	hamlet	U:13:22	24,917.3	2.35						X	X
WW	camp/hamlet	possible camp in the Sacaton phase	*37,159.1*	*4.37*					X	X	
XX	camp/hamlet/ possible hamlet	possible camp in the Sacaton phase; hamlet in the Soho phase; U:13:23	52,474.5	1.49					X	X	X
XX—North	possible hamlet	part of Locus XX or WW	23,491.6	—						X	
Y	camp/hamlet	possible camp in the Sacaton phase	43,697.6	2.81					X	X	X
ZZ	hamlet	part of Locus VV—north	14,938.3	5.48						X	X
Other Settlements along the Snaketown Canal											
GR-590B	camp	on the Gila Butte canal?	28,072.4	0.49						X	
GR-674A	village (with platform mound)	Maricopa Platform Mound	54,798.8	18.32						X	X
GR-948A	camp	U:13:11 (ACS)	4,388.5	1.44						X	X
GR-957E	camp		4,857.1	0.49						X	X
GR-1175	village	U:13:12, U:13:118 (part)	183,195.1	7.33						X	X
GR-1184	possible camp/ camp	Johnson's (1964) U:13:9 Area A; possible camp in the Snaketown phase	14,366.1	1.44		X	X	X	X		
GR-1205A	camp	Johnson's (1964) U:13:9 Area B	*27,628.4*	—					X	X	
GR-1206	hamlet/village	U:13:11; village in the Sacaton phase	73,267.2	—			X	X	X		
GR-1206A	camp	Johnson's (1964) U:13:11	14,366.2	—						X	

[a] Site numbers are ASM numbers unless otherwise noted. ACS = Archaeological Consulting Services, Inc.

the 49 habitation sites in study area include the following types: 3 villages, 12 hamlets, 17 camps, 2 possible hamlets, 2 possible camps, 2 hamlets/villages, 1 camp/village, 6 camps/hamlets, 2 possible camps/camps, 1 camp/hamlet/possible hamlet, and 1 hamlet/possible hamlet.

As noted above, the area covered by each settlement is carefully defined in this study. The actual areas that were occupied changed through time at Snaketown, GR-1157C, and GR-1157I East. For Snaketown, I used the habitation areas through time as drawn by Wilcox et al. (1981:18) (see Figure B.2). The camps were identified first based on the site-function model, and then boundaries were drawn around the portions of those sites and loci that appeared to have been the foci of the camps. Some camps included trash mounds or structural mounds, but others were represented by one or more artifact concentrations. Two camps, at GR-1184 (AZ U:13:9 [ASM], Area A) and GR-1206A (AZ U:13:11 [ASM]), were identified on the basis of a previous excavation project (Johnson 1964).

Settlement Trends through Time

This section describes the settlement trends through time in Study Area 1, with a focus on site function. The figures below display the results of the revised assessment of site function by time period, in conjunction with the definitions of habitation sites (see previous sections above). The boundaries and numerical designations of all the sites and loci are shown in gray in the figures. A site/locus boundary is highlighted in a color representing a specific function for each time period that it was in use. Only the primary site function ("revised site type (1)" in Table B.1) is shown in the figures, because of the limitations of visually depicting multiple site functions. The "intensity of occupation" is depicted by the line width of a site/locus boundary, with the thickest/darkest line denoting the most intense period of occupation (i.e., coded 10 in Table B.1). Another set of symbols were used to indicate the habitation-site areas in the figures. The dashed lines represent the inferred community-territory boundaries. These boundaries reflect the most practical configurations based on applying the principles of the two community models and the boundary-definition criteria described in Chapter 2. Chapter 5 discusses the implications of these boundaries for the two community models.

Pioneer Period

Snaketown was founded during the Vahki phase of the early Pioneer period, and it is the only known settlement in the study area from that time. The site is situated near the end of an 8.1-km canal that was built at the same time. In Figure B.5, the habitation area of Snaketown at that time is indicated in gray. The site measured around 4.61 ha and probably was a hamlet-level habitation in its incipient phase (see Wilcox et al. 1981). No public architecture had been constructed at the site yet. Two roasting pits were found that dated to this early occupation (Haury 1976:156–160). Based on current ceramic-analysis data, no other sites in the study area are known to include Vahki Plain or Vahki Red (however, these pottery types were not systematically identified in the GRIC-CRMP Stage 1 ceramic analysis). Hence, the other sites and loci highlighted in Figure B.5 date to the late Pioneer period. Three loci around Snaketown included Sweetwater Red-on-gray sherds: GR-1157, Loci DDD (n = 2), CCCC (n = 1), and LLLL (n = 1). Although Sweetwater Red-on-gray is a late Pioneer period (Sweetwater phase) decorated pottery type, its restricted area of occurrence suggests that human occupation and activity remained centered around Snaketown during these early stages of development.

By the late Pioneer period (Snaketown phase), Snaketown had more than tripled in size (16 ha) and had certainly reached village size (see Figure B.5). Snaketown residents built the first public architectural mound (Mound 40) at this time, the earliest known platform mound in the Hohokam region. Survey to the west of Snaketown recovered Snaketown Red-on-buff sherds in sufficient quantities (i.e., more than incidental occurrences) to suggest that two probable camps (GR-1157I East and GR-1157C) were established during this time. These new settlements were situated 4.5 and 6.5 km away from Snaketown, respectively (along an inferred extension of the Snaketown canal, as described in Chapter 4). Roughly 6.5 km to the east of Snaketown, a new settlement known as the Gila Butte site was founded, on the eastern side of Gila Butte. This site, which probably was a hamlet at the time, was located at the tail end of a new canal (known as the Gila Butte canal) that headed on the river about 8 km (5 miles) upstream from the butte. I assume that, for the most part, the residents of the Gila Butte site were largely focused on their own canal system for subsistence purposes rather than on the Snaketown canal system. Lastly, two camps were in use to the north of Gila Butte. A third camp might have been established at GR-1184, which was coded as a possible camp, at the southwestern foot of Gila Butte. Although excavation at this site clearly indicated that it was a camp in the subsequent early Colonial period (Johnson [1964], at AZ U:13:9 [ASM]), the site might have been occupied as a camp by the late Pioneer period.

Based on the criteria for defining community-territory boundaries described in Chapter 2, Figure B.5 depicts the inferred Snaketown community during the early and late Pioneer periods. Both boundaries encompass the entire canal system, as the political community was essentially isomorphic with the canal system. Chapter 5 discusses these incipient communities further.

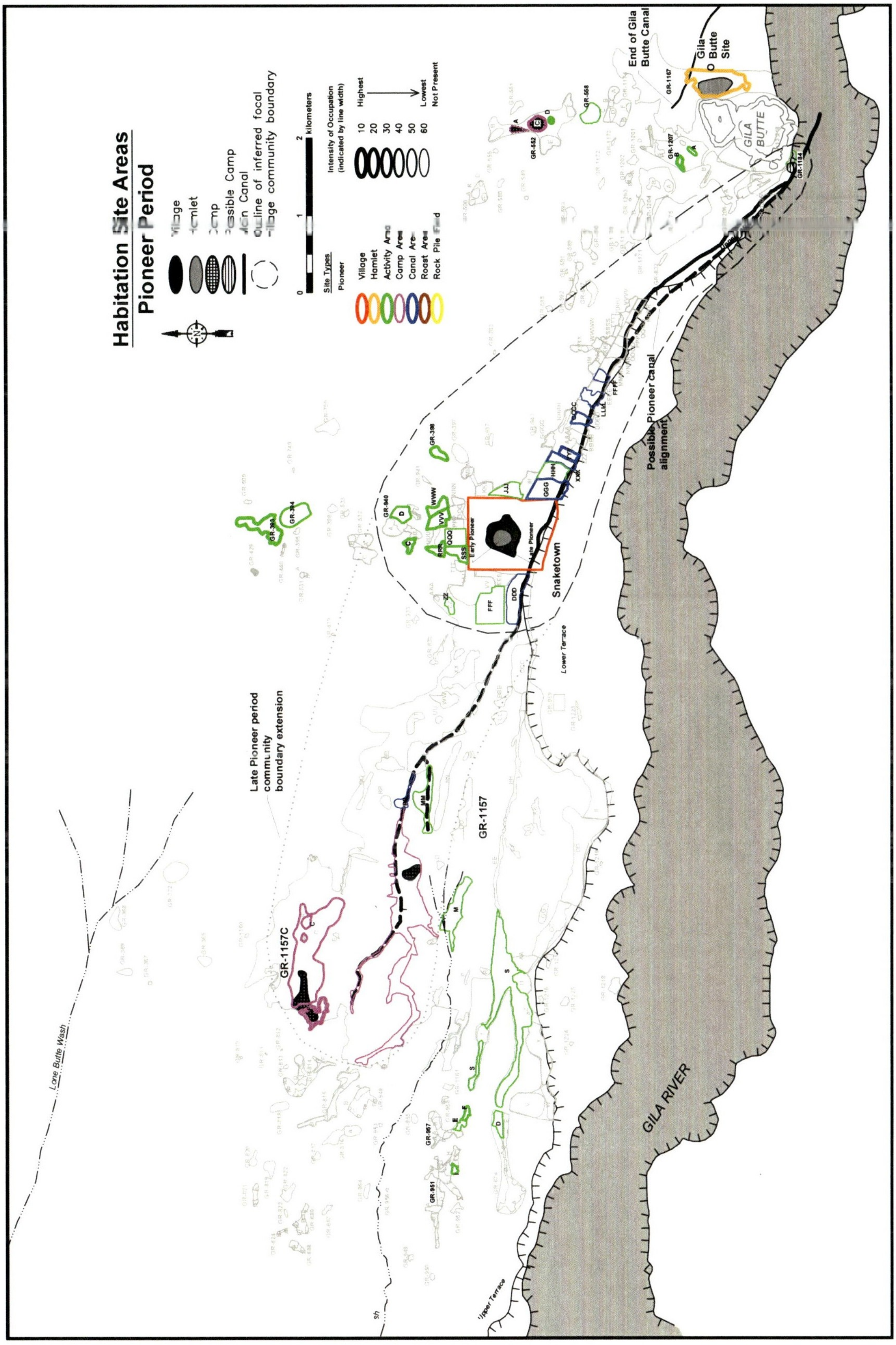

Figure B.5. Map of canals, settlements, and site types in Study Area 1 during the Pioneer period.

Table B.4. Primary Site Types per Time Period for the Snaketown Community

Site Type	Period			
	Late Pioneer	Early Colonial	Late Colonial	Sedentary
Village	1	3[a]	3[a]	4[a]
Hamlet	—	1	1	—
Camp	5[b]	3	2	4
Possible camp	1	2[c]	2[c]	7[d]
Canal area	8	17	16	15
Activity area	14	47	32	43
Roasting area	—	1	1	1
Total	29	74	57	74

[a] Three loci compose Snaketown village (for an actual total of one village).
[b] Four of these loci (GR-1157, Loci A, B, C, and F) are part of one camp.
[c] These two loci (GR-1157, Loci SSSS and TTTT) are part of one camp.
[d] Four loci (GR-1157, Loci QQQQ–TTTT) are part of two camps; one locus (GR-1157LLL) may not have been founded until the middle to late Sedentary period.

Table B.4 lists the numbers of occurrences of each primary site type for the community territory during the late Pioneer period, as well as for the rest of the pre-Classic period. As stated in the table footnotes, in some cases, the counts of sites/loci designated as villages, camps, or possible camps overrepresent the actual numbers of these habitation sites. The remaining sites/loci within the late Pioneer period community include 5 camps, 8 canal areas, and 14 activity areas. These areas are distributed around the village perimeter, with some found along the main canal to the west and east of the village. The canal areas represent the loci where irrigation and agriculture-related activities took place along the Pioneer Canal. Although no distinct roasting areas were defined as sites/loci from this phase, three roasting pits dating to the late Pioneer period were found within Snaketown (Haury 1976:156–160).

The activity areas extending northward from Snaketown probably were situated along a series of trails posited to have existed during the late Pioneer to Sedentary periods (Wilcox et al. 1981). This hypothesis is based mainly on linear features visible in aerial photographs, with some support from the field observations of Wilcox et al. (1981). Recent survey evidence does support the contention that a series of trails were used between Snaketown and points to the north (Wells and Greenspan 2002). These trails would have passed through GR-1157, Loci NNN, OOO, PPP, QQQ, and SSS; GR-940; and possibly north, through GR-393 and GR-394. Wells and Greenspan (2002) noted the presence of linear features that could have been trails at these sites and loci. The secondary site type for these GR-1157 loci and GR-940 was coded as "trail" (see Table B.1), but these sites are not coded as such in the figures, because their primary function appears to have been as activity areas. These trails appear to represent a transportation corridor that extended between Snaketown and the villages in the lower Salt Valley, the closest of which would have been Los Muertos and Los Guanacos.

Early Colonial Period

The number of sites in the study area increased by over 400 percent during the early Colonial period (Gila Butte phase), and the canal system was re-engineered and built out to its maximum extent (Figure B.6). Three primary villages were in the study area at this time. Snaketown grew further in size, and the large, east–west-oriented ballcourt (Ballcourt 1) was built. The camp at GR-1157C expanded to a village-level settlement and added two possible ballcourts. The GR-1157C village actually is represented by a closely spaced pair of settlements that together represent a village. This type of "dual village" was noted by Gregory (1994:185–186) for other pre-Classic period villages upstream from Snaketown (Olberg, Granite Knob, Chee Nee, and Grewe-Casa Grande). Gregory (1994:185–186) suggested that this pattern may reflect a dual division within pre-Classic period Hohokam society and may express aspects of Hohokam sociology, cosmology, and worldview. Also, a new village with a probable ballcourt was founded at the Maricopa Road site (GR-1157V), 7.3 km west of Snaketown (along the newly built south branch of the Snaketown canal). Factoring in the intervals between Snaketown and the other two primary villages in the study area (6 km to GR-1157C, 7.3 km to Maricopa Road, and 3.4 km between GR-1157C and Maricopa Road), the average spacing is 5.6 km. This interval remained constant during the early Colonial, late Colonial, and Sedentary periods (at least through the Middle Sedentary period). If the distance from Snaketown to the Gila Butte site (6.5 km) is considered in this (although it was on a separate canal system), then the average spacing is 5.8 km (which is nearly the same as 5.6 km).

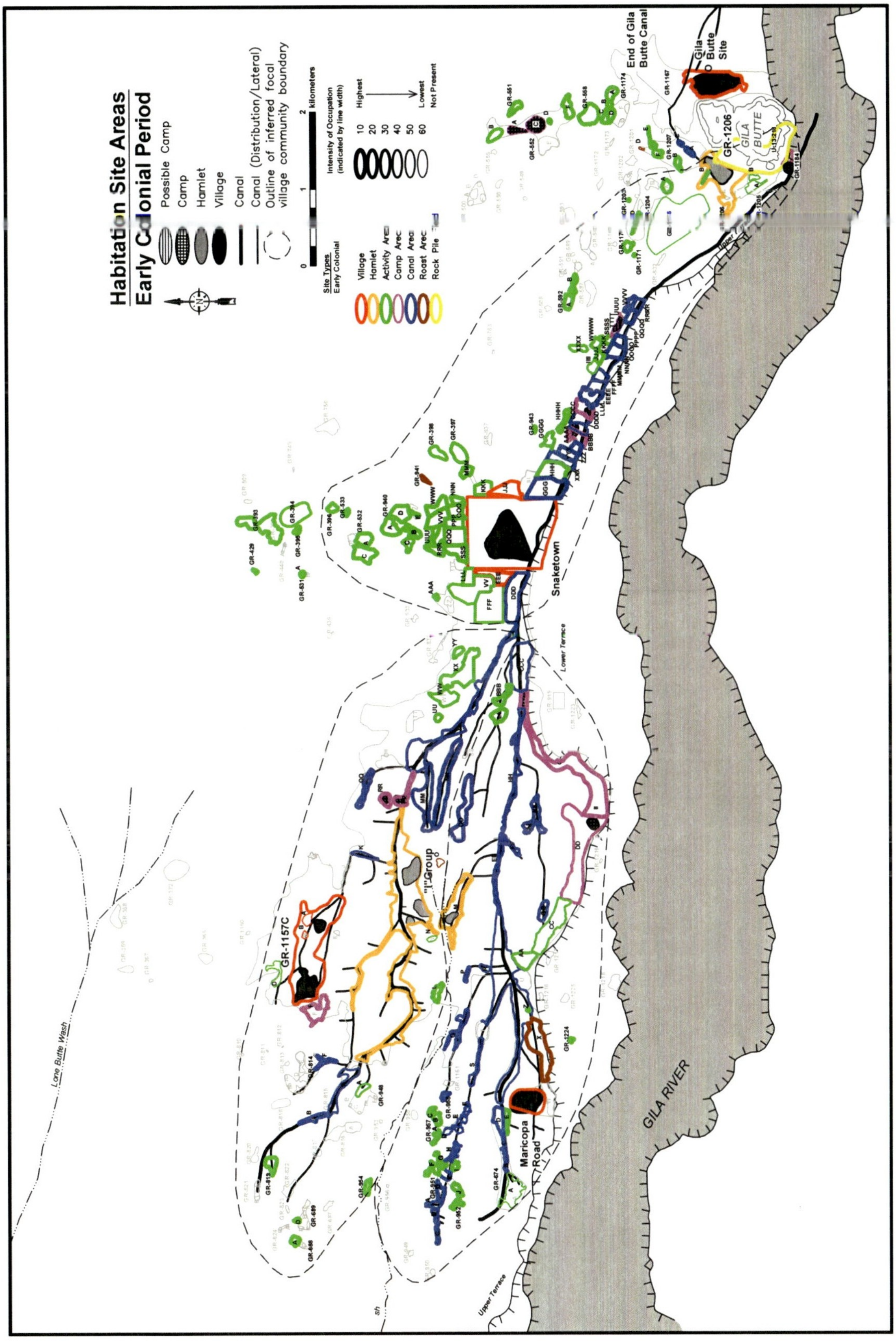

Figure B.6. Map of canals, settlements, and site types in Study Area 1 during the early Colonial period.

Other new habitations developed in the early Colonial period. The camp at GR-1157I expanded into a hamlet, and three additional hamlets were founded nearby, in Locus I and in adjacent Locus M. The I Group hamlets appear to have been more dispersed and less intensively occupied than a village, although collectively, they probably represent a dispersed village (see discussion of this issue above). Another hamlet was founded at GR-1206, on the western side of Gila Butte, 5.6 km upstream from Snaketown and near the canal-system heading. GR-1206 was situated near the end of the Gila Butte canal, which raises the question of whether the settlement was more closely associated with the Gila Butte canal system than with the Snaketown canal system. A camp had definitely been established at GR-1184 by this time, if there was not already one in the late Pioneer period. Finally, six new camps and one possible camp were established during the early Colonial period. Four of these camps were interspersed between Snaketown and the two downstream villages, with two along the north-branch canal and two along the south-branch canal. The other three camps and the possible camp were established between Snaketown and Gila Butte. Two camps to the north of Gila Butte were still in use.

Between and among these habitation sites, as Figure B.6 shows, there was a marked increase in the intensity of use of the landscape in Study Area 1. The vast majority of activity and canal areas were situated in a linear manner along the upper terrace. There were no visible breaks in the distribution of sites and loci, suggesting use of the entire landscape within a distance of about 4.8 km from the river. All three villages and the hamlets are associated with discrete roasting areas, and the camp at GR-1157DD also includes two roasting pits. Additional roasting pits are situated within Snaketown (one pit documented by Haury [1976:156–160]) and the I Group hamlets (two or three roasting pits). As noted for the late Pioneer period, the activity areas emanating northward from Snaketown probably represent activities that were partly related to the trails extending toward the lower Salt Valley. A new line of activity areas is evident near two camps to the north of Gila Butte; their north–south alignment may indicate another transportation corridor extending from the Gila Butte site to the north.

The three inferred community boundaries depicted in Figure B.6 were drawn in accordance with the criteria discussed in Chapter 2, based on the occurrences of three focal villages, and with reference to the three principal main-canal segments. The boundaries were further defined by settlement falloff to the north, south, and west. The GR-1157C and Maricopa Road communities were divided along a natural wash drainage that probably represents a natural boundary during prehistory. Chapter 5 discusses these communities further.

Tables B.5 and B.6 list the numbers of occurrences of each primary site type for the inferred GR-1157C and Maricopa Road site community territories during the early Colonial to Sedentary periods, respectively. As stated in the table footnotes, in some cases, the counts of sites/loci designated as villages, hamlets, or camps either overrepresent or underrepresent the actual numbers of these habitation sites. When compared with the early Colonial period site types in the Snaketown community (see Table B.4), each of the three communities is associated with one to three camps and numerous activity and canal areas. GR-1157C and the Maricopa Road communities included four and three hamlets, respectively, clustered in the I Group. Each of the three communities also is associated with at least one discrete roasting area; Snaketown and the I Group hamlets include additional roasting pits in the habitation areas.

Late Colonial Period

The settlement pattern and canal-system layout during the late Colonial period (Santa Cruz phase) were similar to those of the early Colonial period (Figure B.7). The intensity of use of the landscape remained quite high within a distance of about 4.8 km from the river, with no significant breaks in the site distribution. The exception was that there was a 22 percent overall reduction in site count in the late Colonial period, as noted above in Table B.2. Some or most of that decline likely resulted from sampling error (due to the frequent difficulty in distinguishing Santa Cruz Red-on-buff from Sacaton Red-on-buff), but it might indicate a decrease in intensity of use in the study area. The same three villages (Snaketown, GR-1157C, and Maricopa Road) continued to be occupied, and the average spacing between them remained at 5.6 km. The villages at Snaketown and GR-1157C again grew in size, and probably in population. The village at the Gila Butte site also continued to be occupied, to the east of Study Area 1. Six hamlets were present, including the hamlet at GR-1206 and the five hamlets in the I Group. The I Group, which again probably represents a dispersed village, expanded from the previous period into adjacent Locus N. The camps that were founded during the early Colonial period persisted, except for one (GR-1157DDDD) that did not exhibit evidence of occupation (another case that may have resulted from the issue with identification of Santa Cruz Red-on-buff).

The areas between these habitation sites were still characterized by a nearly continuous array of activity and canal areas situated in a linear manner along the upper terrace. All three villages and the hamlets continued to be situated near discrete roasting areas, except for the Maricopa Road site (the roasting area at GR-1157X—no Santa Cruz Red-on-buff sherds were found on survey, suggesting that it may not have been used, unless buff-ware-type identifications were in error). The camp at GR-1157DD also included two roasting pits. Additional roasting pits were situated within Snaketown (one pit documented by Haury [1976:156–160]) and the I Group hamlets (two or three roasting pits).

Table B.5. Primary Site Types per Time Period for the GR-1157C Community

Site Type	Period		
	Early Colonial	Late Colonial	Sedentary
Village	3[a]	3[a]	3[a]
Hamlet	1[b]	2[b]	1[b]
Camp	3[c]	3[c]	2[c]
Possible camp	—	—	5[d]
Canal area	8	9	9
Activity area	12	8	15
Roasting area	1	1	1
Total	28	26	36

[a] These three loci are part of one village (GR-1157C).
[b] GR-1157I includes three separate hamlets (for an actual total of three hamlets in the early Colonial period, four in the late Colonial period, and three in the Sedentary period, after GR-1157N is added for the late Colonial period).
[c] One locus (GR-1157F) may be part of the GR-1157C village.
[d] Five loci (GR-1157, Loci Y, BB, TT, WW, and XX) may not have been founded until the middle to late Sedentary period.

Table B.6. Primary Site Types per Time Period for the Maricopa Road Site Community

Site Type	Period		
	Early Colonial	Late Colonial	Sedentary
Village	1	1	1
Hamlet	1	1	1
Camp	2	2	2
Possible camp	—	—	—
Canal area	25	19	25
Activity area	16	11	15
Roasting area	1	—	1
Total	46	34	45

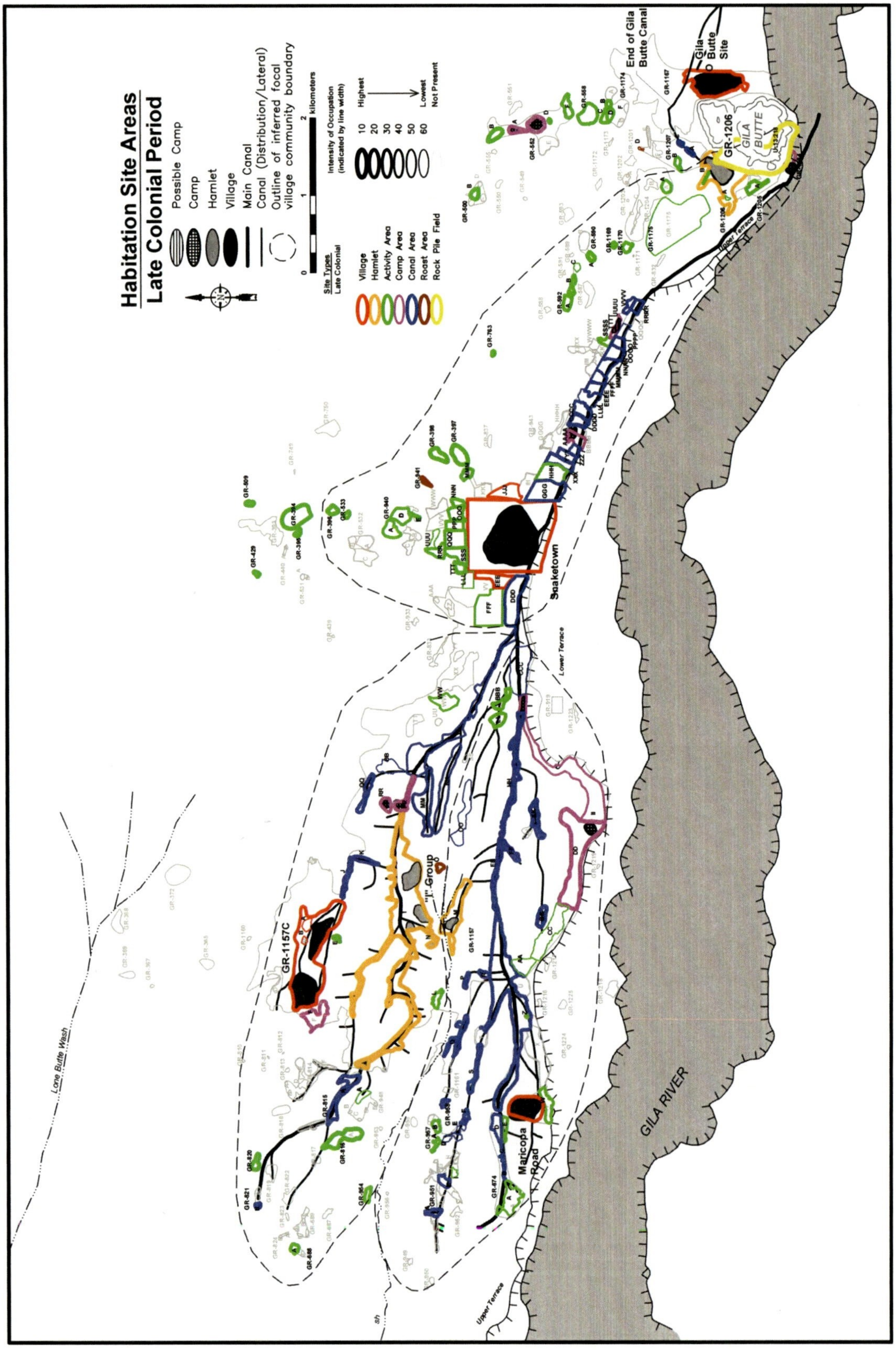

Figure B.7. Map of canals, settlements, and site types in Study Area 1 during the late Colonial period.

The activity areas emanating northward from Snaketown and Gila Butte probably represent continuing activities related to trails extending toward the lower Salt Valley.

The three inferred communities persisted and remained essentially unchanged from the early Colonial period, as defined above. A comparison of the late Colonial period site types in the three inferred communities indicates a similar pattern as for the early Colonial period (see Tables B.4–B.6). One difference, though, is the lower counts in the Snaketown and Maricopa Road communities (again, this possibly was a result of sampling error due to the frequent difficulty in distinguishing Santa Cruz Red-on-buff from Sacaton Red-on-buff). Otherwise, each of the three communities was associated with one to three camps and numerous activity and canal areas. The GR-1157C and the Maricopa Road communities included five and four hamlets, respectively, clustered in the I Group. The roasting-pit areas continued to be used, except the one associated with the Maricopa Road site.

Sedentary Period

During the Sedentary period (Sacaton phase), the intensity of use of the landscape reached a peak for the occupation sequence (Figure B.8). There was a 28 percent increase in overall site count to match the high for the entire sequence (n = 169, which is basically equivalent to the early Colonial period count of 170). Settlement was still focused in the zone within about 4.8 km from the river, with no significant breaks in the site distribution. The entire canal system continued to be used, and a canal in the Gila Butte canal system was extended to the Snaketown canal. The same three villages (Snaketown, GR-1157C, and Maricopa Road) continued to be occupied, and the average spacing between them remained at 5.6 km. The villages at Snaketown and GR-1157C grew to their maximum extents. At Snaketown, residents built two additional platform mounds (Mounds 16 and 39), and possibly a third (Mound 38), as well as a second north–south-oriented ballcourt (Ballcourt 2). The Gila Butte site village remained in use. The hamlet at GR-1206 probably grew to village size, based on its intensity of occupation. The hamlets represented by the I Group were still occupied, except Locus N. Most of the camps used previously were still in use, and eight new possible camps may have been established in the Sedentary period (but see comments below). Six of these new possible camps (GR-1157, Loci Y, BB, TT, WW, XX, and LLL) are situated between Snaketown and the I Group. These camps may have formed the nucleus of a series of hamlets occupied in the Classic period. The other two possible camps (GR-1157, Loci IIII and MMMM) are located midway between Snaketown and Gila Butte.

The areas between the three primary villages and the probable village at GR-1206 were still characterized by a nearly continuous array of activity and canal areas situated in a linear manner along the upper terrace. All four villages and the hamlets are situated near discrete roasting areas, including the Maricopa Road site (GR-1157X showed evidence of use again). The camp at GR-1157DD still includes two roasting pits, and two or three additional roasting pits are situated in the I Group hamlets. The activity areas emanating northward from Snaketown and Gila Butte probably represent continuing activities related to trails extending toward the lower Salt Valley. A new development was the use of activity areas north of GR-1157C, which could represent another trail corridor that would have led to resources in the Lone Butte Wash area and perhaps points farther north.

A comparison of the Sedentary period site types in the three inferred communities indicates a similar pattern to that of the late Colonial period (see Tables B.4–B.6). The main difference is the addition of several possible camps in the Snaketown and GR-1157C communities. As noted above, there is some uncertainty as to whether these possible camps were founded during the occupation span of Snaketown and GR-1157C. It seems more likely that the six possible camps between Snaketown and the I Group (GR-1157, Loci Y, BB, TT, WW, XX, and LLL) were not initiated until after Snaketown was abandoned, and these loci may have been hamlets from their beginnings, rather than camps. Each of the communities is associated with a roasting pit area, too.

Snaketown, along with the other primary villages in Study Area 1 (the Maricopa Road site and GR-1157C), was abandoned by the end of the Sedentary period. The Gila Butte site and other primary villages along the middle Gila River (e.g., the Grewe site, Hidden Ruin, and Villa Buena) also were abandoned or largely depopulated at this time (in some cases, the settlements "drifted" to adjacent locales). These events occurred in conjunction with major social and political changes across the Hohokam region during the Sedentary to Classic period transition (see Doyel 1991). Scholars now contend that Snaketown was abandoned at the end of the Middle Sedentary period, around A.D. 1070, based on the refined typology of Sacaton Red-on-buff ceramics (Abbott et al. 2007; Wallace 2001, 2004). As noted in Chapter 2, that typology allows for the division of the Sacaton phase (Sedentary period) into Early, Middle, and Late subphases based on subtypes of Sacaton Red-on-buff. The Maricopa Road site and GR-1157C probably were depopulated at the same time as Snaketown, but this cannot be confirmed, because the ceramics collected by the GRIC-CRMP during survey were not analyzed using the refined buff ware typology. Further analysis is required, using the revised typology.

The lack of a refined buff ware analysis also presents an issue in properly assessing the timing of the founding of new settlements. For instance, a series of six new possible camps is inferred to have been initiated in the Sedentary period at GR-1157, Loci Y, BB, TT, WW, XX, and LLL, between Snaketown and the I Group (see Figure B.8), based on the occurrence of Sacaton Red-on-buff sherds in sufficient

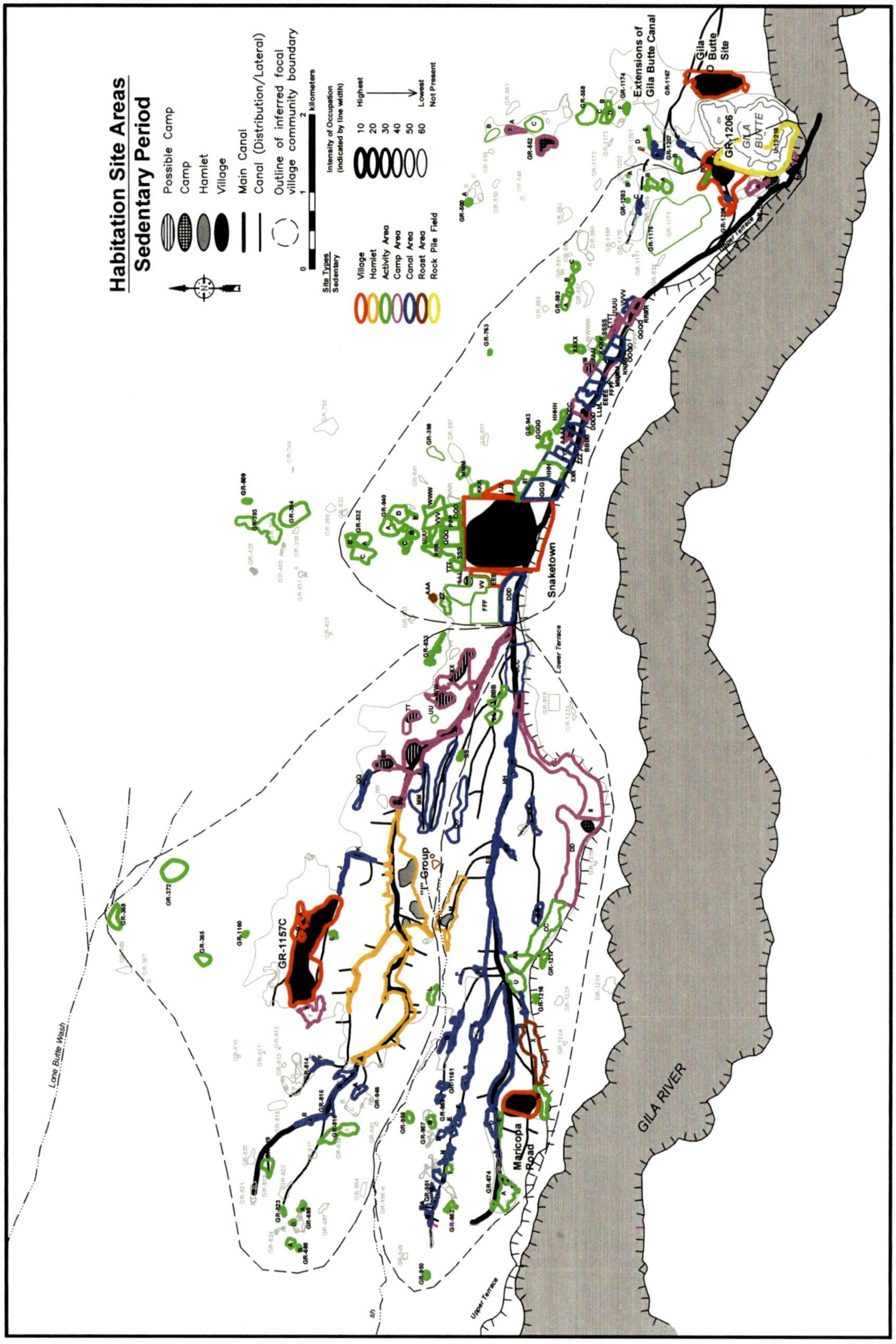

Figure B.8. Map of canals, settlements, and site types in Study Area 1 during the Sedentary period.

quantities to suggest significant use of or occupation at these loci. However, from a settlement-pattern perspective, the founding of six new camps in close proximity to Snaketown—which was at its largest size at the time—does not necessarily make sense. These areas are close enough to Snaketown that residents could easily have walked to and from them in a day. It seems more reasonable to infer, then, that these settlements were initiated either during or after the abandonment of Snaketown, in the Middle Sedentary period, and that the Sacaton Red-on-buff sherds at these loci may have been Middle or Late Sacaton Red-on-buff subtypes. The same situation may pertain to the possible camps at GR-1157, Loci IIII and MMMM, located upstream from Snaketown, which became part of a probable dispersed hamlet in the Early Classic period. Future ceramic analysis with the revised typology will be needed to confirm the validity of these inferences.

Early Classic Period

By the Early Classic period (Soho phase, A.D. 1150–1300), the settlement pattern had taken on a very different appearance (Figure B.9). The 50 percent drop in site/locus counts in Study Area 1 almost certainly indicates a major drop in intensity of use and probably in population, even accounting for some possible undercounting of sites dating to this period (see Table B.2). Despite this decrease, it appears that the entire canal system was still being used, and another canal was extended from the Gila Butte canal to the Snaketown canal. The nucleated pre-Classic period villages at Snaketown, GR-1157C, and the Maricopa Road site had been abandoned, and series of smaller, dispersed settlements were built in their place. One new village with public architecture was built at the Maricopa Platform Mound site, at the far-western side of the study area. One other village was located 13.2 km upstream, at GR-1175, near Gila Butte. Between them were five main foci of habitation, including four hamlet clusters and one cluster of camps. The VV Group may represent a village, whereas the I, U, and Y Groups appear to represent three dispersed villages. The Y and VV Groups feasibly could have been grouped together into one dispersed village. The cluster of four camps between the VV Group and GR-1175 appears to be a dispersed hamlet (FFFF Group). Nine other camps outside these groups were used, including GR-590B, GR-948A, GR-957E, GR-1205A, GR-1206A, and GR-1157, Loci DD, II, CCC, AAAA, and DDDD. Two other possible camps were located at GR-1157TTTT/UUUU and GR-1157QQQQ/RRRR. It is feasible that these two possible camps and the camps at GR-1157, Loci AAAA and DDDD, were part of the dispersed hamlet centered at the FFFF Group. Compared with the Sedentary period, the number of permanently occupied Early Classic period habitation units is dramatically higher—2 villages and 18 hamlets, vs. 4 Sedentary villages and 4 hamlets.

The spacing of primary settlements during the Classic period is difficult to assess. Study Area 1 includes only one "central site" with public architecture (the Maricopa Platform Mound site), which is situated roughly 15.7 km west of Gila Butte. The next-nearest platform-mound site (on the northern side of the Gila River) is at Lower Santan village, located roughly 22 km to the east, on another canal system. The closest "true" village without public architecture is 13.2 km upstream, at GR-1175, or 8 km upstream, at the VV Group (if it represents a village). These are far greater distances than the typical 5-km spacing cited by researchers for Classic period platform mounds (e.g., Fish and Fish 1991:163; Gregory and Nials 1985). If the other permanently occupied habitation units are considered in the analysis (GR-1175 and the I, U, Y, and VV Groups), as well as the possible dispersed hamlet (FFFF Group), then the average interval between habitation sites is 2.8 km, much shorter than the Sedentary period village spacing (5.6 km).

Hence, there is no basis upon which to define a focal-village interval. If the oft-cited average 5-km spacing is applied as a territory length for Maricopa Mound, it would only have encompassed two small camps and the U Group dispersed village along the south-branch canal. If Maricopa Mound was the "center" for a focal-village community that encompassed the entire canal system, it would have covered an area 17 km in length (the length, head to tail, of the Snaketown system) and 4 km in width. To expect such a large territory for one focal-village community would seem to be outside the purview of the focal-village model. In this respect, the Classic period settlement pattern does not appear to conform to the focal-village-community model.

Another consideration is the possibility that the former Gila Butte community may have been integrated into the Snaketown community or the Lower Santan community in the Early Classic period. As discussed in Appendix C and Chapter 6, only two hamlets and two camps are situated along the Gila Butte canal system, and they are located near the GR-1175 village. However, the canal did not have any focal villages. The Gila Butte canal was connected with the Snaketown canal at two points, and it likely was supplying the Snaketown system with a significant amount of water.

Nevertheless, the settlement pattern remained segmented, with three distinct clusters of habitation sites associated with the three main-canal branches. This continued the settlement trend from the Sedentary period, with some key differences: the settlement distribution was more dispersed, only the south-branch cluster includes a focal village, and the Gila Butte canal sites probably were integrated into the upper part of the Snaketown canal. The inferred community boundaries are depicted in Figure B.9. A comparison of the Early Classic period site types in the three inferred communities indicated that the proportion of site types had changed since the Sedentary period (Table B.7). There was still a village in two communities, but only one was a focal village (Maricopa Mound, along the south branch), and the

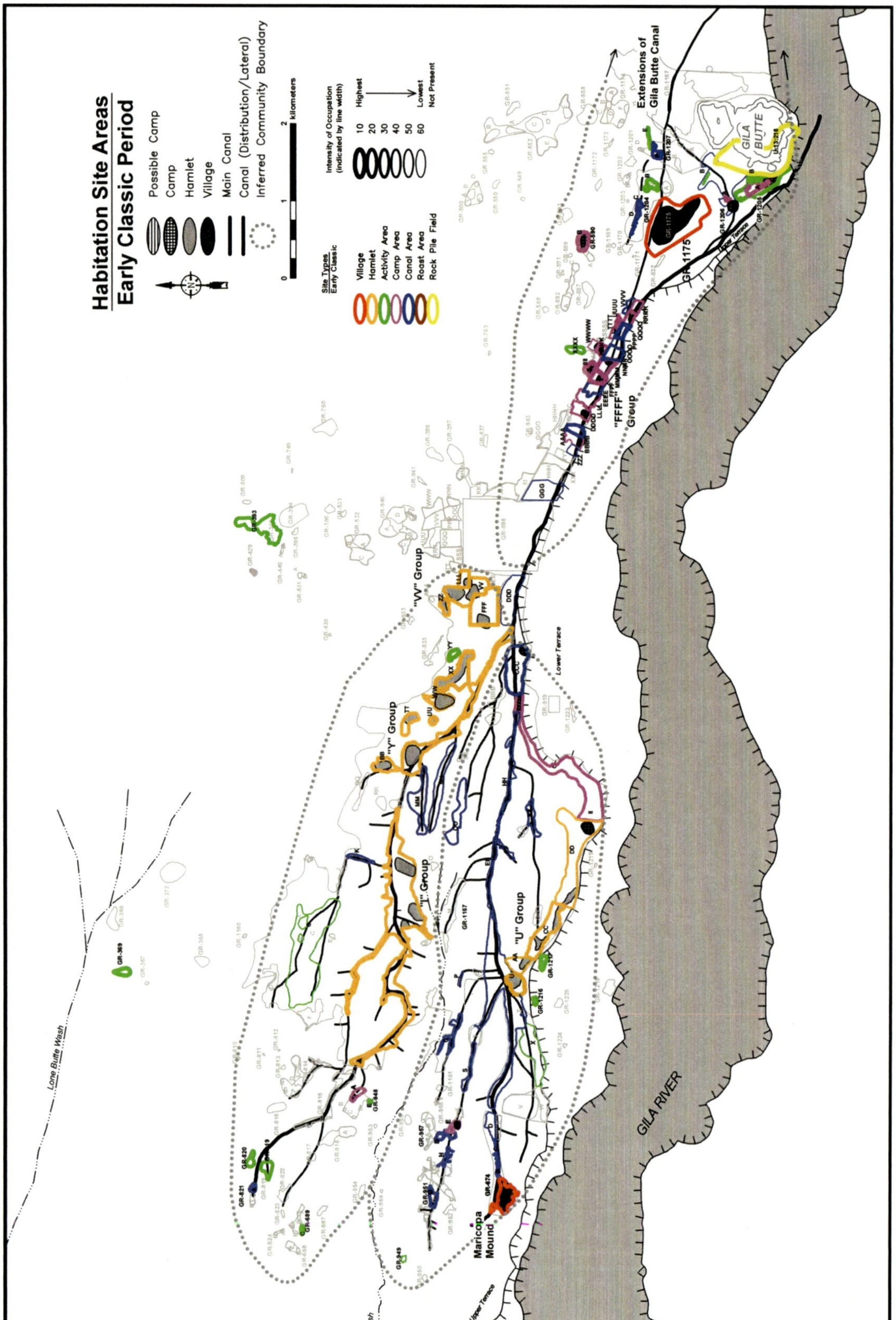

Figure B.9. Map of canals, settlements, and site types in Study Area 1 during the Early Classic period.

Table B.7. Primary Site Types for Inferred Early Classic Period Communities

Site Type	Community		
	GR-1175	North Branch	South Branch
Village	1	—	1
Hamlet	2	11[a]	4[b]
Camp	12[c]	1	3
Possible camp	4[d]	—	—
Canal area	24	4	14
Activity area	18	8	4
Rock pile field	1		
Roasting area	—	—	—
Total	62	24	26

[a] Two loci (GR-1157, Loci I and VV) include 5 discrete hamlets; the 14 total hamlets appear to be grouped into two or three dispersed villages.
[b] These four hamlets may represent a dispersed village; one locus (GR-1157DD) also includes a camp.
[c] Two loci (GR-1157, Loci KKKK and WWWW) are part of one camp that, along with three other camps (GR-1157, Loci FFFF, IIII, and MMMM), probably is part of a dispersed hamlet.
[d] These four loci (GR-1157, Loci QQQQ–TTTT) are part of two possible camps.

north-branch community did not include a clear village. The number of hamlets and camps increased, a reflection of the more-dispersed settlement pattern. However, the hamlets appeared to have been grouped into three or four dispersed villages. There were considerably more camps within the GR-1175 community. Also, the number of activity areas dropped along the north and south branches. Chapter 5 discusses this issue further.

The number of activity areas also dropped dramatically during the Early Classic period. This was probably related to the population's redistributing itself into a greater number of small habitation sites, which were more evenly dispersed and separated by shorter intervals than in the Sedentary period. No discrete roasting areas were indicated by the survey data, but roasting pits occur within several of the habitations (GR-1175 and the I, U, and Y Groups). In other words, activities appear to have been more restricted to the loci of habitation and perhaps the canal areas. This contrasts with the Sedentary period pattern, in which activity areas were arrayed around and between the central village sites. Only one activity area was in use to the north of either Snaketown or Gila Butte—this might indicate a decline in the use of trails extending toward the lower Salt Valley. Lastly, only one activity area was in use to the north of the former location of GR-1157C. This could also signal a decrease in use of this possible trail corridor, although this activity locus also could indicate continued use of the Lone Butte Wash area.

One important point that the recent surveys of the Snaketown area have made clear is that the area was not abandoned during the Early Classic period, as was hypothesized by Wilcox et al. (1981:210–212). Haury (1976:48, 355) observed that Classic period settlements were built to the east and west of the abandoned Snaketown, but he concluded that they dated to the Late Classic period. Along with references to a lack of evidence that the Snaketown canal was used in the Early Classic period (Haury 1976:15), he seems to insinuate that the Hohokam had also abandoned the Snaketown "hinterland." Wilcox et al. (1981:212) wisely recognized the need for more research on the chronology of these settlements, and the current study strongly demonstrates that the Hohokam continued to inhabit the area during the Early Classic period (also see Ravesloot 2007). It is tempting to assume that the residents of the three primary pre-Classic period villages moved to the nearest habitations founded in the Middle or Late Sedentary period to the Early Classic period. If that was the case, then the residents at Snaketown probably established the series of hamlets (the VV and Y Groups) to the west of Snaketown; the GR-1157C residents may have moved into the existing I Group hamlets, or they could have been cofounders of the U or Y Group hamlets; and the Maricopa Road site inhabitants would have moved to the Maricopa Platform Mound site or the U Group hamlets. The village on the western side of Gila Butte (GR-1175) may have been founded by the people who abandoned the Gila Butte site. However, given the steep drop in the number of sites, it seems certain that a segment of the population moved out of the study area.

Late Classic Period

The settlement pattern in the Late Classic period (Civano phase) was similar to that of the Early Classic period (Figure B.10). A probable increase in the intensity of use of the study area is suggested by the 25 percent increase in the number of sites/loci (see Table B.2). As noted above, the amount of increase may be partly artificial, because of

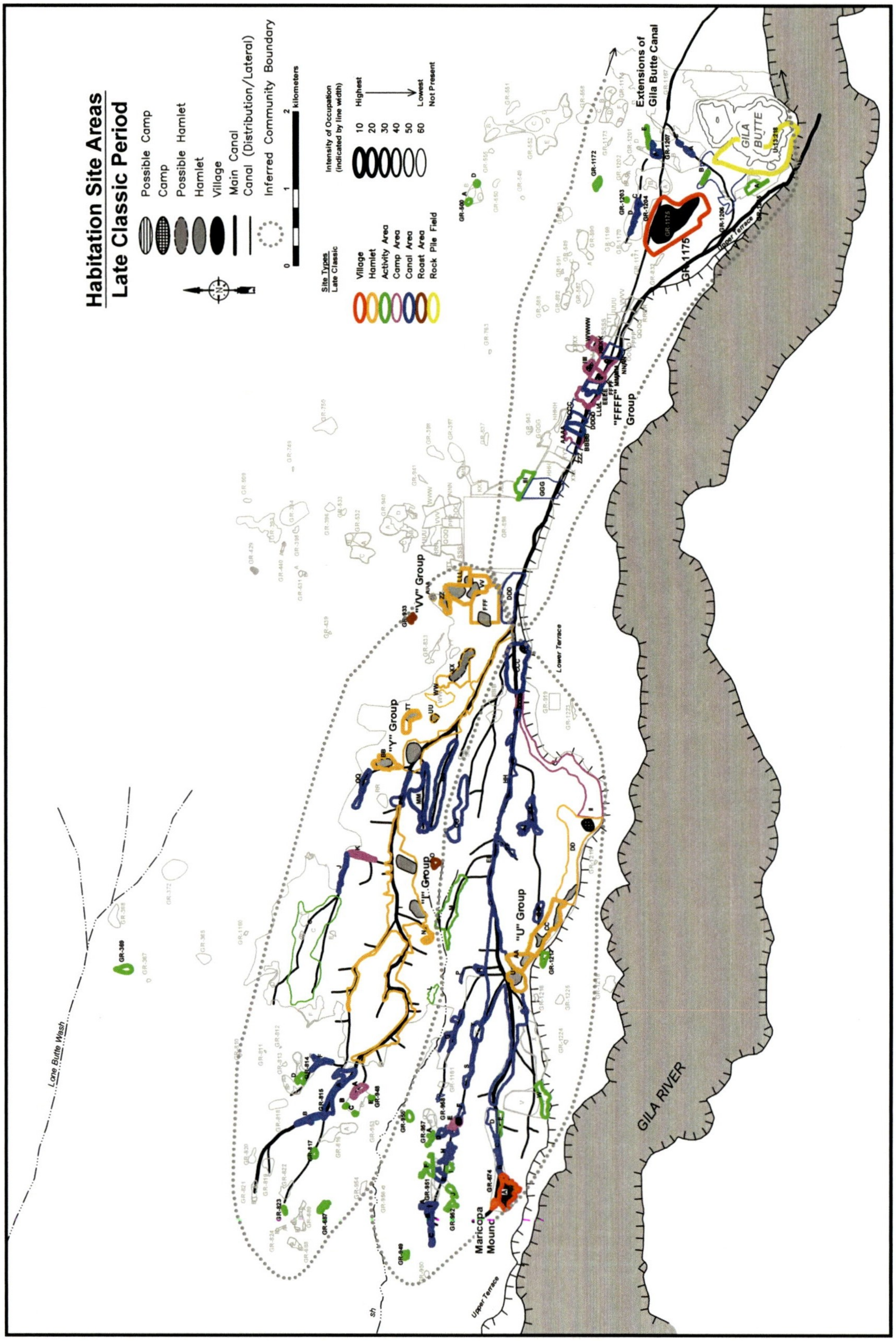

Figure B.10. Map of canals, settlements, and site types in Study Area 1 during the Late Classic period.

the possibly depressed counts of Early Classic period sites/loci. Still in use were the villages at the Maricopa Platform Mound site and GR-1175; the four hamlet clusters, which may be considered "dispersed villages" (VV, Y, I, and U Groups); and the camp cluster (FFFF Group). However, some of the previous settlements were abandoned at this time. Three hamlets between Locus Y and the VV Group hamlets appear to have been abandoned (GR-1157WW), or the intensity of their occupations was dramatically reduced (GR-1157, Loci UU and XX), during the Late Classic period. Four of the camps in the eastern end of the study area were abandoned (GR-590B, GR-1205A, GR-1206A, and GR-1157DDDD), as well as the two possible camps (GR-1157TTTT/UUUU and GR-1157QQQQ/RRRR). This contributed to a slightly more-clustered appearance of the hamlet groups and the camp group. One new camp was occupied at GR-1157K.

Notably, the Classic period settlement pattern still does not appear to conform to the focal-village-community model, as was described above for the Early Classic period. Yet the settlement pattern remained segmented, with three distinct clusters of habitation sites associated with the three main-canal branches. The inferred community boundaries are depicted in Figure B.10. Chapter 5 discusses this topic further.

Between these habitation sites, the number of activity areas in the Late Classic period remained at a low level, in relation to the pre-Classic period pattern (see Table B.2). The number of canal areas increased to a level commensurate to that of the pre-Classic period. Again, assuming that these increases are not inflated by sampling error, they suggest that the canals continued to be used throughout the study area but that other activities still were relatively restricted to the areas around the habitation sites. Roasting pits continued to be located within or next to the habitation sites. The lack of activity in the northern part of the study area suggests a continuing lack or low level of traffic and use along the trail corridors extending toward the lower Salt Valley and the Lone Butte Wash area. The sites in Study Area 1 exhibited no evidence of prehistoric use after the Late Classic period, indicating that the Hohokam had abandoned the area at the end of the period.

Appendix C

Settlements in Study Area 2

This appendix provides additional data on the settlements in Study Area 2 described in Chapter 6. Study Area 2 includes the settlements along the Granite Knob, Santan, and Gila Butte canal systems (Figure C.1). The appendix provides a summary of the settlement-analysis results (including information on site-type designations and habitation sites) and a description of the settlement trends through time. The methods used in documenting the settlements were those described in Appendix B.

Summary of Settlement-Analysis Results for Study Area 2

Study Area 2 includes 359 archaeological sites and loci within sites that are situated along or near the Santan and Gila Butte canal systems and the Granite Knob canal (see Figure C.1). Table C.1 (located at the end of this appendix) provides the data for all sites and loci in the study area. Within 35 of these sites, data were collected separately for the loci, and the overall site number for each of those 35 sites was not used in the analysis, resulting in a total of 324 sites and loci.

Site Function

As described in Chapter 2, I re-evaluated the original site-function designations by Wells et al. (2003, 2004) for all sites and loci in the study area, using additional criteria. More specific identifications now have been made for canals and habitation sites in the study area. Also, the function of some sites/loci appear to have changed over time or exhibited evidence of multiple functions. These situations are accounted for in the "Revised Site Type" columns in Table C.1. The site-type codes utilized in Study Area 2 include *village, hamlet, camp, activity area, canal area, roasting area, trail, rock-pile field,* and *rock art.* The methods used in defining and measuring the site variables are described in Chapter 2. The exception for Study Area 2 was that the relative dominance of a time period (or "intensity of occupation") was not determined for each site/locus, as was done for Study Area 1 (see Chapter 5; Appendix B).

Table C.2 lists the number of occurrences of the primary site types in Study Area 2 for each time period. The footnotes provided for some habitation-site-type counts identify cases in which the "actual" number of a habitation type was less than what is listed, because the boundaries of some habitation sites included parts of two loci. The general trends are worth noting. Similar to the pattern in Study Area 1 (see Table B.2), Study Area 2 witnessed a nearly fourfold increase in the total site type counts from the Pioneer to early Colonial periods (from 41 to 157). That spike in the early Colonial period indicates a surge in intensity of use and almost certainly an increase in population. The late Colonial period count in Study Area 2 was roughly the same as the early Colonial period count. That is in contrast to Study Area 1, which decreased by 22 percent at that time. In Appendix B, it is noted that the decline in Study Area 1 counts might have been due to the lower rate of identification of diagnostic ceramics that date exclusively to that period (Santa Cruz Red-on-buff). In Study Area 2, the count actually increased by 2; so, the suppressed-count issue does not seem to have been a problem. However, as noted by Gregory and Huckleberry (1994) in their analysis of Olberg, Granite Knob, and Chee Nee villages (the former two are in Study Area 2), it is possible that there should have been higher counts for the late Colonial period.

Study Area 2 saw a modest 11 percent increase in site-type counts, to a peak high of 187, in the Sedentary period. Study Area 1 also had a peak high count (n = 169) in the Sedentary period. The Early Classic period count for Study Area 2 reduced by only 8.5 percent, followed by a 7.6 percent decrease in the Late Classic period. That is dramatically different from the 50 percent decrease in the Study Area 1 count for the Early Classic period. As discussed in Appendix B, the decline in Study Area 1 almost certainly indicates a major drop in intensity of use and, probably, in population. In contrast, Study Area 2 did not appear to have seen a steep decrease in intensity of use or in population.

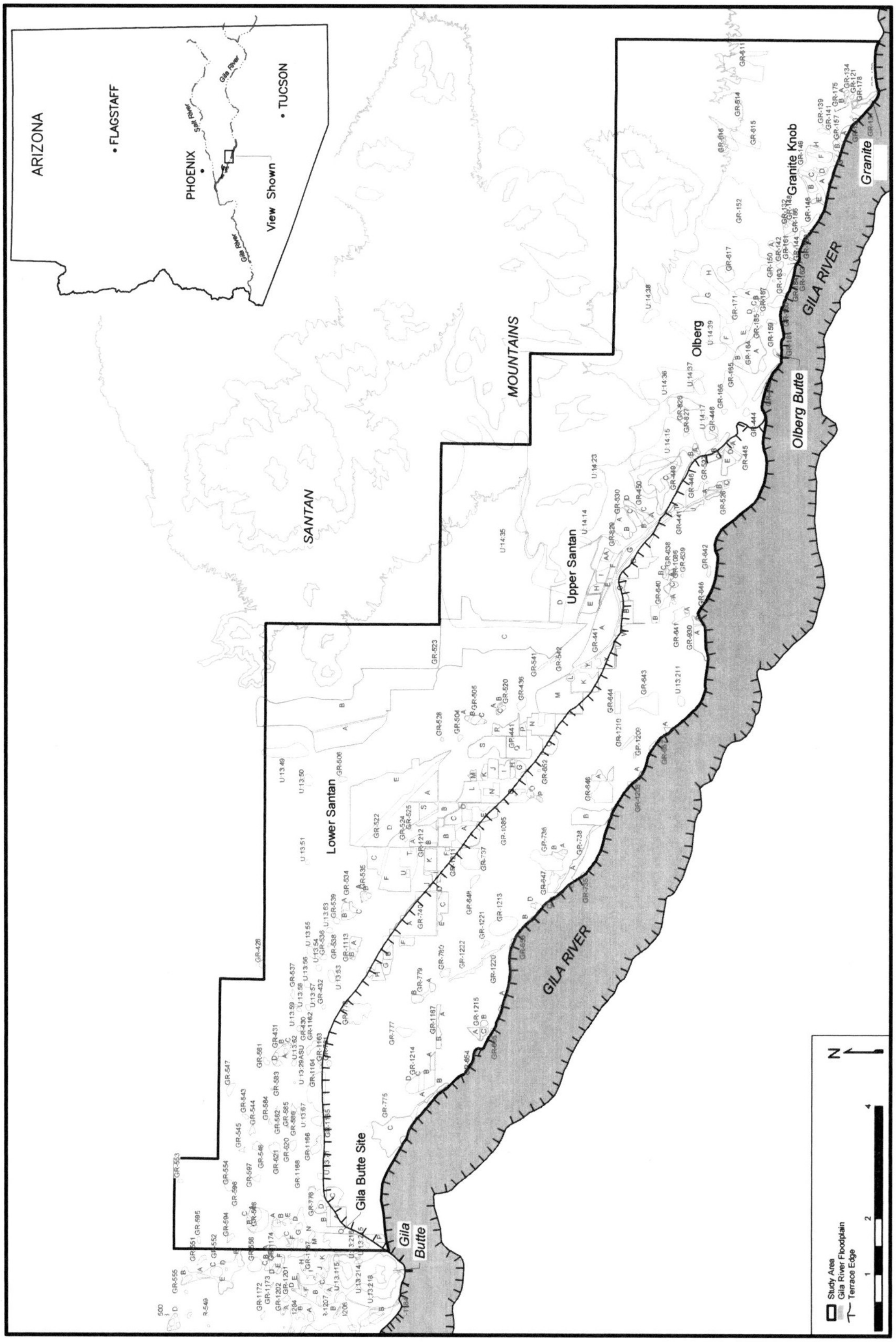

Figure C.1. Map of sites in Study Area 2 that encompassed the Santan, Gila Butte, and Granite Knob canal systems.

Table C.1. Sites along the Santan and Gila Butte Canal Systems

GR- Site/Locus	Area (m²)	Site Type (Wells et al. 2003, 2004)	*Revised Site Type (1)*	*Revised Site Type (2)*	Remarks	Period							No. of TMs	No. of SMs	No. of PMs	No. of BCs
						Pioneer	Early Colonial	Late Colonial	Sedentary	Early Classic	Late Classic	Undefined				
<u>Sites along the Granite Knob Canal</u>																
121			activity area		U:14:246				X	X						
131			activity area	rock art	U:14:256; southwest of Granite Knob		X	X			X					
132	3,205		camp		U:14:257; associated with GR-185				X							
133			activity area	possible camp	U:14:258; possible field house						X					
134					U:14:259											
134A			activity area									X				
134B					historical-period locus											
139			activity area		U:14:212						X					
141			rock-pile feature	possible camp	U:14:213; possible structures				X	X	X					
142	11,865		camp		U:14:261				X	X						
144	35,960		hamlet	roasting area	U:14:263; trails, also				X	X						
146			canal	activity area	Granite Knob canal; U:14:265		X	X	X	X						
148			rock-pile feature	trail	U:14:266							X				
149					U:14:214											
149A			village	hamlet	Granite Knob village; Pioneer period = camp?; Colonial to Sedentary period = village; Soho phase = hamlet	X	X	X	X	X						1
149B	39,710		hamlet		Classic period					X	X					
149C			rock-pile feature						X							
149D	22,426		hamlet		Classic period					X	X					
149E			rock-pile feature									X				
149F	48,701		hamlet	rock-pile feature	Classic period					X	X					

continued on next page

GR- Site/Locus	Area (m^2)	Site Type (Wells et al. 2003, 2004)	*Revised Site Type (1)*	*Revised Site Type (2)*	Remarks	Period							No. of TMs	No. of SMs	No. of PMs	No. of BCs
						Pioneer	Early Colonial	Late Colonial	Sedentary	Early Classic	Late Classic	Undefined				
149G			activity area						X	X						
149H	3,511		possible camp	rock-pile feature	Classic period					X						
150					historical period; U:14:267											
152			rock-pile feature	roasting area	P-MIP 4			X	X	X	X					
152A			rock-pile feature		P-MIP 4; U:14:268			X	X	X	X					
157					Granite Knob village, U:14:215											
157A			village	hamlet	Granite Knob village; Early Classic period, only a few structures (hamlet).			X	X	X						1
157B			village	hamlet	Granite Knob village; Classic period = hamlet.				X	X	X					
161			activity area		U:14:269				X	X						
162					historical-period site; U:14:270											
163			activity area		U:14:271				X	X						
175			rock art		U:14:272; northern end of Granite Knob							X				
178			rock art		U:14:275							X				
179			rock art		U:14:276							X				
180	20,451		possible camp	activity area	U:14:277; possible camp				X							
184			activity area		U:14:278				X							
186	9,368		hamlet		U:14:264				X	X						
611			rock-pile feature		P-MIP 4							X				
614			roasting area		P-MIP 4				X	X	X					
615			rock-pile feature	rock art	P-MIP 4		X	X	X	X	X					
616			rock-pile feature	roasting area	P-MIP 4							X				
617			rock art		P-MIP 4							X				
Sites along the Santan Canal System																
159	10,541		hamlet		U:14:20				X	X	X					
160	42,316		hamlet		U:14:204; Classic period					X	X					

GR- Site/Locus	Area (m²)	Site Type (Wells et al. 2003, 2004)	*Revised Site Type (1)*	*Revised Site Type (2)*	Remarks	Period: Pioneer	Early Colonial	Late Colonial	Sedentary	Early Classic	Late Classic	Undefined	No. of TMs	No. of SMs	No. of PMs	No. of BCs
164	87,223				U:14:2											
164A	189,825		village	hamlet	Olberg village; Sedentary to Classic period				X	X	X		29	12		
164B	14,473		hamlet		Olberg village; mostly Classic period				X	X	X		5	5		
165	174,076		village	hamlet	Olberg village; U:14:18; Sweetwater to Snaketown phase = hamlet; Colonial to Sedentary period = village; Classic period = hamlet	X	X	X	X	X	X		48	27		
166	7,004		hamlet		U:14:205; Classic period					X	X		2	6		
171				roasting area	P-MIP 4				X	X						
171A			rock-pile feature		U:14:43; possible Classic period					X						
171B	1,865		hamlet		U:14:206, GR-169					X						
171C			rock-pile feature		U:14:207, GR-170					X						
171D	2,590		hamlet		U:14:209, GR-182					X						
171E			rock-pile feature	trail	U:14:210, GR-183					X						
171F			activity area	rock-pile feature	U:14:40		X		X	X						
171G			rock-pile feature	trail	U:14:41							X				
171H			rock-pile feature	trail	U:14:42							X				
181			rock art		Olberg Butte; U:14:208							X				
185	1,573		hamlet		U:14:211; Early Classic period					X						
187	3,173		hamlet		U:14:203; Early Classic period					X						
428	12,452				historical-period site											
430	7,348	activity area	activity area						X							
431	45,027															
431A	6,734	activity area	activity area							X	X					
431B	1,856	activity area	activity area									X				
431C	2,000	activity area	activity area									X				

continued on next page

GR- Site/Locus	Area (m^2)	Site Type (Wells et al. 2003, 2004)	*Revised Site Type (1)*	*Revised Site Type (2)*	Remarks	Period							No. of TMs	No. of SMs	No. of PMs	No. of BCs
						Pioneer	Early Colonial	Late Colonial	Sedentary	Early Classic	Late Classic	Undefined				
431D	17,035	activity area	roasting area							X	X					
432	4,469				historical-period site											
436	24,333		canal		north branch, Santan canal		X	X	X	X	X					
441	720,168				areas outside loci									1		
441A	460,374	village	village	hamlet	Upper Santan village, platform mound, U:13:8	X	X	X	X	X	X		15	1	1	1
441AA	38,529		village		Early Classic period compounds					X						
441B	40,711	village	village	canal	northern main-canal branch	X	X	X	X	X	X					
441C	63,131	village	canal	village	northern main-canal branch		X	X	X	X	X					
441D	159,133	camp	canal	village?	may be part of Upper Santan		X	X	X	X	X					
441E	24,294	village	village		Classic period compound; one Sedentary period pit house					X	X			2		
441F	39,014	village	village		Classic period compound					X	X			3		
441G	93,744	activity area	canal	camp	north branch, Santan canal and irrigated fields, field houses		X	X	X	X	X					
441H	37,602	village	village		Classic period compound and small platform mound; U:14:10					X	X			5		
441I	45,808	village	village		Early Classic period compound; U:14:10					X				3		
441J	23,829	activity area	activity area	canal			X	X	X		X					
441K	152,551	activity area	canal		north branch, Santan canal		X	X	X		X					
441L	14,601	activity area	canal		north branch, Santan canal		X	X	X		X					
441M	415,651	activity area	canal		north branch, Santan canal and distribution canals		X	X	X	X	X					
441N	154,296	activity area	activity area	canal	distribution canals?		X	X	X		X					
441O	82,040	activity area	activity area	canal?			X	X	X	X	X					
441P	27,452		activity area	canal?			X	X	X							
441Q	150,951	activity area	activity area	canal?			X	X	X	X	X					
441R	103,271	activity area	canal		north branch, Santan canal		X	X	X	X	X					
441S	192,078	activity area	canal		north branch, Santan canal		X	X	X	X	X					
441T	19,728	activity area	activity area	canal				X	X		X					

GR- Site/Locus	Area (m²)	Site Type (Wells et al. 2003, 2004)	*Revised Site Type (1)*	*Revised Site Type (2)*	Remarks	Period: Pioneer	Period: Early Colonial	Period: Late Colonial	Period: Sedentary	Period: Early Classic	Period: Late Classic	Period: Undefined	No. of TMs	No. of SMs	No. of PMs	No. of BCs
441W	13,272	activity area	village	canal			X	X	X	X	X					
441X	63,932	village	canal		north branch, Santan canal		X	X	X	X	X					
441Y			canal		north branch, Santan canal				X	X	X					
442	57,843	village	canal	possible camp	headward end of the Santan canal	X	X	X	X	X	X					
444	15,004	activity area	activity area	canal?	part of the Santan canal?	X	X	X	X	X	X					
445	62,883															
445A	6,017	activity area	canal		Santan canal, near the branch point		X	X								
445B	49,879	activity area	activity area				X	X	X		X					
445C	41,338	activity area	canal	possible camp	camp = Classic period; north branch, Santan canal	X	X	X	X	X	X					
445D	33,580	activity area	canal	possible camp	camp = Classic period; north branch, Santan canal			X	X	X	X					
445E	47,230	activity area	canal		south branch, Santan canal		X		X	X						
446	77,184				historical-period habitation											
448	10,328	activity area	rock art	trail	bedrock mortars/cupules; U:14:16							X				
449	24,822															
449A	14,273	activity area	activity area		U:14:15 (part)		X									
449B	4,664		activity area									X				
449C	388,184		rock art	rock-pile feature	trails; U:14:15, 21, 22						X					
450	9,494				U:14:19											
450A	13,409		rock-pile feature		U:14:19; historical-period habitation, also		X	X	X	X	X					
450B	9,055		rock-pile feature		U:14:19; historical-period habitation, also		X		X	X	X					
450C	16,864		rock-pile feature		U:14:19		X									
450D	16,990		rock-pile feature		U:14:19			X								
504	8,004	village	hamlet							X	X					

continued on next page

GR- Site/Locus	Area (m²)	Site Type (Wells et al. 2003, 2004)	*Revised Site Type (1)*	*Revised Site Type (2)*	Remarks	Period							No. of TMs	No. of SMs	No. of PMs	No. of BCs
						Pioneer	Early Colonial	Late Colonial	Sedentary	Early Classic	Late Classic	Undefined				
505	20,946															
505A	5,909	activity area	hamlet							X	X					
505B	23,150	activity area	hamlet							X	X					
505C	1,969	activity area	hamlet							X	X					
506	12,048	activity area	activity area		U:13:17 ASU				X							
520	8,362			= SUM (B127:B130)												
520A	142	activity area	hamlet							X	X					
520B	466	activity area	hamlet							X	X					
520C	15,595	village	hamlet	activity area	Sedentary period = activity area or camp				X	X	X					
522	860,488															
522A	161,230	village	village		mostly Classic period		X	X	X	X	X		1			
522B	116,498	village	activity area				X	X	X				1			
522C	119,172	village	village		Lower Santan, U:13:6								1			
522D	355,389	village	village		Lower Santan, U:13:6		X	X	X	X	X		4	1	1	
522E	965,857	activity area	village		Lower Santan, U:13:6		X	X	X	X	X					1
522F	53,696		village	canal	Lower Santan (Hilltop)		X	X	X	X	X					
522G	41,959		activity area				X	X								
522H	26,105	activity area	activity area				X	X	X		X					
522I	55,232	activity area	activity area				X	X	X	X	X					
522J	64,550	activity area	activity area				X	X	X	X	X					
522K	25,262	activity area	activity area				X	X	X	X						
522L	123,159	activity area	activity area				X	X	X	X	X					
522M	20,678	activity area	activity area				X	X	X	X						
522N	48,744	village	possible camp				X	X	X							
522O	13,141	village	possible camp				X	X	X		X					
522P	6,407		activity area				X	X	X	X	X					
522Q	17,690	village	possible camp				X	X	X		X					
522S	69,027	activity area	activity area	canal				X	X	X						

GR- Site/Locus	Area (m²)	Site Type (Wells et al. 2003, 2004)	*Revised Site Type (1)*	*Revised Site Type (2)*	Remarks	Period: Pioneer	Early Colonial	Late Colonial	Sedentary	Early Classic	Late Classic	Undefined	No. of TMs	No. of SMs	No. of PMs	No. of BCs
522T	3,220		activity area				X	X	X	X	X					
522U	260,596	village	village	canal	Lower Santan (Hilltop), small lot		X	X	X	X	X		12			
523	242,942															
523A	426,357	rock-pile feature	rock-pile feature	roasting area	U:13:150		X	X	X	X	X		1			
523B	1,698,727		rock-pile feature	roasting area	U:13:150, U:13:28		X	X	X	X	X					
523C	1,468,324	rock-pile feature	rock-pile feature		U:14:56		X	X	X	X	X					
523D	672,196	rock-pile feature	rock-pile feature	rock art	U:14:10, U:14:11, U:14:19			X	X	X	X					
523E	89,057	village	rock-pile feature	village	part of Upper Santan village, U:14:10				X	X						
524	3,966		activity area		historical-period habitation							X				
525	1,116				historical-period habitation											
526	19,206															
526A	9,910	activity area	canal		historical-period habitation, also		X	X	X							
526B	23,383	village	canal		historical-period habitation, also	X	X	X		X	X					
526C	10,479	activity area	activity area						X	X	X					
527	2,025	activity area	activity area									X				
528	3,710	activity area	activity area		tested			X		X	X					
534	54,953															
534A	1,685	activity area	possible camp		U:13:52			X	X							
534B	781		roasting area		U:13:52			X	X							
534C	14,304	activity area	activity area		U:13:154					X	X					
535	14,288															
535A	7,559	activity area	activity area		U:13:154?		X	X	X		X					
535B	6,846	activity area	activity area				X	X	X		X					
536	9,936	activity area	activity area		U:13:54, 55? U:13:20 ASU				X	X	X					
537	8,515	activity area	activity area		U:13:59?			X								

continued on next page

GR- Site/Locus	Area (m²)	Site Type (Wells et al. 2003, 2004)	*Revised Site Type (1)*	*Revised Site Type (2)*	Remarks	Period							No. of TMs	No. of SMs	No. of PMs	No. of BCs
						Pioneer	Early Colonial	Late Colonial	Sedentary	Early Classic	Late Classic	Undefined				
538	3,298	camp	possible camp		possible cremation			X		X	X					
539	11,827	activity area	activity area		U:13:18 ASU			X	X							
541	9,238				historical-period railroad dock											
542	7,475	rock-pile feature	rock-pile feature									X				
543	6,873	activity area	activity area					X	X							
544	12,612	activity area	activity area				X	X	X							
545	5,207	camp	activity area				X									
546	18,984	activity area	activity area				X	X								
547	22,016	activity area	activity area				X	X								
581	10,357	activity area	activity area				X									
582	1,457	activity area	activity area				X									
583	1,551	activity area	activity area					X								
584	3,569	activity area	activity area									X				
585	960	activity area	activity area									X				
586	10,616				historical-period site, U:13:66; U:13:29 ASU (southwestern part)											
620	21,912	activity area	activity area				X	X								
621	33,898	activity area	activity area					X								
638	14,826															
638A	17,136		canal		south branch, Santan canal						X					
638B	3,480	activity area	canal?		canal to GR-644?		X		X		X					
638C	4,510	activity area	canal?		canal to GR-644?		X		X	X	X					
639	2,921				historical-period site											
640	87,736															
640A	1,505		canal		south branch, Santan canal				X		X					
640B	308		canal?		canal to GR-644? (sherd counts from the whole site)		X	X	X	X	X					
640C	28,363	activity area	canal		south branch, Santan canal						X					
641	43,045		activity area		U:14:10 ASU?		X	X	X		X					

GR- Site/Locus	Area (m²)	Site Type (Wells et al. 2003, 2004)	*Revised Site Type (1)*	*Revised Site Type (2)*	Remarks	Period							No. of TMs	No. of SMs	No. of PMs	No. of BCs
						Pioneer	Early Colonial	Late Colonial	Sedentary	Early Classic	Late Classic	Undefined				
641A	3,709	activity area	activity area								X					
642	10,743	activity area	activity area								X					
643	124,858	activity area	canal		Santan canal, north or south branch?	X	X	X	X	X	X					
644	39,927	activity area	canal		south branch, Santan canal; U:13:212	X	X	X	X	X	X					
646	122,805	activity area	canal	activity area	south branch, Santan canal	X	X	X	X	X	X					
646A	53,820	-	canal	activity area	south branch, Santan canal		X	X	X	X	X					
647	55,251	activity area	activity area		U:13:12 ASU (part)		X	X	X							
648	20,914	activity area	activity area			X	X	X	X	X	X					
652	1,998	activity area	activity area							X						
657	21,407															
657A	14,674	village	camp			X	X	X	X	X	X					
735	8,254				historical-period habitation											
736	147,572	activity area	canal	activity area	south branch, Santan canal?	X	X			X						
736A	1,776				historical-period locus											
736B	17,386	activity area	canal	activity area	south branch, Santan canal?	X	X		X							
737	125,361	activity area	activity area				X	X	X		X					
738	29,321				U:13:201; U:13:12 ASU (part)											
738A	125,640	camp	camp	canal	headward part of the Gila Butte canal; Colonial to Sedentary period dominant	X	X	X	X	X	X					
738B	181,535	activity area	canal		end of south branch, Santan canal?	X	X	X	X	X	X					
740	128,901															
740A	444,146	village	possible camp	canal?	Sedentary and Late Classic period dominant; roasting area; U:13:156	X	X	X	X	X	X					
740B	34,377	activity area	canal		north branch, Santan canal			X	X		X					
740C	63,885	activity area	canal?	activity area			X		X		X					

continued on next page

GR- Site/Locus	Area (m^2)	Site Type (Wells et al. 2003, 2004)	*Revised Site Type (1)*	*Revised Site Type (2)*	Remarks	Period							No. of TMs	No. of SMs	No. of PMs	No. of BCs
						Pioneer	Early Colonial	Late Colonial	Sedentary	Early Classic	Late Classic	Undefined				
740D	5,747	village	activity area		Sedentary period dominant		X	X	X							
740E	10,106	activity area	canal?	activity area			X	X	X							
740F	38,608	activity area	activity area				X	X	X							
740G	40,930	activity area	canal		north branch, Santan canal; U:13:155		X	X	X	X	X					
740H	64,783	activity area	canal		north branch, Santan canal; U:13:155		X	X	X	X	X					
740I	9,620	activity area	activity area	possible camp			X				X					
740J	36,794	village	possible camp	roasting area			X	X	X	X	X					
740K	85,235	activity area	activity area				X	X	X	X	X					
778	115,068	activity area	activity area			X	X	X	X	X	X					
781	7,740	activity area	activity area		U:13:7, 13 ASU (part)	X	X		X	X	X					
826	293				historical-period site; U:14:15 (part)											
827	6,155	rock-pile feature	roasting area		U:14:15 (part)							X				
829	4,462	activity area	activity area		U:14:19					X						
830	18,546				U:14:19											
830A	135,642	rock-pile feature	rock-pile feature		U:14:19				X		X					
830B	4,870		rock-pile feature		historical-period habitation; U:14:19				X		X					
830C	43,130		rock-pile feature		U:14:19; time period unclear				X		X					
846	6,814				historical-period habitation											
930	15,127															
930A	115,860	activity area	activity area		U:14:44		X	X	X							
930B	12,187	activity area	activity area					X	X	X						
1085	2	activity area	activity area		geomorphic testing						X					
1086	55	canal	canal		geomorphic testing; south branch, Santan canal, in GR-638C				X	X	X					
1113	19,962				U:13:232; U:13:33 ASU											

GR- Site/Locus	Area (m²)	Site Type (Wells et al. 2003, 2004)	*Revised Site Type (1)*	*Revised Site Type (2)*	Remarks	Period: Pioneer	Period: Early Colonial	Period: Late Colonial	Period: Sedentary	Period: Early Classic	Period: Late Classic	Period: Undefined	No. of TMs	No. of SMs	No. of PMs	No. of BCs
1113A	40,681		hamlet		Stotonic site					X	X					
1113B	3,335		activity area									X				
1162	26,830	village	hamlet	activity area	hamlet = Classic period; U:13:60; U:13:28 ASU		X	X	X	X	X					
1163	5,071	activity area	activity area		U:13:61; U:13:13 ASU (part)		X									
1164	191,358	village	hamlet	possible camp	hamlet = Classic period; possible camp = Sedentary period; U:13:65; U:13:37 ASU		X	X	X	X	X					
1165	28,074	activity area	activity area				X	X	X	X	X					
1166	38,383	activity area	activity area		U:13:69, 70; U:13:23 ASU		X	X	X	X						
1208	15,743	village	activity area							X	X					
1208A	1,722		possible camp	roasting area			X	X	X	X	X					
1209	3,471				historical-period site											
1210	16,048	activity area	canal		south branch, Santan canal	X	X	X	X	X	X					
1211	88,340															
1211A	138,894	activity area	activity area			X	X	X	X		X					
1211B	107,693	activity area	activity area				X	X	X	X	X					
1211C	66,851	activity area	activity area				X	X	X	X						
1211D	47,065	activity area	activity area			X	X	X	X	X						
1211E	107,321	camp	activity area			X	X	X	X							
1211F	4,422	activity area	activity area						X							
1212	1,284															
1212A	34,321	activity area	activity area				X	X	X		X					
1212B	20,967	activity area	activity area				X	X	X	X						
<u>ASM Sites along the Santan Canal System</u>																
U:13:49			activity area		artifact scatter next to U:13:150		X	X	X	X	X					
U:13:50			activity area		artifact scatter				X	X	X					
U:13:51			activity area		artifact scatter				X							
U:13:53			activity area		artifact scatter					X	X					

continued on next page

GR- Site/Locus	Area (m^2)	Site Type (Wells et al. 2003, 2004)	*Revised Site Type (1)*	*Revised Site Type (2)*	Remarks	Period: Pioneer	Early Colonial	Late Colonial	Sedentary	Early Classic	Late Classic	Undefined	No. of TMs	No. of SMs	No. of PMs	No. of BCs
U:13:54			activity area		artifact scatter					X	X					
U:13:55			activity area		artifact scatter, U:13:21 ASU					X	X					
U:13:56			activity area		artifact scatter				X	X						
U:13:57			activity area		artifact scatter, U:13:36 ASU				X	X	X					
U:13:58			activity area		artifact scatter			X	X	X	X					
U:13:59			activity area		artifact scatter, U:13:35 ASU					X	X					
U:13:62			activity area		artifact scatter			X		X	X					
U:13:63			activity area		artifact scatter					X	X					
U:13:67			activity area		artifact scatter					X	X					
U:13:29 ASU			activity area		U:13:29 ASU (Loci 148, 150, and 151)					X	X					
U:13:211			activity area		artifact scatter		X	X	X	X	X					
U:14:12			rock art	Rock PF	trails, also							X				
U:14:13			rock art	Rock PF			X			X	X					
U:14:14			rock art									X				
U:14:15			rock-pile feature	trails								X				
U:14:17			rock art									X				
U:14:23			rock art									X				
U:14:35			rock-pile feature		grid gardens, check dams; GR-890							X				
U:14:36			rock-pile feature	trails								X				
U:14:37			activity area	possible camp			X	X	X	X	X					
U:14:38			rock art	Rock PF								X				
U:14:39			rock-pile feature	trails								X				
U:14:52			rock art		"Picture Rocks"							X				
Sites along the Gila Butte Canal System																
548	91,094															
548A	42,305	activity area	activity area	possible camp		X	X	X								
548B	12,894	camp	camp			X	X	X								
548C	3,431	activity area	activity area				X	X								

GR- Site/Locus	Area (m²)	Site Type (Wells et al. 2003, 2004)	*Revised Site Type (1)*	*Revised Site Type (2)*	Remarks	Period: Pioneer	Period: Early Colonial	Period: Late Colonial	Period: Sedentary	Period: Early Classic	Period: Late Classic	Period: Undefined	No. of TMs	No. of SMs	No. of PMs	No. of BCs
553	4,950				historical-period site											
554	28,009				historical-period site											
594	12,331	activity area	activity area				X		X							
595	6,305	activity area	activity area				X			X						
596	122				historical-period site											
597	13,414	activity area	activity area									X				
654	3,038	activity area	activity area	canal?	U:13:164		X	X	X							
655	8,128	activity area	activity area	canal?	U:13:163 (part)		X	X	X	X						
656	26,803															
656A	17,277	activity area	activity area	canal?	U:13:163 (part)		X	X	X	X						
656B	31,047	activity area	canal	activity area	headward part of the Gila Butte canal; U:13:158	X	X	X	X	X	X					
656C	11,816	activity area	activity area	roasting area	U:13:158		X	X	X	X	X					
656D	6,935	activity area	activity area		U:13:12 ASU (part)				X		X					
775	44,479															
775A	10,616	activity area	activity area		U:13:84	X	X	X	X	X						
775B	10,845	activity area	activity area		U:13:84		X	X			X					
775C	320,222	village	camp	activity area	camp = Sedentary to Classic period; U:13:80	X	X	X	X	X	X					
776	91,257															
776A	99,100	activity area	canal		Gila Butte canal; U:13:74	X	X	X	X	X	X					
776B	22,098	activity area	canal		Gila Butte canal; U:13:74 (part)	X	X	X	X	X	X					
776C	80,977	activity area	canal		Gila Butte canal; U:13:72, 73, 75 (part)	X	X	X	X	X	X					
776D	33,828	village	hamlet	activity area	hamlet = Classic period; U:13:75 (part)		X	X	X	X	X		8	4		
777	42,928	activity area	activity area			X	X	X	X	X	X					
779	14,286															
779A	13,726	activity area	activity area		historical-period habitation			X	X							
779B	27,227	activity area	activity area					X	X		X					

continued on next page

GR- Site/Locus	Area (m²)	Site Type (Wells et al. 2003, 2004)	*Revised Site Type (1)*	*Revised Site Type (2)*	Remarks	Period							No. of TMs	No. of SMs	No. of PMs	No. of BCs
						Pioneer	Early Colonial	Late Colonial	Sedentary	Early Classic	Late Classic	Undefined				
780	22,445	activity area	activity area				X	X	X	X						
1167	756,214				areas outside loci								2			
1167A	13,796		activity area				X									
1167B	2,479		activity area									X				
1167C	6,826		activity area				X	X		X						
1167D	16,688		activity area				X	X								
1167E	1,231		activity area					X	X	X						
1167F	15,606	activity area	activity area			X	X	X								
1167G	3,199	village	possible camp	activity area	possible camp = Colonial to Sedentary period; U:13:77?	X	X	X	X							
1167H	1,858	activity area	activity area					X		X						
1167I	592		activity area				X	X	X	X						
1167J	3,017		activity area				X									
1167K	24,008	activity area	activity area				X	X	X							
1167M	5,383	activity area	canal				X	X	X							
1167N	15,679	activity area	activity area	canal?	possible alignment of SWCA Feature 7		X	X	X							
1167O	195,035	village	village	hamlet	Gila Butte site, U:13:8	X	X	X	X				38			1
1167P	18,781	village	camp	activity area	south "locus" of Gila Butte Site	X	X	X	X	X						
1168	6				historical-period site											
1187	4,050															
1187A	18,887	activity area	canal?				X		X		X					
1187B	31,875	activity area	canal?				X	X	X		X					
1213	130,379	activity area	canal		end of south branch, Santan canal?		X	X	X	X	X					
1214A	23,227	activity area	activity area	canal?			X		X							
1214B	61,257	activity area	canal		Gila Butte canal; U:13:84		X	X								
1214C	32,061	activity area	canal		Gila Butte canal; U:13:84	X	X	X	X	X	X					
1214D	59,432	activity area	canal		Gila Butte canal; U:13:84		X		X	X	X					
1215	17,830															

GR- Site/Locus	Area (m²)	Site Type (Wells et al. 2003, 2004)	*Revised Site Type (1)*	*Revised Site Type (2)*	Remarks	Period: Pioneer	Early Colonial	Late Colonial	Sedentary	Early Classic	Late Classic	Undefined	No. of TMs	No. of SMs	No. of PMs	No. of BCs
1215A	27,749	activity area	canal?		upper end of the GR-1214 canal		X	X	X	X						
1215B	11,697	activity area	canal?		upper end of the GR-1214 canal		X	X	X	X						
1215C	18,283	activity area	activity area	canal?						X						
1220	10,474	activity area	canal		Gila Butte canal		X	X	X	X	X					
1221	9,855	activity area	activity area	canal?	end of south branch, Santan canal?		X		X	X	X					
1222	37,646	activity area	canal		Gila Butte canal		X	X	X	X	X					
ASM Sites along the Gila Butte Canal System																
U:13:71			hamlet		U:13:24 ASU; Sedentary period = activity area				X	X	X					
U:13:218			rock-pile feature	trails	On the western side of Gila Butte		X	X	X	X	X					
U:13:115			rock art		On the northeastern edge of Gila Butte	X	X	X								
U:13:214			check dams		on the eastern side of Gila Butte							X				
U:13:215			rock art		on the eastern side of Gila Butte							X				
U:13:216			rock-pile feature		on the eastern side of Gila Butte							X				

Site Type (Wells et al. 2003, 2004): If the site-type cell in this column is shaded gray, it denotes that it was changed in the "Revised Site Type (1)" cell.
Key: BC = ballcourt; PM = platform mound; SM = structural mound; TM = trash mound.

Table C.2. Counts of Primary Site Types per Time Period along the Santan and Gila Butte Canal Systems

Site Type	Period					
	Pioneer	Early Colonial	Late Colonial	Sedentary	Early Classic	Late Classic
Village	—	11[a]	12[b]	14[c]	10[d]	8[e]
Hamlet	3	—	—	4	29	21
Camp	4[f]	6[f]	6[f]	10[g]	5[h]	2
Possible camp	1	7	9	9	6	7
Canal area	15	47	41	48	38	43
Activity area	17	79	80	84	68	62
Roasting area	—	—	1	2	2	2
Rock art	1	1	1	—	—	1
Rock-pile field	—	6	9	16	13	12
Total	41	157	159	187	171	158

[a] Together, Loci A, B, and W at GR-441 are one village; Loci A, D, E, F, and U at GR-522 are one village (five total villages).
[b] Loci A, B, and W at GR-441 are one village; Loci A, D, E, F, and U at GR-522 are one village; and GR-149A and GR-157A are one "dual village" (five total villages).
[c] Loci A, B, and W at GR-441 are one village; Loci A, D, E, F, and U at GR-522 are one village; GR-149A and Loci A and B at GR-157 are one "dual village"; and GR-164A and GR-165 are one "dual village" (five total villages).
[d] Loci A, E, F, H, I, and AA at GR-441 are one village, and Loci A, D, and E at GR-522 are one village (3 total dispersed villages).
[e] Loci A, E, F, and H at GR-441 are one village, and Loci A, D, and E at GR-522 are one village (3 total dispersed villages).
[f] Two camps (GR-552, Loci A and C) are actually in Study Area 1.
[g] Three camps (GR-552, Loci A, C, and E) are actually in Study Area 1.
[h] One camp (GR-590B) is actually in Study Area 1.

Habitation Sites

As in Study Area 1 (see Appendix B), specific attention is given to the habitation sites in Study Area 2. The 45 habitations are summarized in Table C.3. The same protocols were used for defining the habitation sites as discussed in Appendix B. Farmsteads and field houses are combined into one type (camps). Hamlets and villages are both permanent residences and were distinguished from each other primarily on the basis of size (area), but other factors were considered. The range of habitation sizes in Study Area 2 was more variable than the range in Study Area 1, largely because of the obscuring of some habitation boundaries from historical-period and modern disturbances. Still, the general size ranges were similar in both study areas: the villages were larger than 10 ha each, and the hamlets were each about 5 ha or smaller. There was some divergence from these ranges: three hamlets were around 8–9 ha (the initial Pioneer period occupations at the Olberg, Upper Santan, and Gila Butte sites), and one village was 6–9 ha (Colonial period occupation at the Granite Knob site; its original extent may have been obscured by historical-period floods that scoured away part of the site). The camps in Study Area 2 also were 5 ha each or smaller, in contrast to Study Area 1, where they were 3 ha each or smaller. Lastly, as with Study Area 1, there are a few cases in Study Area 2 where groups of habitations are considered dispersed villages or dispersed hamlets.

Settlement Trends through Time

This section describes the settlement trends through time in Study Area 2, with a focus on site function. The figures below display the primary site type for each site/locus, for each time period, in conjunction with the definitions of habitation-site types (see previous sections). Another set of symbols is used to indicate the habitation-site areas; the canals also are shown. The dashed lines represent the inferred community boundaries, which reflect the most practical configurations based on applying the principles of the two community models and the boundary-definition criteria described in Chapter 2. Chapter 6 discusses the implications of these boundaries for the two community models. Notably, some sites to the north and west of Gila Butte are actually situated within Study Area 1, but they are shown in these figures to flesh out the picture of community organization along the Gila Butte canal system.

Pioneer Period

Current evidence indicates that no settlements in Study Area 2 were occupied during the early Pioneer period (Vahki phase). As noted in Appendix B, Vahki Plain and

Table C.3. Habitation Sites along the Granite Knob, Santan, and Gila Butte Canal Systems

Site/Locus	Settlement Type	Remarks[a]	Area (m²)	Area (ha)	Phase: Snaketown	Gila Butte	Santa Cruz	Sacaton	Soho	Civano
Sites along the Granite Knob Canal System										
Granite Knob Site Complex										
GR-149A	possible camp	U:14:214; possible Pioneer period	*20,000*	*2.00*	X					
GR-149A	village (with ballcourt)	U:14:214; Colonial to Sedentary period; hamlet in the Early Classic period	57,286	5.73		X	X	X	X	
GR-149B	hamlet	Classic period	39,710	3.97					X	X
GR-149D	hamlet	Classic period	22,426	2.24					X	X
GR-149F	hamlet	Classic period	48,701	4.87					X	X
GR-149H	possible camp	Classic period	3,511	0.35					X	
GR-157A	village	U:14:214; late Colonial to Classic period; hamlet in the Early Classic period	33,832	3.38			X	X	X	
GR-157B	village (with ballcourt)	U:14:215; Sedentary to Classic period; hamlet in the Classic period	25,856	2.59				X	X	X
Other Sites along the Granite Knob Canal										
GR-132	camp	U:14:257; associated with GR-186	3,205	0.32				X		
GR-142	camp	U:14:261	11,865	1.19				X	X	
GR-144	hamlet	U:14:263; trails, also	35,960	3.60				X	X	
GR-180	possible camp	U:14:277	20,451	2.05				X		
GR-186	hamlet	U:14:264	9,368	0.94				X	X	
Sites along the Santan Canal System										
Olberg Site Complex										
GR-159	hamlet	U:14:20	10,541	1.05				X	X	X
GR-160	hamlet	U:14:204	42,316	4.23					X	X
GR-164A	village	U:14:2; Sedentary to Classic period	139,825	18.98				X	X	X
GR-164B	hamlet	U:14:2; Sedentary to Classic period	14,473	1.45				X	X	X
GR-165	hamlet	U:14:18; Pioneer period	91,231	9.12	X					

continued on next page

Site/Locus	Settlement Type	Remarks[a]	Area (m²)	Area (ha)	Phase					
					Snaketown	Gila Butte	Santa Cruz	Sacaton	Soho	Civano
GR-165	village	U:14:18; Colonial to Sedentary period	174,076	17.41		X	X	X		
GR-165	hamlet	U:14:18; Classic period	91,231	9.12					X	X
GR-166	hamlet	U:14:205	7,004	0.70					X	X
GR-171B	hamlet	U:14:206	1,865	0.19					X	
GR-171D	hamlet	U:14:209	2,590	0.26					X	
GR-185	hamlet	U:14:211	1,573	0.16					X	
GR-187	hamlet	U:14:203	3,173	0.32					X	
Upper Santan village										
GR-441A	hamlet	U:14:8; Pioneer period	92,287	9.23	X					
GR-441A, B, W	village (with ballcourt)	U:14:8; Colonial to Sedentary period	413,538	41.35		X	X	X		
GR-441A	village with platform mound	U:14:8; Classic period	92,287	9.23					X	X
GR-441A, E, F, H, I, AA	village with platform mound	U:14:10; Early Classic period	219,370	21.94					X	
GR-441A, E, F, H	village with platform mound	U:14:10; Late Classic period	79,117	7.91						X
Lower Santan village										
GR-522A, D, E, F	village (with ballcourt)	U:13:6; pre-Classic period	*700,000*	*70.00*		X	X	X		
GR-522A	village?	U:13:6; Classic period	31,880	3.19					X	X
GR-522D	village with platform mound	U:13:6; Classic period	166,265	16.63					X	X
Other Sites along the Santan Canal										
GR-445C	possible camp	Classic period?	4,030	0.40					X	X
GR-445D	possible camp	Classic period?	5,690	0.57					X	X
GR-504	hamlet		8,004	0.80					X	X
GR-505	hamlet		51,974	5.20					X	X
GR-520	hamlet		24,565	2.46					X	X
GR-522N	possible camp		48,744	4.87		X	X	X		
GR-522O	possible camp		13,140	1.31		X	X	X		X
GR-522Q	possible camp		17,230	1.72		X	X	X		X
GR-534	possible camp	U:13:52, U:13:154?	71,723	7.17			X	X		

Site/Locus	Settlement Type	Remarks[a]	Area (m²)	Area (ha)	Phase					
					Snaketown	Gila Butte	Santa Cruz	Sacaton	Soho	Civano
GR-538	possible camp		3,298	0.33			X		X	X
GR-657A	camp		14,674	1.47	X	X	X	X	X	X
GR-740A	possible camp	U:13:156	32,013	3.20		X	X	X	X	X
GR-740J	possible camp		37,597	3.76		X	X	X	X	X
GR-1113	hamlet	Stotonic site, U:13:232	23,965	2.40					X	X
GR-1162	hamlet	U:13:60, U:13:28 ASU	27,947	2.79					X	X
GR-1164	hamlet	U:13:65; possible camp in the Sedentary period	40,122	4.01				X	X	X
GR-1208A	possible camp	Roasting pit; Late Classic period dominant	1,722	0.17		X	X	X	X	X
<u>Sites along the Gila Butte Canal System</u>										
<u>Gila Butte Site</u>										
GR-1167O	hamlet	Gila Butte site/U:13:8, Snaketown phase	78,158	7.82	X					
GR-1167O	village (with ballcourt)	Gila Butte site/U:13:8, Colonial to Sedentary period	158,791	15.88		X	X	X		
<u>Other Sites along the Gila Butte Canal</u>										
GR-548B	camp		12,894	1.29	X	X	X			
GR-552A[b]	camp		13,435	1.34	X	X	X	X		
GR-552C[b]	camp		33,676	3.37	X	X	X	X		
GR-552E[b]	camp		40,314	4.03				X		
GR-590B[b]	camp	probably on the Snaketown canal system	28,072	2.81					X	
GR-738A	camp	near Diversion Point 2	49,337	4.93		X	X	X		
GR-775C	camp	U:13:80	37,381	3.74				X	X	X
GR-776D	hamlet	U:13:75	33,828	3.38					X	X
GR-1167G	possible camp	U 13:77(?)	3,199	0.32		X	X	X		
GR-1167P	camp	adjacent to the Gila Butte site	18,781	1.88		X	X	X	X	
U:13:71 ASM	hamlet	U:13:24 ASU	11,340	1.13					X	X

Note: Italicized numbers are estimates.
[a] Site numbers are ASM numbers unless otherwise noted.
[b] Site is located in Study Area 1 but is associated with the Gila Butte canal system.

Vahki Red are not systematically identified in the Gila River Indian Community–Cultural Resource Management Program Stage 1 ceramic analysis; so, it is possible that future data recovery will reveal a Vahki phase occupation in the area. Vahki phase contexts also were not identified at sites between Granite Knob and Olberg Butte (Gregory and Douglas 1994). Rather, settlement appears to have been initiated in the Estrella/Sweetwater phase of the late Pioneer period at Upper Santan and Olberg villages (Figure C.2). These appear to have been hamlet-size settlements upon their founding. The limited occurrences of temporally diagnostic ceramics of this time period suggest that Upper Santan village was founded slightly earlier (based on the presence of both Estrella Red-on-gray and Sweetwater Red-on-gray) than Olberg village (where only six Sweetwater Red-on-gray sherds have been found that represent 1.2 percent of all diagnostic sherds [Gregory and Huckleberry 1994]). Olberg feasibly was used as a camp initially and then occupied as a permanent habitation during the Snaketown phase. The sites were situated roughly 5 km apart. By the Snaketown phase, a camp along the edge of the floodplain also was being used.

The few isolated occurrences of Estrella Red-on-gray and Sweetwater Red-on-gray at the Gila Butte site suggest that it may have been founded during the Estrella/Sweetwater phase, but it clearly was occupied by the Snaketown phase. At that time, the site was a hamlet-size settlement. Three camps to the north of Gila Butte also were being used.

None of the sites between Granite Knob and Olberg Butte had a clear late Pioneer period occupation (see Gregory and Huckleberry 1994). The Granite Knob site (GR-149, Locus A) only included a few Snaketown Red-on-buff/-gray sherds, suggesting low-intensity use as either a possible camp or an activity area.

The inferred community boundaries for the Pioneer period are shown in Figure C.2. The boundaries encompass the entire area around each canal system, because the political community was essentially isomorphic with each canal system. Chapter 6 presents the rationale for considering whether each of these incipient communities was organized as a focal-village community or a linear community.

Colonial Period

During the early Colonial period, the previously occupied hamlets (Olberg, Upper Santan, and Gila Butte) expanded to village-size settlements, and each of the latter two added a ballcourt, marking them as focal villages (Figure C.3). Two new ballcourt villages (Granite Knob and Lower Santan) were founded at this time, resulting in five villages in Study Area 2. Granite Knob was situated 4.3 km upstream from Olberg, and Lower Santan was 5.2 km down the canal from Upper Santan. Granite Knob village actually consisted of two separate habitation areas that, together, represent a small village. The southern edge of the Granite Knob settlement appears to have been partly scoured away by historical-period flooding, which may be the reason it was relatively small for a village (5.73 ha in the early Colonial period and 9.11 ha in the late Colonial period). Notably, Olberg village is not considered a focal village, because no ballcourt has been identified there, despite a concerted effort to locate one (Gregory and Douglas 1994; Gregory and Huckleberry 1994:65). Wilcox and Sternberg (1983) even noted that Olberg included three probable Sedentary period ballcourts. This absence seems surprising, especially since Olberg was located about 5 km upstream from the ballcourt village at Upper Santan, which conforms to the expected spacing of ballcourt villages (see Fish and Fish 1991:163). Also, a number of camps (and possible camps) were added along the Santan and Gila Butte canal systems. All five villages and most of the camps/possible camps in Study Area 2 are situated on the upper (T-3) terrace or on the alluvial fan. Three camps are located on the T-2 terrace, which is the former floodplain; these appear to have been located near Diversion Point 2 and fields along the south branch of the Santan canal.

The dramatic increase in activity areas (including canal areas), as shown in Figure C.3, indicates a marked increase in the intensity of use of the landscape in the early Colonial period. There are few breaks in the distribution of sites and loci, suggesting use of the entire landscape within a distance of about 5 km from the river. The exceptions are a gap between the tail end of the Granite Knob canal and Olberg Butte and a narrow, linear gap between the Gila Butte canal and the north branch of the Santan canal. Another notable change is the use of non-irrigation agricultural fields along the alluvial fan of the Santan Mountains (Gregory and Douglas 1994; Jacobs et al. 2010; Neily et al. 1999). The temporal data recovered from these sites suggest that farming with rock piles, terraces, and check dams on the upslope sides of the villages at Granite Knob, Olberg, Upper Santan, and Lower Santan had commenced by this time.

The settlement pattern and canal-system layout of the early Colonial period mostly were unchanged in the late Colonial period, with only a few exceptions (Figure C.4). These include a second habitation area that was added at Granite Knob village, roughly 0.9 km upstream from the existing habitation area. Gregory (1994:185–186) suggested that this "dual village" pattern may reflect a dual division within pre-Classic period Hohokam society and may express aspects of Hohokam sociology, cosmology, and worldview. Two new camps were established to the west of Lower Santan. Also, several new, non-irrigated agricultural field areas were added along the slopes of the Santan Mountains. The inferred community boundaries were extended to encompass these new farming areas. The general extent and intensity of use of the landscape remained steady from the previous period, and the canal systems kept the command areas at the same levels.

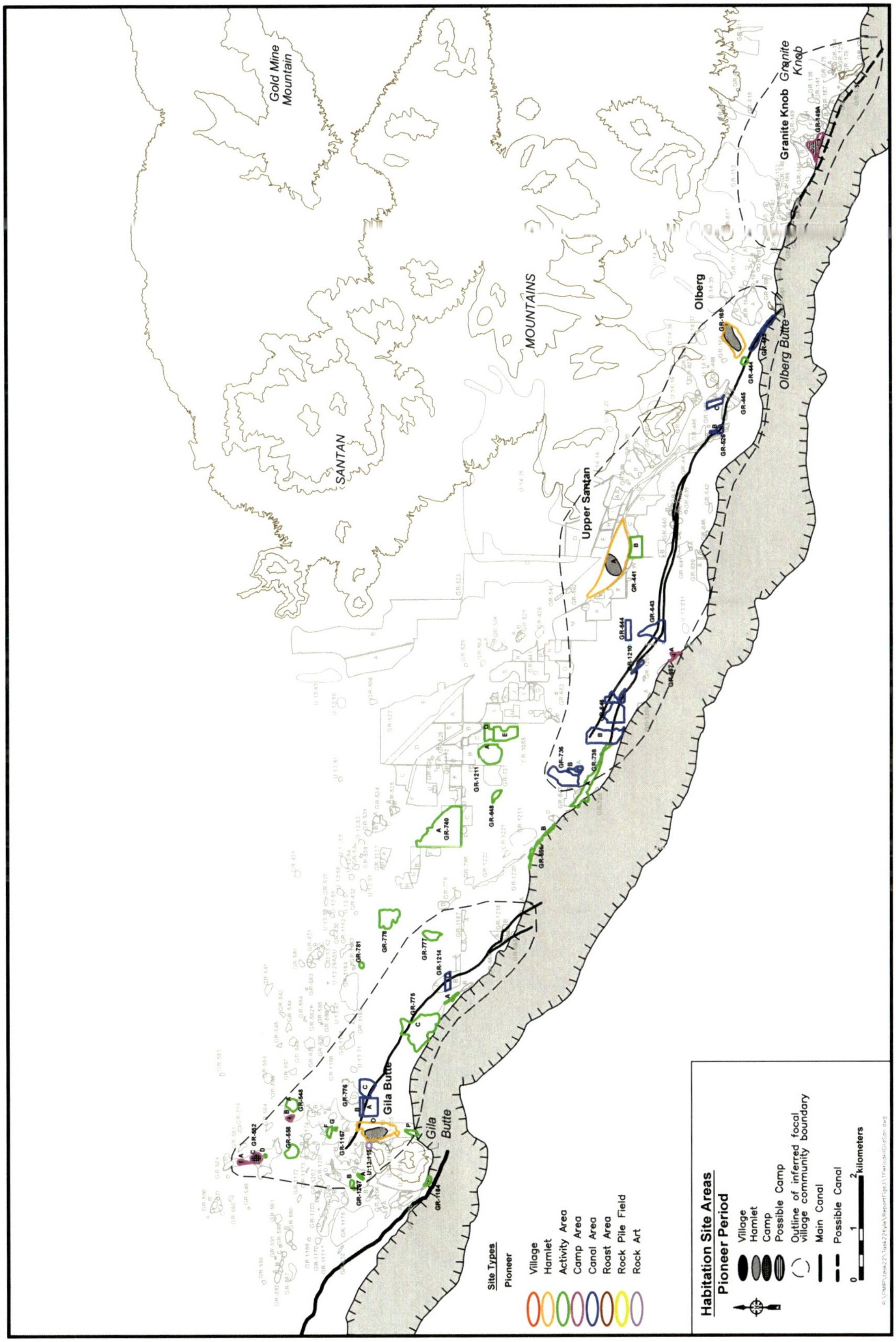

Figure C.2. Map of canals and settlements in Study Area 2 during the Pioneer period.

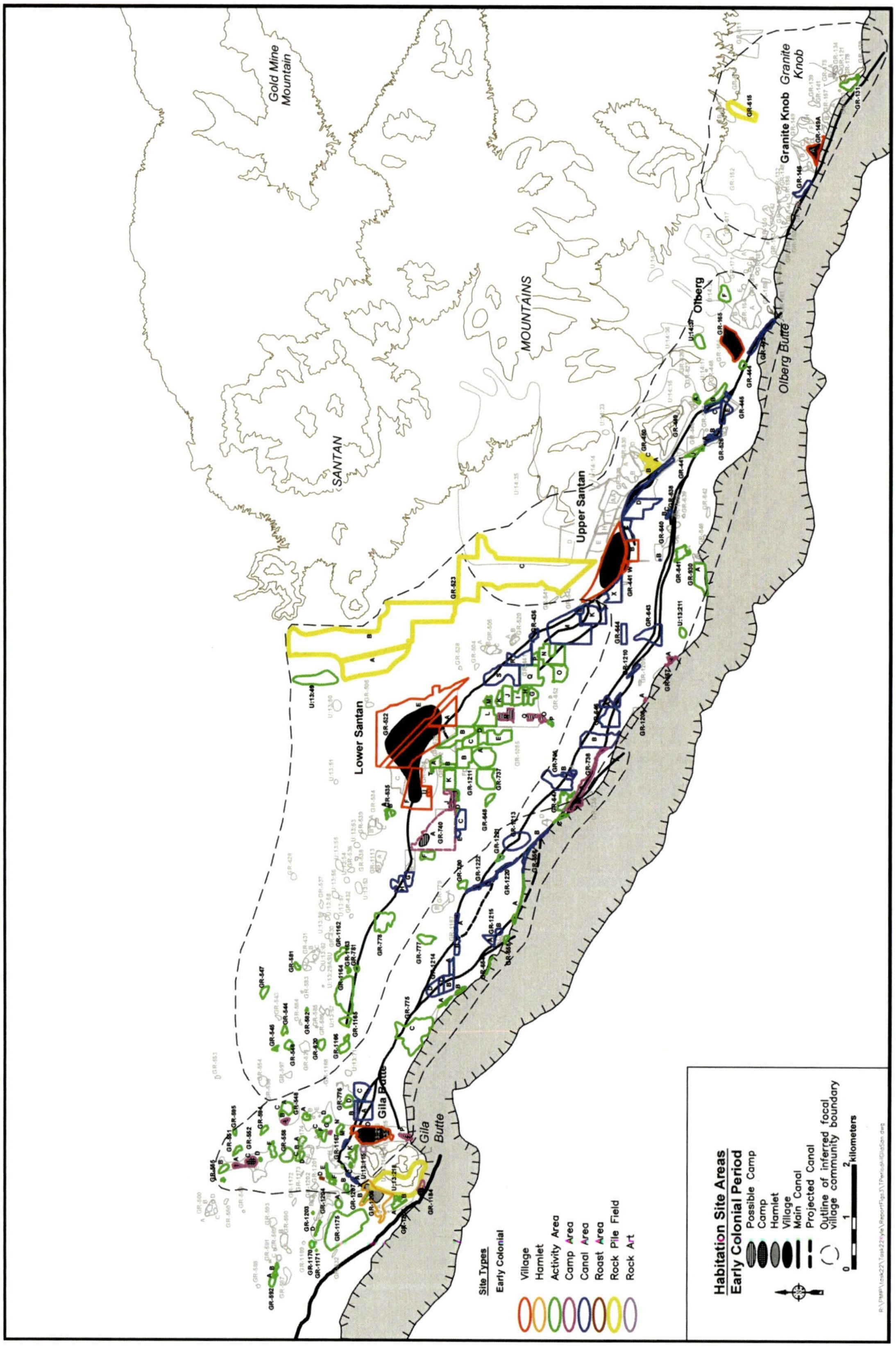

Figure C.3. Map of canals and settlements in Study Area 2 during the early Colonial period.

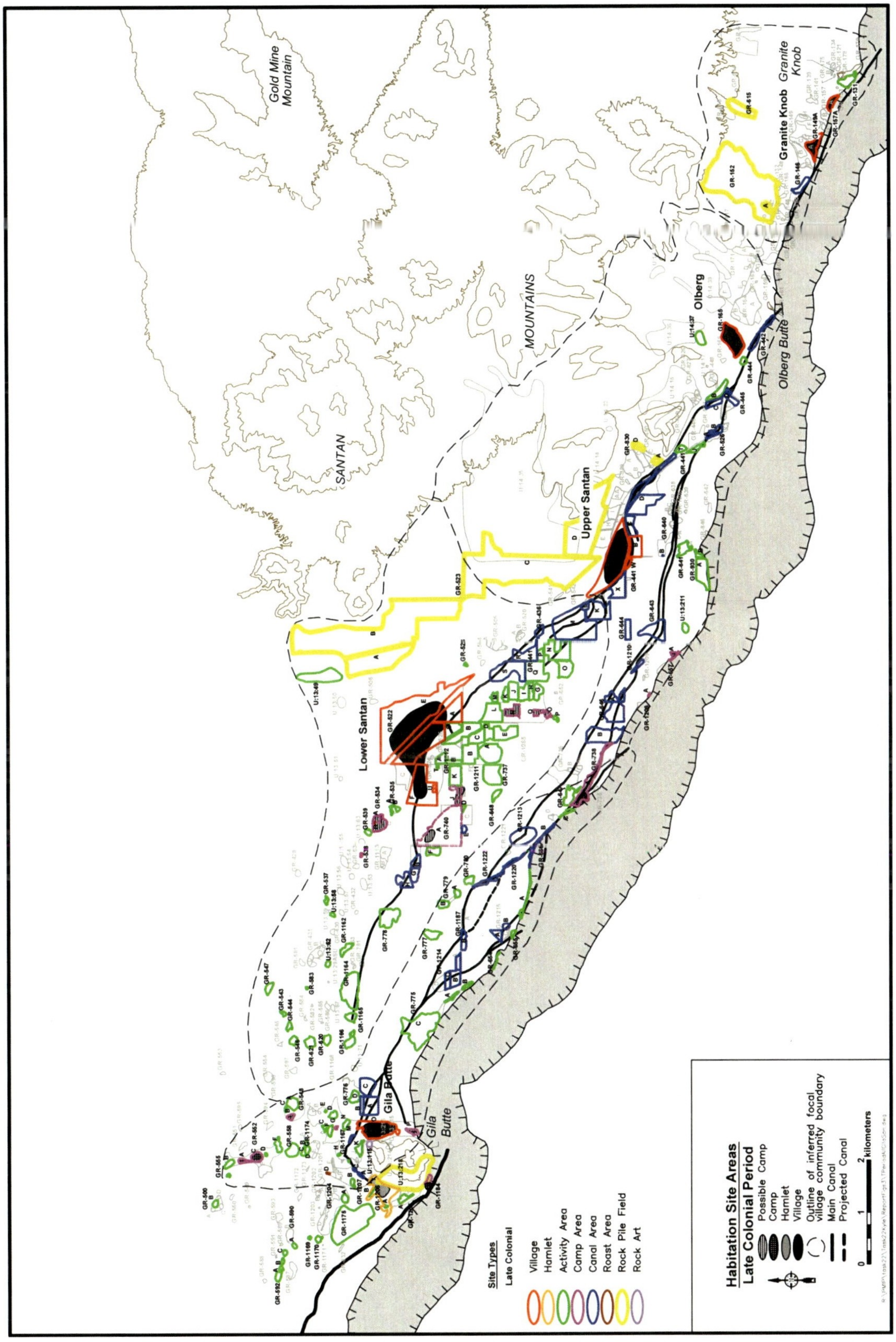

Figure C.4. Map of canals and settlements in Study Area 2 during the late Colonial period.

The inferred community boundaries depicted in Figures C.3 and C.4 were drawn in accordance with the criteria discussed in Chapter 2 and were based on the occurrences of the focal villages and with reference to the main-canal segments. In the cases of the Granite Knob and Gila Butte canal systems, it was fairly straightforward to identify the focal village and associated main canal, since there was one village and one main canal for each system. Also, the linear space between settlements along the Gila Butte canal and the north branch of the Santan canal partly defined a boundary. However, there was not a clear break in the settlement distribution between the Gila Butte canal system and its neighboring canal systems on either end. These boundaries were slightly arbitrary and conformed roughly to the extent of the canal system. The Santan canal system, on the other hand, had two branches, but both focal villages were situated along the north branch, and there was no clear break in the site distribution. These community boundaries were drawn based on the assumptions that (1) the Upper Santan community maintained its original territory from the late Pioneer period (while adding some irrigated area along the upper part of the north-branch canal) and (2) the Lower Santan community encompassed the newly occupied and irrigated areas along the north-branch canal, downstream from Upper Santan. The boundaries of the Upper Santan, Lower Santan, and Gila Butte communities abutted each other because of their proximity. Lastly, it must be noted that the community territories for the Granite Knob community and the two Santan communities encompassed the non-irrigated agricultural fields directly upslope from the focal villages along the slopes of the Santan Mountains. Because there was a relatively continuous distribution of these non-irrigated fields, the community-boundary lines in these areas were somewhat arbitrary and were drawn along topographic features that might have been seen as natural borders (such as washes, buttes, and bedrock outcrops and the perimeters of the steeper parts of the Santan Mountains).

Sedentary Period

During the Sedentary period, the settlement pattern and canal-system layout generally were similar to those of the prior period, with the five villages still present, except for an overall increase in intensity of use (Figure C.5). This intensification was indicated by the expansion of Olberg village to include a second habitation area roughly 0.8 km upstream from the existing habitation area, as well as a probable hamlet between these village segments, so that like Granite Knob, Olberg village represents a kind of "dual village" (see Gregory 1994). Also, three new hamlets, three camps, and three activity areas were established at the tail end of the Granite Knob canal. Two other new camps were established along the north branch of the Santan canal and along the Gila Butte canal. Also, several new, non-irrigated agricultural field areas were added along the slopes of the Santan Mountains. The canal systems in Study Area 2 appear to have been linked together by the Sedentary period: the Granite Knob canal most likely was extended and connected with the Santan canal, the Santan canal definitely had been connected to the Gila Butte canal, and the Gila Butte canal was extended to connect with the Snaketown canal.

The inferred community boundaries still abutted each other and remained essentially unchanged from the late Colonial period, although the boundary between the Granite Knob and Upper Santan/Olberg communities became much less distinct. The latter two communities may, in fact, have been consolidated at this time. This probably was related to the motivation to extend and connect the Granite Knob canal with the Santan canal. Or perhaps the Granite Knob community was equivalent to another main-canal-reach community in the greater Santan canal system.

Classic Period

During the Early Classic period, the settlement pattern changed to a more-linear configuration (Figure C.6). In contrast to the 5 nucleated villages (4 with ballcourts) and 4 hamlets in the Sedentary period, the permanent habitations in Study Area 2 included 3 dispersed villages (2 with platform mounds) and 29 hamlets. The 2 platform-mound villages were located 5.2 km apart along the north branch of the Santan canal. Also, the number of camps declined by nearly half. The ballcourt village at Gila Butte was abandoned and was replaced by only 1 hamlet, unless the new village on the western side of the butte (GR-1175) was considered part of the Gila Butte community rather than the Snaketown community. The Granite Knob ballcourt village became disintegrated and was replaced by a series of dispersed hamlets. The other nucleated ballcourt villages (Upper Santan and Lower Santan) and the village without a ballcourt (Olberg) shrank in size and were manifested as dispersed villages. Two platform mounds were built at Upper Santan and Lower Santan; also, a second, smaller platform mound was built in the eastern part of Upper Santan village.

Despite the change to a more-linear settlement pattern, the intensity of use in Study Area 2 remained quite high, which contrasts starkly with the steep decline observed in Study Area 1. Activity was apparent along the entire lengths of the canal systems, as well as in a large swath of the non-irrigated field areas on the *bajada* of the Santan Mountains. A reduction in activity was evident on the northern side of Gila Butte, though.

The inferred community territories also changed during the Early Classic period. The communities along the Santan canal system probably were organized around the two platform-mound villages at Upper Santan and Lower Santan, a continuation of the pattern from the Sedentary

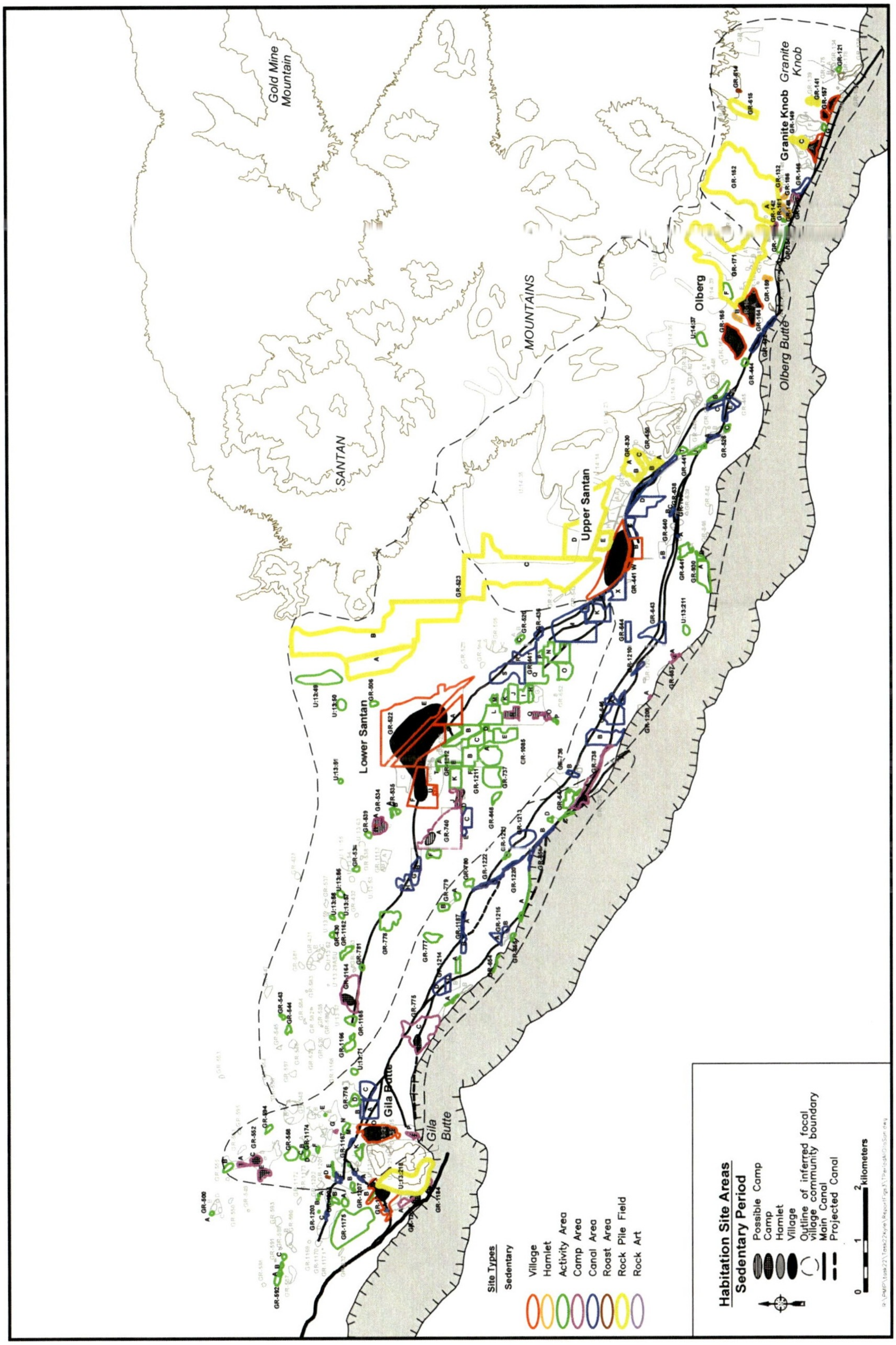

Figure C.5. Map of canals and settlements in Study Area 2 during the Sedentary period.

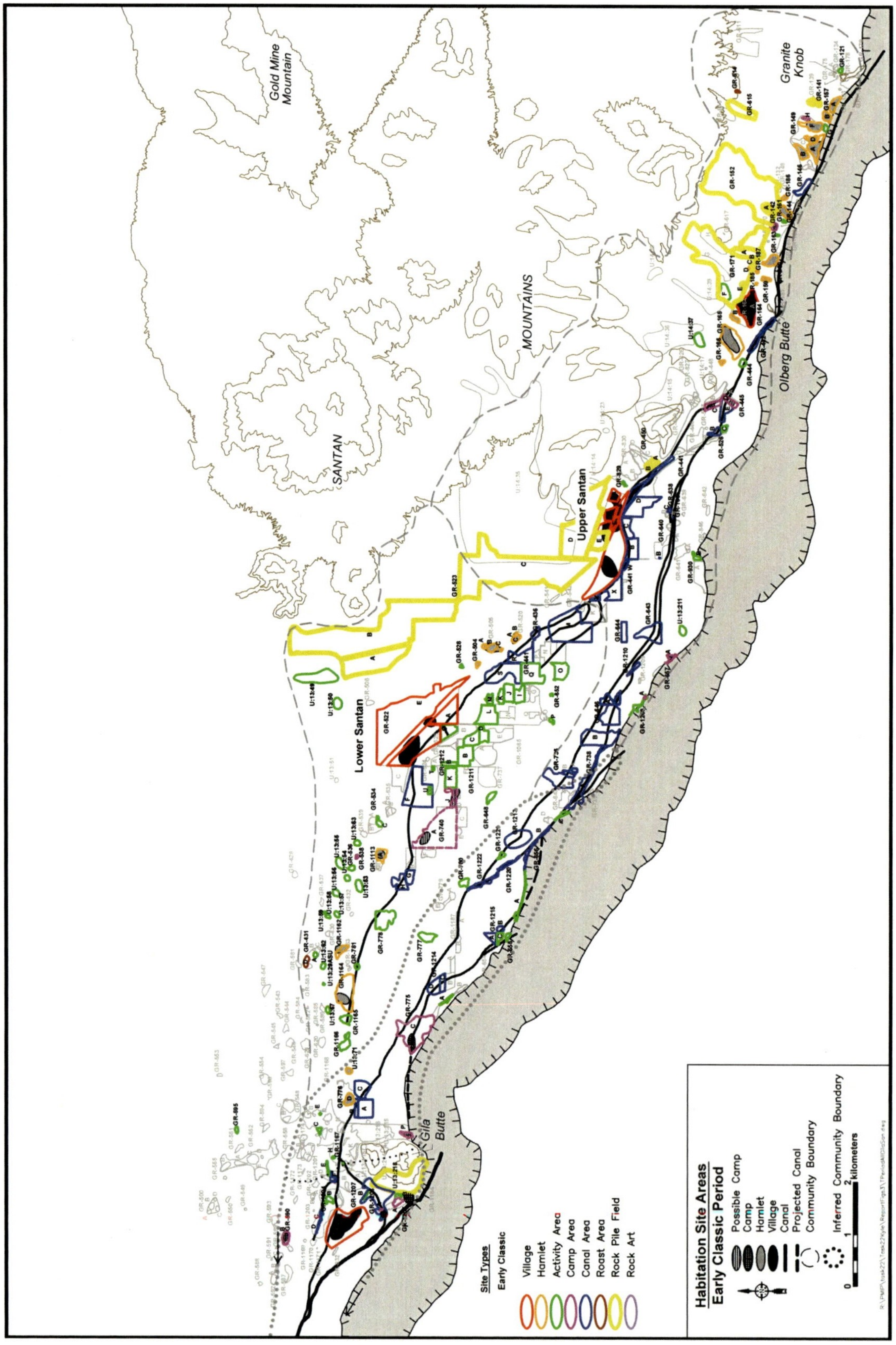

Figure C.6. Map of canals and settlements in Study Area 2 during the Early Classic period.

period, when the communities were organized around the ballcourt villages. The Granite Knob community probably became integrated with the Upper Santan community, if that had not already occurred in the Sedentary period. This conclusion is based on the lack of a focal village along the Granite Knob canal (which had been consolidated with the Santan canal) and the even distribution of hamlets between Granite Knob and Olberg Butte. Likewise, the abandonment of the Gila Butte site left only two hamlets and two camps along the canal system (and no focal village), unless the GR-1175 village was linked to it, instead of the Snaketown canal (see above). Even if that was the case, there were no focal villages directly associated with the canal anymore. Therefore, it is plausible that the former Gila Butte community became integrated into either the Snaketown community or one of the Santan communities (probably Lower Santan, based on proximity). This is suggested by the dotted-line outline of the Gila Butte community in Figure C.6.

During the Late Classic period, the settlement pattern remained quite linear in nature, with 3 dispersed villages (including the 2 platform-mound villages at Upper Santan and Lower Santan) and 21 hamlets representing the permanent habitations (Figure C.7). The Granite Knob settlement continued to be characterized as a dispersed hamlet, but 8 of the previous hamlets and 2 of the camps along the Granite Knob canal were no longer occupied by this time. The only site with a relict segment of the Granite Knob canal (GR-146) had no Gila Polychrome. There was an overall drop in intensity of use along the inferred canal, to the same levels as in the Colonial period. The steep decline in use levels may suggest that the canal had been abandoned and settlement had become more restricted by this time. The inferred community territories appear to have been the same as in the Early Classic period, with the Upper Santan and Lower Santan communities dominating the study area. The settlements remaining in the Granite Knob area probably continued to be associated with the Upper Santan community. Again, the former Gila Butte community did not exhibit the traits expected of an independent community, as either a focal village or a linear community. Instead, it probably remained integrated into the Snaketown or Lower Santan community. The sites in Study Area 2 exhibited no evidence of prehistoric use after the Late Classic period, indicating that the Hohokam had abandoned the area at the end of the period.

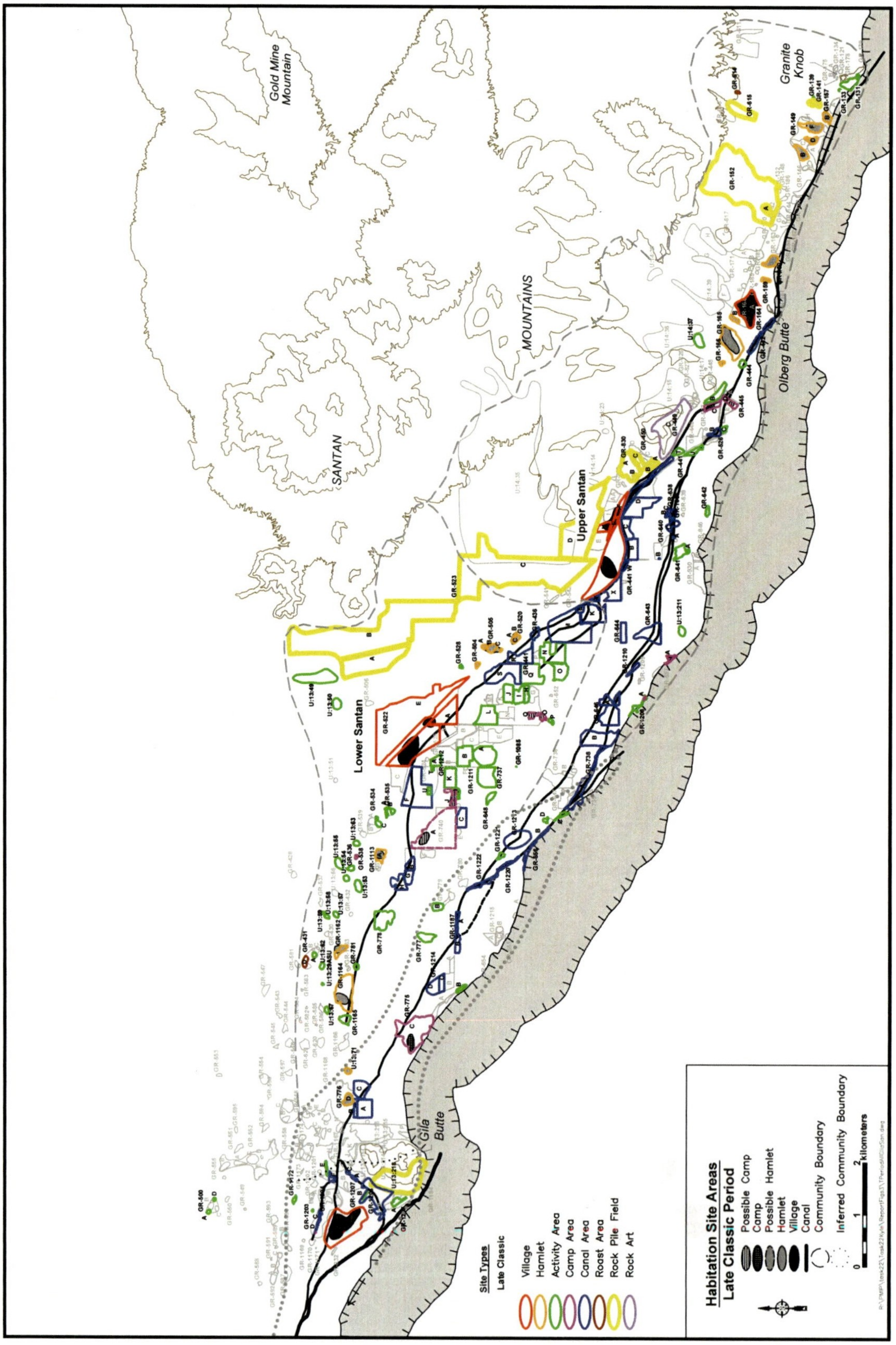

Figure C.7. Map of canals and settlements in Study Area 2 during the Late Classic period.